REFLECTING ON REFLEXIVITY

REFLECTING ON REFLEXIVITY

The Human Condition as an Ontological Surprise

Edited by
Terry Evens, Don Handelman, and Christopher Roberts

berghahn
NEW YORK · OXFORD
www.berghahnbooks.com

Published in 2016 by
Berghahn Books
www.berghahnbooks.com

Library of Congress Cataloging-in-Publication Data

Names: Evens, T. M. S., editor. | Handelman, Don, editor. | Roberts,
Christopher, 1971- editor.
Title: Reflecting on reflexivity: the human condition as an ontological
surprise / edited by Terry Evens, Don Handelman, and Christopher Roberts.
Description: New York: Berghahn Books, [2016] | Includes bibliographical
references and index.
Identifiers: LCCN 2015036423| ISBN 9781782387510 (hardback: acid-free
paper) | ISBN 9781782387534 (ebook)
Subjects: LCSH: Human beings--Philosophy. | Reflection (Philosophy) | Self
(Philosophy) | Philosophical anthropology.
Classification: LCC BD450 .R365 2016 | DDC 128--dc23 LC record available at
http://lccn.loc.gov/2015036423

British Library Cataloguing in Publication Data
A catalogue record for this book is available from the British Library

ISBN 978-1-78238-751-0 (hardback)
ISBN 978-1-78920-092-8 (paperback)
ISBN 978-1-78238-753-4 (ebook)

Contents

❧ Preface ❧

Terry Evens, Don Handelman, and Christopher Roberts

[W]e have to remember that what we observe is not nature in itself but nature exposed to our method of questioning.... [Q]uantum theory reminds us... of the old wisdom that when searching for harmony in life one must never forget that in the drama of existence we are ourselves both players and spectators.

—Werner Heisenberg, *Physics and Philosophy*

I know that I am caught up and comprehended in the world that I take as my object.... In saying that, and in recommending the practice of reflexivity, I am also aware of handing over to others instruments which they can turn against me to subject me to objectivation—but in so doing, they show that I am right.

—Pierre Bourdieu, *Science of Science and Reflexivity*

The Concept in Question

The social sciences are implicitly reflexive, and anthropology explicitly so. In its very nature, anthropology—etymologically, the study of *anthropos* (man)—constitutes a description of humans turning back on themselves in a disciplinary pursuit of "scientific" knowledge. It is not altogether surprising, then, that in the last third of the twentieth century "reflexivity" became a prominent, formal usage in anthropological studies.

In the present collection, we revisit this notion, but now with an eye to reflecting reflexively on the very idea of reflexivity. Over the course of several years of discussion and correspondence, this volume issued from the initial goal of interrogating the notion of reflexivity, interpreting what difference it makes to doing social science, and doing so reflexively.

Finally, given our broad anthropological usage of "reflexivity", much of what appears in this collection has a strong philosophical affinity.

As the reader will see, the concept of philosophy tends to appear often in the volume's contents, including many of the chapter contributions, and is particularly prominent in the postscript. In regards to the common distinction between analytical and continental philosophy, with the latter understood to include some of the traditions from which the topic of reflexivity emerged, such as phenomenology and German idealism, clearly this volume both draws from and contributes to a great many discourses in the continental tradition. That said, the aspirations motivating this volume would contest rather than perpetuate such distinctions that unreflexively segregate fields according to fixed parameters and incontestable premises.

It might appear advisable to have a clear sense of just what a topic means before one introduces it for scholarly discussion. Short of that, a working sense of the term's semantic domain, a sketch of the parameters defining the term's semantic dispersion, or at least an illustration of the range of play in the term's usage seems necessary. But while a number of the chapters in this volume are implicitly critical of the received notions of reflexivity, taken all together the chapters seem to belie a general consensus regarding the sense or significance of this notion for the social sciences. By and large, the different ways that these scholars interpreted the goal of the collection produced a dispersion of topics and agendas. We argue that, *exactly so,* the lack of a general consensus as to its meaning bespeaks "reflexivity's" extraordinary value, and that, accordingly, this notion remains profoundly pertinent, not only to social science, but also to what it means to be human.

Problematics of "Reflexivity" in Academia

It is a fact that for several years the concept "reflexivity" managed to provoke a number of compelling debates in the social sciences. At its peak of interest toward the end of the last millennium, works displaying every kind of textual ingenuity, generic awareness, and epistemological play appeared one after another (the names Clifford, Marcus, Tyler, Latour, Bourdieu, etc., come to mind). Reflexivity was one of many paradigm-defining concepts competing for hegemony, and the effervescent quality of these texts made the appearance of reflexivity one of the most widely desired accessories of scholarly practice. But like so many formerly prevailing concepts, this one too has largely fallen by the wayside. Perhaps the hyperintellectual freight of its academic history made the term seem too avant-garde and precious by far (see Handelman 1994).

In fact, narratives of contemporary scholarship trade on a succession of master terms such as symbol, structure, power, and practice, each of which claims supervening relevance but ultimately fails to make the grade. In this agonistic environment the series of interest bubbles that these master terms inflated eventually popped. Now that so many other institutions are beset by crises just as academic fields have been for decades, scholars seek to hedge our bets as broader sentiments of failure continue to bleed into a sense of theoretical disenchantment. Yet beyond the specific and arguable shortcomings of reflexivity, like few other terms it raises issues about the discursive and institutional conditions of knowledge production in the contemporary academy. What we euphemistically call "new economic realities"—which are not new but have been felt in the academy for decades—make academic labor increasingly precarious, and the often catastrophic economic and political crises of the new millennium make the definition of academic labor an increasingly pressing issue.

In the past, scholars could account for their scholarly labor by referring to an imminent or actual contribution to a particular archive or to the total fund of knowledge production. However, in the fight for funding imposed upon departments in the increasingly technocratic global university system, such long-term incremental rewards add little quantifiable value. In a neoliberal capitalist environment that refuses to grant any status to nonmarket values in human behavior, such contributions to the archive now need to be supplemented with any number of new species of intellectual labor, whether face time with students, public relations for the broader community, or service-learning projects. Over the last several decades, then, as institutions of higher learning have launched increasingly aggressive advertising campaigns to brand their institutional identities and burnish their prestige, a rhetorical premium accrues to qualities like "engagement" and "relevance" in research. It is impossible not to feel this pressure, and with employment so precarious, the status of humanist and social scientific researchers has diminished at significant cost, both in the long-term flourishing of the humanities and in an operationalized, atheoretical immediacy imposed upon the social sciences.

Unfortunately for its advocates, reflexivity emerged formally at a moment when the scientific nature of the social sciences, especially anthropology, needed buttressing during the budgetary conflicts that now seem the norm for contemporary institutions of higher learning. The fault lines and scars that remain after these conflicts both rupture and structure the interdepartmental terrain of academic relations. This agonistic framework has been exploited by a new metastasis of academic administrators, with the proportion of higher education budgets going toward administration instead of instruction increasing at almost every institution. In a sense, then, the textualist and formalist tendencies of reflexivity arrived at an untimely moment when scientistic fetishes like "testable outcomes" and "quantifiable results" began to win more budgetary standoffs. Exactly at the time when a clear demonstration of the "value added" by scholarship appears urgent, arcane notions like reflexivity arrive to make this even more difficult than before. Dropped into an inhospitable environment, with its proponents lauded by some but critiqued by more, at the turn of the millennium reflexivity as a term of scholarly art appeared to sail into its sunset, if persisting at all doing so in the twilight proper to it, eclipsed as an instrument of research to become an object of research, an inert historical datum, a discursive artifact. Ironically, academia is thus bureaucratically remade as positively antireflexive.

But reflexivity is not gone, as if a cultural item could ever wholly disappear. Is reflexivity now simply a baroque development of the heyday of "theory" and irrelevant to sound scholarship? Or was the first iteration of reflexivity's discursive footprint only a broaching period, a moment of instauration to be articulated and developed in subsequent research? Is reflexivity to be an anachronistic master term like any other, with each dispersed across the academic field like contiguous and contending sovereigns, each marshaling resources to defeat encroachments and defend their various claims to autonomous domains? Or might reflexivity even offer a new twist on scholarly labor, a speculative and high-risk form of discourse, a postspecialization specialty?

After the demise of the first "reflexivity" launch and bubble, after the IPO hype and ensuing market collapse, the venture has been variously rebranded, but it is easy to recognize reflexivity as a topic that dare not speak its name. Though it has gone underground, instances of it persist, and its influence is evident in innumerable stylistic turns and rhetorical tactics. But in this afterlife of the notion, its best exemplars know to disavow its relevance if pressed. "Reflexivity" has become a traditional element of a scholar's second nature, but modeled on Heraclitus's first nature—that is, our nature as what we are before we come to know or reflect on our*selves* and the deeds for which we are responsible—in that reflexivity now knows to hide itself, and how. As always, the challenge is that one will have to become more reflexive to recognize it when it occurs.

Surely some help is necessary to facilitate this recognition. Any metatheory or master term poses as a contingent universal, one that translates contingency into universality by means of a paradigmatic claim.

Here we have an editorial dilemma: should the editors exhibit examples, chosen conscientiously and yet ultimately arbitrarily, of scholarly
reflexivity, or cases of reflexivity exhibited by ethnographic subjects?
Advocates of a strong editorial hand might expect a taxonomic apparatus that would help tame this dispersion by speciating the various
instances of reflexivity and grouping them accordingly. However, the
notion of reflexivity itself makes this an almost insurmountable challenge, for the pursuit of a fixed classification and a delimitable essence
is exactly the kind of unreflective scholarly reflex that the notion purports to question.

But the contemporary scholar has options other than the static
premises of Linnaean binomial nomenclature (even if these options
threaten the scholar by ignoring the epistemological status quo). For
instance, one could turn instead to Wittgenstein's notion of family
resemblance, according to which through a variety of overlapping
features (eyes, ears, nose, etc.) the members of the family resemble
one another, yet there is no single trait common to each and every
member. Certainly this could prove a useful heuristic, allowing for
the analytical multiplication of distinguishing features and, no less
fruitfully, the identification of disjunctures that serve to sully the borders between these features (see also Vygotsky [1962: 64–66] on "chain
complexes").

Reflexivity in Social Science and Human Being

If we cannot in the last instance plainly classify the reflexivity speci-
mens in these chapters, perhaps one might embed reflexivity in a brief
discursive history of the concept, which would at least have the virtue
of accounting for the genesis of this variety. This too presents formidable difficulties, for unlike other paradigm-shifting notions such as
"logocentrism" or "phallogocentrism," reflexivity is not a coinage, so
its roots end back beyond recall. While there is a perceptible body of
anthropological literature that has resulted from the fairly recent (the
last three or four decades or so) thematizing of reflexivity in anthropology and the social sciences, most of it—even the best of it, such
as Bourdieu's rich, provocative, and insightful contributions to the
topic—tends to discuss reflexivity as a kind of method, producing the
call by some for more formally reflexive social sciences. Bringing into
question the chasm (one that, although conspicuous, went perfunctorily unnoticed for reasons of scientist pretense) between the discipline's rationalist view of itself and the sociocultural phenomena the

discipline customarily took as the object of its inquiry, the bringing into relief of reflexivity as a basis for a new methodological paradigm arose along with anthropology's prominent shift from the absorption with knowledge and belief as explanatory of peoples' practices to a focus on practice qua practice. It seems evident that this epistemological shift and the awakening to the difference between how anthropology presented itself in theory and how it actually *practiced* its trade go together. Although the anthropological turn to practice as a focus of research presupposes theoretical reflection, this turn could not help but reflexively nudge anthropologists to the realization that their discipline too is a form of practice. Indeed, the link between practice theory and reflexivity is substantial, at least when "practice" is taken to mean, rather than enactment or exposition, action in the face of uncertainty. Still, given that anthropological practice must continue to rely on rationality in some significant measure, the above-mentioned chasm is not perfectly resolvable. Indeed, by intimating a divide between objectivism and subjectivism, and thereby obscuring the incessancy of the reflexive, the chasm furthers the possibility of anthropology as a kind of science.

Like many scholars before us, we too wish to recommend reflexivity, but not in order to advocate a special kind of anthropology or social science. Rather, the idea is to enhance the advantage of a property that *comparatively* distinguishes the social sciences in regard to their objects of study: namely, the conspicuous degree to which reflexivity characterizes the endeavor of humans to study human social life, whether "their own" (as if culture were ever merely a matter of having) or others'. And we wish to do this by elucidating—as is a vital anthropological claim of this volume—reflexivity in its own right as a critical descriptor of human being. Therefore, while we hope our collection will prove of interest to those social scientists who have explicitly promoted reflexivity in their fields—whether on behalf of greater objectivity, as with Bourdieu, or of increased subjectivity, as with the prominent figures in the "writing ethnography" movement—we wish to (a) emphasize reflexivity as a fundamental, even defining, aspect of "human nature"; (b) assess its significance in "sciences," the object of whose study is the life of a species arrestingly characterized by just this property; and (c) highlight the existential ambiguity it cannot help but describe, namely, the body as mindful and the self as other to itself. Above all, it is these aims, when they are considered in their interrelatedness, that stand to distinguish this volume from the relevant literature, even as it builds upon much of these provocative but often maligned resources.

"Reflexivity" and/or "Reflection"

On the whole, the thematizing of reflexivity in anthropology has projected a methodology. This is true whether reflexivity has been prescribed to advance objectivity or to promote the subjective character of ethnographic practice and analysis. When it is understood primarily as a method, not of doubting but of considered self-inquiry, reflexivity is pictured as a matter of reflection qua reflection. This is a legitimate usage, yet it can have the effect of radical reduction: while people can be unreflective in their actions, they cannot be unreflexive. It is necessary to see that reflexivity is not only intrinsic to anthropological science but is also a representative, even defining, feature of humankind (and, more generally, perhaps, of what there *is*). This is because distinctively human consciousness is always self-consciousness, and selfhood, by definition, is reflexive: the *relation* forged and registered in the event of saying "I." Insofar as it is simply taken as method, reflexivity, in its character as a *fundamental* marker of *anthropos*, is itself hidden. As a result, in addition to the analytical benefits it can bring about, such a method carries real dangers to anthropological research. Thus, the focus on reflexivity primarily as method, although meaningful, risks giving short shrift to the anthropological—not to mention the ontological—significance of the phenomenon, for reflexivity continuously probes and questions the ontological.

By making reflexivity a straightforward matter of radical reflection while simultaneously eclipsing, in the sense of keeping from the mind's eye, the prior and more fundamental reflexivity on which reflection of the ratiocinative kind rests, this method fosters rationalization instead of reflexivity. This is because the intrinsic difficulty of gaining access to the substantive contents and ingenuous nature of first-order reflexive operations, the very operations that condition the presuppositional contents identified by means of the methodological practice at point, is compounded. In contrast to rationalization, which centers and closes reasoning, reflexivity continuously decenters even as it centers. It thus eludes itself, thereby broadening and deepening its grounding of the human.

In this collection, our key task is to consider reflexivity in the round, in an effort to grasp its relevance not only as a social scientific concept, methodological or otherwise, but also in its materialization as a distinguishing faculty of humankind.

References

Handelman, Don. 1994. "Critiques of Anthropology: Literary Turns, Slippery Bends." *Poetics Today* 15, no. 3: 341–81.
Vygotsky, Lev Semenovich. 1962. *Thought and Language.* Cambridge, MA: MIT Press.

Terry Evens is Emeritus Professor of Anthropology at the University of North Carolina, Chapel Hill. Email: tmevens@email.unc.edu

Don Handelman is Shaine Professor Emeritus of Anthropology at the Hebrew University. Email: mshand@mscc.huji.ac

Christopher Roberts teaches humanities and religious studies at Lewis & Clark College in Portland, Oregon. Email: robertschristopher4@gmail.com

Introduction

REFLEXIVITY AND SELFHOOD

Terry Evens, Don Handelman, and Christopher Roberts

Our principal thesis is that reflexivity is a fundamental and defining attribute of humanness itself. Here this thesis has it roots, most basically, in the philosophical anthropology of Maurice Merleau-Ponty, and his ontology of the betwixt and between. What we have in mind by "reflexivity," then, is not to be confused with or misconstrued for the relatively recent anthropological movement that also centered on a notion or notions of reflexivity, and had its beginnings in the 1970s.[1] Granting its impact, provocation, and appeal over two to three decades, that movement was for the most part a matter of taking reflexivity as a methodology for rethinking anthropological research in light of postcolonialism and other ethical concerns of ethnographic practice. In contrast, we see reflexivity as significantly broader than a social scientific scholarly performance or a prescription to guard against our own cultural givens. In effect, our notion of reflexivity differs critically from that of the thinking behind the previous uses of this concept in anthropology. Given the understanding that our approach neither rests on nor derives from the basic concerns of that movement, the question of how the latter relates to the sense of reflexivity we propound is somewhat academic.

Insofar as we see a connection, it is this: when considered as a defining feature of the being and becoming of the human, reflexivity emerges as a normally unseen, because natural, platform on the basis of which the word "reflexivity" was, in productive but cognitivistically circumscribed ways, understood by that previous anthropology. Regarding the collected chapters in this volume, while we incline to emphasize the respect in which they are basically attuned to our ontological argument about reflexivity, readers, of course, can make of them what they will.

It is crucial to understand, though, that ours is, rather than an exercise in the history of a certain practice in our discipline, an approach to the human condition as tied inexorably to reflexivity.

Humans are always already reflexive, even if they have not made a conscious decision to think about this or that. Naturally capacitated to think, whether or not they are thinking to do so, humans cannot help but think. It is the extraordinary scope of this dynamic capacity that distinguishes *anthropos* from other creatures. This is the case despite our indubitable continuity with the animal world, continuity all too evident in our finitude, not to mention our corporeality and its fundamental contribution to our capacity for thought.

Famously, Descartes grasped the ontological surprise that *is* this distinguishing capacity. At the same time, however, owing to his heated rationalism and its logical commitment to dualism, there was no place in his mind's eye to see that, for all its cognitivist self-presentation, at the end of the day our capacity for thinking has an illimitable continuing basis in our bodily being. In other words, our cognitive reflections always presuppose our reflexive and affective desires and predispositions. As humans there is indeed a mind-boggling, wondrous amount of play in our ties to the ground, but in the end we are all reduced to that ground (even if the play of which we speak can yield, in the form of ideas, acts, and memories, a relative immortality that transcends the individual).

We also emphasize the recognition of a particular fact: namely, the fact of recognition, which invokes *the inherent doubling* of every cognition directed either within (toward the self as a self-different other) or without (toward the other as a simulacral, similarly self-divided self). This basic ambiguity of selfhood bespeaks the ability to think about thinking, thus marking a sense of reflexivity as conscious thought or reflection, a meaningful metausage to be sure (as was made clear in the late anthropological movement about reflexivity), but one that all too often is taken as reflexivity per se. The cloud-like reflexivity on which we dwell, however, provides the platform for that usage and has its roots directly between immanence and the worldly transcendence of cognitivism.

Our objective, then, is to bring into relief reflexivity as an inherent feature of the experience of being human or, what comes to much the same thing, the experience of selfhood. It is obvious that human beings are born with the capacity to develop, over time, a strong sense of self. Once developed, the "self" is necessarily twofold, comprising, within itself, a self to think with and another to think about—both being expressed, as a matter of course, when saying "I." In other words, developed selfhood describes, paradoxically, the individual as a social or self-other relationship in its own right. However, issuing originally from a self-other relationship in which, by contrast, the other is external to the self, the self-other constitution of the individual presents an inversion whereby the external other is *internalized* as still an*other* self, thus producing the individual self as divided within itself between self and other. In turn, in a continuing dialectic of reflexivity, this fundamentally divided self turns back on the societal relationship from which it originally sprang, thus reconstructing a social order proper, that is, a group "I" comprising more than one individual.

To anticipate, in short, the cosmological meditations soon to follow here, one bright portrayal of the developmental process of reflexivity we have in mind is given in the biblical myth of Adam. Having been created in the image of his maker, the first man was endowed with a feracious seed of selfhood, that is, the life/spirit breathed into him by his creator. Because it remained, in preponderate part, a function of Adam's maker, this selfhood was naïve or innocent in nature, so much so that to realize itself it required enticement. Once aroused by the first woman, however, Adam, in a manner closer to a bodily (serpentine) reflex than a mindful deliberation, "chose" to slacken his ties to his maker (in meaningful measure eclipsing the latter) through an act of disobedience. As a consequence, *his embryonic self was given to appear to itself*, thereby becoming its own sovereign power. Thus, man was born again, this time giving birth to himself—that is, to his *self*. By so doing, he emerged from a veritable garden of innocence, a world in which man's selfhood barely registered, to one in which human selfhood, even if with many different cultural forms and degrees of development, came into its own as a basic descriptor of humankind.

Ethnocentrism and Universals

To make our argument, perhaps the best evidence follows from surfacing implicit reflexivities in primary data, such as, in the following case, religioculturally generated cosmologies. Reflexivity embedded and modeled in cosmology would reveal this primary awareness *of* the cosmos included *in* the cosmos. Yet the strongest obstacle against this robust notion of reflexivity as a human universal is that some will understand it as breaking a widespread professional injunction against ethnocentrism in the social sciences. Are the editors, in fact, offering reflexivity as a universal characteristic of the human species, thus committing an ethnocentric projection of a faux universal?

With so many examples of reflexivity exhibited by or implicated in cosmologies, any example will be rather arbitrarily chosen. To exemplify this primary—or primordial—reflexivity, or to illustrate it with a haphazardly chosen instance, inevitably incurs risks and costs that usually counsel caution. It is difficult to make peace with the arbitrariness of selection, for anyone might translate this arbitrariness (itself neither good nor evil) into the idiom of ethnocentrism. Here, then, lies the risk: the following example could make one point in reference to reflexivity while also being unreflexively ethnocentric. True, if one could rigorously designate an absolute cultural and discursive externality, an illustration from some immaculately defined "outside" of any recognizable relation to the traditions of Western scholarship, this pristine example would virtually prove a wider intercultural provenance for some notion of reflexivity.[2]

Perhaps such a pristine comparative item exists, but it is also possible to forestall these critiques by critically examining the very notion of ethnocentrism, and the slippery nature of the prohibition against it. Certainly this prohibition is widespread: perhaps no other appears so self-evident across the various social science disciplines. But this commonality exposes a fault line: If one eschews ethnocentrism, has one thereby achieved objectivity? That is, is objectivity something more than a rejection of the idols of one's tribe and good faith argumentation with evidence, or is objectivity itself an ethnocentric notion that we would do well to discard as a misconstrual of the nature of social scientific understanding? That the same scholars might oppose both ethnocentrism and objectivity marks the site of the epistemological wound that this volume will address with the notion of reflexivity. Perhaps much of what has been taken prima facie as an ethnocentric prohibition could in fact be a call for reflexivity in disguise.

Two Religiocultural Cosmologies

Aristotle's Transcendental Reflexivity and Cognitivism

This intractable tension between antiethnocentrism and objectivity has established a fault line within and between the various disciplines. When transported from the natural to the social sciences, many scholars treat natural scientific objectivity as a given, and others understand it to be an Occidental fiction. Given the multitude of differences between the natural and human or social sciences, the persistent appeal of natural scientific postures of objectivity in the human and social sciences demands explanation, for the flaws are readily apparent. This volume turns to reflexivity as a solution for the deformations of objectivity that occur when social science researchers actively disengage from others and the human play of mutuality and reflexivity because they are trained to value distance and control more than relation and recognition. But how did the scientistic posture of objectivity become a portable model of immovability? How too did the distance that objectivity requires become an unalloyed good, so that an immunity to affective appeals and a closure against unreasoned influences remains to many an unequivocal advantage to be maintained at any cost? Surely for a pressure so persistent something deeper than a precedent must be at work here; deeper even than a paradigm, it would take nothing less than a world-framing, cosmological model that historically refracts this relation between objectivity and reflexivity.

While there is no single source that can account for the domination of objectivity, a cosmological precedent survives in the "Western" imaginary unrecognized as such because disguised as science, its mythological status denied, its *logos* eclipsing its *muthos*. The preeminent transcultural precedent for a solipsistically cognitivist notion of reflexivity occurs in Aristotle's "Metaphysics," one of the major capstones of classical Greek thought. In the twelfth book Aristotle describes the good life of a divine being whose only adequate and proper activity is to reflect upon itself and think the nature of its own perfection. Aristotle declares that if "God is always in that good state in which we sometimes are, this compels our wonder; and if in a better this compels it yet more." As God's condition is better both quantitatively and qualitatively, Aristotle determines that "the actuality of thought is life, and God is that actuality; and God's essential actuality is life most good and eternal" (XII.7.25). Once anchored in wonder, Aristotle's depiction acknowledges that the "nature of divine thought involves certain problems." For one, Aristotle's divine Mind must take an object if it would not exist in futile isolation, for "if it thinks nothing, what is there here of dignity?" It is not enough for this Mind simply to be; there must be a relation between thought and its object, a relation that reflects well on the Mind as thinker and on thinking in general. At risk of collapsing into either nullity or indignity, to befit its status the Prime Mover "thinks that which is most divine and precious, and it does not change; for change would be change for the worse, and this would be already a movement" (XXI.9.26). With itself alone as its only proper object of thought, Aristotle posits a Mind that relates without movement or mutation through a self-reproducing, autoaffective process. With this cosmological model of divine self-regard Aristotle devised an image of the good life for the philosopher to emulate that integrates metaphysical postulates with astronomical observations. Although this cosmological model of reflexivity long outlived the cultural values and social conditions of its genesis, in light of this model we can broach the issue animating this introduction: is reflexivity an activity, or is it an aspect—something humans do, or something we are?

While discussing whether to consider divine reflection as an act or a capacity, Aristotle presumes that expenditures of labor are onerous. Aristotle's cosmological reflexivity is hermetic and circular, and like the orbits that share this form, perfectly self-reproducing and self-sustaining. This means that the divine Mind's characteristic condition is understood not as an action or laborious effort but as a state of being. He further supposes of the Prime Mover that if what this being exhibits is "not the act of thinking but a capacity, it would be reasonable to suppose that the continuity of its thinking is wearisome" (XII.7.27). As an effortful act, the discontinuous exhibition of a capacity could not be the "actuality of thought" or "life" as such; otherwise the plenitude of God's good life would syncopate to become an intermittent state of being dependent upon expenditures of energy and effort. Ascribing effort to the Prime Mover would render cosmological reflexivity temporal, processual, punctual, and syncopated when it should instead be eternal and continuous. In this way common Greek value preferences for the perfect and the permanent, the closed and the immutable, compromise Aristotle's model and influence received notions of knowledge and objectivity to the present day.

But beyond these broad, framing values, the course of Greek discourse highlights a more specific antecedent. For Aristotle, the divine life of thought remains fully immanent to itself in a transcendence that is not intermittent but enduring, and thus eternally distinct from the movement and mutation that typifies nature as *phusis*. In the way that Aristotle disguises his cosmological speculations as extrapolations from physics, his model depicts metaphysically what had already occurred by the time of Plato's dialogues, for whom preexistent "ideas" were the origin and not the outcome of the social history of knowledge. With Plato the social basis of geometric knowledge in craft technology falls away in favor of an a priori account of true knowledge not as learned but as "remembered" (*anamnesis*) by a soul always already equipped to distinguish truth from opinion.[3] Having gleaned from the crafts their intellectual component, Plato set the stage for Aristotle to leave every residue of manual labor categorically behind. If Plato distinguished the philosophical craft among others and against a vulgar sense of *tekhne* as unthinkingly acquired skills reducible to mere know-how, in "Metaphysics" Aristotle severs thought from action, while effort as the fact of human labor, whether technical or theoretical, shrivels before the value of divine contemplation. As he ascribes mindful reflexivity to the cosmos, Aristotle sloughs off the matrix of social labor against which Plato distinguished philosophical labor. Aristotle sublimates intellectual activity away from all other types of social labor and redefines effortless thinking (a gerund, an activity) as eternal thought (a perfect and unchanging "substance"), which affirms the philosopher's calling as a quasi-divine state categorically unlike the drudgery of human labor. In this way Aristotle finishes the project of distinguishing, against any other type of labor, thinking understood as the reflexivity peculiar to philosophers and God. The connotations evident in this early instance of reflexivity, connotations of aristocratic leisure and elitist self-regard, remain part of the notion's semantic freight to this day.

Aristotle's model exhibits a form of cosmological reflexivity that appears similar to the ontological hypothesis developed in this volume: if the Prime Mover is reflexive, it is so in its state of being and as its life, and not as a distinct and separable action. With effort, work, and expenditure denigrated, Aristotle's path toward understanding divine self-knowledge rejects any retroactive valorization of this process as labor and elides the activities and expenditures, the risks and costs, of knowledge production. To rehabilitate this model it seems simple enough to revise Greek values and, instead of a state of being or capacity, affirm reflexivity as a form of action or labor.

But when reflexivity is construed strictly as a specific type of action or activity, it still resonates too closely with the objective posture understood as a peculiar, not to say sui generis, form of mental labor. In the wake of Aristotle's model, reflexivity seems trapped between the banal notion of reflexivity as self-awareness or self-monitoring and the display of a rare or specialized kind of mental effort. With this cosmological precedent, reflexivity too often appears trapped between antipodal images of a strenuously detached objectivity and a leisurely solipsism.

Once the Aristotelian cosmological construal of reflexivity as an extreme form of solipsistic objectivity is off the table, perhaps we can begin to discern different aspects of reflexivity than have yet been apparent. Might we shake loose of such governing world images altogether? In this volume, instead of an agenda aimed toward the iconoclastic dismantling of any particular world image of reflexivity, we have sought to pluralize the number of possible models and seek ones that recast reflexivity less as a rare feat than as an ontological reality.

Isaac Luria's Mysticist Reflexivity and Basic Ambiguity

After addressing, if not resolving, these possible objections, we turn now to a "beginning," citing, comparatively, two Western devotional accounts of cosmogenesis, one the scriptural account in the book of Genesis, the other an early modern Jewish mystical account. The idea is to show how one of these two cosmogeneses reflects, in a provocative manner relative to the other (as well as to the Aristotelian transcendental conception), the human experience of reflexivity. The one we feature might be said to deconstruct the other, which, being biblical, happens to be a far more familiar account. This is not to say that the standard biblical Genesis fails to reflect the experience of reflexivity, for in its depiction of how Adam and Eve become self-conscious, the story is emphatically about that experience. But because, unlike the biblical story, the account we choose to highlight does not try to conceal the bodily nature of reflexivity, it serves better to bring out the essential ambiguity between self-consciousness and being or becoming, which is to say, between reflection and, in its nature as an autonomic process, reflexion.

On the one hand, according to the familiar Judeo-Christian biblical depiction, starting with absolutely *nothing* the god figure proceeded to create everything that is something: heaven and earth, and all that follows from this binary signification of the emergence of being (spirit and matter, light and darkness, water and land, man and animals, man and woman, etc.). On the other hand, for an ingenious and revealingly contrasting account, one that arrives at creation from neither something nor, in its received meaning as nonexistence, nothing, we can look here to the kabbalistic tradition of Judaism. More particularly, we have in mind Isaac Luria's interpretation of the Hebraic idea of *Tsimtsum*. Whereas this idea originally conveyed the tremendous concentrating of God's creative power into a single, totally inclusive point, Luria interpreted it inversely, to mean God's withdrawal or retreat away from such an all-absorbing presence. Asking himself (in Scholem 1954: 261), "If God is 'all in all,' how can there be things which are not God?" Luria supposed that, by withdrawing from, rather than essentializing, himself, God made room for creation. That is, by limiting or shrinking himself, God allowed for a primordial space-time in which creation could take place and revelation make sense.

It may seem that the conspicuous difference between the two cosmogeneses is academic, since in both the universe is generated by a god figure. But to see it so would overlook a difference that makes a world of difference. Indeed, it might be said that Luria was engaged in a precocious, mystically driven exercise of deconstruction, detecting a fundamental contradiction in the conventional biblical story (how can there be a creationary world if all there is is God) and then addressing himself to its resolution.

In the conventional biblical account, it is the sheer *will* of God that makes creation, whereas Luria describes the world as a product of something more than will, something capable of contraction, that is, a presence of an incandescently numinous kind, but a *presence* nonetheless. By limiting this presence, this "all in all," God makes room for yet another kind of presence—the world as *we* find it, where being qua being looms large. In effect, in the Lurianic account, although God is grasped as otherwise than being, he is not rendered simply as nothing. As Scholem puts it (1965: 101, 102), by contrast to "the so-called rational theology of late Rabbinism," for the kabbalists "there is no room for the *nihil* in this world [the Kabbalah] of the theological conception." Rather, the figure of God is constituted in terms of basic ambiguity. It is helpful here to appeal to a twentieth-century Jewish philosopher, even though this thinker was no friend to mysticism. Discussing the very word "God," Emmanuel Levinas (1991: 151, emphasis added) also arrived at a picture of "the Infinite"—in kabbalism, the *Ein-Sof* ("without end")—in terms of fundamental "ontological" ambiguity: "[God] is an extraordinary word, the only one that does not extinguish or absorb its saying, but it cannot remain a simple word.... The glory of the Infinite shuts itself up in a word and becomes a being. But it already undoes its dwelling and unsays itself without vanishing into nothingness.... A said unique of its kind, it does not narrowly espouse grammatical categories like a noun... and does not incline exactly to logical rules, like a meaning (*being an excluded middle between being and nothingess*)."

This ambiguity manifests itself primarily as a dynamics (in contradistinction to a statics), wherein God, in his epitomical constitution as being *and* nothingness, *a distinctly Janus-faced figure,* is forever "falling back upon" himself (Scholem 1954: 261) to issue in mirror images that are both identical and reversed or inverted. In effect, at bottom the aspects of being and nothingness appear as ever becoming different from and identical to each other, an endless becoming other. Put another way, in Lurianic kabbalism the word *Ein-Sof* or God may be understood as a name for an *ur-* reflex, the arc of which is cosmological, moving continuously between being and nothingness, the visible and the invisible, life and death, and so on. In this light, the Infinite's autoinversion is plainly reflexive, in the sense of both a reflective or deliberative *and* an autonomic action, at once *both* a willful *and* a corporal reflex that rather than (immediately) denying the gravity of being gives way to it. In still other words, we have here a description of a quasi-sacrificial act of self-destruction and creation pictured as direct functions of each other.

Thus, by contrast to the Judeo-Christian scriptural account, in which it is God's will alone that creates the world, Isaac Luria's representation of genesis may be seen to picture a uniquely reflexive event. It is unique because, while will or volition is at the very least an implied feature of this event, the reflexive nature of the god figure's inward collapse or withdrawal and this figure's subsequent creation of what is other to itself have the feel of a physiological phenomenon: it is just as if, having been somehow stimulated, a muscle contraction is followed by an expansion of palpable magnitude and duration in the very same muscle. What, then, is the stimulus that produces this amazing double response? It seems a fair presumption that in Luria's account God wishes to create life, as we humans know it, and is willing to sacrifice (shrink) himself in order to achieve this. In which case the generating stimulus is, as in the second and third chapters of the traditional Genesis, God's autonomous will. At the same time, however, there is in Luria's account an element of heteronomy as well as self-determination about God's act, making it hard to distinguish will from reflex, which is also to say, will from desire, inasmuch as desire is a matter of stimulus. The contraction and creation convey a quasi-autonomic character that suggests bodily necessity, as if they were advanced by need in addition to will. It will be objected that God, being omnipotent, can scarcely have needs or desires. But inasmuch as being, as well as nothingness, enters Luria's picture of God, it is hard to avoid the conclusion that there is something needful about this creative process, an element of self-concern in a conative sense. It is as if the "life" of God depended on the creation of beings that depend on him. When Scholem writes (1965: 104) that "the God who can be apprehended by man is himself the First Man [*Adam Kadmon*]," it would seem as if Luria's God needed to create reflexive beings who can recognize their creator in their own reflection.[4]

The heteronomous and needful character of Luria's god figure is expressed in yet another, more direct, register, namely, the erotic. Kabbalism had no penchant for sexual asceticism. Scholem puts it this way (1954: 227): "The mystery of sex, as it appears to the Kabbalist, has a terribly deep significance." Indeed, in this mystical tradition, even the relationship between God and himself is pictured as a "sacred union" between "He and His Shekhinah," the *Shekhinah* (the feminine principle or, literally, "dwelling place") being one manifestation or face (*partsuf*) of God (Scholem 1954: 227, 1965: 104–5). In other words, the singular figure of God is cast in terms of a self-reflexion, the two poles of which—the self and the self-as-other-to-itself—are the phallic on the one side and the vulvate on the other. Scholem argued (1954: 225) that while kabbalism held fast to monotheism, the androgynous characterization of the god figure threw a wrench into this theological belief.

While agreeing with Scholem about the critical importance of gender dimorphism in the Kabbalah (specifically in the text known as the *Bahir*), another student of Jewish mysticism, Elliot Wolfson (2006: 145), by seeing the feminine element as hierarchically (in the Dumontian sense of the term) subsumed by the male element, makes oneness out of the androgyne. More inclined to understand the hermaphroditic nature of the god figure as a hitch in the kabbalistic theosophy, Scholem sees in this nature an unintended pantheism (1954: 252–53). In respect of this conjecture, even though he agrees there is no question but that the kabbalists saw themselves as holding to a dualism of spirit and matter, Scholem suggests that (1954: 269) they nonetheless entertained "the conception of man as a *micro-cosmos* and of the living God as a *macro-anthropos*." Wolfson's position is based on the kabbalistic grasp of the rite of circumcision as a feminizing (a withdrawing) of the phallus, thus dimorphically transforming the head of the phallic god figure. He (1994: 357ff.) explicates his position as follows:

> [I]t may be said that the crowning of the kabbalists is a ritual reenactment of circumcision, whereby the corona of the penis is disclosed.... [I]n the complex gender symbolism of theosophic kabbalah the corona of the penis corresponds to the feminine aspect of the Godhead, the *Shekhinah*, and hence the act of crowning must be viewed as a feminization.... One should speak, therefore, of an androgynous phallus.... [W]e have here another example of a one-sex theory: the feminine (specifically the clitoris) is but an extension of the masculine (the penis).... [T]he contextualization of the female in the male organ allows the kabbalists to envision the penis as the locus of the union of both genders.... The act of uncovering the corona is mystically transformed into an occasion for the revelation of the divine diadem; indeed, circumcision is understood in kabbalistic literature as a rite of symbolic androgynization as a result of which the feminine attribute of God appears through the semiological opening that is inscribed upon the penis.

Thus, Wolfson saves kabbalism for both monotheism and patriarchalism. Inasmuch, though, as Wolfson's position is an account of the kabbalists' own received conception of the matter, there is no reason to conclude that Scholem's construal of this godly androgyny as troublesome to the kabbalists' adherence to monotheism is necessarily erroneous. Indeed, in light of Wolfson's erudite account of the symbolism, in which the Jewish rite of circumcision appears to be an erotic representation of the Lurianic *Tsimtsum*, it is eminently inviting to speculate that this autocontraction of the god figure amounts to a tacit introduction of the feminine principle as the buried source of Creation.[5]

"Luria is driven to something very much like a mythos of God giving birth to Himself," writes Scholem (1965: 271), who goes on to venture that this logically essential conundrum of reflexivity is the "focal point" of Luria's "rather obscure and inconsistent" cosmogenesis. Obscure and inconsistent indeed. Luria's image of God implicates an ambiguous nature, a *presence* that is nonetheless *not there*, an in-itself that yet remains discorporate and utterly indeterminate. In an apparently selfless act, this figure of the in-between, this infinite Self, contracts, thus occasioning what is other to itself, its complementary image—the Finite. But because it does so solely as a function of "its own self," it sustains and, in a sense, even completes itself at the same time. Although theologically scandalous, this conclusion must be the case inasmuch as the figure of the deity is defined in terms of its capacity to create, that is, as the Creator. Indeed, it is not unreasonable to think of "God" as one name for a veritable creational dynamics. What Luria's genesis account captures is that, for one thing, if God is infinite, if all there is is God, the only way it can effect difference, that is to say, the Creation, is by limiting or sacrificing itself; and, for another, precisely because it is the Infinite, the result of this act of self-sacrifice can only be what seems otherwise than God, that is, finitude. Put another way, in effect the figure of God amounts to an ambivalently sacrificial reflex arc, an open paralogical and dialectical relation in which what there is remains what it is by becoming, in perpetuity, something else. Just so, desire and self-interest are respectively squared with will and other-regard, in a never-ending process of creation.

Commenting on the *Ein-Sof*, here is how Wolfson (2006: 107) intimates the sexual imagery as well as the multilayered reflexive logic of creation in the Kabbalah:

> Time is precisely the measure of this "narrative space" arising from the infinite withdrawing into the sheltering-open of its hidden disclosure.... From a kabbalistic vantage point we can speak of the overcoming of time but only in the timelessness of time's perseverance.... There is no eternity over and against time, but rather the timeless time of temporal eternity measured against the timelessness of eternal temporality... the halo of silence enveloping the periphery of the verbal, the haze of invisibility permeating the showground of the visible.

In this subtle but provocatively telling description of the Infinite, Wolfson discerns in the kabbalist cosmology a narrative that defines what there is as that which is beyond definition. From the point of view of logic as such, this *whatever* presents the paralogical phenomenon of self-causation. As the "infinite withdrawing into the sheltering-open of its hidden disclosure," space-time comes to nothing but ongoing creation or reproduction. Its sameness or permanency—which is to say, its identity—is, then, enigmatically, a matter of ever becoming itself by becoming other to itself. Consequently, its sole measure is itself, continuously turning back on itself, thus *repro*ducing itself by *pro*ducing what is other to itself. What we have, then, is a picture of what there "is" as a cosmological or primordial reflexive relationship obtaining between what the is "is" and what it is not: the verbal determined by silence, the invisible by the visible, space by time, and time by eternity. It is a depiction of what there is as betweenness, a virtual middle, but one that is always already broken, always already changing while all the while remaining the same, a whole no less open than closed, a picture of infinition as reflexivity.

From a strictly anthropological (as opposed to theological) perspective, it is unremarkable that this picture of the *Ein-Sof* can be shown thus to reflect—in the way of a definitively radical refraction—selfhood as we know and experience it in this world. This goes back at least as far as one of the preorigins of modern social science, the most materialist of the German idealists, Feuerbach, who posited that theology is indeed best understood as a form of anthropology. This helped build the bridges between what otherwise appears to be only distantly related, the philological scrutiny of scriptures and anthropological fieldwork, that scholars since W. Robertson Smith have explored.[6] What is more, that divinity and humanity are mutually implicated and reciprocally regarding seems perhaps the only point of agreement among all who would interpret religious claims such as these, scholars, clergy, and laity alike. In other words, to play on the theme of reflexivity and as against Genesis 1:27 ("And God created man in His own image, in the image of God created He him"), man has made the other and otherness the mirror of himself, that is, his *self*. How could it be otherwise, even if it stands to reason that selfhood issues ultimately from otherness?[7] That is, how could man imagine (in the sense of "circumscribe") the figure of god or gods except by self-reference (cf. Deleuze 1994: 136ff.)?

Reflexivity as the Being and Becoming of the Human

Nondualism and the Absolute Individual

In modern anthropology the direct and emphatic study of the self may be traced especially to Mauss's precocious essay (1985) on "person" (*personne*) and "self" (*moi*) and to the intensive comparative writings on the "individual" by Mauss's eminent student, Louis Dumont. Naturally, these studies owe inspiration especially to Durkheim's theoretically pivotal and axiologically asymmetrical distinction between society and the individual. Seeking to attenuate Kant's dualism of reason and the senses (*Homo noumenon* and *Homo phenomenon*), Durkheim (1960: 325–340) identified reason with the social order, thus affording what he regarded as moral primacy to the collective rather than the individual self. As is well-known, according to him, the collective, creating ideals that transcend the individual as such are experienced as an impersonal, external power. But, listing in the direction of nondualism (without formally embracing it), he held that if these ideals are to captivate the individual, they have to lodge themselves in the world of the senses, such that things of material reality come to symbolize this transcendent power. Even so, the tension between, and dialectic of, the individual and society by no means disappear; to the contrary, with considerable prescience, Durkheim thought (1960: 339) it probable that the struggle between reason and the senses—for him society and the individual or, respectively, the sacred and the profane—was bound "to increase with the growth of civilization."

Of the chapters collected here, nearly all raise to critical question, either explicitly or implicitly, the ontoepistemologically deep-rooted presumption of both dualism and the Western sense of self in terms of individual autonomy. They do this by virtue of the very idea of reflexivity, whereby selfhood, whether individual or collective, necessarily defines a relationship between self and other. In our view, the intellectual problematic of selfhood springs from the inexorable experience of oneself as both two and one at the same time: mind/inside *and* body/outside as well as mind/inside *as* body/outside. In addition to the legacy of Aristotle discussed above, another critical backdrop to these anthropological discussions on selfhood and individualism is the abiding question of the relation between mind and body, modern answers to which tend to exhibit the provocation of Descartes's dualism. It seems as if modern scholars have been condemned to wobble through every paradox generated by Descartes's irremediable ontological scission. By ontologically elevating the experiential element of mutual exclusion rather than that of the intertwining characterizing this paradoxical phenomenon of selfhood, Descartes constructed a seeming logical resolution to the felt contradiction. This is his famous cogito, which defines the self transcendentally, in terms of reason alone, that is, as "thinking stuff" (*res cogitans*). During the latter part of the twentieth century, especially with the rise of so-called postmodern thought, the

Cartesian cogito, in its role as a pillar of the Western ideal of the sovereign, individual self, has come under strong, elemental criticism, as has the ontoepistemological dualism accentuated by this luminous French philosopher.

Selfhood entails self-consciousness, and, to reiterate, self-consciousness involves at least two selves, one to think with and one to think about—in which case, one is always other to oneself, a truth that characterizes the collective self-identity as well. Freud's psychological concept of the unconscious, which dovetails with his thesis of the self as divided against itself, captures this. But the Freudian "unconscious" suffers from a certain limitedness of psychologism. We must grasp, with Wittgenstein, that even were one to invent a language that one keeps, hermetically, to oneself, such a language would still not be private in essence. This is because, since its very construction could not but presuppose language as an inherently social phenomenon, it would remain necessarily open to understanding by others (as, indeed, is presumed by ethnographic practice). What is ultimately at stake, then, even with the psychological notion of the unconscious, is a relationship between self and other, in which case it must follow that the unconscious obtains no less between individuals than within them.[8] In other words, for all its intimation of absolute identity, selfhood, like language, is fundamentally a social phenomenon.

Ethics and Human Nature

By the same token, namely, reflexivity or the ambiguous constitution of selfhood, most, if not all, of the various chapters making up this collection disclose, either explicitly or implicitly, the essentially ethical nature of social science and human life. If selfhood, in itself, describes a reflexive relationship between self and other, then it necessarily also describes the essential condition of ethics: the emergent, evolutionary property of responsibility in being. Insofar as humans *conduct* themselves, in the sense of determining their own ends, to that extent they can be held to answer for their actions, at least in significant part, and even if, in any particular case, responsibility can be sensibly distributed equally or unequally as between men. In other words, conduct, as we use this term, is, whatever else it is, always and essentially a question of ethics. This remains true despite the consideration that all human actions follow from reflections that are many times removed from the immediate actors, to the point where we might speak of these reflections as preconceived. In this light, for all its rhetorical power and seeming common sense, Nietzsche's famous analogy (1967: first essay, sec. 13) between archetypically "strong" men (*übermenschen* or overmen) and birds of prey is misleading. While raptors cannot be held responsible for their rapacious behavior, as if they were under an *obligation* to leave little lambs be, humans can. When it comes to human beings, Western politicoeconomic presumption (and its actualization) notwithstanding, it is no more "natural" to prey on their fellows than to refrain from doing so, since human nature is signally second nature. If in being self-responsible the self is ever other to itself, then, logically, by virtue of its very constitution, the self is necessarily responsible to and for others and otherness (other creatures and the environment) in general.

Scientism and Basic Ambiguity

Also running throughout the chapters collected here is a strong tendency to, at the very least, throw open to question scientism and its related notions, such as objectivity, facticity, positivism, materialism, determinism, and the like. This is because, keyed to reflexivity—that is, to an understanding of self-consciousness as a dynamic *relationship* between a person and him- or herself, or a sociocultural order and itself—the chapters are logically constrained to reconsider the received acceptation of self, other, mind, body, subject, and object, which is to say, the ontological acceptation of absolute identity. Unhappily, one result of this reconsideration has been a disciplinary propensity to gloss reflexivity as simply a matter of subjectivity, in this way reproducing the dualism implied by objectivism. It is crucial, though, to bear in mind that the model of reflexivity *most basically* advanced here is not a subject seeing a reflection of herself in the looking glass. Rather, the model is a reflex arc as found, not in biological science or even Gestalt psychology, but in a paradoxical figure of self-negation, a figure that, in its endlessly creative dynamism, holds directly between will and desire. Put another way, the figure limns a zone of relative but fundamental ambiguity between mind and body, and therefore, between subjectivity and objectivity, or, indeed, subject/self and object/other.

Ontology and Reflexivity

Luria's cosmology has shown how different "our" fundamental assumptions might be. Genesis and Luria together demonstrate reflexivity in a radiant way, Luria's account being a transformative reflexion of the biblical Genesis. The latter too, as a narrative of the development of moral consciousness, is in its own right fundamentally about reflexivity. Luria's rewrite, although still within the "same" religious tradition, amounts to a reflexive kind of de- and reconstruction of Genesis, one that in effect throws into question such received notions as monotheism and, given the outright mysticism of the Lurianic story, religious positivism, making Luria an epigone of Maimonides and a harbinger of Kant and Hegel. Indeed, this pair of narratives, the biblical and the mystical, offers inverted cosmogenic recounts constructed by radicalizing divine postulation or denegation, the *via positiva* and the *via negativa*. Such a pairing exhibits what is at stake when one shifts from one embedded cosmology or ontology to the next.

Perhaps one other consequence of this pairing is to associate reflexivity with epistemological modesty, as opposed to the unreflexive hunting for unreflexive moments in others. Instead of abiding by any single prohibition or evaluating a work's lacks and absences against the plenitude of a criterion, perhaps reflexivity allows scholars to assess one another's work along a positive gradient, one that threads the needle between the positively nonethnocentric and the critically antiethnocentric. Different issues raised by reflexivity place the scholar at the limits of once avant-garde but now mainstream notions such as paradigms, epistemes, or *mentalites,* for each of these notions invokes a closed figure, a delineated object with relatively unambiguous demarcations. By contrast, reflexivity is peculiar among this postparadigmatic set. Is reflexivity something subjective and exhibited or discursive and contested, a psychological state or an objective datum in the world? Being a posited topic of uncertain ontological status—at times the quality or effect of a text, the capacity of a subject, or even the being of the human—this apparent shortcoming is in fact its value. Context-sensitive and semiotically ambiguous, reflexivity, despite the ink spilled in its name, remains an open, even paradoxical term of scholarly art. Nevertheless, reflexivity's role as marking the being of the human, that is, the developed and dynamic capacities of exceptional, if still relative, self-consciousness and reflection, ultimately makes possible its semantic flexibility. This is the case even though, *at bottom,* these capacities are more fundamentally perceptual, that is to say, matters of the senses, than they are conceptual or transcendental.

The Contributions

As we turn to the collected chapters, what is crucial to understand is that, however varied and rich they are, they all take for granted the fundamental *indistinction* between reflexivity and both the being and becoming of the human. That is, however disparate the questions and approaches found in the chapters, this volume addresses reflexivity as a horizontal, orienting fact that provides the platform for being human as such, not a recurrent topic periodically rediscovered, and certainly not an epistemological breakthrough to be credited to this or that historical figure. Put another way, it is as if we, in our humanity, exist in a cloud of reflexive particles, a cloud that, because we are literally *of it,* remains *fundamentally* concealed from us, such that when we overtly choose to employ "reflexivity," we understand it as conscious thought. But rather than sheer cognition, the cloud itself holds between body and mind, such that our sensibility and our thought partake of each other, describing a basic ambiguity that is logically irreducible.

The following chapters do not fall cleanly into distinct categories. The fact of the matter is that many of these contributions address reflexivity directly, while others approach it more obliquely. What is more, the meanings attributed to the notion of reflexivity may vary from one chapter to another, as well as within any one chapter (as was also the case with the late anthropological movement that centered on reflexivity). Nonetheless, it proved useful to organize the chapters into four separate sections on the basis of, where possible, a few prominent commonalities. Of course, according to his or her interests, the reader is bound to find still other pertinent connections and differences.

Notes

1. See, e.g., Clifford and Marcus (1986); Marcus and Fischer (1986); Rosaldo (1989); and Tyler (1984). For a strong critique of this movement, see Handelman (1994).
2. A possible example, in terms of alterity and significance, could be one portrait of cosmogenesis found in the *Rg Veda.* See Handelman and Shulman (1997: 45ff.), in which "play" is seen as the springboard of the creation story in this sacred text of Hinduism.
3. In section 9 of *The Crisis of European Science,* Husserl describes the process by which the ancient Greeks gradually separated mathematics and geometry from the social conditions of their emergence in craft technology. In a process that Husserl calls "sense-emptying" (*Sinnentleerung*), even as practical developments facilitated an approach toward ever more ideal shapes in production, the sense or awareness of this craft knowledge basis "emptied" while the ideal, a priori status of mathematical knowledge came to appear more robust and, eventually, independent. The cultural drift of *Sinnentleerung* became explicit in Plato's texts but took place over centuries and across cultures, wherever the influence of Hellenism extended.
4. In this respect, it would appear that Luria's god figure stands as a precursory account of Hegel's master-slave dialectic. One might also think here

of Nietzsche's declaration of the "death of God," by which he meant man's ceasing to believe in such a heavenly figure.

5. For a deconstructive account in which it is argued that the story of Adam and Eve in the biblical Genesis was set out by its redactors so as to put out of sight an implicit subsuming primacy of the female over the male principle, see Evens (1997).

6. For two current examples, see Handelman and Shulman (1997, 2004).

7. We have in mind here, for instance, George Herbert Mead's work (1962: part 3) and, more recently, the philosophy of Emmanuel Levinas (e.g., 1991).

8. Cf. Kenneth Burke's essay (1968: part 1, chap. 4), written with Freud in mind, on the linguistic varieties of the "unconscious."

References

Aristotle. 1984. "Metaphysics, Book 10." In *The Complete Works of Aristotle*, vol. 2, *The Revised Oxford Translation*, ed. Jonathan Barnes, trans. William D. Ross. Princeton, NJ: Princeton University Press, 1074b15–1074b34, pp. 1698–99.

Burke, Kenneth. 1968. *Language as Symbolic Action*. Berkeley: University of California Press.

Clifford, James, and George Marcus, eds. 1986. *Writing Culture: The Poetics and Politics of Ethnography*. Berkeley: University of California Press.

Deleuze, Gilles. 1994. *Difference and Repetition*. Trans. Paul Patton. New York: Columbia University Press.

Durkheim, Emile. 1960. "The Dualism of Human Nature and Its Social Conditions." In *Emile Durkheim, 1958–1917*. Ed. Kurt H. Wolff. Columbus: The Ohio State University Press, 325–40.

Evens, T. M. S. 1997. "Eve: Ethics and the Feminine Principle in the Second and Third Chapters of Genesis." In *The Ethnography of Moralities*, ed. Signe Howell. London: Routledge, 203–8.

Handelman, Don. 1994. "Critiques of Anthropology: Literary Turns, Slippery Bends." *Poetics Today* 15, no. 3: 341–81.

Handelman, Don, and David Shulman. 1997. *God Inside Out: Śiva's Game of Dice*. Oxford: Oxford University Press.

———. 2004. *Śiva in the Forest of Pines*. Oxford: Oxford University Press.

Husserl, Edmund. 1970. *Crisis of European Science and Transcendental Phenomenology: An Introduction to Phenomenological Philosophy*. Trans. David Carr. Chicago: Northwestern University Press.

Levinas, Emmanuel. 1991. *Otherwise than Being or Beyond Essence*. Trans. Alphonso Lingis. Dordrecht: Kluwer Academic Publishers.

Marcus, George E., and Michael F. Fischer. 1986. *Anthropology as Cultural Critique*. Chicago: University of Chicago Press.

Mauss, Marcel. 1985. "A Category of the Human Mind: The Notion of Person; the Notion of Self." In *The Category of the Person*, ed. Michael Carrithers, Steven Collins, and Steven Lukes. Cambridge: Cambridge University Press, 1–25.

Mead, George Herbert. 1962. *Mind, Self, and Society.* Vol. 1. Ed. Charles W. Morris. Chicago: University of Chicago Press.

Nietzsche, Friedrich. 1967. *On the Genealogy of Morals.* Trans. Walter Kauffmann and R. J. Hollingdale. New York: Random House.

Rosaldo, Renato. 1989. *Culture and Truth: The Remaking of Social Analysis.* Boston: Beacon Press.

Scholem, Gershom G. 1954. *Major Trends in Jewish Mysticism.* New York: Schocken Books.

———. 1965. *Kabbalah and Its Symbolism.* Trans. Ralph Manheim. New York: Schocken Books.

Tyler, Stephen A. 1984. "Ethnography, Intertextuality and the End of Description." *American Journal of Semiotics* 3: 83–98.

Wolfson, Elliot R. 1994. *Through a Speculum that Shines.* Princeton, NJ: Princeton University Press.

———. 2006. *Alef, Mem, Tau: Kabbalistic Musings on Time, Truth, and Death.* Berkeley: University of California Press.

Terry Evens is Emeritus Professor of Anthropology at the University of North Carolina, Chapel Hill. Email: tmevens@email.unc.edu

Don Handelman is Shaine Professor Emeritus of Anthropology at the Hebrew University. Email: mshand@mscc.huji.ac

Christopher Roberts teaches humanities and religious studies at Lewis & Clark College in Portland, Oregon. Email: robertschristopher4@gmail.com

❧ SECTION I ❧

REFLEXIVITY, SOCIAL SCIENCE, AND ETHICS

Editors' Preface

Evens's contribution is a cautionary argument against the unquestioning way social activism is taken for granted in so much of today's anthropology. Reflecting on the powerful impact of reflexivity in the discipline itself, he suggests that, ironically, the reflexive turn to activism inclines to conceal from itself a critical lack of reflexivity regarding ethics and the nature of anthropology as a social science. Reflexivity is, Evens argues, always open and never complete. As a consequence, the resulting analyses may prove vulnerable to self-undoing when it comes to their effectiveness as activism. This is because, even if the line between subjectivity and objectivity is essentially equivocal (objectivism amounting to a subjective position), in the absence of duly scrupulous attention to the objective pole of the analytical equation, anthropology qua anthropology becomes refutable as just another partisan stance. In the event, the discipline's offering on behalf of any activist cause is subject to a loss of the leverage the discipline, in its function as social science, can, in fact, offer. But these concerns do not lead Evens to argue that social activism has no place in anthropology. Rather, the point is that the scholar whose anthropology is dedicated to social activism is obligated by profession to assess vigilantly the impact of the activist cause on the soundness of his/her research. Given the intrinsic difference between moral reason and anthropology as social science, Evens concludes on the ethical note that in any particular ethnographic situation, the anthropologist might find her- or himself caught between doing good and doing good research. In effect, he or she will then be compelled to decide, situationally, which of the two choices should serve as *the* "good" under the conflicted circumstances.

Like Evens's contribution, but with a more decided sense of the ethical, Handelman's contribution constitutes a reflexive critique of his own discipline. He argues that anthropology is, for reasons of "ethics," acutely and irredeemably dilemmatic. In light of the preponderantly face-to-face nature of ethnographic research and Emmanuel Levinas's philosophy of ethics, Handelman maintains that anthropology is caught between conflicting ethical demands, ones that do not allow of intermediation: on the one hand, professional ethics, in which the concern for the subjects of study is for the most part "bureaucratized," a function of objectivism and the researcher's careerism; on the other hand, the ethics of face-to-face or intersubjective relations, in which the "other" enjoys ethical primacy. The latter ethics is not a question of a professional moral code but of the self as subject to the other's entreaty, the result of which is the fundamental compromise of the researcher's very self. From this Levinasian perspective, the point is precisely not to grasp, in the sense of take hold of, the other, as if he or she is but an object, but to preserve the other's difference, the other's essential, particular humanity. In the one case, the other is, in Levinasian terms, reduced to "the same" and thereby disappeared; in the other case, the other is experienced directly, through the immediacy of affectivity, which is to say, the *reflexivity* of immanence as against the *reflection* of conceptualization. Because the other is thus basically irreducible and *ultimately* beyond the grasp of the anthropological interrogator, Handelman argues, provocatively, for a disciplinary "ethic of being wrong," and finds that anthropology is subject to fundamentally schizophrenic ethical demands. In contrast to the bureaucratic legalism of a professional code of ethics, he holds that bringing Levinas to the ethnographical field places the ethical onus of responsibility in fieldwork immediately on the anthropologist, in the most personal of ways.

In his contribution, Koenraad Stroeken distinguishes between two kinds of reflexivity, cosmopolitan and destructive. Broad and complex, his argument constitutes a critique of traditional anthropology and certain of its current trends. Whereas *cosmopolitan* reflexivity reflects what Stroeken calls the "psychic unity" of humankind, *destructive* reflexivity continues to hew to the positivism on the basis of which anthropology established itself as a bona fide social science. It is the difference, he contends, between seeing culture and meaning as mechanistic and understanding them in terms of events rather than objects (a distinction similar to Handelman's). In this connection, his critique of Latour's actor-network theory is particularly provocative. It is not the case, Stroeken argues contra Latour, that we have never been modern but, rather, that people everywhere and always have themselves naturally exhibited elements of what we, conceitedly, call modernity. Stroeken backs up his general argument with two case studies from his ethnographic research on the Sukuma of Tanzania, the one case on healing ritual and the other on gender equality. With these cases, he shows that the Sukuma are patently reflexive in their own right, and that this reflexivity displays openness that is indigenously modern and hence cosmopolitan. Attributing this kind of reflexivity to the "psychic unity" of mankind, he finds that there is continuity between this people and modernity. The notion of psychic unity (originally coined by the nineteenth-century ethnologist Adolf Bastien, from whom Carl Jung developed the idea of the collective unconscious) remains rather ineffable, but not ineffective. With this notion, Stroeken seems to suggest that the ethical dilemma between anthropological "science" and ethnographic fieldwork, discussed in different ways by both Evens and Handelman, is resolvable.

More so than most fields, the reflexive turn in the discipline of religious studies has rendered theoretical critiques of religions such as those penned by d'Holbach, Feuerbach, or Freud almost obsolete. On this terrain, Roberts, a religious studies scholar, turns to the philosophical distinction between using language in first-order human interactions and mentioning it in the sense that referring to language facilitates reflection upon language as a distinct human phenomena, and generates metadiscourses such as rhetoric, linguistics, poetics, and semiotics. The use versus mention distinction is critical to understanding a US Supreme Court ruling that scholars of religion cannot use religion to persuade or proselytize, but should instead only mention them, in effect rendering the persuasive features of religions temporarily inutile through reflexive scrutiny. The broad provenance this opened for scholarly practice has been restricted, Roberts argues, because of a moral as opposed to a semiotic interpretation of this ruling. He illustrates this critique by turning to Geertz's influential essay on religion, showing how that anthropologist's widely embraced perspective leaves religionists profoundly ill equipped to deal with anyone but the utterly naïve religious other, deeply entranced by authorized factuality and incapable of perceiving a cultural drama or social panic as spectacle and not reality. In particular, as shown finally by a case study from the author's youth, during which a deacon orchestrated a moral panic to prevent the desegregation of a white church in postsegregation suburban Atlanta, Geertz would have religionists miss the Machiavellian believer, the one who willfully and strategically uses religious and cultural resources, often for quite idiopathic purposes. Given Roberts's critical emphasis on a particular conception of the moral as dramatically manipulable, situationally sensitive, context dependent, and ultimately empty of content, every "value" becomes vulnerable to unscrupulous use and exploitation by the Machiavellian believer. As this figure leverages mentions of the moral to pursue the immoral use of religion, the Machiavellian believer marks the spot of a metaethical problem for religious studies as a field and for societies struggling in the agonistic atmosphere of the postsecular world.

❧ 1 ❧

IS THERE A DIFFERENCE BETWEEN DOING GOOD AND DOING GOOD RESEARCH?

Anthropology and Social Activism, or the Productive Limits of Reflexivity

Terry Evens

This notion emerged as de Kooning was recalling the Great Depression and how his well-meaning New York colleagues had attempted to make art relevant to social problems by depicting "strikes and poor people." It may have been good politics, but it was bad art, said de Kooning—and therefore, in the long run, bad politics.

—Richard Shiff, "Willem de Kooning: Same Change"

Focus and Problem

At its etymological broadest, "reflexivity" (Latin: *reflexus*) denotes "bending back." Obviously, this term can yield a very broad spectrum of usages. In the field of anthropology, it has always been implicated in the concept of ethnocentrism, the disciplinary proscription on measuring other cultures and societies by the standards of one's own cultural and social order. Perhaps needless to say, this proscription cannot oblige the ethnographer to wipe his or her mind clean, for we have no choice but to interpret otherness by *starting with* what we already know and understand. Rather, the rule against ethnocentrism entails the effort to turn back on one's preconceptions in order to interrogate them in the light of what one is observing and experiencing ethnographically. This reflexive act is phenomenological.

In this chapter, I am concerned with a related but more recent anthropological usage of reflexivity, pertaining to a heightened self-awareness of the limits of the ethnographer's objectivity. The recognition of these limits as largely inherent in anthropological research has brought into added relief the question of the ethnographer's participatory impact on the social order under investigation. My focus is on one of the reactions this question has stimulated in current anthropology, namely, social activism.

A self-critique of anthropology as a discipline bent on aggrandizing the self by epistemologically subjecting the other has been developed monographically and theoretically with some regularity in recent times. Although I would argue that all anthropology is innately reflexive and comparative, critiques that today take reflexivity as an explicit theme enjoy a salutary importance. Nevertheless, it seems to me that there can be a faint odor of the "politically correct" about them. Of course, since such critiques vary greatly in analytical sophistication and perceptiveness, my intention is to speak here in very general terms alone. Plainly, though, particularly when their analyses proceed more or less chiefly on a basis of sociopolitical causes, critiques of this kind are not just bent on theoretical contestation—they then also connote moral superiority.

My aim here is not to condemn this reflexive turn in current anthropology, but rather to sketch a cautionary picture of it. On the one hand, the turn is constructive: it opens conventional anthropology to serious question and highlights its nature as inherently valuational. But on the other, it inclines to collapse to an excessive degree the distinction between doing good and doing good research, thus putting both objectives at risk. My argument revolves around the understanding that although, for ontological reasons, purely value-free research is not an option, there is such a thing as relative objectivity, and anthropological research, even when it is undertaken with explicitly political intent, necessarily demands a determined objectivity in this sense. Put another way, even though in the final analysis research is always predicated on values that are irreducible to positive fact, doing good and doing good research remain *relatively* separate and distinct, and *insofar as the difference between them is allowed to go unattended,* the carrying out of research on behalf of the good is likely, perhaps even bound, to be self-defeating.

My argument proceeds as follows. First, I draw attention to the irony that activist self-contraction on behalf of the ethnographic other can be, in respect of the other anthropologist, a moralizing exercise in self-expansion. Second, I argue that this perverse twist in the activist's selfhood goes hand in hand with the reflexive turn's characteristic preoccupation with the discourse of power, and that this discourse is prone to totalism and the erasure of any difference between objective research and political commitment. Third, I highlight the irony that this same discourse presupposes the very dualistic sense of reality on which rests the vulgar empiricism reflexive anthropology intends to overcome. Lastly, seeing social activism as but one of two principles of an inescapable double bind (the other being positive science), I begin to address the question of its place in anthropology.

Activism and the Anthropological Self

As I see it, in its efforts to make the other intelligible, anthropology has tended gradually to erode the otherness of the other. This intellectual evolution seems to have reached a tipping point in much current anthropology. In its effort to deal remedially with the discipline's own unwanted proclivity to "colonize" the other by exoticizing and eroticizing it, this anthropology has turned sharply inward. In doing so, it has found that, like the "other" cultures of anthropology's yesteryear, the professional anthropological enterprise is, far from being a matter of truth, principally a system of beliefs, values, and ideas, in a word, a kind of culture or ideology—only in its case, one with a strong, but secreted, political bent. In effect, anthropology has, reflexively, "otherized" itself.

As a result, by discerning and disclosing the discipline's hidden complicity in subjecting the other, it would seem that the anthropology that has helped to promote this recent reflexive turn has positioned itself to address the disciplinary problem at issue. Moreover, because this problem is seen as essentially political, so too the proposed solution is plainly political in nature: social activism. Accordingly, the anthropology in question may well appear as having transcended the problem altogether. Indeed, practitioners of this anthropology look as if they have kept their ethnographic authority pure—precisely because it is openly and pointedly political, their anthropology tends to present itself as self-transparent and untainted by any need to subject the other.

Coupled with this exception to the discipline's alienation from its established self is the following consideration. The charge against the older anthropology is typically leveled against the ethnographer in his or her relation to the representative other (primitive, preliterate, traditional, atheoretical, etc.). In other words, the charge is aimed at the anthropologist in his role "abroad," as a kind of would-be other. Excluding the experience of female members of the profession, who have themselves been made to feel as a category the relegation to otherness, the charge is not leveled at the anthropologist in his professional capacity in relation to other anthropologists, when he is at home, in academic residence.

The point is that the principled restriction of the accusation of "othering" to the relation between the anthropologist and the ethnographic other enables the critic to conceal from her- or himself (if only thinly) the consequences of the critique in respect of his or her own professional relationship vis-à-vis, instead of the discipline's usual others, other anthropologists. It generally does not occur to such a critic that his pointed appraisal of his colleagues, by depicting them as not simply theoretically wrongheaded but *ideologically* backward (or worse), may well implicitly project him as their ethicopolitical superior. To be sure, this failure of reflexivity also marks a generational function whereby the position that is fresh and new—for example, postcolonialist anthropology—is inclined to see itself as enlightened relative to the "dark ages" of the "politically naïve" anthropology that preceded it. But, tellingly, this generational function displays an expansion of self that plainly runs contrary to the overt ethicopolitical claims of the new anthropology.

In the same vein, this sense of superiority is predisposed to consign a great deal of anthropology, including classics, to the dustbin of history. In his compact critique of what he calls the "postmodernist mood" of much current anthropology (a critique in which he bemoans the Foucauldian fetishism of "power" in today's anthropology), Marshall Sahlins, with his typical caustic wit, comments as follows (2002: 26): "I don't know about Britain, but in America many graduate students in Anthropology are totally uninterested in other times and places. They say we should study our own current problems, all other ethnography being impossible anyhow, as it is just our 'construction of the other.' So if they get their way, and this becomes the principle of anthropological research, fifty years hence no one will pay the slightest attention to the work they're doing now. Maybe they're onto something."

Is it really the case that our discipline is so unlike philosophy (to choose an obvious example, and even if we grant significant differences) that we need not bother to read and reread the anthropological masters and many others who followed them? After all, a great deal of philosophy, perhaps even the bulk, from the Greeks through Kant and the moderns, is, although not by the surface lights of formal disciplinary boundaries, anthropological in a sense in which we deeply share. Does our discipline really advance, theoretically and ethnographically, at a pace so swift that its ancestors, both distant and near, are simply no longer relevant, mere relics worth looking at only to highlight by contrast how far we've come? Does not this sort of scientistic pretension to the accumulation of knowledge run contrary to the political and ethical tenor of modern anthropology, ironically the very tenor these critiques—with their defining focus on value no less (if not more) than on fact—propose to cherish?

These observations, about a distinct lack of reflexivity within reflexive anthropology, suggest that there is something still secure, even comforting, about *alter*izing ourselves in our ethnographic role as would-be others. In that role we remain still, as it were, at a fairly safe distance from ourselves. Although it is serious and can threaten the anthropological identity in a useful way, the recent charge against the ethnographic authority of the anthropologist does not quite hit home, does not kick the professional self where it really lives—in the hallowed halls of the academy.[1] If this observation runs true, then an ethnography of an association or department of anthropology would make a salutary piece of epistemological violence. By accessing ourselves where our otherness to ourselves is most immediate and closest to home, where reflexive observation becomes peculiarly threatening to the anthropological self, we stand to alter the terms of our discourse in such a way as to extend our away-from-home reflexive endeavor to reflect on itself and its own professional as well as intrinsic limitations. Of course, for the very reasons I have just adumbrated—that is, the need to keep a safe distance from our*selves* in their pretense of professional self-righteousness—we should not expect to see, barring the rare exception, an ethnographic undertaking of the kind.[2]

Activism and the Discourse of Power

In point of this somewhat skeptical picture of the anthropological activist's well-intentioned self (the sincerity of whose avowed intentionality is not in doubt here), we have no more reason to think that today's anthropologists are not themselves significantly informed with the "colonization" of self characterizing the Western episteme than we have to presume that the anthropologists of colonialism's heyday managed to free themselves cleanly from the gravity of colonialist and rationalist presumption and design. The self in question is conceived of in terms of sovereignty, an independent (Cartesian) subjectivity that ideally enjoys supreme power over what it is not. While it is true that anthropologists have been duly taken with the argument regarding the fallacy of such autonomous selfhood, if Foucault and others are right about this selfhood's a priori status and its epistemic depth and reach in Western self-identity, then our sense of self will scarcely change overnight. It would be a gross disciplinary conceit to think that, because of our theoretical and critical insight into this sense of self, we anthropologists have transcended it. Insofar as we have not, it is bound to show up in our work, including our self-critiques (the present one, as goes without saying, not excepted).

In the past several decades, anthropology has been characterized by a driving concern to expose hegemonic power structures that foster oppression and injustice.[3] It is easy to sympathize with this concern, which, as a form of resistance in its own right, has largely proceeded as a monologue of power. But even though the resulting analyses of power can be acutely insightful, they tend to remain, in respect of their work of resistance, theoretically self-defeating. For, if power alone is at work, if it is the sole operative force, then one cannot help but wonder what legitimates the movement of anthropological resistance and what social forces other than power per se are ethnographically obscured. Are all social conditions reducible to power as such? Does justice too reduce to terms of power? Does the academic discourse of resistance spell yet another would-be or emerging power structure? Without *explicit* acknowledgment and theorizing of something other than power per se, can there be a meaningful sense of moral inquiry or even, to invoke Durkheim's elementary sociological insight, moral force and order?[4]

The turn to the discourse of resistance has encouraged a concomitant interest in dissolving the distinction between academic anthropology and social activism. Although the notion of participant observation has long been a shibboleth in ethnographic research, generally it has conveyed earnest observation but token participation. It is only in recent decades that the discipline, in line with twentieth-century philosophy of science, has come fully to realize that there is no observer who is not in some fundamental way participant in what he or she observes. However, this important realization—that there is no such thing as a view from nowhere, or that pure objectivism is chimerical—appears to have ushered in an at least tacit conclusion that between anthropological research and social activism there is no difference to speak of. And from this conclusion, it is a mere baby step to reckon not only that it makes sense to try to choose one's bias in an overt and considered manner, but also that one's research ought to proceed altogether as a function of this bias.

In fact, though, the assumption of simple identity between research and activism is fallacious, for a premise of imperfect distinction does not logically entail a conclusion of total indistinction. What is more, monistic collapse of the distinction at point reveals the very dualism that cultivates the Western sense of self in question, the hermetic, sovereign sense predicated on the exclusion and domination of others and otherness. The collapse results from the same logic of reification that holds that wherever two mutually exclusive phenomena coexist (mind and body, self and other, subject and object, and so on), one of them must be reducible to the other. In other words, this Cartesian logic inherently excludes *relative* difference, making this organon a logic of power.[5]

Activism, Empiricism, and Ontology

I suggest that insofar as this development in anthropology threatens the quality and validity of research in the discipline, to that same extent it undermines the discipline's unique ability to assist social causes. In this event, it would be perverse and self-defeating. The activist development of which I speak is predicated on the idea of the beholder's—in the present case, the ethnographer's—share in the determining of what there is. This idea constitutes a distinct caution against the vulgar empiricism that tends to lurk beneath the general idea of empirical research. Whereas, loosely speaking, empirical research prescribes close and exacting observation that *aspires* to objectivity, vulgar empiricism, as I use the term, holds that the facts speak for themselves (see Evens 1995: 196ff.).

What is striking about the reflexive turn in anthropology is that while it has occasioned an acute awareness that there is no such thing as an unbiased ethnographic perspective, it has only rarely grasped that the biases the ethnographer brings with him or her necessarily carry a taken-for-granted picture of reality *as a whole*—which is to say, an implicit ontology. Instead, correlative to the disciplinary rise in importance of such limited—even if vital—topoi as women's and postcolonialist studies, emphatically the tendency has been to take the biases as primarily political in nature, as matters of power. In reaction to the realization that the effort to maintain sheer ethnographic objectivity and impartiality is naïve, the anthropologist—revolving dualistically—has been inclined on the whole to expressly politicize the discipline. As I suggested earlier, this shift appears to follow a logic to the effect that if implicit political bias is unavoidable, then one may as well assume, albeit with due deliberation, an explicit political position.

Speaking generally, the resulting positions, the bulk of which move to empower and dignify the relatively powerless, cannot, in my view, be gainsaid. Nevertheless, and notwithstanding the consideration that perfect objectivity is indeed a chimera, this politicization may itself be naïve, insofar as it saps the life from the consideration that without the *bias of relative objectivity* ethnographic practice per se has no "scientific" or special warrant. It takes very little reflection to see what we all experience on a day-to-day basis anyway—that although "[o]ur aspiration towards objectivity can only proceed from the admission of subjectivity" (Berger 2001: 421), the "distance" between observer and observed is nonetheless patently relative and varies precisely with the nature of the subjective perspective the observer takes. That is to say, while it cannot afford the observer a view from nowhere, objectivity can be methodically assumed, to efficacious effect, as just one such subjective perspective. The critical point is that if, when adduced on behalf of a political position, ethnography (qua ethnography) is to serve effectively, it must take scrupulous care not to impugn its own relative objectivity, for its special force in relation to political argument must rest with its comparatively objective determinations. Without this force, anthropology becomes just one more political discourse, duly susceptible to refutation as, rather than wrong or inaccurate or unsound, simply partisan.

But here what I particularly want to bring out about this politicizing movement is that, ironically, for all its attention to the hidden biases of objectivist ethnography, it seems not to have alerted the discipline substantially enough to the problem of empiricism as an unspoken dogma implicating the view from nowhere, and underlying ethnographic interpretation. Indeed, arguably the emphasis on power as the defining concept of this reflexive anthropological turn continues, at least tacitly, to lend support to this dogma. The presumption of power is itself an inherent bias, one that bears a picture of reality consistent with the positivist idea of objectivity from which such empiricism issues. The empiricist dogma that all knowledge is reducible to brute facts presupposes the clean (Cartesian) differentiation of an object world (and hence, naturally, of a subjectivity equally sui generis). On this positivist conception of the world, "power," in turn, is afforded a driving phenomenological purchase: because for its operation, as Hegel famously spelled out, power requires an object *in itself*, an ontology of absolute objectivity is bound to breed an epistemology of absolute power.

For a full-blown example decidedly telling in respect to the rise of modernity, we can cite Baconian empiricism, according to which, in Horkheimer and Adorno's interpretation ([1972] 1998: 4, emphasis added), "What men want to learn from nature is how to use it in order *wholly* to dominate it and other men." Bacon aside, the point is that empiricism comports effortlessly with power, whether we have in mind a Hegelian/Weberian sense, in which power obtains interpersonally, or a

Nietzschean/Foucauldian sense, in which power is atmospheric. In line with Horkheimer and Adorno, Foucault's conception of unspecified power that produces subjectivity for the purpose of *subjection* implicates the enclosure of the subjective by the objective, since the subject's subjectivity (mimicking the fate of the master in Hegel's master-slave dialectic) then consists in treating itself as an object.

This analytical fixation on power gives reason to think that the relatively recent and conspicuous reflexive turn in anthropology, with its strong political bent, has not confronted directly the shadowy but suffuse presumption of empiricism that has characterized ethnographic anthropology's rise as a social science and has helped to eclipse from view the absolutely critical extent to which ethnographic inquiry is also and always an exercise in intervention, metaphysics, and the attribution of ultimate value.[6] It is notable that the ontological implications of Foucault's notion of power do not seem to have been perceived as such by anthropologists. Insofar as they limit their grasp of the Foucauldian notion simply to the idea of the political, anthropologists risk blinding themselves to the ontological preconceptions underlying the very idea of power, and therefore, as I go on to explain, to the possibility of opening the reflexive turn itself to critical reflection. As a result, ironically, like the anthropologists they rightly fault for blind faith in the possibility of value-free research, such critics might be implicitly predisposed to present themselves as self-transparent, as if their truth is eternal and represents the limitless view from nowhere.

In conceiving of power in terms of production as well as repression, Foucault had in mind the creation of the real. Although his work tended to concentrate on the constraining force of the reality thus produced, in view of power's creative function, he also saw power in a positive as well as a negative light. This affirmative understanding of power points directly to the importance of ontology for anthropology, to the way in which humans in their relations to things and to one another (including, of course, the ethnographic interaction) participate in the creation of reality. Because Foucault's usage of "power" lends itself too readily, at least in today's conceptual universe, to the eradication of *any* distinction between ethics and power, I prefer not to use the term in this (Nietzschean) way. Nevertheless, this usage, wherein creation and constraint are two aspects of the same phenomenon, plainly and forcefully suggests that at the end of the day anthropology is ontology (whether its practitioners know it or not and despite its quite proper credentials as social science), and that, therefore, ontological preconceptions, both those of the studied and the student, should be an explicit and pivotal concern of anthropological inquiry.

As they are constructed through experience, such preconceptions plainly are historical. Yet precisely because they are *pre*conceptions, they serve also to produce and reproduce reality. On the one hand, like deductive truths, or, to use Kant's term, "analytic a priori," such preconceptions are held as necessarily true; but on the other hand, like Kant's "synthetic a priori," they are arrived at on the basis of experience instead of logical deduction and its censorious principle of noncontradiction. As such they mark a zone of ambiguity between theory and practice, or between mental act and bodily action. As a result, under most quotidian circumstances, their hosts are in no position to tell these preconceptions from concrete reality, including the reality of the hosts themselves. In effect, as Bourdieu theorized with his notion of habitus, the preconceptions are innocently enacted in the "natural" course of everyday life.

If this is correct, then it suggests that it is to our great advantage to seek to isolate and identify these ontological preconceptions, which reveal themselves in their own existential and discursive practice. And since the ontological preconceptions of the anthropologist are critical to his professional inquiry, it is in his direct, expert interest to do the same for his own as well as those of others, taking advantage of the disruption offered by ethnographic confrontation to jar his reflexive insight and rethink reality. It is a central contention of my argument that of anthropology's preconceptions, dualism remains one of the most, if not *the* most, stubborn and comprehensive, and that it has worked and continues to work to restrict profoundly—at the heart of the discipline's defining purpose—the anthropologist's ability to plumb the reality of other cultures. It is only by seeing beyond dualism, to comprehend boundaries as both separating and connecting, that we can position ourselves to grasp power as also otherwise, and to realize that every act of power presupposes ethical generation or the construction of value.

The Place of Activism in Anthropology: An Ethical Double Bind

I have argued that insofar as current reflexive anthropology fails to reflect carefully on the difference between doing good and doing good research, it risks sabotaging both its anthropology and its social activism. I am not contending, then, that activism has no place in anthropology, but rather that it must not be introduced in such a way as to vitiate relative objectivity. How, then, should it be brought into social science?

Max Weber provided to this question one of the most developed and deeply reflexive responses by a social theorist. In essence, he argued (1949: 82) that the notion that social scientific conclusions derive from the "facts themselves" is indeed "naïve," for, he observed, in cultural science all facts presuppose "evaluative ideas" or, if you will, ideas of the good. Nevertheless, he maintained with no less force that it is critically necessary to preserve a conceptual distinction between fact and value, which is to say, in his own terminology, between the objective and the subjective. The apparent contradiction in his thinking here is, I think, workable if we take it to imply that objectivity is a relative rather than absolute property, and that it constitutes a value in its own right, the good and importance of which rests with its instrumental fruitfulness (in Weber's argument, given ultimate values, objectivity can distinguish the most likely means to achieve them). I would argue that this way of reconciling his apparently contradictory assertions (that facts are both distinct from values and yet never free of them) is nicely consistent with his famous notion of "ideal-type" (1949: 91–92), according to which objectivity would amount to a heuristic model against which a researcher could measure his or her finally limited but by no means negligible ability to observe with disciplined detachment.[7]

In a self-commentary pertaining to political activism vis-à-vis his own intellectual project of deconstruction, Jacques Derrida captures something like the existential tension implicated in Weber's penetrating phenomenological understanding of the relationship between, on the one hand, taking a stance on what is just and good and, on the other, rigorously analyzing the extant nature or logic of things. "But the difficulty," writes the late French philosopher (in Bernstein 1991: 214), "is to gesture in opposite directions at the same time: on the one hand to preserve a distance and suspicion with regard to the official political codes governing reality; on the other, to intervene here and now in a practical and *engaged* manner whenever the necessity arises. This position of dual allegiance, in which I personally find myself, is one of perpetual uneasiness. I try where I can to act politically while recognizing that such action remains incommensurate with my intellectual project of deconstruction."

I can also enlist, with Weber's argument in mind, the support of a key philosophical influence in anthropology's recent reflexive turn, another famous French thinker: "The project, tactics and goals to be adopted," Michel Foucault emphatically declares (in Gutting 2001: 262), "are a matter for those who do the fighting. What the intellectual can do is to provide the instruments of analysis.... But as for saying, 'Here is what you must do!,' certainly not."[8] With reference to the clause "The project, tactics and goals to be adopted," it is well here also to recall Foucault's stated position (in Rabinow 1984: 343) regarding the critical purport of his thought: "My point is not that everything is bad, but that everything is dangerous.... If everything is dangerous, then we always have something to do. So my position leads not to apathy but to a hyper- and pessimistic activism." One conclusion that follows from this wonderfully wise and discerning position, I should think, is that while resistance and reform can be effective, they always carry acute dangers of their own, and they scarcely ever prove as salutary as they are hopeful.

On the other hand, where objectivity is conceived of as absolute rather than relative—that is, in terms of the logical perfection defined by dualism or mutual exclusion—it too courts disaster, as Weber himself, in his profuse writings on rationalization, made clear. But to see the potential inhumanity of unqualified rationalization, it is only necessary to cite figures the likes of Adolf Eichmann and Donald Rumsfeld, whose devout but banal bureaucratic actions and self-justifications have done so much to advance what, from the perspective of ethics, can only be regarded as geometrical evil.[9] It is crucial to understand, then, that limitedness is no less an absolute condition or sine qua non of objectivity than it is of reflexivity.

In light of this picture, the issue of the relation between anthropological research and politicoethical commitment can be resolved only situationally, never once and for all. This is because, objectively speaking, we find ourselves, as professional social scientists, always and representatively caught between deciding when to strive for an objective perspective and when to intervene "in an engaged manner." It is just this sort of double bind, wherein we are intrinsically and continuously condemned to mediate and decide (wakefully or not) between equally vital courses of action, that describes what it means to depict the human condition as ethics (politics being, paradoxically, a continuation of evaluative decision making in the realm of power). If objectivity is taken as an absolute, then it is bound to foster inhumanity, and in this sense undermine the human condition (even if being inhuman—by contradistinction to "nonhuman"—is something humans alone can aspire to and achieve); and the same holds for reflexivity, which, when seen as a completed state of being instead of a continuing dynamic, describes nothing if not the Western ideal of sheer (godlike) self-transparency, a sense of selfhood that defines away the very act of reflexivity, seeing as that act always and necessarily *deforms* or contracts the subject.

The revelation that the ethnographic observer participates in the observed makes the former partially responsible for the latter. More generally, it marks our capacity to determine in part reality itself, including, of course, the reality of our*selves*. If, though, the contradiction between perceived reality and the reality we deem desirable proves flagrant and grotesque, as it became in the twentieth century (with all the talk of human rights, in the midst of military and industrial slaughter), then our responsibility becomes peculiarly politicized. In view of the state of human reality today (the staggering amount of exploitation and unnecessary man-made suffering), the need to become politically engaged is urgent. But for the anthropologist as such, the responsibility that issues from the realization of the observer's share is not only political but also—in the sense in which science representatively demands the methodical attempt to achieve an imposing degree of objectivity—scientific.

Hence, the responsibility of the anthropologist qua anthropologist is basically divided between engagement and disengagement. Here it is deeply edifying to bear in mind that that which marks us as peculiarly human, namely, the incomparable amount of play in the "intentional threads" that tie us to our ground (Merleau-Ponty 1962: xiii), signifies nothing if not a defining, existential mode of disengagement.[10] It is this singular looseness in our being, constituting a certain distance from the world, that makes us conscious of the world as if it were somehow outside of ourselves, and thereby gives us the power of choice and something to choose between. As Rousseau put it (1950: 208): "Nature lays her commands on every animal, and the brute obeys her voice. Man receives the same impulsion, but at the same time knows himself at liberty to acquiesce or resist: and it is particularly in his consciousness of this liberty that the spirituality of his soul is displayed." In light of this picture of the human condition as ethical process, it seems fair to say that for us social scientists, as for all humans, the characteristic mode of engagement is relative disengagement, which is why political commitment is, in an important if limited sense, a matter of choice for us. But as social scientists what distinguishes us is the burden of attending methodically to the mode and measure of disengagement.

Weber concluded that value judgments cannot be derived on the basis of empirical knowledge. Since scientific inquiry looks into what *is* rather than what *ought to be,* surely Weber's conclusion is correct. But it is also in a notable sense excessive, for there is one value—more precisely, hypervalue—that may be inferred from the realization of relative objectivity (Evens 1995: 205–7). I have in mind the value on the possibility of engendering ends and values. If, as Weber maintained, all empirical research is ultimately predicated on value judgments, then a value on making such judgments and, correlatively, on fashioning meaningful worlds may be deduced from the very possibility of such research. Being derived from the fact of what is (the irrevocableness of value as such in human life) but at the same time representing a judgment as to what ought to be (the *particular* ideal it communicates), such a value stands directly between nature and artifice, making it (an oxymoron if ever there was one) a "natural value." But a value on creating values can ensure only that we remain always caught between conflicting ends and obligations, such that we have no choice but to live our lives as a dynamic of choice or "unnatural" selection. In this chapter, my cautionary contention has been that, given the double bind of research and activism, without the concern for relative objectivity anthropology (qua anthropology) has nothing unique to offer politicoethical ends, and that therefore the *anthropologue engagé* needs to give his or her science its relative due and take care to allow political purpose to eclipse his or her science neither altogether nor overmuch.

Acknowledgments

I am indebted to Don Handelman, Lee Schlesinger, and Jim Peacock for their thoughtful and constructive readings of this chapter.

Notes

1. Of course, Bourdieu's grand study (1988) of the French academic world must be counted here. For another example, in his *Academia and the Luster of Capital* (1993), Sande Cohen, a self-designated "ex-historian," provides a powerful critique of the "high university." In the third chapter in particular, detailing a case of a grievance filed by a faculty member (Cohen served on the grievance committee), as well as his own tenure case, Cohen fairly skewers the institutional process, leading him to arrive at conclusions of the following kind (1993: 35): "There isn't a faculty in the United States that offers resistance to its Officer Corps and bureaucratic 'center'"; "[W]e can say that this Officer Corps ensures that the university will not be contaminated by acts of reading that undermine its own consistency." For a book-length historical (and notorious) case study of an iniquitous dismissal of a faculty member at Rutgers University, see Oshinsky, McCormick, and Horn (1989).
2. In connection with reflexive memory slippage, whereby self-criticism fails to reflect on political implications of its own endeavor, allow me to note a

concrete possibility pertaining to the anthropologist in academic residence. Many of us have heard of or observed departmental conduct that constructs others out of fellow members who seriously question the institution's or discipline's professional integrity, identity, and authority. These members are commonly labeled "difficult," "irrational," "unrealistic," "troublemakers," "loose cannons," "whistleblowers," and the like. Important here is not the accuracy of these epithets in any particular instance, but rather the process of power they betray. Of course, this sort of thing is hardly confined to the institutional setting of the discipline of anthropology. But if our discipline is to be truly reflexive, then it must be prepared to analyze conduct of this kind in the departmental and organizational settings of the profession. These days few anthropologists would hesitate to conclude that other social and epistemological orders run on a basis of power (we have become exquisitely expert in our ability to uncover power at work in social orders), including now the order composed by the ethnographic relation. But few also are inclined to admit, if only to themselves, the open secret that their own professional orders at home may be similarly characterized.

When I began my field research in the kibbutz Timem, a few members of the community asked me if it was my intention to treat them like "guinea pigs." Once I thought about it, I replied that I intended to treat them in the only way open to me to treat any human being (including myself): as a "subject-object." This response was significantly imprecise, however, for the polarity of subject and object admits of degrees of direction as between the two poles, and given that my primary goal in being there, in the kibbutz, was ethnographic research, these apprehensive and inquiring members had a substantial point. But there was more to the question than that of overobjectifying other human beings, for members also wanted to know, in a related vein of inquiry, if I was after their "dirty laundry." Can there be any doubt that we, as anthropologists, have similar apprehensions about being scrutinized ethnographically, apprehensions compounded by our self-identification as experts on the nature of society and its operation? Indeed, do we not readily understand Timem's members' concerns about objectification and scandal precisely because we have experienced them at home?

3. Apropos of my point about the relevance of anthropological classics, political ideals along these lines were not really missing from bygone anthropology. For example, as especially Kapferer (2007: 85ff.) has argued about the Manchester School, Gluckman and his colleagues were fundamentally moved in their ethnographic endeavors by just such ideals. The difference is, though, that far from taking anthropology to be a primarily political enterprise, they were basically disposed to take its science at face value and therefore to see it as a powerful documentary and practical tool in relation to their political persuasions. Another example is M. G. Smith, who gave up his headship of University College London's anthropology department to become special advisor to the prime minister of Jamaica, in order to give something back, in the way of political ideals and sociological expertise, to his native land (Hall 1997: chap. 6). To be sure, from the perspective of the

modern critics in question here, it is just such an unreconstructed view of anthropological inquiry that is politically naïve. But, as I am arguing in this chapter, modern critics too seem to display a diffuse ingenuousness of their own.

4. Given his inspired Marxian reflexive sociology but prodigious practice of social scientific method, Bourdieu's work is exemplary in combining activism with research. But even he fails to address directly the question of the legitimacy of his sociological activism in relation to the prevailing disciplinary emphasis on power (cf. Evens 1999).

5. In connection with such a logic, it is worth reminding ourselves of Agamben's explication (1998: 86) of the Western tradition of governmental sovereignty: he speaks of a "zone of indistinction" by virtue of which the sovereign stands both within and outside the law, and is therefore possessed of unlimited power.

6. As I am claiming only a loose but pervasive hold on anthropology by vulgar empiricism, I do not have in mind "true believers" (few if any of which could be found today). The kind of adherence I am concerned with is more in the nature of a subtle and insidious prejudice against theory, where "theory" continues to be seen in shrill opposition to "empirical observation." For example, some years ago, seeking constructive commentary from a distinguished colleague, I sent to him my (then) unpublished reanalysis of a particular ethnographic problem found in Evans-Pritchard's (1956) Nuer ethnography. Although he was trained (as was I) in the anthropological tradition of British empiricism, and therefore placed great value (as do I) on intensive field research, I have little doubt that he would reject empiricism as I have defined it for present purposes. Yet he responded to my reanalysis of the Nuer data by suggesting that further fieldwork alone could suffice to resolve the problem. I was taken aback by this response, for two reasons. First, given the awkward fact that almost fifty years had gone by since Evans-Pritchard had gathered the relevant data among them, surely the Nuer were no longer the Nuer as Evans-Pritchard had found them. Second, my reanalysis was plainly predicated on the consideration that the data were basically in, and that—as in principle is the endgame with all ethnography—the problem was of a nature that what was needed were not more data but a fresh way of looking at them, in this case an ontological way. As I see it, my colleague's response revealed nothing more than the sort of vague and uncritical empiricist presumption that concerns me here, and that serves needlessly to close off theoretical possibility.

As to empiricist anathema to ontology, I may as well cite Evans-Pritchard, who (although a gifted theorist) in *Nuer Religion*, a book fairly bursting with ontological implication and ontologically relevant Nuer notions, explicitly refrains from discussing the ontological question (1956: 124, emphasis added): "I do not discuss this ontological question here beyond saying that were we to suppose that such phenomena are in themselves regarded as God we would misunderstand and misrepresent Nuer religious thought, *which is pre-eminently dualistic*." Although this (tautological) avoidance appears as such in only one place in the book, it is, in my view, equally applicable to the whole of his analysis. I find the avoidance ingenuous but also convenient, for it permitted Evans-Pritchard to impose a dualist ontology he bore with him to Nuerland, all the while supposing that he was deriving it from his empirical ethnographic observations. I cannot do here the close analysis of Evans-Pritchard's great monograph that is necessary to demonstrate this. But as the quotation might suggest, in his fierce concern to show that the Nuer were not hypostasizing the godhead but, rather, were speaking figuratively, Evans-Pritchard was inclined to preempt ontological discussion in favor of presuming what he wished to find out, namely, whether Nuer religion is or is not dualist.

7. In an illuminating critique broadly akin to the present one, Bickerton (2006: 14–15), a historian, speaks of the "moralization of historical inquiry." He finds that there has been in his chosen discipline a shift of focus "from history to memory," memory being a form of bearing witness whereby, as Bickerton puts it, "those excluded and marginalized in the conventional stories told about the past can be included and recognized." Although he admires the fact that this shift opens "official" or conventional histories to question, he also thinks that it has "laid the basis for the abandonment of history altogether." This is because the focus on memory "instrumentalizes facts as a tool for the construction of identities and as means with which moral judgments can be made," but history "is concerned not with remembering, but with establishing these very facts." Bickerton's critical discussion of memory in relation to the moralizing of historical inquiry is pointed. However, because he does not see that this shift of focus goes hand in hand with a turn to reflexivity, Bickerton overlooks the consideration of which Weber, as we have seen, was aware: that in "establishing" the "facts" the historian in some measure, but necessarily, shares in their creation. That is to say, Bickerton gives us no reason to think that he does not still take for granted the empiricist dogma that the facts speak for themselves.

Focusing on the meaning of academic freedom with respect to college teaching, Stanley Fish (2006) too seems prone to make too little of the innately fuzzy line between fact and value. In an opportunity editorial distinguished by its clarity and incisiveness, Fish takes up the case of a lecturer at the University of Wisconsin at Madison who was inclined to share with his students his belief that the attack on the World Trade Center was a Bush administration conspiracy. Whereas the university's provost argued that it would be an infringement on the principle of academic freedom to censor what ideas could be taught in a classroom, critics maintained that "crazy or dangerous" ideas are not entitled to protection under that principle. Rejecting these arguments, Fish points out that academic freedom has nothing to do with the content of what is taught. He proposes instead that the relevant distinction rests between "studying" an idea and "proselytizing for it": this distinction, he declares, "is crucial and can be generalized; it shows us where the line between the responsible and irresponsible practice of academic freedom should always be drawn. Any idea can be brought into the classroom if the point is to inquire into its structure, history, influence and so forth. But no idea belongs in the classroom if the point of introducing it is to recruit your students for the political agenda it may be thought to imply." The point is satisfyingly put and makes an admirable rule of thumb. But, while it roundly matches Weber's own position on the duty of teachers (in Gerth and Mills 1946: 145ff.), the point glosses too easily over the consideration—again, one that Weber seems to have intuited, despite his insistence on the conceptual differentiation of fact from value—that the very choice of materials "to inquire into" has a rhetorical force of its own. (For example, it is hard to imagine anyone teaching about Holocaust revisionism without informing the inquiry with an evaluative point of view, either pro or con.) When Fish asserts that the exercise of setting personal conviction aside while in the classroom "may not always be total, it is both important and possible to make the effort," he implicitly acknowledges the problem. And although I concur with his judgment that the effort is both possible and important, it seems to me that the elegant simplicity of his solution is achieved at the cost of omitting to address the underlying problem that fact and value are only relatively, not absolutely, separate and distinct from each other.

8. "Foucault's history of madness," writes Gutting (2001: 262), "although taken up by Laing and others in the anti-psychiatry movement, was not intended as a call to abolish asylums or for any other specific reforms in society's treatment of the mad. In Foucault's view, decisions about how to deal with political and social problems are the province of those immediately involved in and familiar with them. Disengaged intellectual analysis is important but only as a background suggesting possibilities, not as a normative summons to action."

9. The allusion is to Primo Levi's (1993: 51) cutting idea of "geometrical madness," which he joins to the lethal rationalism of the Nazi death camps, or, as he says, "the voice of the Lager."

10. This conception of disengagement as well as the expression "intentional threads" is due to Merleau-Ponty. It is worth quoting him in full (1962: xiii): "Reflection does not withdraw from the world towards the unity of consciousness as the world's basis; it steps back to watch the forms of transcendence fly up like sparks from a fire; it slackens the intentional threads which attach us to the world and thus brings them to our notice; it alone is consciousness of the world because it reveals that world as strange and paradoxical."

References

Agamben, Giorgio. 1998. *Homo Sacer*. Trans. Daniel Heller-Roazen. Stanford, CA: Stanford University Press.

Berger, John. 2001. *Selected Essays*. Ed. Geoff Dyer. New York: Vintage International.

Bernstein, Richard J. 1991. *The New Constellation*. Cambridge, MA: MIT Press.

Bickerton, Chris J. 2006. "France's History Wars." *Le Monde Diplomatique*. February, 14–15.

Bourdieu, Pierre. 1988. *Homo Academicus*. Trans. Peter Collier. Stanford, CA: Stanford University Press.

Cohen, Sande. 1993. *Academia and the Luster of Capital*. Minneapolis: University of Minnesota Press.

Evans-Pritchard, E. E. 1956. *Nuer Religion*. Oxford: Clarendon Press.

Evens, T. M. S. 1995. *Two Kinds of Rationality*. Minneapolis: University of Minnesota Press.

———. 1999. "Bourdieu and the Logic of Practice: Is All Giving Indian-Giving or Is 'Generalized Materialism' Not Enough." *Sociological Theory* 37, no. 1: 3–31.

Fish, Stanley. 2006. "Conspiracy Theories 101." *New York Times*, Op-Ed Contributions, 23 July.

Gerth, H. H., and C. Wright Mills, eds. 1946. *From Max Weber*. New York: Oxford University Press.

Gutting, Gary. 2001. *French Philosophy in the Twentieth Century*. Cambridge: Cambridge University Press.

Hall, Douglas. 1997. *A Man Divided: Michael Garfield Smith*. Kingston, Jamaica: University of the West Indies Press.

Horkheimer, Max, and Theodor W. Adorno. (1972) 1998. *Dialectic of Enlightenment*. Trans. John Cumming. New York: Continuum.

Kapferer, Bruce. 2005. "Situations, Crisis, and the Anthropology of the Concrete: The Contribution of Max Gluckman." *Social Analysis* 49, no. 3: 85–122.

Levi, Primo. 1993. *Survival in Auschwitz*. Trans. Stuart Woolf. New York: Macmillan.

Merleau-Ponty, Maurice. 1962. *Phenomenology of Perception*. Trans. Colin Smith. London: Routledge and Kegan Paul.

Oshinsky, David M., Richard P. McCormick, and Daniel Horn. 1989. *The Case of the Nazi Professor*. New Brunswick, NJ: Rutgers University Press.

Rabinow, Paul. 1984. *The Foucault Reader*. New York: Pantheon Books.

Rousseau, J. J. 1950. *The Social Contract and Discourses*. Ed. G. D. H. Cole. New York: E. P. Dutton.

Sahlins, Marshall. 2002. *Waiting For Foucault, Still*. Chicago: Prickly Paradigm Press.

Shiff, Richard. 2006. "Willem de Kooning: Same Change," in Karen Painter and Thomas Crow, eds., *Late Thoughts: Reflections on Artists and Composers at Work*. Los Angeles: Getty Research Institute, 38.

Weber, Max. 1949. *The Methodology of the Social Sciences*. Trans. and ed. Edward A. Shils and Henry A. Finch. Glencoe, IL: Free Press.

Terry Evens is Emeritus Professor of Anthropology at the University of North Carolina, Chapel Hill. Email: tmevens@email.unc.edu

2

THE ETHIC OF BEING WRONG
Taking Levinas into the Field

Don Handelman

Fieldwork anthropology is a unique discipline in academia because it desires and often requires unmediated contact between the anthropologist as subject and the native other as subject—subject to subject. This relationship of subject to subject hardly is respected in the formal codes of ethics that dominate the public spaces of the discipline, in universities, professional associations, grant-giving foundations, and the like. In contrast to the formal codes of disciplinary ethics, I argue that what I call "the ethic of being wrong" is a special virtue in relation to much of interpersonal face-to-face fieldwork in anthropology. In fieldwork anthropology, being wrong is to be appreciated and valued with patience and endurance (in contrast to being wrong in numerous other academic disciplines). In arguing for an ethic of being wrong in fieldwork anthropology, Emmanuel Levinas's work can offer some thoughts that are helpful. Just as I argue for an ethic of being wrong, so I intend this brief chapter as a think piece whose rightness is open to question.

Scholarly disciplines insist that their practitioners be right in their academic work. The purpose of scholarly work is to discover, uncover, refine, and polish knowing and knowledge. Knowledge of the highest quality is knowledge known with certainty from every angle, through every dimension. Objective knowledge, knowledge that is totalized and totalizing, encompasses the phenomena it describes, analyzes, theorizes. Given its Enlightenment foundations, the intention of scholarship is to bring the unknown or the less known from darkness into light, to illuminate through the scholarly gaze, through the scholarly mind, deciphering, clarifying, exacting (Handelman 2005). This, in commonsensical academic understanding, is the work ethic of scholarship.[1] It holds no less for research directed toward living social beings than for research on phenomena in the biological and physical sciences.

Scholars in all disciplines know what it is to make mistakes in research design, in analyzing data, and so forth. The iterated understanding is that being wrong is part and parcel of scientific and interpretive processes. The usual solution—its bottom line—is often the same: scholarship and research improve with experience; expertise accrues; the gradient of acquiring knowledge may be gentle or steep, but through time it always moves upward, toward sources of illumination. Scholarly effort and work is thought to develop, to evolve in an upward gradient. The seasoned, expert scholar learns to be less and less wrong in the research process and more and more right in understanding the data.

But (to my knowledge) in no scholarly discipline is there an ethic of being wrong—a discipline saying that being wrong is a virtue, one even to be cherished, especially in research that finds its way through intersubjectivity. Instead, across the scholarly boards, ethical dilemmas— usually about being morally upright in research—are to be dealt with by codes, rules, guidelines, committees, and Helsinki committees, each in its own way specifying what a researcher must and must not do in order to be ethical. Or, perhaps I should say, in order to have one's ethics validated with bureaucratic stamps of approval (see Lambek 2012).

The only value of being wrong in scholarly work is tutelary, part of the ongoing education of scholars and researchers. Therefore, one strives to learn from one's errors, to untie these knottings of ignorance, these blocks to progress in the accruing of knowledge, as speedily as one can, to straighten and make more effective the gradient of acquiring knowledge. One should get away from, depart from, being wrong as quickly as one can. If one is consistently wrong, then one is incompetent in research and should leave academic work.

Nonetheless, I argue here that interpersonal fieldwork anthropology should be informed by an ethic of being wrong. Being wrong is commonplace in fieldwork anthropology (and is referred to under a multitude of euphemisms), yet it is no less the ethical ground and ethical response to doing fieldwork. To put forward this point of view, I will argue the following:

- Ethnography has created unusual intersubjective conditions in the universe of scholarly research, conditions that though not fully unique in academia do approach this.

- Being wrong is integral to intersubjectivity; and, no less, to the radical intersubjectivity at the heart of ethnography, one that should not be erased.
- Emmanuel Levinas insists that ethics is intersubjective and, thus, that ethics originates social relationships.
- Thus, the ethnographer, the Other (*autri*), and other (*autre*) are originary creators of relationships; and ethics is basic to the ethnographic relationship.
- Being wrong through ongoing intersubjectivity is a ground for the radical relatedness so common in ethnographic work, and this has its ethical aspects.

So, the ethnographer-scholar has the responsibility to be wrong in the face of the other and otherness; only in this way can he behave ethically toward the subjects of his research. Whether the ethnographer should consistently be wrong in research, in relation to others, is an open question. Perhaps ethically he or she should never consider themselves entirely correct, for through that trajectory lies the hubris of the objectification of native others, as if they are captured by the ethnographer as taxidermist of human spirit.

Accepting these premises as part of the grounds of ethnographic fieldwork would upend ways in which the doing of anthropology is taught and institutionalized in universities and research institutes. This position in anthropology would insist, reflexively, that the ways in which knowing qualities of otherness have come to be positioned—primarily through the qualities of selfness of the anthropologist—be altered.[2]

The Distinctiveness of Anthropology

Two decades ago I argued that fieldwork anthropology has constituted an utterly radical break with all other academic disciplines that study the human condition, in relation to otherness in its individual and collective dimensions (Handelman 1994). Unlike other academic disciplines, anthropologists have pursued the living presences of others in order to study these face-to-face. Fieldwork anthropology has insisted on facing the face of otherness rather than effacing this, and trying to learn about others as members of living collectivities rather than as members of categories invented by social scientists. In this discipline, how the ethnographer perceives otherness is formed interactively through the practice of relationships that *subject* each to the other.

Through ethnographic fieldwork, *anthropology was (and still is) the only scholarly discipline to put, in the first instance, otherness-as-subject before otherness-as-object, and thereby shift toward an implicit ethics in the Levinasian sense of the idea.* Nonetheless, ever since, anthropology has strained to straddle the enigmatic shifting of others from active subjects in their own lives to passive objects in anthropological texts. The paradox of the presence and absence of otherness has tantalized and vexed fieldwork anthropology from its beginnings in the early twentieth century. Anthropology's openness to otherness in its own right is its strength and its frailty, since its loss of the subject (through textual objectification) is easily criticized by disciplines (particularly by critical theories in cultural studies and by postmodern literary criticism) that know their so-called subjects *only* through representation and metaphor (Handelman 1994). Fieldwork anthropology is an *experimental moment* in scholarly disciplines of the human condition, one that should be nurtured, yet one that may be extinguished as research is increasingly theorized and rationalized, and as the duration and skills needed for fieldwork are diminished in significance in the teaching of students.

The dimensions of this experimental moment are evident on reflection. Consider the humanities. History relates to human beings and their endeavors, but always through textual remains, through representation. Philosophy creates theories of the human condition, yet even when purporting to relate to real human beings, these theories are hypothetical conventions or provisional simulations of the human. Literature has only representation, the text, through which to find and interpret the human (and one readily can add other media of interpretation—film, video, digital art, and so on—to this listing).

Consider the social sciences. Psychology makes the individual the essential unit of being, a unit to be examined under controlled experimental and semiotic conditions, often through representations like tests and other devices of measurement. Even clinical psychology—today no more than a substream of dominant experimental, quantitative psychologies—rarely has gone beyond the study of the individual, and then often uses tests of various sorts. Sociology in the United States did develop fieldwork perspectives, mainly through the Chicago School, but in present-day sociology these are definitely minor rivulets, though at times vibrant ones. Mainstream sociology stresses the absence of scholars from those sites where others live, replacing these with mediating devices of interrogation (interviewers, the closed question, the open question), measurement, statistical analysis.

Fieldwork anthropology broke with all of these disciplines, in whole or in part, since their conditions of knowing and their creation of knowledge were always *mediated* by objects, particularly by text, indeed, by textism. This point is so embedded as common sense that it is not given the attention it merits—yet the role of textual mediation in scholarship is stupendous in scale. In all of the disciplines mentioned above (and, of course, in others), scholarship either begins with or speedily passes on to texts of various kinds: scholars start from persons as constructed objects whose fictional qualities may be highlighted or suppressed, but their fundamental premise of scholarship is the necessity of distance from otherness, even when (and not by accident) they call these people-objects "subjects."

Alterity is reduced to the ontological status of *passive object*, one whose nearness and subjectivity are indeed subjected, to be reimagined more or less at will (the passive subject is another matter). All these disciplines move information from one kind of text (archive, diary, biography, statistic, questionnaire, test result, poem, novel, film, photo, etc.) to another (monograph, book, article, essay, DVD, etc.). All these disciplines conflate living persons in their social worlds with representations of persons and worlds. All construct people as objects and then breathe life into them, as if they were or are alive independently of the scholarship that constructs and represents them. Scholarship in the social sciences and humanities is, with few exceptions, text mediated—people are present in scholarly work as *representation*, as if all of us live in worlds of representations rather than in worlds of others, and as if we live through these representations rather than first and foremost through others.

The only discipline qua discipline that I can exclude almost entirely from these comments is that of fieldwork anthropology. Anthropology moves contrarily, from unmediated alterity, immediately present in all its enigmas, to the problematic objectification of alterity as text. Other disciplines expand the human object into simulacra called subject, learning from this objectness (which not infrequently is no less abjectness). Their ethics hardly involves the objects they call subjects. Should the scholar of history be "ethical" toward historical characters in archives? Should the scholar of literature be "ethical" toward fictional characters in a novel? Should the quantitative sociologist consult his respondent-subjects (whom he likely has never seen) on the significance of his questionnaire entries and their responses, once they have signed their willingness to be interviewed? The ethics of all of these is oriented toward contacts between professionals and positioned in institution and association.

In counterpoint, anthropology begins with the other as subject. *This is why the ethics of anthropology should be positioned at this conjuncture of self and other, where the anthropologist as subject learns from the other as subject.* What is called ethics, positioned in the home world of the anthropologist, in the bureaucratic codes and regulations of committees and institutions, and purporting to apply to fieldwork, is another matter, not to be conflated with the ethics of fieldwork. The ethics positioned in the home world of the anthropologist are constituted by that which Levinas calls the "said," the normative frozen in time and constituted entirely by representations, while the anthropologist in the field is "faced" with the continuous dynamics of that which Levinas calls the "saying," which cannot be caught and cannot be represented.[3]

Only through fieldwork anthropology are scholar and other intersubjective to one another from their first meeting. Yet too often the anthropologist is overly self-grounded, perceiving otherness through selfness shaped in a world of professional achievement and institutional advancement, of publications, prizes, and prestige, a world of individualism at center stage where the other is too easily instrumentalized as a tool of this selfness. The selfness of the anthropologist becomes its own anchor and touchstone for understanding, rather than, in a special contextual sense, coming into existence through or perhaps together with an other. As noted, Levinas (1998: 5–8) distinguishes between the saying and the said. Saying is doing; it is practice toward others that is responsible, for better or worse, for others. Saying is active, interactive, yet as Michael Polanyi (1966) argues, saying is always more than we can tell, always beyond itself (indeed, its self), interiorly, exteriorly. And so, saying leaves an accessible remainder of itself, of its doing, which is the "said." Yet this is only a remainder, and so is always representation, armored ontologically, normatively, morally, textually. Thus, saying is made subordinate to its own remainder, the said (Levinas 1998: 6).

The anthropologist can approach the said with the aim of getting this "right" because it is frozen as a leftover of practice, of the bodies that are its origination. Therefore, getting fieldwork "right" through the said is getting hold of remainders, of representations, left in the wake of the dynamics of doing that includes Levinas's saying. Levinas (1998: 6) writes that "the subordination of the saying to the said, to the linguistic system and to ontology, is the price that manifestation of the said demands." This is where Geertz, the doyen of interpretative anthropology, retarded American anthropology for a generation by mandating the idea of culture as text (Handelman 1994). Even if the anthropologist gets the "said" right, this is hardly more than grains of sand caught in the fluidity of a sea current.

The reflexivity that became embedded in anthropological writings during the latter decades of the twentieth century has done little or nothing to critique versions of selfness grounded in academia, versions that too easily glide between institution and field. The professional ethics of anthropology reflects this embeddedment of reflexivity. In various versions the ethics is grounded first and foremost in the academic institutions and professional associations of the discipline. The ethics is what matters to the profession and to institutions, yet not to the other. The codes of ethics, the Helsinki committees, the codes of subject rights and intellectual property are primarily bureaucratic law-generated taxonomies that cover the asses of institutions and their members. They reflect a radical positivism demanding that the inquirer be *right* about other and otherness. Contrarily, an inquiry that begins with other as foreground must first be *wrong* about otherness, since the anthropologist cannot directly grasp and represent "doing-saying," but only the "said." The anthropologist may well continue to be wrong, not as nihilistic pessimism, but as an accurate refraction of the complexity and confusion of human social and cultural formations and their relations to selfness—a refraction of the humanness of human being.

Therefore, being wrong should not be passed over lightly, en route to perfecting knowledge of otherness. This wrongness should not be forgotten, indeed, should be cherished as human. Being wrong is not antipositivist or negative. Being wrong is not against being right and discovering truth. Being wrong *is* about the pursuit of qualities of otherness by selfness made doubtful, softened, uncertain, and through this, valuing otherness above selfness, selfness as a multiplicity of perspectives even while wondering about the return to hardened edges of knowledge and certainty in the world of institution and discipline. Being wrong is apositivist, perhaps indexing the potentially infinite realities of Deleuzian virtuality (Handelman 2013). Here the perspective of Levinas on ethics may serve as a fruitful corrective to the individualistic self(ishness) of much fieldwork anthropology. Here too the ethic of being wrong becomes relevant.

The Ethics of Levinas

Strongly influenced by phenomenology, Levinas pioneered an independent course in arguing that the *relationship* does not begin with the I (the ego, the self) as sentient and knowing, but rather with the other (indeed, all others) "facing" him directly and indirectly—the other, unknown, dimly perceived, potentially infinite, yet demanding (finite) response that is unknown. Levinas's thought opposes Western philosophy's "systematic reduction of the 'other' (*l'autre*) to 'the same' (*le meme*)" (Benson and O'Neill 2007: 32). That which characterizes the other is "absolute otherness" (Benson and O'Neill 2007: 32). In the very *face* of otherness, Levinas sees a trace of the other, a trace that cannot be retrieved, synthesized, or objectified—a trace that may be infinite. Otherness as saying rather than as said, yet as more than we can say. In my view this formulation is especially poignant in face-to-face interaction, which is always dynamic, always pregnant with the potentiality of generating emergent phenomena from within itself, reaching beyond itself (Handelman 2006). Meeting more than can be said over and again. Facedness "becomes the basis for an ethics that departs from the self-centering attitude that Levinas regards as the hallmark of Western philosophy" (Benson and O'Neill 2007: 33).

In developmental terms, Levinas argues that otherness is present prior to the coherent existence of the I-ness, of the selfness, of the baby. Thus, I am other prior to self. Yet I inevitably forget this. Nonetheless, I am forever responsible to otherness that I cannot remember yet that made me. Selfness is other-created. Created by otherness, self is enabled (and enjoined) to identify with others. As Wall (1999: 41–42) puts this, "Before myself, prior to any desire to be... the self happens to me... the *who* that I am (as opposed to the what) is *formed*... [and] the other has access to me before I do.... The ego proper... [the] healthy, articulated identity—is not its own.... Its *self* is borrowed, eaten, absorbed from others."

Otherness is prior to I-ness. Otherness forms I-ness from its own qualities, and therefore I have "an exceptional obligation to the Other whom I, in fact, incarnate" (Wall 1999: 43). Wall (1999: 37) points out (or, rather, points in) that "[f]or Levinas I *am* only insofar as I am other, only insofar as I am identified/substituted for this other.... This no one other than I.... The Other obsesses me because I *am* that Other, who is... now one other than my self *itself*." Though I forget that I am other prior to self, I am forever responsible to the otherness (all otherness) I cannot remember. "Ethics, in Levinas' sense, is the very event of the self" (Wall 1999: 37). Yet having forgotten the intimate presence of otherness within our selfness, otherness comes to us from "an outside all the more exterior in that it precedes [the existence of] any interiority" (Wall 1999: 37).

As fieldwork anthropologists we come face-to-face with otherness, forgotten. All the more sensuous reason not to hide the attraction of the exoticness of otherness. Our ethics, then, is the recognition of the precognition of our responsibility to otherness, that is, our responsibility no less to ourselves to respond responsibly to the infinity of the otherness before us. In my terms, for fieldwork anthropologists thus is grounded the infinity—impossibly, yet always potentially—within which the ethic of being wrong is formed.

This is not the taking of the role of the other, seeing oneself through the eyes of the other, as in George Herbert Mead's basic formulation, but rather seeing ~ feeling the infinite otherness of other. Levinas's (unspoken) command is that in forming relatedness the infinite other takes precedence over the self—thus too is ethics "grounded." In the instant that relating comes into existence, so do ethics; ethics are always relational, always social (Levinas 1985: 85–86). Thus, selfness (let us say, of the anthropologist) is obligated to otherness for its existence (let us say, in the field).

Levinas's positioning of otherness as taking precedence would insist, I think, in the (Western) self trying to put aside (momentarily, temporarily) those of its qualities that have been formed to consume the world: individualist, capitalist, that of the scholar aggressively competitive in salary, publications, position, status (see Wall 1999: 40). Anthropology, as I implied in the previous section, is something of a utopian discipline in its face-to-face striving to apprehend otherness, and in this endeavor the baggage of institution and profession gets in the way. Let me put this another way: unlike most academic disciplines, in anthropology there should exist an elementary contradiction (often unrecognized), perhaps a tear, between the academic home where the individualist, economistic, achieving anthropologist makes his or her career, and the field, where otherness takes precedence, in Levinas's terms.

The best of fieldwork anthropology constitutes a (not romanticized) *quest* for comprehension that never will be completed in itself, through itself, given the ever present more than one can say (about virtually everything). In this regard, anthropology is something of a "mistaken" academic discipline, one that should put into question social science academia, yet that is unable to do so because of all the institutional and careerist baggage, pressures, and commitments. Simply put, the endeavor of quest cannot stand before an instrumentally corporate academia.

The rupture between home and field is profound and should not be synthesized, despite the prevalence of triumphal fieldwork narratives, triumphal in that their protagonists solve the puzzles of otherness through being there, through dialogue, and, far from the least, through suffering. Taking on Levinas as part of the way recognizes that the capacity to apprehend the living of others is limited and likely will continue to be so. Distant indeed from the insistence on positivist certainty that is endemic to academia, including those parts of it that imagine themselves as critical in a fragmented world.

The rational capacities of the academic self, driven by universal values, produce *knowledge,* as this is perceived in Western tradition. Levinas understands this knowledge as "disinterested contemplation" (1989: 76). Producing knowledge of the other depends on *intention,* in Husserlian terms, a consciousness of something, "and so... inseparable from its 'intentional object'" (Levinas 1989: 77). The intentionality of knowledge production is the disinterested reduction of self and other to the same level of being, creating their potential relationship through *sameness* (self and other share essential qualities, so that both are variations on a theme of humanness, differing through socialization and the sociocultural forms that order them). Sameness is the vector that actively drives self at other in order to capture the essential qualities of alterity. In this movement toward otherness, the rationality of the universal seizes and reduces the other to finite, knowable dimensions that as such are captured and encompassed by the self (of the anthropologist) (Levinas 1989: 76–77).[4] The known, argues Levinas (1989: 76), becomes "appropriated by knowledge, and as if it were freed of its otherness." Then, he continues, nothing may remain *other* to knowledge.

In Levinas's perception, modernity becomes the shift from the appropriation of being *by* knowledge (the early Foucauldian position) toward the identification of being *and* knowledge. The cogito of knowing supersedes and encompasses whatever is out there, "the otherness of things and men" (Levinas 1989: 79); swallowing and digesting this knowledge, strengthened by this in-corporation. This *is* especially the anthropological dilemma of otherness, consonant with that which I referred to beforehand—fieldwork anthropology as the only academic discipline whose research begins with the unmediated face-to-face encounter of anthropologist qualities of selfness and native qualities of otherness. In my view, this condition of interaction with the naked face of otherness, in Levinasian terms, demands of us different thinking, but perhaps no less different feeling, about an ethics of otherness that in its lines of flight does not touch institution, profession, and bureaucratic regulation as its ground and touchstone.[5]

This apprehension is in keeping with Levinas's refusal to relate ethics to universal moral law, to the very universality of law, to Kant's relating to ethics through a rational system (Levinas 2001: 114)—Levinas thereby rejects sameness as the grounds for enabling selfness to relate to otherness. Sameness in Levinasian terms is akin to essence, to essentialism. For my purposes, this refusal of the universality of law has two consequences: first, otherness eludes capture by the rational capacities of self; and second, if this is so, all that self (of the anthropologist) and other have together is the *present* they inhabit in relation to one another (Levinas 1987).

If other cannot be reduced to sameness with self and so eludes seizure, then the future of the present that self and other inhabit is ineluctable—it cannot be known or predicted with consistency by the self (of the anthropologist). Selfness and otherness exist through ongoing duration but cannot exist outside this without self totalizing other. However, self cannot totalize other through the duration of their relatedness. Thus, just as otherness is unknowable because its infinitude takes precedence, so too the (infinite) future of otherness is unknowable. To predict futurity is to set horizons for this future, and thereby to reduce alterity to sameness (Levinas 1987: 90). Here, then, in terms of a Levinasian ethics, is a great difficulty for field anthropologists: how to relate to otherness as otherness, not sameness, through an ongoing present yet without anticipating, predicting, judging the other.

In relation to selfness (of the anthropologist), otherness has enigmatic qualities of uncertainty and indeterminacy; as noted, in Levinas's terms, the other intimates infinity, and therefore the question of knowing. These properties are crucial to Levinas's ethics, for, through them, again as noted, otherness preexists and precedes selfness, yet only *if self refuses to reduce other to sameness, and so does not capture nor fully and completely conceptualize other* (see Wyschogrod 2004: 143). Selfness (of the anthropologist) thereby has *responsibility* to otherness precisely because self will not reduce and capture alterity, even though reduction and capture would be fully in keeping with professional, institutional, and disciplinary principles.

Therefore, the *responsibility* of the anthropologist is to the freedom of the other, indeed, to the habitus of this freedom. Self is responsible not just for what *he and she* do, but beyond this, is responsible for the other, indeed to all others, as a responsible being, that is, as a social being. For Levinas (1985: 96), "This means that I am responsible for his very responsibility." On these grounds, self *has responsibility to respond to* other without reducing and capturing alterity—and therefore *self* (of the anthropologist) *has the responsibility to be wrong about the nature of this alterity*. Getting the infinitude of otherness "right" (quite a trick) depends on getting it wrong, time after time, refusing the primacy of the selfness of the anthropologist, and refusing the capture of alterity that this primacy would enable.[6]

In relation to Levinasian ethics, self-reflexivity as this is generally (mis)understood in academia is somewhat misnamed. Self-reflexivity is not done deep within the self of the subject (anthropologist), in the solitudes of self-contemplation (as Heidegger proposed). Instead, self-reflexivity is done with otherness unmediated before oneself, yet not as the existence of separate coexisting freedoms (side by side, as Levinas puts it, Buber's I and Thou). Rather, self-reflexivity is done through ongoing face-to-face contact with the mystery of alterity that is not resolved simply through capture, reduction, and understanding, nor through simple relativism, nor through any union of opposites through transcendence (see Levinas 1987: 92–94).

Ethics, writes Levinas (2001: 114), begins primordially with the incomparable; that is, with "the irrecuperable shock of being-for-the-other-person before being-for-oneself, or being-with-others, or be-ing-in-the-world" (Cohen 1985: 10); and responding to this shock with the *response* of *compassion* for other and otherness, compassion that is not romantic, not guilt, not outrage as such, but rather the recognition of humanness before oneself. Perhaps a kind of "culture shock," as anthropologists once called this, as the medium of entry into otherness; perhaps the culture shock of recognizing reflexively that the tools one was taught in graduate school (including theory and the theorizing of everything) could encompass all otherness as knowledge yet could not comprehend this. Levinasian ethics have neither thingness nor essence. Unalterably present at the shock of being-for-the-other, of the other as uncompassable, and the precedence of other and otherness in this, ethics disturbs, disrupts, unsettles essence, disrupting the beingness-of-self (of the anthropologist). Ethics, here, is a radical grounding of and attitude to otherness. Thus, "Ethics is precisely ethics by disturbing the complacency of being (or of non-being, being's correlate)" (Cohen 1985: 10). This, of course, is no less the complacency and righteousness of being right. Levinasian ethics *alters* the anthropologist with qualities of alterity—long an issue in fieldwork anthropology.[7]

The Ethic of Being Wrong

Consider being right, in standard academic parlance. Being right is inextricably related to knowledge, and to the truth value of knowledge—to discovering, uncovering, excavating, experimenting, and testing for the presence of truth in knowledge achieved through research. Scholars lust after and are greedy for knowledge and its truths. Absolute knowledge is, as Levinas (1985: 91, emphasis added) puts it, "a thought of the *Equal*. Being is embraced in the truth… it consists in making the other the *Same*." This is the Enlightenment project of academia (and in his own way, ultimately may have been that of Levinas). To hold up truth, to prove truth, to interpret closer to the truth, are all replete with the moral authority of scholarship, garnering accolades for research. In the humanities and social sciences, rewards for successful research and publication, and for creativity more generally, are individualist.[8] Despite disclaimers of modesty and good fortune, official authorship of publications and intellectual property rights to research are crucial to the career of the scholar. Moreover, the will and intention of the scholar as qualities of the individual are commonly understood to be important in his or her success. The ideological continuation of Enlightenment ideals casts the individualist scholar as standing against the world, wresting from it knowledge and truth and answering to it from within his or her deep interior contemplation.

This is no less so in anthropology. The successful fieldworker is often understood to wrest knowledge from recalcitrant conditions and informants. As noted, fieldwork narratives—including hardship, misunderstanding, disaster, reciprocity, friendship—are commonly put together as triumphalist stories of individual endurance and intelligence, intended for the settings of institution and professional association to which the anthropologist returns, and in which the great bulk of anthropologists spend most of their professional time.[9] All of this is distant from the ethics proposed by Levinas in which, in my understanding, being wrong is indeed ethical. I emphasize that Levinas's ethics depends nonsymmetrically from the intersubjective relation that is unequal, the other preceding the self (of the anthropologist) and eschewing the reduction to sameness that is so critical to much of scholarly research, and that enables the sovereign I, as Levinas (1985: 101) puts it, to reign within self-reflexivity.

The other makes ethical demands of the anthropologist, yet, as Judith Butler (2004: 131) writes more generally, Levinasian ethics have created consternation because "we do not know [indeed, cannot know] which demand [the ethics] makes." For the anthropologist, this is as it should be, for if he thinks he knows otherness, if he is not discombobulated by otherness, why is he bothering to do fieldwork? Not knowing can be considered the prelude to and the grounds for anthropological practices of fieldwork, in which being wrong is an ethical response to otherness. However, one should note that fieldwork anthropology, given its potential totality in the life of the anthropologist who practices anthropology in this way, is infinitely expandable in its potentiation. Thus, the ethics of being wrong in fieldwork may expand into the life of the anthropologist outside of fieldwork, colliding with the standards and contexts of institution, corporation, and citation indices. What happens then…

Consider being wrong, in standard academic parlance. Being wrong, except for its educative consequences, is the actualization of error, a turning away from righteous paths to achieving knowledge and truth. Being wrong over a lengthy period is an index of poor analytical or interpretive training, an index that the scholar or researcher in question should seek other ways of making a living. Wrongness may well be seen as chaotic, as scholastic wildness and impetuousness lacking discipline, as the inability to grasp what is so obvious to others in the discipline, and therefore that the scholar in question is not a member of the discipline's thought collective, as Ludwig Fleck ([1935] 1979) put it. In short, being wrong in career-driven academia is unrewarding and denigrating—simply bad.

Consider being wrong, in my usage of Levinas's ethics. His ethics emphasizes the unmediated relatedness of self and other, face-to-face, face-to-infinitude, the priority of other over self, the ethical demand made by other, the unmediated demand that cannot be known, and the necessary response of self to the unknowable. The anthropologist does fieldwork in order to learn about otherness, in as unmediated ways as possible. He or she is trying to relate to others they do not know, others who have priority because they are living their lives in their own habitus in which the anthropologist is an interloper. If they are going to learn, they (wittingly or not) must put the other before themselves, because they can only learn from others living in their own life. In doing so, they can only be surprised, be unsettled, make mistakes, and be wrong, as Jean Briggs (1970) has shown so sensitively and profoundly in her classic study of living with an Inuit family.

Being wrong in the field, in field research, is *the* ethical response to others and otherness, because it acknowledges their precedence over the anthropological self, and because being wrong responds to their demand that the anthropologist cannot know in its depths, that is, from within itself. The ethical height of the other is *the* way of understanding for the anthropologist, since it highlights his or her ultimate inability to know fully, completely, totally; finally, it is the anthropologist's inability to encompass the complexity of otherness. Indeed, *it is in being wrong (rather than right) that the anthropologist opens to and makes space for the plenitude of otherness, yet is ever unable to encompass this.*

In relation to Levinasian ethics, it is not erroneous for the anthropologist to be wrong in field research—it is ethical to be so. However, when once more in institution and profession, quite the opposite holds—here the presence of Levinas would be fragile and uncertain, and of no relevance in judging the ethics of the anthropologist in the field. Here codes of ethics are user-friendly for professional associations and institutions that reduce ethics to positivist judgments of rightful and wrongful action, of the true and the good against the false and the bad. The ethic of being wrong against the ethic of being right—anthropology as an experimental moment in academia has produced a profoundly schizophrenic moment in its ethics.

Acknowledgments

I am indebted to Einat Bar-On Cohen and Terry Evens for their critical comments.

Notes

1. That scholars play in and with their work is rarely mentioned. Yet without the playfulness of rearranging thoughts and data, with fooling around with their potentialities, much scholarly effort would come to naught. As philosopher of science Isabelle Stengers (2004: 93) writes: "Ethics, as I feel it is relevant for the scientific adventure, is first linked with keeping alive the sense of wonder." Levinas's theory of otherness offers much space-time for playing in scholarship.
2. I usually prefer to use "qualities of selfness" and "qualities of otherness" rather than "self" and "other," since the latter infer bounded closure and the unity of *the* self in a thoroughly monotheistic, albeit secular vein, while the former infer the dynamic openness of selfness and otherness, which then may open to ideas of the dividual (Strathern 1988; Wagner 2001; Busby 1997). McKim Marriott, a pioneer in thinking of dividuality (Marriott and Inden 1977; Marriott 1989), writes: "The 'solidarity' that Durkheim... presumes as a normal, healthy social state in the Western world may be extraordinary or pathological for the inhabitants of a Hindu world which 'moves' (*jagat*) or 'flows together' (*samsara*); for them, 'fluidarity' may be preferable" (Marriott 1989: 3). On "selfness" rather than "self," see Handelman (2002).
3. On questions of dynamics in anthropological theorizing, see Handelman (2007).
4. For example, see Rapport and Stade (2007) on the supposed sameness produced by "cosmopolitanism."
5. Indeed, an ethics of otherness that rejects two prominent positions on ethics through institutions of anthropology. One, represented by Roy D'Andrade (1995), argues that rational, scientific anthropology should establish moral models that support the viability of objective research. The other, represented by Nancy Scheper-Hughes (1995), argues that the primary act of anthropological research occurs through ethics, and therefore that this is

political, demanding the active involvement of the anthropologist so that "we can position ourselves squarely on the side of humanity" (1995: 420).

6. Matan Shapiro (personal communication, 25 October 2014, emphasis added) has put to me an attractive argument that an ethical anthropology is "a counter-romantic endeavor to semi-stabilize your selfhood through partial exposure to alterity in ways that are never too submissive nor abusive… [an ethical anthropology is] the strive, the drive for *stoicism*, rather than being anything in concrete ways [and thereby 'bound']."

7. There is one great drawback for fieldwork anthropologists in thinking with Levinas. His thinking is unabashedly monotheistic, even as he always opens to the individual (and so, to the Christian) and to the relational (and so, to the Judaic). Ultimately his higher Other is God, who is infinite yet enclosing normatively the cosmos of his creation. Ideas such as the dividual, such as partible and permeable persons, have no potential existence in Levinas's thinking.

8. Yet, not always. Writing of Bengali *jatra* playwrights, Seguin and Farber (1978: 343) comment: "While they are paid to write plays and while they relinquish claims over them [they] do not keep copies of their plays, do not expect to be cited when the play is either rewritten or sold for 'movie or performance' rights, do not remember the titles they attribute to their plays, and do not assert the right to control the deployment of their literary energies." Seguin and Farber attribute these characteristics of authorship to Bengali conceptions that creative energy is part of cosmic energy that cannot be owned but merely possessed or shared.

9. A critical domain of Levinas's ethics that I do not address is that of passivity. Levinas (2004: 15) writes of "a passivity more passive than all passivity, and exposure to the other… exposure of exposed-ness, expression, saying.… The frankness, sincerity, veracity of saying." Radical passivity, writes Wall (1999: 1), "is passive with regard to itself, and thus submits to itself… it is always outside itself and is its own other." When this occurs, "[t]he self becomes passive to contingency and spontaneous marking" (Benson and O'Neill 2007: 48). This at times is critical for ethnographic observation. In my own early ethnographic experience it was something like my letting go and my openness to contingency that by accident enabled a Washo shaman, Henry Rupert, to speak to me about his shamanism (Handelman 1967, 1993). Similarly, becoming passive in watching closely enabled me to see the unexpected and silent emergence of an invented nonverbal game in a Jerusalem workshop, which opened me to discover the whole domain of play and playfulness (Handelman 1977: 154–74).

References

Benson, Peter, and Kevin Lewis O'Neill. 2007. "Facing Risk: Levinas, Ethnography, and Ethics." *Anthropology of Consciousness* 18, no. 2: 29–55.

Briggs, Jean. 1970. *Never in Anger: Portrait of an Eskimo Family*. Cambridge, MA: Harvard University Press.

Busby, Cecilia. 1997. "Permeable and Partible Persons: A Comparative Analysis of Gender and Body in South India and Melanesia." *Journal of the Royal Anthropological Institute,* n.s., 3: 261–78.

Butler, Judith. 2004. *Precarious Life: The Powers of Mourning and Violence.* London: Verso.

Cohen, Richard A. 1985. "Translator's Introduction." In *Ethics and Infinity: Conversations with Philippe Nemo,* by Emmanuel Levinas. Pittsburgh: Duquesne University Press, 1–15.

D'Andrade, Roy. 1995. "Moral Models in Anthropology." *Current Anthropology* 36, no. 3: 399–408.

Fleck, Ludwig. (1935) 1979. *Genesis and Development of a Scientific Fact.* Chicago: University of Chicago Press.

Handelman, Don. 1967. "The Development of a Washo Shaman." *Ethnology* 6: 444–64.

———. 1977. *Work and Play Among the Aged: Interaction, Replication and Emergence in a Jerusalem Setting.* Assen: Van Gorcum.

———. 1993. "The Absence of Others, the Presence of Texts." In *Creativity/Anthropology,* ed. S. Lavie, K. Narayan, and R. Rosaldo. Ithaca, NY: Cornell University Press, 133–52.

———. 1994. "Critiques of Anthropology: Literary Turns, Slippery Bends." *Poetics Today* 15: 341–81.

———. 2002. "Postlude: The Interior Sociality of Self-Transformation." In *Self and Self-Transformation in the History of Religions,* ed. David Shulman and Guy G. Stroumsa. New York: Oxford University Press, 236–53.

———. 2005. "Epilogue: Dark Soundings—Towards a Phenomenology of Night." *Paideuma* 51: 247–61.

———. 2006. "The Extended Case: Interactional Foundations and Prospective Dimensions." In *The Manchester School: Practice and Ethnographic Praxis in Anthropology,* ed. T. M. S. Evens and D. Handelman. New York: Berghahn Books, 94–117.

———. 2007. "How Dynamic Is the Anthropology of Chaos?" *Focaal: European Journal of Anthropology* 50: 155–65.

———. 2013. "Bruce Kapferer, Deleuzian Virtuality, and the Makings of a Ritual Masterstroke." *Religion and Society* 4: 32–40.

Lambek, Michael. 2012. "Ethics Out of the Ordinary." In *The Sage Handbook of Social Anthropology,* ed. Richard Fardon, Olivia Harris, Trevor H.J. Marchand, Mark Nuttall, Chris Shore, Veronica Strang, and Richard A. Wilson. London: Sage, 141–52.

Levinas, Emmanuel. 1985. *Ethics and Infinity: Conversations with Philippe Nemo.* Pittsburgh: Duquesne University Press.

———. 1987. *Time and the Other.* Pittsburgh: Duquesne University Press.

———. 1989. "Ethics as First Philosophy." In *The Levinas Reader,* ed. Sean Hand. Oxford: Blackwell, 75–87.

———. 1998. *Otherwise Than Being or Beyond Essence.* Pittsburgh: Duquesne University Press.

———. 2001. *Is It Righteous To Be? Interviews with Emmanuel Levinas.* Stanford, CA: Stanford University Press.

———. 2004. *Otherwise Than Being, or Beyond Essence*. Pittsburgh: Duquesne University Press.

Marriott, McKim. 1989. "Constructing an Indian Ethnosociology." *Contributions to Indian Sociology*, n.s., 23: 1–39.

Marriott, McKim, and Ronald B. Inden. 1977. "Toward an Ethnosociology of South Asian Caste Systems." In *The New Wind*, ed. Kenneth David. The Hague: Mouton, 227–38.

Polanyi, Michael. 1966. *The Tacit Dimension*. London: Routledge & Kegan Paul.

Rapport, Nigel, and Ronald Stade. 2007. "A Cosmopolitan Turn—or Return?" *Social Anthropology* 15, no. 2: 223–35.

Scheper-Hughes, Nancy. 1995. "The Primacy of the Ethical: Propositions for a Militant Anthropology." *Current Anthropology* 36, no. 3: 409–40.

Seguin, Margaret, and Carole Farber. 1978. "Whose Who's: Possession and Ownership in Hindi and Bengali." In *Papers From the 4th Annual Congress (CES)*, ed. Richard Preston. Ottawa: National Museum of Man, Mercury Series, 337–44.

Stengers, Isabelle. 2004. "The Challenge of Complexity: Unfolding the Ethics of Science—in Memoriam Ilya Prigogine." *E:CO* 6, nos. 1–2: 92–99.

Strathern, Marilyn. 1988. *The Gender of the Gift*. Berkeley: University of California Press.

Wagner, Roy. 2001. *An Anthropology of the Subject*. Berkeley: University of California Press.

Wall, Thomas Carl. 1999. *Radical Passivity: Levinas, Blanchot, and Agamben*. Albany: State University of New York Press.

Wyschogrod, Edith 2004. "Levinas' Other and the Culture of the Copy." *Yale French Studies* 104: 126–43.

Don Handelman is Shaine Professor Emeritus of Anthropology at the Hebrew University. Email: mshand@mscc.huji.ac

3

COSMOPOLITAN REFLEXIVITY

Consciousness and the Nonlocality of Ritual Meaning

Koenraad Stroeken

Summate the factors that gave rise to this first sentence, from English vocabulary and academic idiom, over many personal experiences, to the neural networks activated in my brain, the sinews in my fingers, the chips in this laptop, and the particles and ink on your paper: the chance of anyone reproducing this event is infinitely small. And yet we may comprehend each other. The reason is called meaning. This simple fact points to a basic asymmetry between meaning and the network of summated elements commonly described as matter.

Meaning is another way of saying that we are satisfied with less—or better, with something else—than an exact copy of an event before feeling to have reproduced the event. Is our feeling unwarranted? Phenomenologists insisting on the irreducible nature of experiences may argue so. They may say that cultural events can only be *interpreted*, deficiently, through a writing tainted by the author's cultural bias (Geertz [1973] 1993). In choosing to write about culture anyway, a part of the author signals to know better: comprehension takes place. Comprehension requires not concepts, metaphors, and other carriers of meaning that copy the total network, the complex sum listed above of intramental and extramental interactions and mechanisms. Human sciences are not striving to build the ultimate computer to approximate the network. That would be to *explain* culture from nature (cf. Sperber 1996). No, culture is reflexive, changing with every interpretation we make of it. The newly arisen "culture" can only be interpreted further (*verstehen*, not *erklären*, according to Weber's methodology of the humanities). In a mechanistic worldview this might come across as a show of weakness, because the new "culture" resulting from the change we as researchers caused would be eluding us; we are always interpreting the erstwhile culture. Some social scientists might therefore be willing to consider their job not as science but as a sort of art or an act of creation. This article recovers the phenomenologist's stamina by developing a reflexivity that does not believe in the absolutely "new" of any meaning or culture. Rather than piling up data like building blocks, the fieldworker "gets into" the meaning of an event, and this by starting from the whole, from the unspoken layer of consciousness that all humans share and that can be further differentiated.[1] In this approach the verb "to situate" in the often repeated mantra "meaning is situated" becomes an act of situating, an active converging of the whole into a here and now, instead of a summation of atomistic causes. For the researcher this shifts the emphasis in a positive way from desperate interpretations to a special method, which I will term the *comprehending* of culture. Ethnographers go out "in the field" to capture the meaning of an event by linking up their biography with the event (including the intentions of the participants). Ethnographers transform themselves by making the field part of their experience, which latter radically broadens. In short, they seek to both *com*prise and *ap*prehend—which together makes "comprehend"— the event. Reflexivity indeed applies to the change undergone by the fieldworker, by the subject studying rather than by the object studied.

The Place of Consciousness

The comprehending fieldworker, this bit of epistemological arrogance, is bound to be the major foe of both modern and postmodern theorists. According to the dominant view, which insists on the historicity and locality of meaning, we could never capture the meaning of the words Socrates spoke twenty-five hundred years ago before he reached for the chalice of poison. And yet, we all feel we can. Or, to move from a crossing of distance in time to one of distance in space, an ethnographer could never comprehend life in a place she has only known for a year or so; she could never approximate the sum of intramental and extramental interactions this place has piled up. Anthropology and the ethnographic method have a long tradition of coping with this objection. As Winch (1958) saw it during the rationality debate of the late 1950s, how could Western anthropologists capture the meaning of witchcraft if meaning depends on the culture it is part of? In relativist terms, cultural backgrounds are "incommensurable," like two separate networks of events.

I want to argue that the postmodern skepticism about bridging these networks is based on the positivist worldview of the natural sciences. Jameson (1991) has already pointed to the continuity between modern and postmodern thought. The anticonformist position of the comprehending fieldworker, in my view, is to defy the mechanistic worldview by making an epistemological claim: despite entirely distinct backgrounds, diverging in the ideas and emotions embodied and socialized, in the neurons, the cognitive dispositions, and the environments they grew up in, humans can converge in the same meaning. Interpretations about an event can be radically different; the one regards it as just, the other not; and while both feel indignation at suffered injustice, the feeling can vary as well; even the meaning of justice, indignation, suffering, and so on, is historically and culturally specific. However, each of these meanings is comprehensible. The meanings are each universal, in the sense that they can be "apprehended" and "comprised" by any other human—even if only to a certain extent. If not, we would not even make the attempt of talking across cultures or discussing ideas reappearing in history. The reason why we can is the *psychic unity of humanity*.

To argue, as I have in the opening paragraph, that the meaning of an event does not coincide with the sum of its constituent atoms is to situate meaning at the very opposite of those atoms (whose principle would lie in their ever smaller constituents), namely, as originating from consciousness, a fullness of meaning. Events structure this fullness into specifics, which leaves the researcher of meaning with no option but to settle for a degree of inaccuracy. Those ignoring the whole of consciousness, which is indeed as invisible to us as the sea is to fish, will not settle for "extent" or "degree." The positivism surfaces in Lévi-Strauss's approach to meaning as a permutation of elementary monemes as well as in the cognitivist's interaction of psychobiological modules. But, surprisingly, it lingers on too in the phenomenologist's location of meaning in an experiential "now" that has come and will go, forever gone like a point in time. I approach meaning as a place, a topos, that the subject can enter, again and again, together with others, although never exactly on the same spot. The more specific one wants a meaning to be, the fewer people will share it. That impossibility of exactitude, the firmer the grip the smaller the catch, is the condition of doing anthropology. (It is also what separates our theory of meaning from Platonism.) Rather than upsetting us, as it should those seeking a mechanistic reconstruction, it should reassure us that when releasing our grip we do not end up with empty hands but with the fullness, if diffuseness, of consciousness. This nonlocal dimension, which follows from (atomistically far apart) humans converging in meaning, is about the last thing social scientists, repeating the mantra of situated practices, would want to consider. Every meaning is local, and the author should retain an amoral position. In this chapter I argue the exact opposite: meaning is nonlocal and always has a moral dimension, as it arises from the unity of consciousness.

From Cultural Critique to Epistemological Critique

Anthropology began in the nineteenth century—"The Internationale" playing in the background—with this belief in the psychic unity of humanity, a principle that separated our anthropological ancestors, cultural evolutionists, from racists (Eriksen and Nielsen 2001: 17). This chapter argues that the growing number of hybridist and globalist approaches from different corners of the social sciences have their analyses crippled by ignoring—more passively than actively, so rather, by forgetting—this anthropic unity. Their solution to the discipline's crisis of representation and the author's problematic authority is a specific type of reflexivity, namely, the self's increased awareness of its biases. The result is a destructive type of reflexivity, whereby consciousness is directed against itself. Following the socialization paradigm of established figures such as Giddens (1991) and Bourdieu (1980; on the dialectic of social structures, producing as well as produced by agency), the ultimate goal of reflections bending back on themselves and becoming reflexive has become something like the sociologist's blank slate, namely, a pure structure devoid of all biases (read: of all culture). An equivalent to that blank slate is the one anthropological truth defended in their theories: the equilibrium of structure (macro) and agency (micro), which amounts to the logic of a rat spinning its wheel. Giddens's famous third way is this imaginary center, after the slants of meaning have been pulled toward their collective middle.

A more plausible alternative seems to me a decentered view where every meaning, including the seemingly neutral sociological analysis, is equally cultural (biased, if you like). Of course, none of the above authors would deny that the social sciences, like all academia, are a cultural product. It is another thing to admit that the diversity of opinions within the discipline is mere varnish over the one Western cosmology they share. At one time, anthropologists thematized this fact and developed what Marcus and Fischer (1986) called a "cultural critique," juxtaposing another culture to our own in order to question the latter. However, since a decade or two after the birth of globalization theory, we are in the era of the critique of this cultural critique. We reproach our essentializing of cultures, described as "theirs" and "ours." Gupta and Ferguson (1992) have remarked that the "we" juxtaposed to another culture stands for a little club, the West. Their shift of attention from cultures—stuck to places such as "the Nuer in Nuerland"—toward things traveling across "cultures" certainly gave rise to fascinating studies of social fluidity such as Appadurai's (1996). It obscured, however, an important matter that cultural critique did take into account and that its critics never managed to refute, or even tackle, and therefore now increasingly threatens to undermine the whole effort of globalization theories, turning them into globalist ideologies: anthropologists have actually been quite right about the "we," namely, about their theories being cultural and following from a particular perspective on the world, embedded in a history of rationality debates, Cartesian dualism, Enlightenment, and romantic reaction. Of course, Gupta and Ferguson objected to the juxtaposition because they wanted to emphasize the sheer diversity of and within cultures. And they were right about that part being neglected (or, I would say, sacrificed) by the cultural critique adepts who were too preoccupied with a comparative stance permitting the criticizing of Western society. But in the same go, globalization theorists neglected those adepts' (and perhaps our whole discipline's) original concern: the possibility of radical difference, hence of another perspective, of another epistemology than the anthropologist's—indeed, than "our" epistemology. In my view, the faulty *cultural* critique, essentializing cultures, should therefore be recast as an *epistemological* critique, discerning between or within cultures different, possibly opposite perspectives (more generally, cosmologies) concerning similar issues. That would make the gradual, deeper comprehension of another culture again a very worthwhile exercise. Globalization theorists lapse into globalism when they give the last word to society conceived as one global social structure in which culture can only appear in the form of diversity (identities), culture in the weak sense, and not as radical epistemological difference—culture in the strong sense. It is in this strong sense that the author can be interrogated and the culture concept raises the issue of reflexivity.

As announced in the opening paragraph, the basis for the culture concept I propose is a relative independence of meaning from mechanistic interactions and the network they form. Such independence of meaning from matter is in direct conflict with the by now established position of figures such as Latour (2005), DeLanda (2006), and a long list of social theorists, all focusing on the network made of material interactions, calling for a hybridist as well as globalist approach.

The Power Concept Resisting Reflexivity

A major objection to the established globalist view seems to me its emptying out of the culture concept, in the first place by reducing culture to identity and "imagined community," because it disguises the unconscious experiential structures of culture. It is striking that whenever globalists reintroduce the concept of culture, as Chabal and Daloz (2006) did recently, they do not think of having culture bend back on their own analysis, that is, of verifying how the analysis may be the product of a certain culture. The ubiquity of power as an explanatory model in their studies is suggestive, though, of what that culture might be. Globalization theories describe practices in terms of power, and more precisely one *continuum* of power (from low to high) spanning the globe, whereby magic would be the desperate means of the poor to cope with capitalism (or funerals would be a way for the subaltern to publicly assert their cultural identity). True, as Radcliffe-Brown (1940: 4, 10–11) argued already three generations ago, there cannot be more than one society on earth. But surely, there exist many cultures, not necessarily coinciding with any geographical area, but nevertheless producing a difference in logic and meaning whose epistemological challenge could never be detected from treating the world as one globe or as a multiplicity of modernities. Is the role attributed to power, or resistance amid disempowerment, not a typically academic construct disinterested in the proper principle and cosmology of magic (or, in the other example, ignoring the emotional concerns of funeral participants)? Is this construct not a sign of epistemological closure rather than of cosmopolitan openness? As a young prophet from Palestine once alluded when cornered ("Give the emperor what belongs to the emperor, and God what belongs to God") there can be more valid explanatory frames than power. To not, or no longer, consider that possibility is indicative of a decline in reflexivity, that of the good (or what I will call "cosmopolitan") kind.

In short, globalization theorists can be commended for rediscovering the multiplicity of cultural flows but have been imprudent to snub the anthropological sensitivity to hegemony and the dualism of "us" and "them." The first-person plural in that pair referred to the culture of Western academia (and more exactly anthropology) that fieldworkers should be aware of when approaching another epistemology. The downplaying of the dualism during the last decade has relaxed the demands on participatory, long-term, and epistemologically trying fieldwork. I would dare suggest that in the practice itself of globalization theory, Marx's historical materialism eerily rings true: the economy's higher demand of efficiency has transformed the way we think about fieldwork, privileging short, multisited stays in urban environments and cosmopolitan borderlands (not requiring the time-consuming language training of a linguistically homogeneous site), while the economic infrastructure's need of extended markets makes us think in a globalist manner, diminishing the significance of cultural difference, rephrasing it as diversity (cf. Spivak 1988).

A final remark in this respect. The dualism of subject and object, us (author) and them (researched culture), against which anthropologists used to warn, cannot be refuted by the globalization and growing cultural diversity of the scientific community. That would be to overestimate the difference between African, Indian, and Western academia. To think these fundamentally challenge each other rather illustrates how the concept of cultural difference has eroded. By thinking intercultural skirmishes among scientists are the issue does one not suggest that real conflict could not be possible with outsiders to academia? Could the magical cosmology of some Sukuma healers I will talk of shortly never be an epistemological match to science? Anthropology should remain a discipline preventing such an elitist view from dominating academic cultures.[2] The so-called ontological turn exemplifies that concern.

Cosmopolitan Anthropology and Moralism

Another major problem of the established globalist-hybridist view, which I will clarify further toward the end of the chapter when discussing Latour's actor-network theory, is its banning of morality from meaning. The ban is inherited from the natural sciences (again) and rooted in the Kantian divide between theoretical and practical reason, science and morality. Is obeying the Cartesian and Kantian divides not in itself a form of morality? Are physicists not acting morally by keeping culture out of their study of nature? Are sociologists not making the moral claim that physicists should not be dealing with culture? In any case, the consequence of the divide is moral. Globalist thought does not believe in what I call comprehension (comprising the other's experience in order to improve apprehension), which aims to enrich thought through practice. Globalist analyses treat ethical principles as absolutes, external to thought. The recent plea for a "cosmopolitan anthropology" illustrates this. Echoing Gupta and Ferguson, Stade asserts in Rapport and Stade (2007: 229, their italics):

[I]t is unethical to turn the other into an *object* of knowledge. This means that the days of "the Nuer," "Muslim women," "Europeans," and other categorical designations of human beings are over (which they, at least in metropolitan-style anthropology, are anyway).... It goes without saying that anthropologists still will want to make sense of why and how human beings themselves (including anthropologists) use collective and categorical terms for other human beings.

Catch a categorizer and you have a violator of the principle. While I for one am sympathetic to a "cosmopolitan" approach, I very much doubt this is an example of it. Being contemporaneous with this author and his interlocutor, Rapport, who both in fact do no more than divulge what most of us have been teaching our students for the last decade, one is very much tempted to agree at first. Are there not many kinds of Nuer, Muslim women, and Europeans? I correct myself: "kinds" is still categorizing. I would probably agree with Rapport (in Rapport and Stade 2007), who cites Beck ("cosmopolitanism presupposes individualization") and says that there are as many kinds as there are individuals. But is this the only way we can speak of "kinds"? What in the eyes of these authors makes an anthropology cosmopolitan is the option for one kind or category only, that of "the human species." I wonder whether this pronounced category (opposed to other animal species) is the kind our ancestors, such as the alluded Evans-Pritchard, were thinking of. If he were so categorical about the "Nuer," how could he have thought to be learning at a more fundamental level about human society at large when describing segmentary organization and conflict management through witchcraft concepts in particular societies? Might *we* today not have become the beholders of a segregationist, categorical definition of culture, after rejecting and eventually growing unaccustomed to our discipline's dialectic of the particular (cultures) and the universal (*anthropos*)? We once banned "the human" (for its universalism). Now we ban "cultures" (for its essentialism). Might we suddenly have lost this dialectical, hence provisional, understanding of cultural knowledge, bridging theory and practice, which in the end prevented our precursors from turning people into "objects" of knowledge? One reason we lost it is that somewhere along the way (After the Holocaust? With the growth of the Cartesian divide in the social sciences?) we gave up on the psychic unity of humanity, which our precursors did not, and so categories began to frighten.

The upshot of our ethical stance against categorization is to exclude the possibility of cultural difference. Such cultural difference in the radical sense made our study of other cultures relevant for other disciplines, for it suggested that we as Western authors might be over-looking something in our understanding of humanity (including our-selves). In contrast, Stade's passage quoted above permits the study of culture only on the condition that culture is reduced to a public marker of identity, a collective categorical term. The metropolitan-style anthropologist is happy to note that cultural difference has vanished over time, so that history allows us now to be so ethical as to reject the concept of cultures—and to despise our discipline's ancestors, who in studying them did the allegedly dirty job for us. Can this qualify as an epistemological advance?

The only plausible reason in my view for not studying "a culture" would be that a consensus exists on there being no such thing as cul-tural difference; that there could be no, say, magical lifeworld defying the academically educated mind. I never heard of such a consensus, and—at the risk of breaking yet another new taboo (on the possibility of rural lifeworlds challenging our academic epistemologies more than urban lifeworlds do)—authors such as Stade and Rapport specializing in urban realities could hardly be the judge. In fact, the proof of radical cultural difference requires the study of groups on a generalist level as "cultures," the very thing our self-declared cosmopolitans regard as unethical.

In the ethical prohibition, first on thinking about the human, now on thinking about cultures, I see a destructive form of reflexivity at work. It despises the qualitative, insecure status of anthropological knowl-edge and its hopes of eliciting unacknowledged cultural difference, which once motivated us to do good fieldwork, to participate better, to experience more and live closer with our informants than our teachers did. The cosmopolitan anthropology advocated by Rapport and Stade (2007: 229) crushes all hope; or as one might view it, finally rids the dis-cipline of all that rubbish: "[Cosmopolitan anthropology] will not only object to collective categories for human beings, it will also desist from the sort of claims to intimacy with the other that appear here and there in the ethnographic record. Such claims are forged from pretending to take hold of someone else's otherness and then marketing this other-ness to the rest of the world." Our admiration for this ethical position, and our fear of the excesses hinted at, might obscure the contradiction between the two quotes: our fieldwork concerns "individuals" alone, but they could never be intimate with us, or more/less open? Surely, qualitative research implies degrees of qualitative depth. Cosmopolitan openness should be rewarded. Otherwise, the practice of "fieldwork" slumps into a mere token administered by a cast of high priests. Does a reflexivity that distrusts the discipline's specialty, namely openness for cultural difference through qualitatively rich personal experiences, not betray its self-destructive nature?

Is the kind of reflexivity sought by social scientists the same as the technical reflexivity of engineers taking into account their effect on what they are examining? (I hold in my hand the latest issue of a journal, the *IEEE Sensors Journal,* wherein authors serve the industry by developing a technique for detecting oil reserves that more accurately takes into account the bias effected by the measurer on the measured.) The reflexivity this chapter explores is not self-destructive or technical, like a well-socialized academic reflex. It is cosmopolitan and moral, because the self it bends back on is not an isolated individual but a self embedded in a moral universe. That is the *cosmos* in cosmopolitan. Hybridists feel they have to (morally, in fact) reject cultural difference because of the segregation within humanity it implies. But the segregation they imagine is based on a positivist framework denying common consciousness. In contrast, I consider cosmopolitan those anthropologists able to live with radical difference, something they can do thanks to their acceptance of an encompassing consciousness all meanings derive from. A real cosmopolitan recognizes meanings that are of all times, connecting us to our earliest ancestors. This is the same sense of affinity I found among healers who *recognized* spirits in the experiences of people of diverse backgrounds. The whole point of fieldwork is not to supplant the brains or mental connections of our interlocutors into our bodies, but to accept the nonlocal basis of meaning that connects us to our interlocutors. Meaning grows deeper or more specific as the ethnographer undergoes a transformation in the field, whereby her point of departure remains relevant, permitting reflexivity as she takes note of her transformation. The transformation, a shifting from one state into another rather than an arbitrary change, again suggests that meaning is partly lying in wait, hence more than a local and historical product. The reason seems to me nothing more than our unity of consciousness, the canvas on which every historically unique event is painted.

I am aware that the argument has been explorative, anticonformist, and tricky at times. The ethnography supporting the argument will be presented in two parts. The nonlocality of meaning appears from the fact that a "modern" value, such as gender equality, can in certain contexts be as much a "Sukumese" value (and not because of Western influence). Conversely, I show in the second part that there exists a level at which the meaning of spirit mediumship can be equally relevant to a Western ethnographer as to a Sukuma healer. Inspired by the spirit medium's cosmology, I define a reflexivity that is cosmopolitan—*non-locally instead of globally encompassing*—and contrast it with the kind of reflexivity advocated by contemporary sociologists such as Bruno Latour.

Modern Sometimes

Equal rights for men and women: what could better qualify as a modern value? Sociologists such as Giddens point to a process of democratization of social relations whereby macrochanges such as the decline of institutional authority went hand in hand with women's sexual liberation and their personal dissatisfaction with old models. The sociologist observes a change here of one type of culture into another. The temptation is to subsume non-Western cultures under the former, old type. Anthropologists have warned about such "metanarratives of modernity," as these ignore the diversity of cultures and unify these in function of a Western process and thematic (cf. Englund and Leach 2000). I want to explore the alternative to both approaches. Due to our psychic unity, I argue, the meanings in two cultures are inevitably related. They are not just different, but should have a relation, for instance, one of *opposition*. The example of gender equality I shall clarify next does not oppose two sorts of culture (modernity as a universal process), nor present a value proper to one culture, unrelated to that of other cultures (diversity instead of the metanarrative of modernity). I will show that the value and meaning of gender equality is familiar to Sukuma farmers in Tanzania as well, but emerges in certain experiential contexts. These contexts are rather exceptional, yet stimulated by social institutions that can be termed "modern."

Democracy and gender equality are some of the modern values whose origins we habitually attribute to the dissolution of old Western hierarchies since the late seventeenth century (Israel 2001). These values are not unknown to Sukuma-speaking farmers, and probably have never been, going by the form in which they materialize. Long before Sukuma people were in contact with Europeans they shared this idea of gender equality, an idea that is too semantically rich to be attributed to biological disposition alone and, at the same time, too universal to be explained from cultural diffusion. Where, then, lie its origins? I agree that in the dominant topos of Sukuma society the value of gender equality remains very implicit. Sukuma compounds reproduce a peaceful settlement whereby, if I may simplify, men and women live in largely separate worlds, and men hold most forms of formal power, while women hold the informal ones. A very different topos is the situation of crisis, such as mourning or anxiety over the outcome of illness.

In such circumstances something happens to the beliefs we deemed so deeply socialized. Then these same farmers appear to believe in the absolute equality of men and women.

In times of crisis the Sukuma patients I worked with rid themselves of the central norms they were socialized into. Their "bewitchment," which they articulate and act out to the full in the healer's compound, came with a rationalist perspective on the world. The most striking example was how they reinterpreted the tradition regarding the duty of a woman to move to another clan in return for bride wealth so as to allow her brothers to marry and continue the patriclan. In analogy with the Western concept of gender equality, the bewitched felt that women are treated unfairly. They saw the bride as making a sacrifice that entitled her to their life (or their children's life), an idea they admitted at the same time to be absurd, since it is the bride's duty to do so; it is a cultural norm, a tradition. How to account for this harsh compensatory logic that in their minds manages to overrule tradition? Whence this birth of the value of gender equality? We have no reason to attribute it to Western influence. The situation itself of crisis holds a logic that generates the construct of the witch. All the people concerned partake of the meaning, defined here as a topos or place they found themselves in. The particularity of this one topos is the people's deep conviction of a truth irreducible to anything else. After Descartes, who threw himself into a crisis of radical doubt—a process still replayed in our schools and in scientific skepticism and self-criticism—which by itself generated "clear and distinct ideas," the victim of witchcraft constructs a witch pure in reason (in the double sense: pure in reasoning as well as in motive): she is entitled to the victim's life. We could not be further away from the socialization model by Bourdieu (1980), Giddens (1991), and other classic sociologists, depicting a subject externalizing an internalized meaning. The event molds consciousness into a meaning which is neither historical nor local (*in casu,* the value of gender equality). This meaning generated by the network is asymmetrical to the network— connected to it but of another order.

The Sukuma witch construct is modern in the etymological sense of *modo,* "the recent." Modern reason is *modo*-oriented for distrusting past convictions, wisdoms and anything traditional or once taken for granted that conflicts with rational logic and calculus (cf. Gellner 1992). The proposition implied in the witch construct, of a person morally entitled to the life of the indebted receiving bride wealth, expresses this rational logic as well as neglect of tradition and acquired wisdom. That, not coincidentally, is the destructive kind of reflexivity I am arguing against, the one whereby consciousness turns against itself. Bewitchment is its

sociotope. A truly cosmopolitan anthropology should desert the socialization model, which lets comprehension depend on individual disposition, accumulated cultural influences and local background. If we
break away from this historicist and cognitivist perspective, and try to
look at the meanings themselves, we realize that the moral power of
the witch draws on the (a-historical) values of democracy and gender
equality and that, paradoxically, these values have much affinity with
the merchant's logic of commodity trade, that is, a chain of debt and
credit not attenuated ("unpolluted") by traditional principles such as
the solidarity of kinship. The opposition between commodity and kinship logic is nonlocal, instead of locally socialized.

Geschiere's (1997) claim about "the modernity of witchcraft" thus receives a new meaning. He need not have limited the meaning of modernity to its historical sense of contemporaneousness: witchcraft belief is
contemporary with late-modern capitalism. He could have gone for the
full experiential sense of modernity as a commodity logic and defined
the belief in the life-claiming witch as an event proper to "modern" situations (Western or other, now or before). We can observe modernity at
work outside Western history, since its meaning is not socialized (programmed) by people but arises from events, the meaning characterizing the situation as a whole. Therefore, we may invert Latour's (1993)
famous formula. All humans are modern—sometimes. Only, Western
modernity has chosen to organize and sustain some form of these existential crises through school, media, and science (via self-criticism,
skepticism, social critique, Bacon's search for idols bugging the mind,
continuous debates in politics and the media about moral responsibility, and so on).

Meaning should not be localized, incarcerated by history. I have
shown that a value deemed Western (gender equality) concerns Sukuma culture as well, without cultural diffusion accounting for it. To
prove the nonlocality of meaning, the other direction of recognition
should apply too, as demonstrated next: some Sukuma healing rituals
speak to an ethnographer from the start, rather than need socialization
to be comprehended. They even affect the body. How to explain this
relative universality or nonlocality of the healer's meanings?

Cosmopolitan Healers

Sometimes the social begins with a greeting. The situation of living in
the city calls for the speediest greeting, the lowest common denomina-
tor, "Hi." Greetings among Sukuma farmers are elaborate references to

the clan and the grandparents' generation. They seek to give the foreigner a place in the social network, mostly by reflexively adapting the network. With every greeting, the network of kin and allied expands and reorganizes. Cultures choose the extent to which they will be reflexive about this restructuration. An outsider may suspect materialist ulterior motives behind the renowned African tradition of (classificatory) extensions of kinship (which used to help Western ethnographers in getting adopted by their hosts). This section considers the philosophy of life behind classificatory extension, which is cosmopolitan and reflexive.

Cosmopolitan reflexivity would be my entry point to characterize the group of Sukuma healers I regularly traveled with, in search for medicine and an answer, the first time during the spring of 1996. On that trip one healer was Solile, a handsome, somewhat stubby man in his early fifties with sparkling eyes, a contagious smile, and charismatic presence. His sonorous voice led the singing we regularly yielded to at night and during our shaky drives in our rusty 1978 Land Rover "short chassis." Mostly quiet but enjoying the ride was Lukundula, an elderly healer, tall and stout. Although used to heading the healers' convention (*isambingula*) and more respected than Solile because of his family's healing tradition (and less mercenary bearing), he had become Solile's patient. He needed to be treated for what looked like elephantiasis. Diviners had attributed it to *mitego,* a "magical snare," supposedly laid by his new wife. Lukundula himself did not believe it. The diviners in turn attributed his disbelief to the "denial" medicine (*lemaga*) she probably kept on mixing in his food. This I got to hear accompanied with sniggering innuendo from his nephew and adopted son, Mashala (this is the name he requested me to use for this chapter).

Mashala had been extensively treated at Lukundula's place for a not uncommon case of bewitchment combining mental and physical disorder (i.e., psychotic episodes and paralysis of the arm). Pending the oracle that would finally discharge him, Mashala now assisted his classificatory father in his search for a cure. He had avidly learned along the way about new medicines and about the extensive medicopolitical network of practitioners propelling much of the talk and excitement in these western parts of Tanzania. I only knew Solile, but would soon become closer with Lukundula and with Mashala, whose wit and curiosity I found most congenial.

Solile lived in a village neighboring the small town of Misungwi. Among his many clients, some were traders looking to be divined about their fortune. They bought magic of "attraction" (*samba*) to expand business. Like most healers I knew, Solile was open to any creed or denomination that could serve the purpose of curing his thirty or more patients. One day he called me over. He was beaming with expectation about the exorcism he allowed two Pentecostal ministers to perform on a psychotic young man who in the past year had made little progress. The frantic invocations of God and Bible eventually did not convince Solile, to say the least. He had not been able to contain his laughter when observing the exorcism. But he had given it a chance. Likewise, he had earlier on acquired some ingredients of Muslim magic on his annual trips to "the West," *ng'weli*, at the border with Rwanda and Burundi. Especially the Tanzanian town of Kigoma is renowned for developing such new recipes to combat the ever innovative attacks of witches. Lukundula's new wife was presumably versed in such sophisticated magic. That is what had brought Lukundula to his colleague Solile for treatment in the first place.

My arrival with the old Land Rover to visit Solile seemed the perfect excuse for Lukundula to ask to be discharged. Not that he felt cured. The chicken oracle was not too affirmative either about him leaving. But the old man had made up his mind about healing prospects at Solile's. His promise of divulging a secret recipe in return helped to loosen Solile's grip. So after a few days they decided to drive off together with me: Lukundula, Mashala, and Solile. The latter in the last instance had invited a young female patient for the trip to get divined by Seele, Lukundula's daughter. That this patient reached the higher notes of Solile's songs with her amazing voice was perhaps just a happy coincidence.

Suddenly a somewhat bogged down ethnographer found himself in the company of a vibrant bunch of ritual specialists, who would turn out to guide him until the end of his research; to initiate him in the society of elders and show him the forty medicinal ingredients, to teach him to sacrifice and divine chickens, to perform rites of expulsion, and toward the end of two years of fieldwork commence the initiation as Chwezi spirit medium, to complete it three years later. Despite my different upbringing, it seems that Lukundula and Mashala did not exclude me from that world populated by spirits and by mediums of the most diverse demeanors.

One might argue that their meanings are very much localized and that a slow process of integration helped me to approximate these, or at least give the impression to. That would be to confirm the socialization model, fieldwork as gradual programming by the local culture. I propose to turn the tables on that reasoning. How localized could meaning be if a few paragraphs (say, the last five) sufficed for me to evoke some of that other culture? Moreover, how many of the words and their combinations were new to the reader? Very few, I think.

Does this undermine the value of the ethnography? I do not think so. Rather, it acknowledges that meaning is a nonlocal as much as local affair, intercultural as much as cultural. The model is not socialization but *initiation*. Meaning has a wide, shared canvas it draws on, in which we can be initiated.

In the Chwezi cult I witnessed tangible moments of enthusiasm by members holding my hand to talk and share their experiences of spirit mediumship with me. Cosmopolitan is the sense of affinity experienced by people from disparate backgrounds who never met before. Among mediums that sense is reflexive, because the felt affinity concerns a difference so radical that these people have long been ashamed to articulate it; no matter what culture they grew up in, they are aware of having something they are not supposed to have. That is why not everyone is a healer or shaman, and people invent names for these social roles. The concept of spirit expresses this difference that is nonlocal. The Chwezi mediums were happy to hear about spirits from my experience as well and thus to encounter them in other parts of the world, the cosmos. Let me further clarify this reflexivity and what is cosmopolitan about it.

Reflexivity as Inclusive, Nonlocal, and Systemic

The first trait of cosmopolitan reflexivity is its radical inclusion. It represents the very opposite of the destructive reflexivity that excludes people unable to face their cultural biases and apply Ockham's razor to these on top of other mental obstructions. The Chwezi spirit cult exemplifies the cosmopolitan, inclusive approach to culture. The cult is geographically of Rwandese origin, referring to a dynasty ruling four centuries ago, and has for a long time spanned the region of western and northern Tanzania and southern Uganda. Nominally, dozens of cultural groups have adopted the cult at some time. But the experience of spirit is virtually boundless. Because of this nonlocality, a Belgian ethnographer could be part of it.

A second trait illustrated by the Chwezi spirit cult is the hidden complexity of "ternary" (or rather quaternary) reflexivity. All participants ritually express that spirit possession requires from the subject an acceptance of something not commonly accepted. The possessed becomes medium by overcoming the socialized (or natural) tendency to prohibit and expel intrusive thoughts, experiences, or voices that manifest spirit. The overtaking by the spirit may produce silence, screams, or loss of consciousness, but these forms of "noise" harbor a more complex experience and meaning. Instead of domesticating the otherness of the spirit in an altar or exorcising it, the medium opts for the difficult path of synchronizing with the intruder (Stroeken 2010). This expansion of self is possible if the self our reflexivity bends back on is not an individual but a larger reality linked to human consciousness, articulated by the spirit. This reflexivity is (qua)ternary, for it overcomes and uses the binary dialectic of self and other. It overcomes the self-destructive reflexivity of bewitchment whereby victims reproach themselves for causing jealousy (which gives birth to their witch). They are unable to see the world other than through themselves. The witch of their imagination addresses them with a look that kills. Her curse is called "the look" (*ibona*), in analogy with "the evil eye" haunting the indebted in other cultures. The victim is "tied" (*litunga*), too localized. Why might membership into a spirit cult be the antidote? It introduces nonlocality, an extension of the self into a spirit that keeps the X, the unknown, in place. Epistemologically, the medium's position counts four layers: if the normal situation is for self and other to exchange (first layer: initiation, greeting, alliance), and in rare instances of breach the other intrudes the self (second layer: constructing the witch), yet this intrusive other can be expelled (third layer: exorcism, sacrifice), then the medium can suspend the urge to expel and instead become one with the outside, thus expanding toward the cosmos (fourth layer: spirit possession). This is not the binary reflexivity of (post)moderns confronting and attacking their own thoughts, hence sustaining the state of crisis (see second layer). Nor is it the ternary reflexivity of these moderns (especially anthropologists) adapting their "all too localized" Western beliefs after the confrontation with new facts (see third layer). Cosmopolitan is the reflexivity of those accepting the nonlocality of all meaning, so that a wide range of meanings or values (e.g., ethnocentrism, dualism, feminism, democracy, colonialism, liberalism) are encountered in any culture, like spirits (see fourth layer).

The third trait of cosmopolitan reflexivity is, as argued earlier on, that it is thoroughly systemic. It operates on the fact that our words can sicken or heal—that meaning is matter. This systemic reflexivity shows in Sukuma diviners assuming their own diagnosis of a condition to alter that condition. A quick illustration, which brings us back to Lukundula's homecoming trip, may suffice. In the days before setting off, Mashala had been telling me about Lukundula's daughter and his classificatory sister, Seele; how she as a young mother of seventeen had for days on end been "climbed upon" by the spirit speaking in a voice that summoned her to become a healer; how Mashala had failed to keep her from running from her husband's home; how she had roamed the bush for weeks, singing songs she had actually never heard before. When we arrived at Lukundula's place, Seele was expecting us. A slender mother in her late thirties, she paid respect to the elders entering, while stealing the scene with her poise and laughter. All at once she told Solile that she had dreamed about the patient he had brought along. She would prepare for divination at the ancestral altars outside the fence. The drums sounded. The old coins in her winnowing basket rattled. Solile and his patient sat down on the ground before her. The girl handed to the diviner a euphorbia twig (*inala*), with its milky juice on one end, on which she had spat. Then the oracle began. Seele spoke in grim incantations, slowly building up to a climax. When did the girl's nightmares and stomachache start? Had she not recently lost one of her favorite dresses? The girl nodded. That dress had been used as *shingila*, literally "access" (from *-ingila*, to enter). The thief was a jealous neighbor aiming to hurt her, so the oracle stated. The girl had come well in time for divination, so the counterattack by the healer's magic would be successful. Seele, this frail woman who had charmingly welcomed us, had transformed into a warrior in what seemed like a combat of life and death. The first step of her countermagic was this divinatory séance. Sharing the discovery of the purloined dress and identifying the culprit were acts bound to corner the witch and ruin her plans. Some diviners claim that the witch actually overhears the séance (which used to be public but is private nowadays). So the diagnosis itself of the situation is thought to affect the situation. Divination is reflexive. And it uses a systemic logic to get a grip on events, as Seele's spirit had shown everyone once again how everything holds together: the dress, the desires attached to it, also by those members of the social network who possess little, the theft, and the contiguity of the witch by holding in her hands this dress, a direct connection to the victim. The advantage of this play on perspectives, and their shift, is that its possibility for expansion through reflexivity is unlimited. In biomedical therapy the hospitals, diagnoses, and cures convey a logic one can only at the price of its destruction be reflexive about.

Ethnographers have for a long time been recording how rituals use mind to affect matter, how these manipulate the senses and heighten reflexivity, as well as how rituals exploit collectivity—the social—to prompt and stabilize the process. It is ironic that the height of intellectual advance today should be Latour's actor-network theory (ANT), which denounces as illusory people's distinction between mental, biological, and social dimensions. This is something else than rejecting their *segregation* (a rejection I support). It is to claim that there could be no such dimensions and hence no meanings connecting these dimensions in ways that provide humans a source of agency. For Descartes, this systemic play envisaged by magic and ritual, working on a mental layer to set another layer in motion, was not impossible. He thought this kind of agency was mysterious (he spent a lot of time inventing bridges to mind and matter, such as the spinal gland). Today we are rigidifying the evolution begun by the modernist illusion. Whereas Descartes could still grant the subject a minimal "scopic" advantage, such as the ability to know the object, the disempowerment of the subject is complete with ANT. We and our objects are rolled together in a network trading in one currency: the positivism of matter connected to matter.

The reflexivity our discipline opted for, to resolve its infamous "crisis of representation" since the 1980s, has not reached a cosmopolitan level, because we could not take seriously the ancestral spirit of the people we study. Our reflexivity is not cosmopolitan, since their cosmology could not affect ours. The Chwezi spirit could not actually enter our bodies, thoughts, and theories, and bless (or curse) them. The modern reflexive stance stipulates that we include ourselves as authors in the analysis, in order to reinforce our awareness of the gap with the other culture, with people believing in spirits. The emphasis is on our position as outsider and intruder: How can we know another culture? How can we avoid affecting this culture by our very presence and the questions we ask, as Lévi-Strauss (1955) wondered in his famous reflexive moment about anthropology's "entropology"? How can we prevent the researcher writing about another culture from reproducing the colonial position of authority? A sense of crisis prevails in the social sciences, this sense taken as an auspicious sign for the merit of its theories. And so we obscure the other side: Westerners have a culture too, dealing with existential issues in ways that concern Sukuma farmers and spirit mediums, as their ways concern us.

Latour's Turn (*Le tour qu'il nous a joué*)

A central tenet of ANT is to reject the distinction between causality and intentionality, which since Dilthey and Weber motivated social scientists to separate the study of culture from the study of nature. Latour showed that things and people, which "the modern constitution" artificially distinguished to invent technology, form networks of hybrids proliferating, especially since industrialization (and so "we have never been modern"). This failed artificial constitution may explain the consecutive, massive social and ecological disasters Europeans have been surprised to find themselves in during the past century.

At the same time, it should be remarked that this critical analysis is possible thanks to a meaning asymmetrical to the network. I agree with Latour (2005: 76n88) about the hybrid "nature-culture" associations forming when people play pool in a bar:

> Psychologists have shown that even a two-month-old baby can clearly differentiate intentional and non-intentional movements. Humans and objects are clearly distinct.... But a difference is not a divide. Toddlers are much more reasonable than humanists: although they recognize the many differences between billiard balls and people, this does not preclude them to follow how their actions are woven into the *same* stories.

Where I part is his choice to italicize the word *before* "stories." This obscures the crucial fact that things and persons enter into a *story*. The things and persons are selections and abstractions arising from the work of meaning, which cannot be accounted for by the mechanistic reality of the network, as I have argued from the onset. The relevance of the chemical constitution of beer and billiard ball depends on the story the researcher wants to tell (a selection that sooner or later depends on the dimensions of biology and sociology that Latour rejected as artificial). Let us cite Latour (2005: 75–76) at length to appreciate both the advance and the price paid by ANT:

> To get the right feel of ANT, it's important to notice that this has nothing to do with a "reconciliation" of the famous object/subject dichotomy. To distinguish a priori "material" and "social" ties before linking them together again makes about as much sense as to account for the dynamic of a battle by imagining a group of soldiers and officers stark naked with a huge heap of paraphernalia—tanks, rifles, paperwork, uniforms—and then claim that "of course there exist some (dialectical) relation between the two." One should retort adamantly "No!" There exists no relation whatsoever between the "material" and "the social world," because it is this very division which is a complete artifact. To reject such a divide is not to "relate" the heap of naked soldiers "with" the heap of material stuff: it is to redistribute the whole assemblage from top to bottom and beginning to end.

Who would not agree that we should not remove the uniforms from the soldiers to put them back on? Yet, for the comparative work and assembling to begin, we must first differentiate the meanings behind the two realities (uniform and person). Merely assembling a formula of textile onto a military order, and so on, will not do. Unless. Unless, indeed, we integrate the formula and the order into one story. That story could, for example, recount the lack of reflexivity marking both military speech and the formula of a homogenous piece of textile. That lack of reflexivity is a meaning cutting across the assemblages of the system.

This meaning corresponds to a value, which places today's army in a critical light. ANT, reassured by the anthropologist's cultural relativism of the 1970s, undermines such a basis for social critique. Yet, it cannot account for the nonlocality of meaning, namely, that this one problematic value or form of reflexivity, although not specific to the army, permeates the army's assemblages in the wider world, "from top to bottom and beginning to end," as well as in other assemblages that have nothing to do with the army.

But there is more. Should we agree with Latour that the division between the material and the social world "is a complete artifact" if the manipulation of the one (physical health) through the other (collective ritual) is the trick of the healer, one that works? Natural scientists, perhaps like alchemists before them, display a special variant on the same trickery. They benefit from this division, yet this time (on the contrary) by isolating one half of it.

To reject the phenomenological distinction between intentionality and causality, and to build a theory on the exclusion of that distinction, rather than keep the possibility open, is an ideological move exacting a price. ANT's symmetrical anthropology (the symmetry of people and things) proposes a constructivism that takes the mechanistic method for granted: detect the many minute elements and their associations and you will obtain the network that is reality. No wonder the materialist worldview of physicists was perhaps stirred but never shaken by Latour's theory. He does distinguish between, on the one hand, the cause and effect of "intermediaries" and, on the other hand, the unpredictable negotiations by "mediators," and does not mind this slight weakening of his hybridist position. But he could not admit to a fundamental asymmetry within the network, which is the dimensional difference between matter and meaning. Another word for it might be what Terry Evens (2008) calls nondualism, an ambiguity that keeps social scientists on their toes, reflexive, that is, aware that their meanings, which their writings may present like objectified matter, teem with the uncertainty of value. Without this asymmetry the physicist can rightly smirk that the mediator is nothing more than an intermediary the sociologist (or symmetrical anthropologist) failed to compute.

What would be the adequate way of approaching initiation into a spirit cult? Could I pretend to be one of the Chwezi pilgrims I wrote about? Interpretive anthropologists should be happy with Latour opposing "the old sociology" (which explains phenomena from "social forces") to his descriptions of hybrid associations populating our world, forming and collapsing. Compared to sociologists explaining the pilgrim's reference to the Virgin Mary in terms of delusion and pretext, anthropologists may want to sympathize with Latour (2005: 48) seeing "the diversity of agencies acting at once in the world." But can diversity evoke the depth of tension that asymmetry does? He adds: "If it is possible to discover today that 'the Virgin' is able to induce pilgrims to board a train against all the scruples that tie them to home, that is a miracle indeed."

Now here is the choice. As much as we need not believe in the pilgrim's miracle, should we seek other reasons, like Latour does, to still speak of a miracle? Is our job to treat meanings like billiard balls (causality), or should we consider their intentionality? In case intentionality is given consideration, we should find a language in which the miracle is related to experiences we as researchers and readers recognize. Is this universalizing and valuating gesture not the only way in which researchers could respect the pilgrims they study? That is the cosmopolitan reflexivity I have defended here. It is the option closest to the ethnographer's participatory experience, something between interpreting culture (Geertz and ANT) and explaining it away (cognitive anthropology). Taking the example of the Chwezi cult, we are not doing the mediums a favor by taking the existence of their spirits literally. True, for them the spirits exist. But in the cultural experience of this author and his readers, existence has another connotation, as in an empirical fact or a religious dogma—generally put, as in a belief that the believer is willing to defend. The Chwezi medium is not concerned with the existence of her spirit in that sense. For her the spirit is an experience in the first place. Therefore, taking the belief literally (and describing its many associations, like Latour) is as much a cop-out as the cognitivist's or sociologist's reduction of the belief to a set of factors. The typical alternative has been to depict the medium's experience as too different for us to grasp, given our socialization and culture. I have argued that such wallowing in impasse has a positivist basis and disguises the psychic unity that relates the Chwezi medium to the author. That, after all, is how the value of gender equality arises among the healer's patients: not socialization or Western influence but an event molds consciousness in this way.

So, instead of interpreting/explaining, why not perfect something we are doing anyway: *comprehending* culture? That is to take the practice seriously by considering what it would mean in terms of a very different culture such as ours. This is something else than gaping at the miraculous number of people the Virgin Mary sets in motion, like the observer does who sticks to the positivism of networks. The comparative exercise I thus advocate relies on the nonlocal reality of meaning and value. Values have since time immemorial inspired healers, philosophers, and social commentators eager to define "the states of the system" and speak the truth about "the world." A relational reality subtends these values. This nonlocal dimension is what the constructivism of ANT opposes. Latour is explicit about phenomenology and ANT being irreconcilable because of the former's humanist liking for intentional beings. Yet, this (perhaps mistaken) humanism follows from a concern more basic to phenomenology, known as the hermeneutic circle, which Latour has not refuted: the parts of a text, as much as the parts of a network, have no meaning without reference to the whole, and vice versa. Yes, ANT is right that our *state*ments—on the *state* of the system—fail to accurately represent the system, but no reconstruction of the many assemblages can be meaningful without such a comprehensive act. ANT's own concepts of hybrid and network obviously derive their meaning from the contrast with their opposites, because meaning making has this profoundly social character of relating part to whole. Like DeLanda, Latour excludes that nonlocality. He sides with Gabriel Tarde, who criticizes Durkheim for believing that "the source and foundation of every social coordination is some general fact from which it descends gradually to particular facts" (2005: 14). Tarde claims we should "explain collective resemblances of the whole by the massing together of minute elements" (2005: 14). Enter Latour's microscopic assemblage. Interpreted in this Platonic way, of a general law and its particular reflections, aversion to Durkheim's whole and by extension to any macroscopic analysis is understandable. But the more common reading of holism is of something crosscutting the ever changing network and permitting a macroscopic take. The examples we came across were the reciprocity in greetings and the intrusive logic of witch constructs. Sure, we may wonder about the veracity of a theory such as Durkheim's, whose concept of traditional society (mechanistic solidarity) perfectly predicts his description of modern society (organic solidarity) and vice versa. Structural contrasts can rarely avoid moral connotations and can never capture the complexity of events. Yet, how else do our writings make sense? There is a marked preference today for Weber's explanation of capitalist modernity from the asceticism of the Protestant ethic. The historical localization of the analysis attracts. But the attraction comes from preventing the next question: Where did or does this ethic originate from? Could we not snap out of history's incarceration for a moment and consider the nonlocal? Would the rigid logic behind the self-inflicted asceticism and behind the idea of deserving heaven in proportion to investments sacrificed be so different from the Sukuma fearing the witch's moral power and regarding her bridal sacrifice as credit, moreover opting for an initiation through seclusion and ordeal to get better? Protestant and bewitched both strive to become initiates. "Christianity," like "modernity," often serves as a final explanation, as if its beliefs and practices would be grounded on divine introduction and not have a history that goes back infinitely—a nonlocal basis. Latour contrasts "prerelativist" sociology with his "relativist sociology", and "local" sociology with his "dislocal" sociology, in what he calls "a somewhat tricky parallel from the history of physics" (2005: 12). Perhaps he suddenly remembered that Einstein, the man whose theory but not name he cites, made one notorious mistake: he excluded nonlocality. (Quantum experiments have later shown twin particles to be nonlocal, as they make the same arbitrary choices light years apart.)

The "symmetrical anthropology" of ANT is a missed opportunity in that it has the intention of crossing the Cartesian dimensions but refrains from any positive formulation on what it is actually doing. It refuses to revel in this unlikely human capacity to sweep across the system and define it—to go nonlocal. According to ANT, there is no way that a meaning could capture a whole cross section of reality. However, is the healer wrong to apply the meaning of "intrusion" to define both the poison (nature) and the guilt feelings (culture) her patient copes with? Is she wrong to combat this encompassing state of the system through another meaning, that of "expulsion" applied to both the plants (nature) and the ritual (culture)? The healer does more than bridging the Cartesian gap between body and mind, nature and culture. The Kantian divide shrivels away. At this level meaning and value merge into one another. Is our discipline ready for cosmopolitan reflexivity?

Spirit possession, I have argued, integrates four interrelated values: if social exchange (value 1) is impossible, then all modes shift into intrusion (value 2); either the breach is restored through a ritual following a code that sets the modes into expulsion (value 3), or instead of exorcising the spirit the breach is denied through the code of synchrony: "the spirit is my destiny" (value 4). Since Kant's division of practical and theoretical reason, Western epistemology has assumed that thought can be purified from moral values. Social scientists do not distinguish good from bad; at most, they determine what pertains to society and what does not. On closer look, though, their position is far from value-free. Why do sociologists generally dislike the idea of biological evolution determining society? Conversely, why would biologists not want to hear that society determines their theories of nature? Both sides seem to sense how intrusive the other may be (value 2). They sense that they are better kept apart (value 3). Hence, the Cartesian split of nature versus culture can hardly conceal its moral stance.

The contrast is painfully glaring between ANT's localism and the pilgrim or the believer in magic trusting in nonlocality, of which the Cartesian division still bore some traces. Denying the asymmetry of matter and meaning, ANT erases the last trace of the morality of its own thinking. ANT has blinded itself to the moralism of claiming pure symmetry, for it prides itself in treating as numerous props equivalent to any other thing in the network of hybrids the "spirit," "soul," or "gods" (or "mind" versus matter in consciousness studies at the periphery of Western academia) by which cultures the world over, on the contrary, are realistic enough to keep the unknown in place and accept nonlocality and asymmetry. Social theory takes place in a topos further than ever from the lifeworld of Sukuma healers. Maybe fortunately indeed, the social scientist's interest in that lifeworld is rapidly fading. In its positivist relativism the forerunner of the social sciences signals to the rest of humanity to have reached a position of absolute certainty.

Conclusion

This chapter has explored possible avenues to a cosmopolitan reflexivity, one that envisages something else than the technical form of reflexivity achieved by a mechanism integrating the observer's effect in the chain of cause and effect. Reflexivity becomes cosmopolitan when it crosscuts these (mental, physical, and social) mechanisms with a nonlocal dimension. Healing rituals, I have argued, are after such nonlocal meanings.

I concluded that the process of reflexivity characterizing the social sciences of late is heading in the wrong direction. Not only has it eroded radical difference to eventually signify mere diversity. Social scientists deal with cross-cultural meaning all the time, but translate it into localized, mechanistic terms. They have progressively denied the asymmetry of matter and meaning, system and state, experience and culture, words said and their intended meaning. It was once obvious that humans, unlike machines, have nonlocal meanings such as moral values that apply to their networks without having to be activated in particular assemblages. The "social" was a way to evoke that (cf. Kapferer 2005). In ANT the asymmetry has vanished; the material associations rule without the analyst having to care about the asymmetry known as intentionality, which used to keep us on our toes as to the meaning of statements. I cannot help thinking about the following joke, attributed to the Irish comedian Spike Milligan.[3]

> Two hunters are out in the woods when one of them collapses. He doesn't seem to be breathing and his eyes are glazed. The other guy whips out his phone and calls the emergency services. He gasps, "My friend is dead! What can I do?" The operator says, "Calm down. I can help. First, let's make sure he's dead." There is a silence, then a shot is heard. Back on the phone, the guy says, "OK, now what?"

Freud's ([1905] 2002) essay "The Joke" explains why we laugh. We obtain pleasure from getting away with the transgression of a moral value. An extra reason to laugh is what the panic-stricken hunter does, which on second look is what Latour expects social scientists to do: to ignore the intentionality of meaning. "Making sure" he is dead was intended to mean "checking" whether he was. The stroke, the phone, the words, the gun. They all added up to reproduce the event's actor-network. And yet, something very basic was missing. Call it meaning. Value. Something nonlocal crosscutting the network.

That absence makes us laugh. Adding the degree of humor interlarding Latour's writings, we may begin to suspect that he never meant us to take his symmetrical anthropology seriously either.

Acknowledgments

My deepest gratitude goes to my hosts from Wanzamiso and Misungwi. *Wabeja, banamhala na bagiikulu!* For their comments and the marvelously stimulating atmosphere they created, I thank Terry Evens, Don Handelman, Einat Baron-Cohen, Christopher Roberts, Sverker Finnström, Bruce Kapferer, and the participants at the EASA 2008 panel "Reflecting on Reflexivity" in beautiful Slovenia.

Notes

1. For an elaborate argument on consciousness as a shared meaning system, compared to nonlocality in quantum physics, see Stroeken (2011), also retrievable at <https://www.academia.edu/1108925/Why_consciousness_has_no_plural>.
2. Can we grant our academically uneducated compatriots the benefit of deeper insight in philosophical issues? Has it become more difficult today to consider this possibility in African rural communities now that we are busy combating the neocolonial habit that sought to undermine urban African elites? For a more nuanced take on this issue than I could offer in this limited space, see Apter's (1992) discussion contrasting Hountoundji's and Mudimbe's positions regarding ethnophilosophy and the requirement of a reflexive critical stance to speak of philosophy or epistemology.

3. It came out as the winner from Richard Wiseman's public survey rating over ten thousand jokes worldwide at http://www.laughlab.co.uk.

References

Appadurai, Arjun. 1996. *Modernity at Large: Cultural Dimensions of Globalization.* Minneapolis: University of Minnesota Press.

Apter, Andrew. 1992. "'Que Faire?' Reconsidering Inventions of Africa." *Critical Inquiry* 19, no. 1: 87–104.

Bourdieu, Pierre. 1980. *Le Sens Pratique.* Paris: Minuit.

Chabal, Patrick, and Jean-Pascal Daloz. 2006. *Culture Troubles: Politics and the Interpretation of Meaning.* London: Hurst.

DeLanda, M. 2006. *A New Philosophy of Society: Assemblage Theory and Social Complexity.* New York: Continuum.

Englund, Harri, and James Leach. 2000. "Ethnography and the Meta-Narratives of Modernity." *Current Anthropology* 41, no. 2: 225–48.

Eriksen, Thomas Hylland, and F. S. Nielsen. 2001. *A History of Anthropology.* London: Pluto.

Evens, T. M. S. 2008. *Anthropology as Ethics: Nondualism and the Conduct of Sacrifice.* Oxford: Berghahn Books.

Freud, S. (1905) 2002. *The Joke and its Relation to the Unconscious.* New York: Penguin.

Geertz, C. (1973) 1993. *The Interpretation of Cultures.* London: Fontana Press.

Gellner, E. 1992. *Reason and Culture.* Oxford: Blackwell.

Geschiere, P. 1997. *The Modernity of Witchcraft: Politics and the Occult in Postcolonial Africa.* Charlottesville: University of Virginia Press.

Giddens, Anthony. 1991. *Modernity and Self-Identity.* Cambridge: Polity.

Gupta, Akhil, and James Ferguson. 1992. "Beyond 'Culture': Space, Identity, and the Politics of Difference." *Cultural Anthropology* 7, no. 1: 6–23.

Israel, J. 2001. *The Radical Enlightenment: Philosophy and the Making of Modernity, 1650–1750.* Oxford: Oxford University Press.

Jameson, F. 1991. *Postmodernism: Or, the Cultural Logic of Late Capitalism.* London: Verso.

Kapferer, Bruce. 2005. *The Retreat of the Social: The Rise and Rise of Reductionism.* Critical Interventions 6. Oxford: Berghahn Books.

Latour, Bruno. 1993. *We Have Never Been Modern.* London: Prentice Hall.

———. 2005. *Reassembling the Social: An Introduction to Actor-Network-Theory.* Oxford: Oxford University Press.

Lévi-Strauss, C. 1955. *Tristes Tropiques.* Paris: Plon.

Marcus, George E., and Michael M. J. Fischer. 1986. *Anthropology as Cultural Critique: An Experimental Moment in the Human Sciences.* Chicago: University of Chicago Press.

Radcliffe-Brown, Alfred Reginald. 1940. "On Social Structure." *The Journal of the Royal Anthropological Institute of Great Britain and Ireland* 70, no. 1: 1–12.

Rapport, Nigel, and Ronald Stade. 2007. "A Cosmopolitan Turn—or Return?" *Social Anthropology* 15, no. 2: 223–35.

Sperber, Dan. 1996. *Explaining Culture: A Naturalistic Approach.* Oxford: Blackwell.

Spivak, *Gayatri* Chakravorty. 1988. *In Other Worlds: Essays in Cultural politics.* London: Routledge.

Stroeken, Koenraad. 2010. *Moral Power: The Magic of Witchcraft.* Oxford: Berghahn Books.

———. 2011. "Why Consciousness Has No Plural." In D. Aerts, B. D'Hooghe, and R. Pinxten (eds), *Worldviews, Science and Us: Interdisciplinary Perspectives on Worlds, Cultures and Society.* Singapore: Worldscientific Press.

Winch, Peter. 1958. *The Idea of a Social Science and its Relation to Philosophy.* London: Routledge.

Koenraad Stroeken is an associate professor of Africanist anthropology at Ghent University. Email: koen.stroeken@ugent.be

4

RELIGIONIST REFLEXIVITY AND THE MACHIAVELLIAN BELIEVER

Christopher Roberts

At the dawn of a new millennium, this chapter addresses the present age of academia, the twilight of the paradigms. Only recently many educated people accepted some form of Kant's analogy between personal maturation towards autonomy and general social enlightenment (1996: 13-22), though the indices and criteria of these advances would differ. Such a faith in secularization made the historical transition beyond religious heteronomy toward rational autonomy both incontestable and inevitable. But the inevitable reign of a univocal science and a unilinear trend of secularization have both gradually fragmented in disparate, historically contingent patterns. Scholars of the human and social sciences today confront multiple competing paradigms, no one of which seems likely to displace or eliminate all its rivals. With so many contending frameworks and narratives, any possibility of a consensual account of the academic vocation seems foreclosed. Today a critical study of one's own academic field virtually compels some modified position of paradigm relativity.

As if an exemplar of this situation, the field of religious studies appears engineered for the epistemic fog of the contemporary academy. If paradigms form an epistemological assemblage operationally sustained by a relatively univocal scholarly community, religious studies remains a field undefined by paradigmatic parameters. Since religious studies addresses the rise, fall, and transmutation of religious microparadigms, scholars of religions, or religionists (an odd word for an odd bird), cannot but adopt a multiparadigmatic methodological toolbox. Since a religionist wielding a paradigm employs an unviably absolute demarcation between the belief claims of religion and the truth claims of science, to this day religious studies as a discipline resists calls for "paradigm orthodoxy" and other rebrandings of scientism that seek the simplistic imposition of natural scientific models of knowledge on all academic fields.

Although in ways beneficial, this flexibility also leaves the paradigmatically unmoored religionist vulnerable to moral suasion and prestigious scholarly exemplars, as this chapter will show. Turning, then, to the symptomatically illuminating field of religious studies with this caution in mind, this chapter will reflexively scrutinize the religionist's vocation and its projected religious other, as this vocation depends less on its methods than on the particular otherness of this construct. Specifically, this chapter will explore the religionist's faith in the self-identical "I" of the believer and the univocal "we" of the religious community by tracing a dual reading of two documentary sources: a US Supreme Court (hereafter USSC) ruling that sanctioned the teaching of religious studies courses in public schools, thus serving as the academic charter of the field in America (the case of *Abington v. Schempp* [1963], hereafter referred to as Abington), and Geertz's "Religion as a Cultural System" (1966) (hereafter RCS). Both these texts are decisive, as USSC rulings constitute the nation's last recourse for democratic unanimity, and RSC has been read by many as an exemplary demonstration of a post-Abington consensus that pivots religionists' attention from the clergy to the laity. With the focus now on the laity, the agonistic relation between scholars and clerics inherited from the Enlightenment *philosophes* transforms as both turn toward the laity as their object of scrutiny and concern. As the laicized religious other appears without religious or social authority yet full of belief, the metanarrative of secularization constantly threatens the subaltern authenticity of this projected other. With the religious other now less an agonist in the historical secularization narrative than its unwitting victim, the tenor of research has shifted from scientistic objectivity toward humanistic neutrality. But when the field focuses on this or that type of religious other—and especially when defined by default as a member of the laity—the relational nature of religious authority vanishes from view. Hence, this reflexive reading will look beyond Geertz's example to recover what it occludes, for RCS's analysis takes place at the beguiling but hexed crossroads of humanism and scientism, where both the other's full reflexive humanity and the empiricism that "saves" the phenomena are betrayed.

From Husserlian Reflection to Semiotic Reflexivity

Reflexivity has proven a pivotal if protean component of social research, sometimes as a method to adopt and other times as an essential feature of the human world. As a term of art, reflexivity thus exhibits an extreme plasticity, making it a marked notion suggesting at times a concept, a faculty, a mode of knowledge, and even a writing style. This variation has helped make reflexivity a lightning rod for polemical debates on diverse epistemological, aesthetic, and moral issues, especially those concerning the existence and nature of the "postmodern condition" and the validity of poststructuralist thought. Most often this has left the topic muddled in polemics that statically oppose the clarity of objective scholarship to the sophistry of its postmodern critiques. But if reflexivity only "makes the objectivation of the subject [in the sense of *agent*] of objectivation the necessary precondition for scientific objectivation," as Bourdieu suggested (2004: 93), the paradigm of scientific objectivity itself would limit analysis in religious studies to static object switching between the religious other and the religionist, while leaving the same hermeneutic infrastructure in place. Threatening everything but changing nothing, reflexivity is in danger of becoming a null term, a floating signifier to attract the uncathected anxiety of the contemporary scholar.

The first step of this analysis should distinguish reflexivity from received notions of reflection to clarify a minimal working sense of the term. But to speak of reflexivity *itself* immediately raises problems of mediation and access to this "object," especially since the semiotic innocence of object construction is precisely what reflexivity, if such a "thing" exists, would challenge. Moreover, reflexivity could supply a platform of parity to allow the discursive portrayal of the religionist through relations with the projected religious other. But because reflexivity includes virtual and nonempirical aspects, it has accreted quasi-gnostic connotations that skew attention from semiotically mediated—hence empirical—interpersonal relations in favor of solipsistic projects to acquire understanding of alienated others. Although the psychologically oriented scholar in any field might excavate the other's motivational and affective structure with great insight, the idea that scholars can readily "catch" reflexivity at work as a marked mode of awareness suggests a naïve view of self-knowledge. In this light, *introspective beholding* construed as an act of phenomenological *reflection* must be distinguished from the sense of semiotic reflexivity at work in this chapter.

To illustrate this distinction, Husserl set forth a refined but still rather commonsense notion of reflexivity that served as a point of departure for his phenomenology. Husserl claims for the ego an essential "possibility of a 'reflexive' directing of the mental glance towards itself naturally" (1952: 111). To specify this natural possibility, Husserl begins with a distinction between "intentional experiences," described as "transcendently directed" (these include all cognitive "acts directed towards essences, or towards the intentional experiences of other Egos with other experience-streams; likewise all acts directed upon things, upon realities generally"), and others that are "intentional experiences immanently related," which "include those acts which are essentially so constituted that their intentional objects, when these exist at all, belong to the same stream of experience as themselves" (Husserl 1952: 112). Something like this phenomenological capacity for self-relation often passes as the "faculty" of reflexivity. Although Husserl's sense of phenomenological self-transparency could be construed as solipsistic, it remains a tempting premise for humanistic hermeneutics because it usefully renders every subject self-immanent—and thus tautologically self-explanatory—even as all "other Egos" become as alienatingly transcendent as a geometrically ideal triangle.

Equally abstract is Husserlian reflexivity's perfect self-relation, an immanent "nexus of two intentional experiences" the "self-containedness" of which allows "perception and perceived" to "essentially constitute an unmediated unity, that of a single concrete cogitatio" (1952: 112). Instead of reflexivity as a specialized or elite capacity, Husserlian reflection promotes an antignostic, demotic view, but overshoots the mark by collapsing a mode of self-relation into a self-transparent "unmediated unity." Husserl portrays as a recursive fold what actually exists as a processual folding, the dynamic nature of which is invisible in such portraits. By shattering a dynamic phenomenological folding into moments of immediate self-identity, each of which then becomes an "unmediated unity," reflexivity would face no intrinsic limit to the positivistic optimism of "know thyself." On the basis of reflection as a detemporalized and immediate unity, even hitherto unconscious obtrusions upon the ego can become conscious because "every cogitatio can become the object of a so-called 'inner perception,' and eventually the object of a reflexive valuation, an approval or disapproval" (Husserl 1952: 112). Husserl's "reflexive valuation" takes as given the mimetic adequacy of the self-speculum relation and ignores the mediating semiotic detours, deferrals, and delays to which any putative immediacy succumbs. Denying the post-Kantian ontological rupture between knowledge and thing, even when this "thing" is an experience of oneself as such, Husserl predicates reflection upon a capacity for proliferable and epistemically adequate automimesis, with no anomaly in the copy or corruption in the simulacra.

Inattentive to the self-difference of identity generated by the iterations intrinsic to any repetition, Husserl's phenomenological faith in self-awareness occludes the ambiguity between reflection construed as a self-identifying act immediately executed by the brain's evolved capacity for self-sensation and self-reference, and reflexivity as a virtual, dually articulated relation between this reflective experience of self-immanence and temporally iterative experiences with myriad socio-semiotic prostheses encountered *in* and *as* the world. That is, instead of an immediate self-reflection, post-phenomenological, semiotic reflexivity begins with knowledge of the mirror's dual-patterned complexity as a referential device that functions through indexical and iconic semiosis. Similarly, it is only by empirically scrutinizing signs, symptoms, and other indications of the subject's idiosyncratic evaluations that we can refer to the other's reflexivity at all. But with only the self's immanent reflections to counterpose against the other's transcendence, Husserl never supplemented these initial premises with enough intersubjectivity to make phenomenology a viable foundation for social theory. That is, the phenomenological *epoché* "brackets" the ontological "thing-in-itself" but in doing so downplays the role of heterogeneous and dispersed semiotic prostheses, the socializing and acculturating deployment of which humans require for intersubjective recognition. Hence, a shift from phenomenology to semiotics interrupts the reflective illusion of immediate self-capture to examine reflexivity in reference to the traces of a datum, artifact, or some other semiotic detour. This virtuality extended beyond the silhouette of the isolated subject broaches a posthumanist analysis of reflexivity that opens the scrutiny of subjectivation-effects to include autopoietic conjunctions with state institutions, religious organizations, cultural arenas, aesthetic artifacts, and other material-virtual assemblages

Beginning, then, with an automimesis that does not achieve self-identity, we witness it split at once between the phenomenological and the semiotic, between a minimal, quotidian sense of reflection and a robust, semiotically proliferative sense of reflexivity. The turn from Husserlian "reflection" as a distinct cognitive act now requires a broader framework that can include, not only sincere reports concerning experiences of self-identity, but also misdirecting or distancing gestures, conspiratorial winks and motivated mentions, the revelatory moments when the noncoincidence of conventional expectations and performed iterations publicly appears. As all these semiotic events observably proliferate, heterogeneous types of reflexive significations indicate their conventionality to solicit the addressee's recognition of this distance signal as a reflexive supplement to the content of the message. By transforming the semiotic systems with(in) which humans communicate into proliferating objects of scrutiny, this autoapplicative capacity to *mention* what we would usually only *use* fragments the apparent continuity of the dual articulation of subjectivity-effects and socio-semiosis, thereby iterating ambiguity between—and ambivalence about—the psychologically aspective and the semiotically prosthetic. Postreflective reflexivity thus does not exclude but is premised upon conditions of epistemic ambiguity and semiotic polysemy, as well as an acceptance of the impossibility of perfect mimetic capture or fidelity in repetition. Hence, this reflexivity will not lead to psychologism but toward semiosis, rhetoric, aesthetics, and any other generic and conceptual clearings where appearing as such can appear.

Reflexivity and the Second-Person Plural

This reflexivity typified by semiotic refraction moves beyond discourse as the topic's basin of attraction. Still, ours remains an age arguably defined by a newfound reflexivity concerning discourse. According to Tyler, one of the pivotal heralds and provocateurs of the reflexive turn, "Postmodern anthropology is the study of man—'talking,'" which means that "[d]iscourse is its object and its means. Discourse is both a theoretical object and a practice, and it is this reflexivity between object and means that enables discourse and that discourse creates" (1987: 171). Tyler's analysis presumes that any scholarly practice requires a reflexive approach that strives to take distance from methods employed while at the same time acknowledging the scholar's dependence upon this equipment as well as the phenomena that he or she would scrutinize.

But given that scholars both study and inhabit disciplinary institutions and discourses, how does one reflexively relate to our professional prescriptions, given what the social sciences have revealed about the impact of conflicting signals on interpersonal relations, or the ongoing role of contestation and antagonism in social reproduction? A reflexive approach to the scholarly unconscious no longer denies the role of desire and even transgression in scholarship. Indeed, any community might exploit the discursive capacity to conjure ideal-types and utopian values as asymptotes toward which we might orient our desire—this a reflexive scholar forthrightly acknowledges as opposed to the quarantining discourse of objective disinterestedness. But an openness to neological creativity and utopian invocations comes at the cost of their permanent virtuality. We now enter an age when the viability of any second-person plural address falls under erasure, making any scholarly "we" increasingly difficult to invoke because of our chronic inability to convoke sufficient constituencies under the aegis of fragmenting disciplines, fields, and paradigms. But is it still possible to seek consensus even on this point, effectively redeeming a reflexive sense of community on the basis of a shared awareness of semiotic conventionality?

Tyler posits just such a discursive community predicated on the historical emergence of this semiotic reflexivity. Invoking implicit metanarratives entangled with notions of reflexivity, Tyler's account hinges on the epoch-making turn that he assumedly helped steer. This crisis of representation itself marks the advent of a new consensus, a disenchanted, etic awareness of linguistic and semiotic conventions. Tyler even provides a performative license for this emergent community of scholars, in that "[d]iscourse is the maker of the world, not its mirror, for it represents the world only inasmuch as it is the world. The world is what we say it is, and what we speak of is the world" (1987: 171). The desire to achieve this consensus requires the rhetorical invocation of a "we" hermeneutically united about Tyler's discursive sense of reflexivity. But whom does Tyler mention when he speaks in the second-person plural? There is a tacit community of autopoietic discursive agents invoked, but who exactly is this "we" who participate(s) in this discursive self-construction? Truth among "us" becomes a matter of rhetorical invocation, so which of many possible second-person plurals is it who utters the world? Finally, what self-actualizing vocalization is this "we" to utter, and who in the end would hear it?

Tyler exploits the openness of rhetoric, especially the semipermeable membranes of the "we" around which the rhetorician convenes the audience, a systolic and diastolic fracturing and suturing of every "we" that we mention. If Durkheim went too far toward social unanimity with his notion of collective representations (1995), Tyler also courts this danger, for every ad hoc "we" is but a contingently construed projection of discursive practices that stray across the boundary between religion, culture, and aesthetics. At its limit this impossible "we" emerges through the socially constructed nature of any language community but exists as such and immediately only under elision or erasure. This casts a mark of suspicion upon all façades of consensus and every invocation of unanimity, for persuasion is never total, and the struggle to convey or depict consensus should never be mistaken for the reality of unanimity. This dearth of consensus gives a simulacral quality to any "we" that "we" might invoke, for one will always find among the backbenchers some role-players, winkers, dissidents, and other defectors from social contracts both explicit and implicit.

Nonetheless, as if entranced by reflexivity itself, Tyler forgets the rhetorically constructed nature of every possible second-person plural, and ignores the plurality of the many "we's" to come, to make a prevailing sense of discursive conventionality the binding element of the scholarly community. Arguing that "[t]o represent means to have a kind of magical power over appearances, to be able to bring into presence what is absent," Tyler describes human mimeticism as a religio-aesthetic capacity that fashions a beguiling sense of factuality. But one might become reflexive about this capacity too, as contemporary scholars have come to know that the "ideology of representational signification is an ideology of power. To break its spell we would have to attack writing, totalistic representational signification, and authorial authority, but all this has already been accomplished for us" (Tyler 1987: 208). One can forgive Tyler's sense of accomplishment, but he approaches this event as an "attack" that, once executed, constitutes an irreversible historical break or rupture. As survivors of this passage between paradigmatic systems, our contemporary unanimity depends on the otherness of those who once believed or anachronistically believe in "the ideology of representational signification." This model of a temporal distinction predicated upon a detraditionalizing or secularizing discovery assumes that the postideological scholar has accomplished much through mere reception and inheritance. Meanwhile, this attributes a great deal of naïvete and gullibility to all those who still believe in "totalistic representational signification" and faithful mimetic capture. With Tyler's "we" he seems to miss that a great many mimetically immersed scholarly others probably work just down his hall. Thus, Tyler fails to reference any viable consensus for his second-person reflexive plural, for just as the "I" as a self-identical subject has fragmented, so this semiotically enlightened "we" coheres only through the projection of its benighted scholarly other.

From the Loss of "We" to the Projection of the Other

Turning now to one of the youngest humanities, religious studies is a loosely defined field that pursues the secular and/or scientific study of religions. As an interdisciplinary field, religious studies draws from many irreconcilable epistemological paradigms; hence, it exhibits characteristics of a "discipline" in the pursuit of an organized body of knowledge, provided one has a generous sense of "organized." Yet of all the various fields of the human and social sciences, religious studies has an illustrative role because of its late emergence within the university system, as well as the period of its American emergence at the dawn of the "postmodern" era. For the first several decades of its disciplinary history, debate has centered on many intractable issues, such as the hidden theological and humanist premises of the field. With such fundamentally different and conflicting theoretical agendas and methodological resources contained within the same field, scholars who begin the study of religions are quickly humbled regarding the scope and type of truth claims they might make, as epistemological modesty is enjoined with a devotional zeal. Steeped in the history of so many paradigms fallen and traditions crumbled, the entire field seems temperamentally attuned to this modesty, perhaps as much from the influence of ancient wisdom literature as from Heisenberg or Wittgenstein. Neither are we hopeful about the religionists' "we," for we have learned from the religious other that every second-person plural at once evokes a community and marks an exclusion.

Because of its legal instauration with a series of USSC decisions, the history of religious studies in the United States has required a judicial charter like no other discipline in the university. In this secular nation-state with many publicly funded educational institutions, the USSC had to differentiate the religionist from the cleric. In the landmark Abington case, the petition alleged that the school district had students "read from the King James version of the Bible." Because "the exercise was sectarian," it was in violation of the Disestablishment Clause of the US Constitution. Writing for the majority, Justice Clark noted that "even if [the exercise's] purpose is not strictly religious, it is sought to be accomplished through readings, without comment, from the Bible," and "[s]urely the place of the Bible as an instrument of religion cannot be gainsaid" (USSC 1963: 224). With remarkable insight into the role played by repetition in religious practices, the trial court held that even without overt proselytizing religious repetition is insufficiently distinctive, for "the reading of the verses, even without comment, possesses a devotional and religious character and constitutes in effect a religious observance" (210). As the USSC distinguished religionists from the religious, it is as if the self-evident "tool-being" capacity of scripture to inscribe tipped the case. To clear a place for teaching about religion in the public sphere, Abington demands signals from the religionists that they are mentioning and not using religious resources.

For the religionist, then, clarity regarding the use versus mention distinction is enjoined at the outset. Long familiar in the philosophy of language as one of the field's necessary premises, the use versus mention distinction is in fact integral to scholarship as a whole. Just as the bedrock philological practices of quotation and citation allow a writer to capture allotextual discursive elements, so this distinction allows us not only to *use* a word *for* referring to an object as a discernible thing in the world but also to *mention* a word *as* a virtual object to scrutinize. Just as a quotation distinguishes its mention from a use by means of orthographic marks, according to Abington this signaling must take place whatever the media, not only when religionists read scripture but also when they exhibit devotional images. Abington thus requires the religionist to develop and employ broader strategies of *mentioning deutilization* than simple intertextual quotations; indeed, it apparently requires multiple operations to transform an aspect of religious semiosis into an inutile object of knowledge. Moroever, this scholarly skill set stems from a fundamental semiotic reflexivity by means of which any human can indirectly mention as well as directly use various semiotic media, thereby, for instance, analyzing the operations of rhetoric instead of simply exercising or experiencing them.

Abington's vocational premise of religionist reflexivity requires a metadiscursive mentioning that enacts a recursive, autoapplicative movement to provide an initial, minimal taxonomic purchase on a source flow of religio-cultural semiosis. Moreover, instead of the resemblance that descriptions and transcriptions promise, mentioning acknowledges refraction and iterative difference, thus providing the religionist with a vocational program that does not reduce to a reduplicative amplification of the voice of the religious other. This plausible interpretation makes Abington a license for religionist reflexivity to ground a robust set of postconventional practices that proliferate religious objects of scrutiny through generative mentions that mark and distinguish without stigmatization.

It is a mistake, however, to see in Abington's vocational charter only an alienation or distanciation from religion. This reflexive capacity to use semiotic media in a way that both negates the naturalness of these media and affirms human recognition by taking distance from these media constitutes a double movement, an alienation that is also an approach. When transparent these media appear given, or rather, as given they do not appear as such but instead disappear into the flow of praxis. But like Heidegger's broken hammer that suddenly emerges from its equipmental nexus to become a distinct object of scrutiny, discursive practices, when refracted by means of atypical usage or a de-utilizing, bracketing mention, suddenly appear and become available to us for consideration (1962: 95–101). The work of disemploying the tools of religion to hold them up to scrutiny could constitute a true revolution that builds upon the epistemological egalitarianism that typifies religious studies, with an efficacious practical distinction to establish the interdisciplinary credibility of the field.

Religionist reflexivity that employs semiotic refraction in the form of the use versus mention distinction here serves a juridical role and also offers a broad charter for the religionist vocation. Abington does not resolve the practical issues concerning how a scholar is to demonstrate and differentiate this vocational mentioning from a proselytizing utilization of religious resources. But what is clear is that for we religionists, mentioning these resources is our only permissible use for them. Moreover, this initial restriction grants us the vocational liberty to scrutinize what our mentioning manifests. But if this reading of Abington is plausible, why is it so rare to see this vocational license exercised with the latitude that it seems to encourage?

Most religionists in America would read Abington as a charter of vocational distinction, fewer though as a manual for practice. But the moralizing frame of the ruling carries weight too, such as the observation that we have learned through "bitter experience" that the "place of religion in our society is an exalted one," which informs the decision that "the State is firmly committed to a position of neutrality" (USSC 1963: 226). Hence, in post-Abington America one might expect religionists to exhibit neutrality and remain outside any religious polemics so that they can help manage the public sphere's interreligious détente. This gives reflexive neutrality both an epistemological and an ethical aspect. Abington echoes precedents that blend neutrality with paternalistic concern, as in *Minor v. Cincinnati Board of Education* (1870), when Judge Taft offered his account of American religious liberty as "absolute equality before the law, of all religious opinions and sects," while avowing that the "government is neutral, and, while protecting all, it prefers none, and it disparages none" (cited in USSC 1963: 215). The court marks two forbidden poles, disparagement at one and preference at the other, and religionists thread this same needle by exhibiting respect for the belief claims of others. Indeed, while the religious other's interreligious tolerance and respect is situational and context dependent, they are criterial characteristics for the religionist.

Yet the court's reverence for religion is rarely experienced as a constraint, though the field plays a civil-religious role in most every nation that permits the secular study of religion. For instance, when Geertz proclaims that the "whole point of a semiotic approach to culture" is for "gaining access to the conceptual world in which our subjects live so that we can, in some extended sense of the term, converse with them" (1973b: 24), this focus on the other, cleansed of scientistic ambitions, forms the fundamental compact between the scholar's vocational reflexivity and the consensus-building agenda of the nation-state's civil religion. In fact, this implicit complicity shaped the field from the beginning, as did a broad premise held by both scholar and citizen that posits individual religious beliefs as private and beyond critique. This rejection of disparagement discourages any overtly critical employment of Abington's vocational liberty through the religionist's mentioning. But a robust reading of Abington need not conflict with neutrality; indeed, mentioning transforms neutrality from a position or perspective into a practice of *neutralization*. Hence, in lieu of legal restrictions, what trimmed the sails just as the religionist set out to sea?

Geertz Mocks the Village Atheist

To explore this restricted reflexive turn in religious studies, after Abington in 1963 this chapter now considers the second of the two key if heterogeneous influences on religionists in the United States, Geertz's 1966 essay "Religion as a Cultural System." When read together Abington forms the legal charter for the religionist's vocation, while Geertz demonstrates a way of relating to the religious other that, though influential, falls short of the robust agenda for religionist reflexivity that Abington broached. RCS impressed upon generations of religionists the many ways that religions construct an orienting sense of reality for their adherents, and also provide them resources for handling the existential insults that beset us all. By developing a positive portrayal of the religious other, Geertz held out the promise of a clearer sense of ourselves as religionists. Eager to locate the prestigious in the interdisciplinary field, when Geertz attributed to the religious other a sense of factuality so overriding that it made any awareness of art as semblance and not reality impossible, we applauded the way he took the religious other "seriously". But this applause was symptomatic of a problematic consensus. The rest of this argument will develop a reading of Geertz's omissions and avoidances to show how his analysis of religion foreclosed mention of its aesthetic dimensions for generations of religionists.

Perhaps we religionists should have picked up on the troubling ambiguity of the title: difficulties might be expected when an author alludes to "pure" and "applied" (1973a: 121) religion in an essay whose title implies that religion will be treated on "improper" terrain anyway, "as" something other than what it is or has been, namely, a cultural system. This ambiguity is not resolved but exploited, as the title promises both an anthropologist's updated, postromantic consideration of religions and their cultural or "value" dimensions, as well as a restricted inquiry that excludes social "fact" aspects like rank, status, and kinship that were the principal concerns of the British structural-functional school. This ambiguity allows Geertz to consider factuality but only through the detour of valuation and the cultural system. To derive the factual from the virtual, Geertz treats authority as anonymous and factuality as given while exhibiting a persistent disinterest for the human intermediaries who produce this anonymity and givenness by disguising the way things now are as how they have always been. Strangely, the counterfactual *as-ness* mentioned in the title is rejected in RCS, committed as it is to a thoroughgoing occlusion of the aesthetic and other human fingerprints on religious phenomena.

Even though Geertz announces his famous definition of religion with the words of an impresario ("Without further ado"), the definition itself barely mentions the aesthetic production of factuality. Yet when Geertz addresses religion, his descriptive prose includes repressed aesthetic aspects that are sharply excluded from his definition of religion. The language of rhetoric and aesthetics roils irrepressibly to the surface when he speaks of religion creating "an aura of utter actuality" and a "sense" of the "really real," or of how "religion tunes human actions to an envisaged cosmic order and projects images of cosmic order onto the plane of human experience." Tuning and projecting would inevitably involve the senses, aesthesia, and thus the aesthetic mode of experience, and Geertz even admits that it is "the essence of religious action" to construct a "persuasive authority" (1973a: 112). But even as Geertz describes the aesthetic nature of religious persuasion, he aggressively misinterprets the actual appearance of aesthetics in his case study. In RCS semiotic reflexivity, with its simulacra, refractions, and dissimulations, is present in description but repressed in theory.

Geertz presents a hermeneutically generous approach to religion, one that he is eager to distinguish from a hostile, secularizing attitude. In this way Geertz shifts the religionist's vocational principle from objectivity to Abingtonian neutrality, which entails not only a shift in attitude but also the performance of a style. Seeking the mean between the vicious extremes of the debunker and the proselytizer, how can the religionist rhetorically convey *neutrality*? Geertz considers this one of the "main methodological problems in writing about religion scientifically" (1973a: 123). Seeking neutrality instead of objectivity, Geertz encourages religionists "to put aside at once the tone of the village atheist and that of the village preacher, as well as their more sophisticated equivalents, so that the social and psychological implications of particular religious beliefs can emerge in a clear and neutral light" (1973a: 123).

Geertz defines his others by their tone, but speaks for himself in terms of a way of writing ("scientifically") and a type of light ("clear and neutral"). Moreover, in American English one generally speaks not of village preachers and atheists but of the "village idiot." In this overt detour from the idiom Geertz makes the association between the atheist, the idiot, and the pseudocosmopolitan bigot unmistakable. Far short of a neutral portrait of his neutrality, Geertz approaches discipline-specific reflexivity indirectly through a caricature of those who fail to exhibit such neutrality, since neutrality and fairness naturally have their limits.

Professional imperatives like Geertz's evoke a scholar who, being culturally unbiased if not scientifically objective, is always already reflexive. Indeed, Geertz assumes reflexivity in the ability to "put aside" one's tone and demeanor without any express "putting on" of anything else. This noncommittal ethic overrides epistemological commitments to consider matters of tone and propriety. Even as epistemological mastery has lost most of its authoritative claims, ethical responsibility provides supplemental justification for the religionist's drift from objectivity toward neutrality. At this vanishing point epistemology blurs into ethics, giving the scholarly crisis of knowledge a moral payoff, for in our uncertainty we can defer to study those who still have convictions.

Beyond this putative equality, however, the scholar emerges burdened with the duty to avoid offence through the reflexive performance of secular deference. The neutral, nonpolemical style of the scholar is thus the wink that others easily mistake for a blink. That is, though perceived as a lack of distinction by most others, Geertz's rejection of proselytizing for neutrality subdues religionist reflexivity and shapes it for service to an ethically charged sense of epistemic egalitarianism that has become the religionist's fundamentally moral distinguishing feature.

Geertz's Retreat from Wink to Belief

Perhaps Geertz's most significant contribution to the social sciences has to do with the aesthetics of his writing. To distinguish "what anthropological analysis amounts to as a form of knowledge," Geertz makes clear that it "is not a matter of methods," calling it a "kind of intellectual effort" and "elaborate venture" in the practice of "thick description" (1973b: 6). As an exemplification of the post-Abington consensus, in the wake of RCS many religionists have opted for thick description as a form of robust neutrality. But if Geertz established the modest work of description as the primary scholarly task, why does he characterize it as "elaborate"? There is a peculiar generosity at work in Geertz's hermeneutics, as it posits an other to be understood, but to justify the effort the other must be *so other* as to become a mysterious object of scrutiny whose alienated distance needs a full-fledged discipline to overcome. In a more negative light, modest, homely description becomes the sole scholarly task instead of a platform of initial discursive capture upon which basis the more theoretical projects of analysis and interpretation can take place. Moreover, by making description "thick" Geertz ensured that it would be labor-intensive enough to leave no remainder for other projects. As Geertz flattened Abington's neutralizing deutilizations into neutral descriptions, this gave cover to well-mannered scholarly analyses that reject critical and theoretical approaches on principle.

In our enthusiastic embrace of Geertzian hermeneutics, we religionists overlooked how, if we compared Geertz's two most famous essays, the winks discussed in "Thick Description" and the beliefs in RCS do not appear to harmonize. Winks and beliefs share invisibility, since "from an I-am-a-camera, 'phenomenalistic' observation… one could not tell which was twitch and which was wink," and obviously, "the difference, however unphotographable, between a twitch and a wink is vast" (1973b: 6). Since the retreat to hermeneutical interiority remains the religionist's primary temptation, this shared invisibility was beguiling, but there are no mentions of winks or twitches in RCS. Further, if the task is description, does the religionist describe belief itself, or what belief is about, its object? Geertz himself shifts from the wink to consider what informs the wink, making the "object of ethnography" the "stratified hierarchy of meaningful structures" (1973b: 7) that produces this nonmimetic difference between photographable appearances and the experience of social meaning. But whether the agent's interiority or the system that structures it, a focus on "belief" posits a relation between durability and truth that privileges the given, the static, and what appears to reside or passes for permanent. With religion cast as the "having" or "holding" of beliefs, at the outset this privileges the traditional, the repeated, and the fixed as the properly religious, with no regard for the resources for contestation, quickening, and change that religions also supply.

As the wink's nonphenomenal status defies mimetic capture, Geertz could have broached a post-Husserlian, nonmimetic species of reflexivity. As Geertz offered us the apple of the wink, we saw the future set for an interdisciplinary, humanistic hermeneutic concerned with the confessed intentional states of the religious other. In fact, Geertz's question—"What does 'belief' mean in a religious context?" (1973a: 109)—set the stage for decades of scholars who sought to combine the modesty of description and transcription with a concern about the other's non-empirical interiority. But with belief center stage, Geertz must ignore the religious wink, which is just as well, since privileging the wink's *meaning* would still amount to a retreat away from the semiotic indices that are the sole traces of subjectivity that we have publicly available for scrutiny, toward an interiority where meaningful belief dwells in all its aniconic—not to say solipsistic—glory. What is worse, the next section will show that Geertz's factuality-transfixed religious other appears to miss winks not accidentally but categorically. Geertz's failure of reflexivity pivots on his failure to recognize reflexivity in the religious other, and in this Geertz himself missed the biggest wink of all.

Geertz's Retreat to Distributed Factuality and Anonymous Authority

An other who winks would make the referent of religionists' descriptions inherently unstable, if not unknowable entirely. This is unthinkable for Geertz, as it is the unknowable that his postulated notion of religion must therapeutically address. I will take from Geertz the *nonmimetic nature of reflexivity* as illustrated in the difference between the blink and the wink. But to have something to describe, Geertz's famous definition of religion retreats from winked meanings to durable religious moods and motivations which depend upon the impressions of "factuality" that the religiocultural system produces. With religion Geertz turns from the wink to factuality, authority, and performances that exhibit the "really real." These terms mark the sites of serial vanishing points in RCS, each of which appears for a moment as if to serve as an explanation, only to recede in turn from the text.

Geertz's *first recession* moves from facts to factuality. To avoid a picture of the gullible native, Geertz makes the religious other like us, concerned about the really real. The asymmetrical reciprocity between the religionist and the other hinges on scholars recognizing the fragmentary and incomplete nature of "our knowledge" even as we commit to describing the systematic coherence of "their belief." Geertz thus bases his construction on the scrutiny, not of their winks, but of their construals of "factuality." Referring to *factuality* as a concern posits a durable systematicity to beliefs because one's sense of reality does not depend entirely on any one *fact*. Instead, the warrant for any one fact derives from a distributed system of factuality no one element of which, if proven wrong, is focal enough to discredit the system as a whole. By redefining religious authority as a holistic sense of factuality, RCS emphasizes the scope, systematicity, and even scientificity of the other's belief, because expanded to designate the other's experience of reality as a whole and not only specifically religious phenomena. As opposed to the originating fiction of, say, a social contract, a quasi-agreement between preexisting agents who are, paradoxically, already socialized enough to understand what a contract is, Geertz points to (and unreflexively participates in) the perpetual complicity whereby authorities conjure anonymous, often supernatural others as guarantors of a posited factuality that mediates collective assumptions. This more implicit agreement mediated through factuality should permit more heterogeneity and division than explicitly formulated contracts would allow. Like earlier social contract theorists, Geertz plausibly treats society's minimal cohesion as a premise, but then implausibly makes little room for contestation and conflict in his theory.

Geertz's *second recession* disregards the sources that project authority, whether agents who might be named or observable practices that might be mentioned. Geertz proclaims the disembodied authority of factuality to be the nebulous glue holding everything together, for "religious belief involves not a Baconian induction from everyday experience—for then we should all be agnostics—but rather a prior acceptance of authority which transforms that experience" (1973a: 109). Abstracting away from the contested field of authoritative claims within society to reach a level of general consensus allows Geertz to obviate any choice on his part regarding whose acceptance or belief he will choose to describe. The definitive priority of factuality renders power faceless, always already acknowledged as authoritative by all, an authority that is never fully present and demonstrated but instead looms behind the present as given and established, its shadows cast long before the living came to be. This therapeutic givenness, a religio-cultural placebo effect of *authoritativeness without authorities*, forms Geertz's *geistliche* commons from which theodicizing effects inevitably flow.

Recognizing only a specular relation between the social world and its religious reflection, Geertz retracts religion self-identically into its own self-subsistent realm with no leaching from or leaking to other sources and channels of social power. To acknowledge this embeddedness would make the religious other's sense of factuality the contingent outcome of socially observable processes that could end in failure. Geertz's dilemma is that acknowledging *religious contestation as itself religious* would relativize and contest the consensual façade of many religious traditions. As if to avoid conflict with this traditionally clerical perspective, which marks *religious dissent as irreligious*, Geertz derives belief from an acculturated sense of factuality unmediated by social others, in effect depoliticizing truth. Geertz never acknowledges that "whose" authority prevails might be an issue that concerns the religious other. However suitably Geertz's sense of religion might apply to indigenous cultures or relatively homogeneous societies, even among these, key components of religious capital (myths, rituals, sacred names, and prerogatives) tend to be owned by specific clans or secret societies. Because even universalizing religious claims originate from a particular social location, as power shifts among these groups, the society's overarching religious ecosystem undergoes periodic shocks and reequilibrations. While this is common enough in small-scale societies, it is virtually constant in more complex, stratified societies. In his eagerness to attribute an epistemological thickness to the religious other that he can describe, Geertz allows little to no role for endogenous religio-cultural critiques of hegemonic, authorized simulacra of factuality.

Geertz consistently diminishes the sense that actual humans are involved in the production and reproduction of the religious authority that he claims grounds a group's sense of factuality. To this end, Geertz's language retreats to the passive voice with his description of religion in action, whereby "a group's ethos *is rendered* intellectually reasonable *by being shown* to represent a way of life ideally *adapted* to the actual state of affairs the world view describes, while the world view *is rendered* emotionally convincing *by being presented* as an image of an actual state of affairs peculiarly *well-arranged* to accommodate such a way of life" (1973a: 89–90, emphasis added). The passive parallelism helps Geertz exclude any sense that social power fractures the smooth façade of factuality. Moreover, he orients religions more toward nature than society in a way that obscures how religions might generate conjunctions between endogenous religio-cultural critiques and social scissions between authoritative and subaltern agents. In consequence, Geertz abstracts religions from the systole and diastole of validating and contesting social authority.

To make up for this lack of human agency, Geertz symptomatically claims that "the world view describes" reality—as if it were not itself a particular description, one reified portrait of reality among others produced from traceable sources. Geertz also attributes an autoaffective power to rituals themselves, as "the acceptance of authority that underlies the religious perspective that the ritual embodies thus flows from the enactment of the ritual itself" (1973a: 118). The advantage here is a certain semiotic realism, in that ritually patterned behaviors produce predictable effects despite the variability of actors and participants. But this extreme formulation of self-executing performances of authority ignores the real channels of power connecting this performance to quotidian social action. In this way Geertz constructs a hermetically sealed circuit flowing between authority wielded by no one in particular, factuality that is given and incontestable, and autoauthorizing performances that produce of themselves alone an impersonal, non-perspectival, putatively objective, and thus authoritative sense of factuality, the "really real."

To install a permanently therapeutic cultural function for religion Geertz must derive a systematic effect of distributed authority that does not depend on anything in particular for its legitimacy. This is the *third recession*, as Geertz aligns himself with all religions in the defense of *order as such* against chaos, without acknowledging the plurality of possible orders one might endorse. Geertz holds that religion from the native's emic perspective "moves beyond the realities of everyday life to wider ones which correct and complete them" (1973a: 112). Perhaps Geertz means that religions pass beyond the social to more existential dimensions or supernatural realms. Geertz does not claim this himself, but safely ensconced in the subjunctive mood he does humbly suggest that "[i]f one were to essay a minimal definition of religion today," it would be the "relatively modest dogma that God is not mad" (1973a: 99). This epistemological modesty shows how Geertz's recessions—to factuality, authority, and finally rituals depicted as self-executing performances—underscore religion's incontestability by shifting expectations. When religions maintain only a minimal sense of the world's explicability, this factuality's reasonableness stands impervious to discredit because no one fact or claim is authoritatively focal enough to disturb the web of belief. Meanwhile, the plausibility of any particular interpretation or the success of any prediction confirms the minimal sense of order necessary to produce religion's therapeutic effect. Geertz's desire to present a holistic portrait of religion as culture leads him to emphasize the holistic and therapeutic aspects of religion, a consonance and parity between the claims of religious traditions and Geertz's definition of "religion" that only produces the semblance of an explanation.

Geertz's Provincial Aesthetics

Geertz's portrayal of a zero-degree, effaced authority deposits social power in a spiritual commons from which placebo effects flow, but in doing so ignores the authoritative vocations occupied by particular agents in this contested social field. Geertz's religions equip people to confront the more natural challenges of life (illness, aging, death, the unjust distribution of good fortune), but there is much less attention paid to religions as primary channels of social power. That is, religions apparently never disturb or fragment anyone's sense of reality, a telling omission. Geertz would have us understand religious authority without any reflexivity concerning the appearances of authority qua appearances; indeed, the entire post-Machiavellian sensitivity to the semblance of authority and power becomes irrelevant to Geertz's study of religion. Hence, Geertz does not only make authority anonymous, he ignores the counterfactual, the reflexively aesthetic, as well as the therapeutically homeostatic tension that cultural performances maintain between persuasion and coercion.

Perhaps every "we" is held together by nothing more than a wink, a complicity that, unlike the contract, entails neither publicity nor recognition; nor can complicity ever become unanimous, since its premise is the secret's exclusivity. As our secrets sift us from them, we who are in the know get the joke and catch our own winks. But Geertz's religiously authorized factuality transforms each religious believer into an unwinking placeholder for a univocal construal of reality, immune to the confusing deceptions of aesthetics because unaware of that cosmopolitan mode of experience. As opposed to religious rituals, the "spectacularly theatrical cultural performance from Bali" that Geertz analyzes "can be most readily examined by the detached observer" (1973a: 114)—a temporary inversion of authority that only seems to empower the social scientist. But if Geertz has religiously authorized factuality take center stage, what this displaces requires clarification. Not only are cultural performances more public than specifically religious rituals, these displays are so religious for the Balinese that they become rituals that are "aesthetically appreciated" (1966: 113) only by visitors who are locked out of the authentic Balinese experience. As factuality becomes spectacular in these privileged performances, Geertz makes the cultural even more religious than religion, for a cultural performance "objectivizes moral and aesthetic preferences by depicting them as the imposed conditions of life" (1973a: 89–90), and "[i]n these plastic dramas men attain their faith as they portray it" (1973a: 114). Disregarding the aesthetic refractions that depicting and portraying entail, just as thick description remains enthralled to the positivistic promise of perfect referential capture, Geertz's believers remain immersed in semiotic media immediately and by definition in a way that obscures the other's appearing.

At times, even as he treats Balinese factuality as closed and settled, Geertz seems to acknowledge the sleight of hand whereby the aesthetically constructed becomes the ontologically given. How could he not, since even in the laboratory processes of dissimulation play their part. According to Latour and Woolgar, the "process of fact construction" requires "the escape of a statement from all reference to the process of construction." To emphasize the finality of the fact the process of production must disappear, so that it "is not just that facts are socially constructed," but more to the point, "the process of construction involves the use of certain devices whereby all traces of production are made extremely difficult to detect" (1986: 176). Here the aesthetic becomes an irreducible component of epistemology, as the dissimulation of production traces proves integral, and not accidental, to the construction of facts. Whenever simulation appears, dissimulation does as well, so if Latour and Woolgar discover the aesthetic at work even in a laboratory, how can Geertz miss it in Bali? If every truth claim carries the counterfactual as freight, one always finds a rhetoric, a poetics, and a stylistics in play, whether we choose to mention these or not.

The Geertzian model allows the Balinese an authoritative sense of religion's factuality, but no sense of art because they lack a working concept of the aesthetic. Practically this means the Balinese only use their media and cannot mention or otherwise take distance from them for scrutiny and reflection. The religious other might blink in the blinding light of the facts as presented to them, even onstage, but they can never wink about what is represented to them. The Balinese cannot themselves enjoy these *as performances*, for Geertz's sense of actuality is too emphatic, of ceremony too public, and of religion too pure to account for the subtleties of Balinese performances. Unfortunately, Geertz doesn't "save the phenomena" *as phenomena*. This primitivizing depiction of the Balinese should raise alarms about missed winks, since these constitute Geertz's utmost concern whenever religion is not the focal topic. How strange that Geertz did not expect the reader to be concerned, as if a projected lack of an aspect of humanity on others is no loss, so long as it is only, merely, art. If poetry makes nothing happen, according to Auden, then to Geertz the aesthetic will not be missed where it is lacking—and for the most part, Geertz's readers have not noticed.

Geertz's Anaesthetic Panic

By analyzing a "cultural performance," Geertz does not observe the Balinese in everyday settings, but in a theater, a highly specific site separated spatially and conceptually from quotidian social life. This places the religionist as a spectator uncomfortably close to the religious others in the audience. To avoid experiencing the performance as a crisis of ambiguation with this religious other, Geertz disregards members of the audience who are not taken in by the aesthetic illusion. Obliterating traces of their aesthetic distance is necessary because Geertz's empha-sis, "the main point to be stressed" aside from the authority of factual-ity, "is that the drama is, for the Balinese, not merely a spectacle to be watched but a ritual to be enacted. There is no aesthetic distance here separating actors from audience." This he knows because before the ritualized "encounter has been concluded a majority, often nearly all, of the members of the group sponsoring it will have become caught up in it not just imaginatively but bodily" (1973a: 116). There is much to query here, yet when we turn to the Balinese performance itself, Geertz claims that "the relations between [the lead characters] are what [the performance] is about" (1973a: 115). Speaking of the characters on the Balinese stage as "genuine realities," Geertz insists that the roles are "not representations of anything, but presences," so much so that "[t]o ask, as I once did, a man who has been Rangda whether he thinks she is real is to leave oneself open to the suspicion of idiocy" (1973a: 118). Geertz himself plays the role of the village idiot here by questioning the religious other's beliefs, for if the wink signals awareness of a gap between appearance and reality, the religious other apparently does not and cannot wink about religion, art, or theater. But is it possible that the performer stared in bafflement at this interloper who asked bewilder-ingly naïve and inappropriate questions about art?

The case for this reading gets stronger with the specifics of the char-acters. As Geertz describes them, "Rangda is a satanic image, Barong is a farcical one" (1973a: 114); moreover, as opposed to Rangda, who embodies fear, Barong "incarnates the Balinese version of the comic spirit," an attitude marked by "playfulness, exhibitionism, and extrava-gant love of elegance" (1973a: 118). In each term of Barong's description one finds the awareness of the disjunction between appearances and re-ality, the noncoincidence of which is a premise of the aesthetic perspec-tive. But despite his reliance on aesthetic terms, Geertz never identifies Barong with the aesthetic. Geertz's descriptive prose again hits closer to the mark than his theorizing does when he admits that "[t]his odd counterpoint of implacable malice and low comedy pervades the whole performance" (1973a: 115). Even though the performance itself stages the aesthetic, or at least mentions it by placing it on the stage, Geertz misses the mention, blinks at the wink, and otherwise manages to miss the most plausible reading of the performance. With the ultimate point always being authority and factuality, Geertz consistently refuses to view this as a struggle between the religious and the aesthetic. In fact, he cannot do this, because the religious other he has constructed cannot truly bear witness to a cultural performance that depicts a battle be-tween religious and aesthetic principles. Yet it is an incredible conjuring feat to interpret this performance "for the believing Balinese" as "both the formulation of a general religious conception and the authoritative experience which justifies, even compels, its acceptance" (1973a: 118), effectively subsuming Barong's undefeated spirit of ostentation and semblance into the "really real" of the performance's holistic, not to say totalitarian, effect.

Readers of RCS are thus entitled to skepticism regarding Geertz's domestication of Barong's carnivalesque aestheticism to the service of inculcating religious authority. In fact, by minimizing Barong and the laughter he provokes, Geertz doubles his rejection of the cross-cultural reality of the aesthetic mode of experience by misconstruing evidence of aesthetic reflexivity both onstage and in the audience. That is, despite Geertz's rhetorical approximation of unanimity ("a majority, often nearly all"), there are Balinese in the audience who preserve aesthetic distance even as "[m]ass trance, spreading like a panic," eventually "hovers, or at least seems to hover, on the brink of mass amok" (1973a: 117). The concession to the aesthetic marked by "seems" could be a wink that Geertz is wittingly overselling his position. He should wink, because parallel with the battle onstage are "the diminishing band of the unentranced striving desperately (and, it seems, almost always successfully) to control the growing band of the entranced" (1973a: 117). The aesthetically informed minority in the audience should be of great interest, as they "keep the frenzied activities of the entranced from getting out of hand by the application of physical restraint if they are ordinary men, by the sprinkling of holy water and the chanting of spells if they are priests," but Geertz is only concerned with "believing Balinese" (1966: 118). To Geertz it is less important that some do not undergo mimetic immersion than that some do take spectacle for reality. Even though the indigenous response is bifurcated, split between the panicking religious and the therapeutic aesthetes, Barong and the unentranced spectators who preserve aesthetic distance recede from view. When Geertz mentions the therapeutically inclined aesthetes at all, it is to minimize them as anomalies, since there is "an extraordinarily developed capacity for psychological dissociation on the part of a very large segment of the population" (1973a: 116). Instead of turning to Belo's then recent work (1960) examining the trance as a set of existing relationships that transform in the course of the performance, Geertz psychologizes—and thus biologizes—this as a racial or cultural capacity, which makes the trance element of the performance an initial condition and not the outcome of an aesthetic performance that so obviously employs religious trance in tandem with recognizably aesthetic themes.

Geertz's emphasis on the authoritative construction of factuality does no justice to the positive sense of illusion and aesthetics in this Balinese performance. With the dramatic mise-en-scéne normatively regarded in terms of fourth-wall aesthetic distance, Geertz's explicit references to theater as an aesthetic medium were surprisingly provincial, in effect normalizing nineteenth-century European dramaturgical conventions. He thus lacked the resources to theorize the aesthetic issue of the audience's complicity in the counterfactual pretense of reality. The Balinese stage this issue in a transgressive framework closer to Nietzsche and Artaud than Ibsen and Chekov, much less Eliot, whom Geertz directly mentions. The ostentation and aestheticized foppery of Barong serves as a comic foil to the terrorizing realism of Rangda, and both elements are included onstage. Since the performance depicts a standoff between the two characters, could this be read as a depiction of religion in a counterbalancing ontological dance with aesthetics, or as the dreadful weight of authoritative, historical factuality lightened by the insouciance of counterfactual play? Geertz treads close to this by noting that "the performance begins with an appearance of Barong, prancing and preening, as a general prophylactic against what is to follow" (1973a: 117). Geertz seems to admit here that, for the Balinese, the aesthetic provides an important "prophylactic" to religion's sense of real terrors. This is so obvious as to pass for a description rather than an interpretation, since the Balinese themselves have staged this therapeutic capacity of aesthetic counterfactuality, and instead of letting it pass unmentioned have incorporated this mentionable feature of their culture reflexively into the performance. But Geertz does not let this affect his theory, apparently mentioning this prophylactic interpretation only as a prophylactic measure to dispense with it and argue the opposite, that the performance is not in fact a mocking corrective to Geertz's extreme sense of religion's exclusive grounding in factuality.

Post-Machiavellian Analysis of the Religious Other

Arguably, then, for the Balinese the therapeutic value of the aesthetic, with its comic discontinuities between appearances and reality, offers an important counterprinciple to the emphatic depiction of the "really real" that Geertz identifies as the proper function of religion. Opposed in this way, the performance becomes unwieldy evidence at best if Geertz's argument is to conform to the civil-religious and vocational expectations of the post-Abington religionist, who needs a knowable type of religious other to study. This is why the aesthetic as a category is shunted offstage despite being personified by Barong, for the aesthetic cannot appear as such to Geertz's Balinese, whose theater can only provide certainty and factuality, not entertainment, illusion, or therapeutic pleasure. As Geertz himself kicks the aesthetic as a category offstage, lurking behind the curtains one can discern another religious other, one whose "mood" and "motivation" deviates from those prescribed by the prevailing, authorized sense of factuality.

By means of RCS's recessions, Geertz counterposes the sincerity of belief against the complicity of the wink, and on the terrain of religion, opts for the former. Geertz's conceptual shell game of serial recessions obscures the Balinese performance's exhibited connections between therapeutic reciprocity and aesthetic semblance. With a religious other depicted as a fervent adherent to incontestable factuality and susceptible to panic when faced with the ambiguation of art and reality, Geertz's benevolent regard for the other is not what is in question here (though it is highly questionable), but that the other he constructs is irremediably naïve, and we religionists must also be naïve to believe in this naïveté. When Geertz declaims with the intonations of a manifesto that studying religion without reference to belief is like staging *Hamlet* without the prince, this rallying cry, sonorous as it was, led subsequent decades of religionists in precisely the wrong direction, toward psychologism instead of a more distributed set of analytical interests. But never one to have it only one way, Geertz himself winks at this point when, in total opposition to his own agenda, he observes that, "if the anthropological study of religious commitment is underdeveloped," one must conclude that "the anthropological study of religious noncommitment is nonexistent." Undoubtedly the religionist is often compelled to take people of faith on faith, to give the benefit of the doubt to the idealism and altruism of the faithful. From the testimony to the archive, the sincerely believing and reporting other is the only true subject of humanist hermeneutics. But this religious other renders invisible the strategizing other who uses without scruple the religious resources that religionists can only mention. As if noting this lack, Geertz claims that religionists will only have "come of age when some more subtle Malinowski writes a book called 'Belief and Unbelief (or even 'Faith and Hypocrisy') in a Savage Society'" (1973a: 109). Since the post-Abington charter for this work exists, Geertz here acknowledges that the study of belief need not foreclose other, even opposed, inquiries. Of course, Geertz's own analysis ignores many noncommittal aspects of the performance, such as the *therapeutically reciprocal complicity* that he misrecognizes as chaotic panic. Depriving the other of their aesthetic and mimetic reflexivity, once Geertz catches his believer winking they are either ignored, like the therapeutic aesthete in the audience, or dismissed, like the village atheist, who lives in the village like others but somehow counts less. Whether backbenchers who mock the pieties or duplicitous authorities who exploit them, both types of religious other have been excluded from the field. While reminding us that our concepts must keep pace with phenomena, it is remarkable that Geertz mentions this topic for "some more subtle Malinowski" in the very essay that aggressively forecloses this possibility.

When postsecular scholars ascribe a sincerity and fixity of belief to religious others that is unavailable to themselves, this is a condescending projection of a simpler form of subjectivity onto another. Reflexivity as a human universal attributes to every other a properly conflicted subjectivity like "our" own. Rather than assigning them the anonymous authority of unanimous factuality, we can save the phenomena by noticing the play of contestation and persuasion that fragments every "I" and "we." Just as any scholarly "we" fragments at the first mention of premises or principles, so with religious others as well. But far from debunking the others' beliefs or disrespecting the purity of their motivations, to locate an agent in a heterogeneous cultural field of conflicting interests and ambivalent desires has a deothering effect that engages them on a reflexive plane of consistency. If we extended this awareness of the conventional and plastic nature of semiosis beyond the confines of Tyler's scholarly "we" to the devotees of religions themselves, religionists might then witness more reflexivity at play among their subjects. Moreover, unless religionists assume that the other is reflexively strategic, and thus Machiavellian to a degree, one cannot account for the inevitable traces of secrecy, complicity, and cunning that close social scrutiny reveals. Winking satirists, duplicitous hypocrites, and cunning Machiavellians thus participate in every religious group, however rarely they appear in religionists' typically antiseptic descriptions. Instead of the naïve authenticity of Geertz's believer, which invokes a model of subjectivity leashed by group-bound sincerity and geared towards authentic commitment, the religionist must acknowledge the post-Machiavellian reality that while every religio-cultural niche places a premium on piety, what tends to prevail is the *appearance of piety*. Any religious other will aestheticize the display of their religious commitment and belief, first and foremost because it most always pays social dividends. For the Machiavellian believer in particular, this requires concealing self-serving actions and strategically obscuring the role of semblance in the reproduction of religiosity. Insofar as religionists also obscure the aesthetics of religious authority, we remain complicit in its reproduction.

The East Point Congregational Holiness Church Urinal Cake Panic

Despite the thrust of his analysis, Geertz is right that we religionists remain in a self-subjected tutelage and will not "come of age" until we are bold enough to acknowledge the existence of the religious hypocrite. To make a minor contribution to this still-broaching project (see Houseman 2002), this religionist can admit that the present chapter's counterreading of Geertz stems in part from events that instilled a long-borne sensitivity to the asymmetric relations, postures, and personae that are intrinsic to religions, each of which is institutionally and discursively stabilized but remains prone to moments of ambiguation, crisis, and panic. The details of this case merit reporting for their reflexive dividends, since the author—born and raised in the American South in postsegregation Atlanta—is also a "religious other" for the American religionist. What would the American religionist make of this religionist as a religious other, whose discovery of the backstage from the back pew disclosed the reality of the Machiavellian believer?

In the countryside houses and churches are less distinct. With similar gables and building materials, if trees obscure the steeple the two are easily confused. The child's quasi-cubist perspective on architecture fragments these buildings and blurs conceptual distinctions between a place of worship and a place of dwelling. It seemed then that the church was the nicest house we entered all week. The tall brick church left in the wake of urban "white flight" (Kruse 2005) and suburbanization helped us feel propertied, but the location left the all-white congregation in a tense relation with the increasingly African American neighborhood.

Racial desegregation came slowly to the American South, and finally in the 1950s and 1960s only through federal enforcement. In Atlanta what persisted of the slave past was a hate that had slowly begun to know shame, but for some not yet remorse, nor for a few even repentance. Because of the film *Gone with the Wind*, one thinks of Atlanta together with the American Civil War, and General Sherman's burning of Atlanta in 1864 marked a crucial turning point in modern warfare. Sherman undertook a war of attrition on his own nation's citizens in the South, which meant that his goal was less to defeat an army than to break the popular will. The South's will was broken, but its resentments over this will outlast us all, a fact that could serve as a cautionary tale about the real costs of war, but has instead become a constant energy source for conservative, reactionary politics in the United States.

The American conservative movement's "Southern Strategy" began in the early 1970s. With racialized media projects and other tactics, it cultivated this region as a crucible of durable resentments to serve as a bulwark against the progressive social movements that emerged in the 1960s. In this period antisecular Christians again began to circulate persecution narratives and reorient their worship and doctrine around their alienation from and animosity toward the "worldliness" of American culture. The prophetic chastisement of the jeremiad became less a sermonic device than an ontological posture. Alongside the glamorous rise of the televangelist in the early 1980s, in most Pentecostal fundamentalist churches one found a percolating cottage industry of pamphlets, posters, and sundry audiovisual material, the sole aim of which was to create moral panics about the satanic perils of American government and popular culture. These would periodically sweep through the congregation and even the denomination as a whole, carving the schism deeper between the church and the world that antagonized it. As the Abington decision worried that "the breach of neutrality that is today a trickling stream may all too soon become a raging torrent" (USSC 1963: 225), this ruling itself counted as such a moral breach to the congregants of the East Point Congregational Holiness Church. The white Southern Pentecostal fundamentalist could thus feel doubly aggrieved, once dishonorably ambushed at home by the Northern Union army, and recently victimized by a federal government whose rulings seemed to render familiar Christian customs suddenly illegal.

Within this broad historical framework the more immediate context for this disclosure of the Machiavellian believer was a string of child murders in Atlanta from 1979 to 1981, to this day one of the worst cases of serial murder in American history, eventually listed at twenty-eight deaths and almost all still unsolved. The entire city was terrorized, and the fact that all the children were African American did not stop white families from living in ever escalating fear.

During this postsegregation period of white flight, black murder, and low-boiling panic, our church's youth pastor suggested a radical act of outreach: invite all the families in the neighborhood, of whatever race, and use the aging and unused church bus to make good on the invitation and provide rides to the proverbial neighbor. The youth pastor presented this opportunity to desegregate our church as a spiritually rejuvenating response to this time of crisis. What likely went unmentioned was that, because the church was property-rich but congregation-poor, this was not only a moral project. The congregation consisted mostly of older people who attended without much extended family, and single-parent families with missing or heretical spouses. Like many fundamentalist churches in this period, the devotion expected was too morally severe to appeal to extended families, so the church's doctrines divided families as much as they united a congregation. That was especially true at East Point, where the enthusiasm typical of Pentecostals made our worship too ecstatic and our doctrines too intransigent to reproduce ourselves as a congregation. These dynamics between demographics and doctrine rendered the youth pastor's initiative both an act of conscience and a rational effort to increase his clientele.

One morning the hibernating bus spluttered to life and children's voices filled the hallways. For the next few Sundays it appeared that this church had a future, and one that was certainly multiracial, as all the new children were African American. But only a few weeks later a general unease had pervaded the congregation. People's ears became hypersensitive to the volume of the children's laughter, and their movements came to seem chaotic and discomfiting. Then the next week, without explanation, the bus stopped circuiting. The head deacon was in the spotlight, but at first we children only heard hurried whispers in the parking lot.

This religionist's initiation began here with a sense of dissimulation and disjunction. If the murdered children on the evening news were all African American, then why were white parents so afraid? This implied equality. But why were the new African American children such a problem for people at church? None of the new children misbehaved like the deacon's own grandchildren, who had defaced the walls with markers and crayons, forcing the deacon to paint the hallway's wood paneling white. In hindsight, perhaps this portion of the deacon's devotion spent cleaning up after his own kin should be regarded more as necessity than virtue. In this equilibrium, did the church's sudden desegregation disturb the deacon by adding an element of racial equality (or, in his mind, submission) that would have demanded "real" virtue?

Whatever the answer, the clergy quietly quelled such questions while the congregation remained unwilling or unable to mention what was in play. Soon gossip brought it all out: the deacon allegedly found a broken urinal cake in the men's restroom, one that was not just cracked by happenstance but intentionally crushed. This putative transgression the deacon inflated into the threat of clogged pipes, burst septic systems, and the flow of interracial waste from the auditorium into the sanctuary, all caused by these dark children who could not distinguish the playroom from the toilet. Perpetually short of money and threatened by such catastrophic risk, virtue bowed to necessity: as the spiritual succumbed to the material, despite the history of communitarian promise symbolized by the Eucharist wafer, the potent affective resonance of the urinal cake helped a religious authority engineer a moral panic that kept the church racially segregated for years to come.

At East Point, that beautiful church gradually came to feel toxic, and the congregation drifted apart. Some never looked back, but like Lot's wife, this religionist cannot help but return to this episode. While together an entire terrain of secrets required the congregation's complicity, and anyone whose secrets were known by others felt obliged to silence by the shared desire to keep stones unturned. This suggests that complicity as a relation of silence is more important than the content of any contract or "secret" as a message in itself. Because the whites at this church managed in this postsegregation era to endure de jure desegregation while maintaining segregation's de facto continuation, modernity began with a sense of untimeliness, a keen sense that we were still what we should have long been past. Religionist reflexivity began, then, not in natural wonder or collective effervescence but in social incongruity and dissimulation. Would that it were otherwise. As it is, for this religionist the field-specific temptation is to join my peers in ignoring the religious other's Machiavellian capacities, for this would require passing as more credulous than experiences like these have allowed.

References

Belo, Jane. 1960. *Trance in Bali*. New York: Columbia University Press.

Bourdieu, Pierre. 2004. *Science of Science and Reflexivity*. Trans. Richard Nice. Chicago: University of Chicago Press.

Durkheim, Emile. 1995. *The Elementary Forms of Religious Life*. Trans. Karen Fields. New York: Free Press.

Geertz, Clifford. 1973. *The Interpretation of Cultures: Selected Essays*. New York: Basic Books.

———.1973a [1966]. "Religion as a Cultural System." *Anthropological Approaches to the Study of Religion*. Ed. Michael Banton. London: Tavistock Publications, 1–46. Reprinted in *The Interpretation of Cultures: Selected Essays*. New York: Basic Books, (87–125). Page references are to this reprint edition.

———. 1973b. "Thick Description: Toward an Interpretive Theory of Culture." In *The Interpretation of Cultures: Selected Essays*. New York: Basic Books, 3–30.

Heidegger, Martin. 1962. *Being and Time*. Trans. John Macquarrie and Edward Robinson. New York: Harper.

Houseman, Michael. 2002. "Dissimulation and Simulation as Forms of Religious Reflexivity." *Social Anthropology* 10, no. 1: 77–89.

Husserl, Edmund. 1952. *Ideas: General Introduction to Pure Phenomenology*. Trans. William Ralph Boyce Gibson. New York: Macmillan.

Kant, Immanuel. 1996. "An Answer to the Question, What Is Enlightenment?" In *Practical Philosophy*. Trans. and ed. Mary J. Gregor. Cambridge: Cambridge University Press, 13–22.

Kruse, Kevin. 2005. *White Flight: Atlanta and the Making of Modern Conservatism*. Princeton, NJ: Princeton University Press.

Latour, Bruno, and Steve Woolgar. 1986. *Laboratory Life: The Construction of Scientific Facts*. Princeton, NJ: Princeton University Press.

Tyler, Stephen. 1987. *The Unspeakable: Discourse, Dialogue, and Rhetoric in the Postmodern World*. Madison: University of Wisconsin Press.

US Supreme Court. 1963. "School District of Abington Township, Pennsylvania, et al. v. Edward Schempp, et al.; Murray, et al. v. Curlett, et al., Constituting the Board of School Commissioners of Baltimore City," 374 U.S. 203 (1963). Argued 27–28 February 1963. Decided 17 June 1963. http://www.law.cornell.edu/supct/html/historics/USSC_CR_0374_0203_ZO.html (accessed January 8, 2015).

Christopher Roberts teaches humanities and religious studies at Lewis & Clark College in Portland, Oregon. Email: robertschristopher4@gmail.com

ᘚ SECTION II ᘚ

Reflexivity, Practice, and Embodiment

Editors' Preface

In his chapter, Horacio Ortiz mounts a critique of positivism while embracing ethics as a focus of social science. He does so by focusing on how three well-known thinkers, Wittgenstein, Bourdieu, and de Certeau, conceive of reflexivity in the study of humankind. Wittgenstein held that to explain human behavior in terms of representation, as if behavior could be adequately understood by reference to rules of conduct that are normatively depictive, is seriously misguided. Because the reality of human conduct is situational and beset by uncertainties, explanation of this kind supposes that, as Wittgenstein pointedly penned, "one's mental act is capable of crossing a bridge before one comes to it." If behavior is thus irreducible to representation, then the nature of talk of rules must be reconsidered. For Wittgenstein, at bottom talk of this kind should be understood as a mode of practice—like walking or playing, a way of negotiating the world practically. In which case, the social scientist's claim to reduce behavior to rules is, for all its provocation, essentially misleading. It must also follow that Wittgenstein's talk about "talk about rules" is itself basically no different from the social scientist's talk about rules. In effect, then, Wittgenstein's position about "talk about rules" constitutes a transparent exercise in both reflexivity and ethics. Influenced by Wittgenstein, Bourdieu, in his turn to practice theory, rejected the scholastic picture of behavior as rule-bound. He argued, against this picture, that behavior—including his own in the service of social science—issues from dispositions (the habitus) coupled with one's position in the relevant social field of practice. Unlike Wittgenstein, however, Bourdieu continues to attribute to his sociological

practice a positivistic superiority, tied to objectivity, over other practices. Ortiz finds that de Certeau's position remains closer to Wittgenstein because it does not elevate social science above other meaningful
forms of practice. In sympathy with de Certeau, Ortiz concludes by
suggesting how such reflexivity affected his own field research.

In his richly descriptive account of Thai boxing, Paul Schissel shows
how reflexivity holds not only within and between humans but also
between the latter and nonhuman animals. By focusing on the pointed
way Thai boxing reflects Thai cockfighting—the way in which instead
of dominating these birds Thai fighters join or "become" them—Schissel
is enabled to bring into relief culturally thematic reflexive relationships
between the living and the dead, masculinity and femininity, interiority
and exteriority, selfhood and otherness, the visible and the invisible,
space and time, and more. Schissel bolsters this demonstration of Thai
holism and reflexivity with terse but insightful juxtapositions of Western philosophical ontophenomenological thought (especially Hegelian)
to the nondualism of Theravada Buddhism. Substantively, the demonstration is keyed to the supremely subtle but stunningly forceful ani-
mal-like movements found in Thai boxing, movements that Schissel, as
a trainee of Thai boxing, has not only observed but also experienced.
In effect, what is most basically in play is carnal rather than reflective
reflexivity, a fundamentally intercorporeal, temporal dynamic, one that
amounts to ritual sacrifice in which death issues in rebirth, thereby
re-creating difference (that between winners and losers) and history.
Insofar, then, as this holism describes unity, the latter is dynamic and
moving, hence open rather than closed, making it allness rather than
oneness. As in Ortiz's discussion, Schissel's emphasis is on a form of
practice, not consciousness per se.

Like Schissel's chapter on Thai boxing, Bar-On Cohen's studied (she
is a long-time practitioner of the martial arts) account of aikido, the
pacific Japanese martial art, argues for a somatic form of reflexivity, one
that critically features bodily motions. In addition to the obvious consideration that both her chapter and Schissel's feature martial arts and
the pervasive significance of bodily movements, the two pieces have
in common an interest in the difference between Western dualism and
Buddhist nondualism. The chapters differ, however, regarding the question of regeneration: whereas Schissel argues that Thai boxing makes
for regeneration through the reality of difference, in aikido regeneration is, in Bar-On Cohen's analysis, presumptively flawless, a perfect
resolution of difference. Aikido aims, as a matter of ethics (and, we
surmise, aesthetics), to transform the constituting opposition into positive harmony—"perfect praxis," as she says. Thus, somatic reflexivity

implies making sense of the "other," not by trying to *understand* him, but by *becoming* him through a dynamic of kinesthetic circularity or reciprocity in which opposition resolves itself into indifference or undividedness. Aikido, then, presents an acute theoretical and ontological challenge, since it defies examination in terms of the individual alone. Speaking of a "nondual"[1] *body*-self, Bar-On Cohen criticizes social scientific privileging of discourse. Similarly to Handelman's understanding of objectivist ethnography, she maintains that discourse introduces a semiotic gap between a thing and its representation, and therewith a bias for the cognitive over the somatic. Whereas reflexivity usually is thought of as a problem stemming from a categorical, discursive, disembodied, and dualistic outlook, aikido as a social enclave insists upon a somatic reflexivity that manifests its nonduality by participating in a resonantly pacific cosmology embodied in the practice itself. For this reason, she intimates not only that aikido is liberating from the ideology of absolute selfhood, but also that it constitutes a practice from which anthropology can, reflexively, benefit in addressing some of its own epistemological challenges. This is a provocative claim, one the utility of which might seem to depend on whether or not the argument for perfect praxis and immaculate somaticism excludes cognitive deliberation as a relative truth in its own right. Possibly, the emblematic *neutralizing* "smile" in aikido bespeaks a vertiginous wildness that is indeed irreducible to the rationalizing horizons of self-management. But in light of this vertigo, suggested by Bar-On Cohen's desire to overcome the "semiotic gap," it is worth asking if the play of aesthetic distance communicated in the gap will only add to the dance.

Notes

1. To avoid confusion down the road, it is necessary to comment here on Bar-On Cohen's use of "duality" as synonymous with "dualism," and as juxtaposed to Deleuzian "multiplicity." In the postscript to this volume, whereas "dualism" is defined in terms of mutual exclusion, "duality" (which, of course, can signify absolute opposition) is understood by contrast as a form of multiplicity.

~~ 5 ~~

WITTGENSTEIN'S CRITIQUE OF REPRESENTATION AND THE ETHICAL REFLEXIVITY OF ANTHROPOLOGICAL DISCOURSE

Horacio Ortiz

This chapter attempts to highlight what can be drawn from Wittgenstein's late philosophy for an ethical reflexivity about the production of anthropological discourse. Wittgenstein's critique of the positivist notion of scientific representation of reality can be used to analyze his own philosophical endeavor. In a similar way, the description of the regularity of human action undertaken in anthropological discourse can be used to describe what this discourse itself does. This reflexivity is ethical in that it is concerned with the way in which anthropological discourse defines agency, be it how it explicitly imputes causality, or by what it implies, develops, and proposes as "human action" in the description of what are considered to be its regularities.

I will compare the work of Wittgenstein around these questions with how Pierre Bourdieu and Michel de Certeau mobilize his reflexivity about the discourse concerning the regularity of human action in different and partly conflicting ways. I will try to show that anthropological discourse never really leaves the ground of positivist representation, that is, that of a discourse that purports to represent reality as it was when we observed it. Yet, by doing this, anthropological discourse goes beyond the positivist satisfaction with this notion of truth, and uses representative description in at least three ways.

According to Wittgenstein, anthropological discourse brings human action closer to the reader, situating it in the realm of his own action. Bourdieu explores how, by the same token, this description also creates a distance from what is described, which allows for a specific critical stance. De Certeau encompasses these two potentials of anthropological discourse in order to show that anthropological discourse can also show the way for new, unknown forms of action, having thereby a poetical force. I will end the chapter by exploring the questions that this raises concerning the ethical content of the methods of imputation and the agencies that we assume and mobilize in the way in which we describe what we see. While Wittgenstein's philosophical endeavor had as a major negative aim to criticize the ambitions of positivism in philosophy, the poetic aspect of anthropological discourse leaves us in a realm much more full of content, yet one in which we have no more warranted ground, and where we have to ask ourselves why we propose what we do.

Wittgenstein and the Negative Critique of Positivist Representation

Wittgenstein's late critique of the positivist conception of scientific representation is partly a critique of his own earlier positions concerning the relation between representative language, logic, and the empirical world. From a critique of parallelism, he develops the idea that representation is just one of the many things that we can do with words, and that it is always integrated in some action where we use it to do something. Analyzing and criticizing Frazer's *Golden Bough*, Wittgenstein considers that anthropological description aims to render other people's lives closer to the reader's, in a way that goes beyond the language of causality that science uses to describe the world.

The Inner Limits of the Representative Conception of the Description of Regularity in Human Action

In the *Tractatus Logico-Philosophicus,* Wittgenstein considers that propositions are images (*Bild*) of reality (2000: 3.1, 4.01).[1] The logic of propositions presents the scaffolding of the world (Wittgenstein 2000: 6.124). There is, therefore, a "parallelism" between "language" and "world," in that the limits of the world and those of language are the same. This is what is considered Wittgenstein's "atomism" (Lock 1992: 67 ff.): the meaning of a name is the object in the world that it represents (Wittgenstein 2000: 3.203). The meaning of each proposition is, therefore, its representative relation (which must be either true or false) to the object of the world that it represents (Wittgenstein 2000: 2.201). All propositions are, therefore, representative if they are to have any meaning.

This understanding of representation exposes in a very clear way the assumptions of a discourse, which pretends to be able to be a faithful representation of reality, or which constitutes an ideal for a scientific endeavor such as that of anthropological descriptions.

Wittgenstein's strength in clarifying and criticizing the presuppositions of this language game is that he does it by exploring its inner limits, without entering into the methodological discussions about the way to reach faithful representation. He does this through the analysis of an example that directly touches on the activity of anthropologists: the use of language to describe human activity as though it were regular, as though it could be accounted for in terms of rules that are followed in one way or another.

In the *Philosophical Investigations*, Wittgenstein attacks the idea that we can describe regularities in human action as if it was the result of rules, which would be either the direct cause of it, or which would effect it because the actor has them somewhere and interprets them in order to act (1965: § 201). This is the case for the rules of mathematics, for instance: when a student learns to make additions, we say that she is actually integrating a rule. When she makes additions correctly, we say that she is interpreting the particular rule and applying it correctly to the particular case. We therefore consider that we describe correctly the regularity of the action of the student if we describe the rule of addition. Wittgenstein is concerned with the last proposition: describing the rule of addition is not describing the empirical act of the student making additions. These are two different descriptions, and for any action, we could find any kind of rule that could be thought of as a description of it.

Kripke has developed this last argument at length as "Wittgenstein's paradox" (1982: 7 ff.). The rule of addition holds, for instance, that 68 + 57 = 125. Yet, someone could say that the rule of addition is exactly the one we think we use when we add, except for the particular case of 68 + 57, in which the rule would hold that the result is 5. Kripke remarks that we cannot rule out such cases from the rule of addition as we use it: this surprising result could be the case for the addition of numbers that are, for instance, so big that a whole human life would not suffice to think them, least of all to add them. The "rule" of addition is therefore not "describing" the regularity of the action of someone who is adding, but is a "rule" telling how to add correctly in a particular way. For less clear-cut cases of the regularity of action, the same reasoning holds. There is, therefore, a logical impossibility for the talk of "rules" to "represent" in an absolutely faithful manner in language the regularity of human action.

The Meaning of the Talk of Regularity in the Way It Is Used

Wittgenstein thus shows that the use of language to describe human action in terms of rules cannot achieve the representative character that science expects it to deliver. This is not due to the methodological limits of the observation of human action, but to the inner limits of any attempt to encompass the world with the talk of regularity. This does not mean that, since that talk does not represent faithfully any relation between objects in the world, it would have no meaning. Actually, in everyday life we use the language of regularity in many ways that seem quite meaningful. But the meaning is not inherent in the relation of representation between language and world: the meaning is the way in which we use that relation in specific situations.

In the *Philosophical Investigations,* the meaning of a word is not an object in the empirical world that it would represent, but what we can start to do with it when we use it (Wittgenstein 1965: § 31, § 43). The meaning, therefore, is constituted in the situation, in space and time (Wittgenstein 1965: § 108), in which the proposition or the word is used. Language can, of course, be used to "represent" objects, that is, to designate them with words. This "ostensive" use of language is one among many others, and can itself be multifarious (Wittgenstein 1965: § 6). It does not designate any particular essence or primary use of language. And it is a practice, not an intrinsic characteristic of language: language works as representing empirical objects in particular situations, where people who use it in such a way do something with it (Wittgenstein 1965: § 291). In the particular case of teaching and correcting an addition, and in many other cases similar to it, according to Wittgenstein, we could say that the rule is indeed an image, yet not a picture (*Bild*), but a signpost (*Wegweiser*; Wittgenstein 1965: § 85). In that particular case, the talk of rules is a use of representative language ("this is how one proceeds when adding") in a normative indicative way ("this is what you must do if you want to add correctly").

A Negative Critique of the Ambitions of the Positivist Conception of Representation

When we describe human action in term of rules, Wittgenstein would hold, we are therefore engaged in an action toward those who would receive our description. The talk of rules does not make any sense as the representation of reality in a realm other than that of the actual practice of its production. What is, then, the situation of its production? This is a question that Wittgenstein does not seem interested in answering, for a reason consistent with his own use of the talk of rules. If the talk of rules is not simply a representation of reality, then this also holds for Wittgenstein's own use of the talk of rules, for instance, for the argument according to which the meaning of a word is its use in an interaction in a particular time and space. When he is describing such regularity of the practice of language (and the "language game" is never only a use of "language," but includes gestures and so forth, that is, all action [Wittgenstein 1965: § 7]), Wittgenstein is trying to do something with his readers, and not just find an adequate way of representing a particular empirical reality.[2]

What is Wittgenstein trying to do? Where do his signposts point to, in our practices, when he speaks of language in terms of rules? Before answering this question, we can already consider that it shows how Wittgenstein introduces the language of regularity back into normal practice, and therefore in the ethical realm, from which it seemed it could be detached so long as it seemed to be self-sustained in an independent, or at least very autonomous, epistemological realm of representative truth. He thus seems close to Kant's pragmatist anthropology, which does not describe human action as part of nature, that is, as an ethically inert element within the ethically neutral laws of nature, but as what the human being can do, can become (2002: AK, VII, 119). This kind of description can only be made by a person, who considers the action as made by a person like him- or herself and not by something other than human (1998: A 353/AK, IV, 223). Yet, Wittgenstein breaks with the positivist reading of Kant, which would hold that the use of logic in such description is transcendentally bound to the structure of what is described. Closer to William James's pluralism, Wittgenstein seems to follow the path according to which there are infinite possible descriptions, and that each can be more or less adequate according to how they work in the situation in which they are produced. According to James, pluralism could be an ontological claim, albeit one that would be content with other ontological claims, since it would consider them as acceptable in their own particular situation (James 1977a, 1977b). James would still hold on to his pluralist ontology, considering it the most supple and adaptable to the complexity of human life. Wittgenstein would hold against James that he transforms his talk of rules in his studies on psychology into an underlying reality, in the same way as the positivists do (1965: § 413). Against James, Wittgenstein is then eager to remain consistent with his analysis of language and avoid asserting a pragmatist *Weltanschauung*, which could seem backed by his understanding of practice (1976: § 422).

This concern with avoiding the assertion of a *Weltanschauung*, or for that matter any ethical value, as a product of philosophical reflection is part of what could be considered Wittgenstein's ethics of the talk of rules (Wittgenstein 1993). While the talk of rules, Wittgenstein tells us, is always an action in a situation, his own talk of rules aims at preventing us from falling into unsolvable linguistic problems that we mistakenly consider as practical ones (1965: § 109). It is a language pointing to the impossibility of the talk of regularity or of logic to change the crucial things in our lives, which can only be changed by changing our lives themselves (1984: 27). How to effect such change, Wittgenstein would not say. His representation of the use of the talk of rules in philosophy has only a negative aim: it is a critique of attempts to say what we cannot say, so that we stop looking in the wrong place for that which we need to solve our problems.

This raises, then, the question of the use of the language of regularity in social sciences. When we say that someone follows a rule in a particular situation, what are we trying to do? Do we pretend that the rule (for instance, shaking hands, voting, following a military command) is in the head of the person who acts and who interprets it in a particular situation (like when we "interpret" the indications of a manual in order to use a complicated machine)? Or that the rule is the adequate description of the action, and faithfully represents the regularity observed in empirical reality? Analyzing Frazer's *Golden Bough*, Wittgenstein writes that speaking of the regularity of the action of other people is just a way to render their actions closer to what I could do, to render them plausible (Wittgenstein 1987: 3–6; Bazin 1996). The possible meanings of a situation are not exhausted by the analysis of their regularity in terms of the reasons of the action, or of the procedures to follow for the action to ensue in a particular manner, or of the sequence of actions to be done without other justification than "this is simply what I do" (Wittgenstein 1965: § 217). But what is the meaning of bringing actions "closer" to what I could do? In an obvious way, anthropological discourse does with the action it describes what Wittgenstein does with philosophical language: it puts it in the same plane as any other action, including that of the anthropologist. But Wittgenstein was not concerned with this issue, since he was mainly interested in showing what positivist philosophers pretended and could not achieve. Two major answers can be explored in the works of Pierre Bourdieu and Michel de Certeau, who develop an ethical reflexivity of anthropological discourse where they mobilize Wittgenstein's critique of positivist representation.

Bourdieu's Ethical Reflexivity as an Immanent Critique of Positivist Representation

Just as Wittgenstein's analysis of the language of representation can be used on Wittgenstein's own language in order to clarify his project, Pierre Bourdieu analyzes the field of social sciences with the tools of his own sociology. In doing so, he counters, like Wittgenstein, the idea that representation is a self-standing property of language. Bourdieu's unified methodology allows for putting all social action at the same level and thus effect that "coming closer" that Wittgenstein had pointed out in anthropological discourse. But the purpose of this action for Bourdieu is to allow us to distance ourselves from our own practice and thereby change it. Bourdieu retains the notion of truth used by social sciences, since his sociological reflexivity gives it the specific social position from which truth itself would be possible. This immanent critique of scientific representation is then mobilized to uphold the Kantian moral project that Bourdieu links to scientific universalism, and that he sets as the norm toward which social change should strive, stemming from his critical endeavor. Yet, this attempt to ground a normative project on the scientific representation of the social world makes him go beyond the limits that Wittgenstein had shown for positivism and that Bourdieu had accepted in the first place.

A Critical Upholding of Scientific Truth as Representation

Part of Bourdieu's critical practice is explicitly inspired by Wittgenstein's reflexivity (Bourdieu 2002). Bourdieu analyzes the practice of social scientists[3] with the same tools he develops in order to account for regularities in human action: field, habitus, distribution of positions and dispositions, and so forth. This analysis leads him to consider that social sciences compose a field with its own particular logics of power relations (Bourdieu 1997b). These logics are, at least partly, the use of argumentation in order to prove the truth of the assertion of any participant to the field. In the particular field of science, the power struggles do not disappear, but they result in the realization of the Habermasian myth of communicational rationality (Bourdieu 2001: 161).

This leads to a particular methodological reflexivity. Bourdieu stresses and shows with examples how the sociological analysis of the researcher's own habitus and position in the field can lead to the correction of particular biases in the definition of the object and the tools of research. This reflexivity helps the researcher to erase those biases and come closer to the absolutely universal *point of view from everywhere and from nowhere* that science strives for. But the truth thus produced is not simply the reproduction by language of a particular reality by a particular person. It is the production of the whole field, through past research and present objections and refutations. It is the field, and not God, like in a Leibnizian metaphor, that realizes scientific truth, because it stands in the very particular social position where it can produce an objective discourse on social reality (Bourdieu 1997a: 27–34).

This production is itself true because it is held as such by the participants to the field (Bourdieu 1997a: 141, 164–65). It is therefore in competition with truths about the social world that are produced in other fields (the media, politics, etc.). Yet, Bourdieu holds that given its mode of production, anthropological discourse is indeed scientific, contrary to that of its opponents, which nevertheless try to usurp its legitimate position (Bourdieu 1996: 17, 2000: 66). This opposition to other fields that also produce a representative discourse on the regularities of human action does not only concern the possibility of scientific truth, but also the social norms that should be accepted as stemming from it.

The Critical Upholding of Scholastic Values

This reflexivity leads Bourdieu to exert a particularly Wittgensteinian critique on what he sees as the scholastic tendencies of the intellectual fields. This tendency consists in considering that there is a correspondence between the logic of logicists and that of the empirical social world (Bourdieu 1997a: 64–66). Instead of observing the concrete rationales and regularities of everyday life, the scholastic observer will consider that actors have, in their heads, or that society has, as a whole, particular logics of action, which correspond to the logics developed in particular scholastic fields, like those of philosophy and economics. This blind universalism does not want to see that it is itself not omnipresent in all social actors, but on the contrary that it is particularly socially situated in certain fields. This is Bourdieu's contention with Habermas's theory of communicative action. But this critique of scholasticism does not lead Bourdieu to a rejection of the particular ethical values of scholasticism, or to an avoidance of any talk of such values, as Wittgenstein would do. Bourdieu develops a critical reflexivity about them.

The scholastic values considered by Bourdieu are more or less akin to those of Kantian morality (Bourdieu 1997a: 80 ff.). Bourdieu contends, against the scholastics, that these values are rarely realized, and that people act most of the time out of determinations by their dispositions and by their positions in the fields. The Kantian free conscience is therefore hardly anywhere to be seen. Without realizing this fact, scholastics like John Rawls or Jürgen Habermas project their own dispositions and positions in their social fields onto all other actors (Bourdieu 1997a: 80–81, 94–95). His methodological reflexivity leads Bourdieu to recognize that he holds on to similar values as these scholastics. He upholds an existentialist view of human life, in which we are constantly searching for meaning in our relations with others, since the death of God. This search finds its resolution in our participation in the fields. This participation is nevertheless alienating, since instead of realizing ourselves as free subjects, we play out our social dispositions and are unconsciously dominated by the logics of the fields (Bourdieu 1997a: 280–85).

According to Bourdieu, the values of universality, equality, solidarity, and freedom as historical constructs by particular social groups are some of the greatest achievements of humanity (1998: 43). Sociology, the talk of the regularity of human action, as a critical scholastic endeavor is a practice aiming at expanding the values of its own field. The critique of the alienation due to the logics of social fields and to one's own disposition is an endeavor to awaken the free consciences of the readers or receivers of the sociological discourse. By showing how we are not acting as free subjects, Bourdieu hopes to help liberate us from sociological constraints, by avoiding them in ourselves and by mastering them in our social relations (1994: 238–41). Yet, this critical upholding of scholastic values is not enough if one wants them to be realized. The scientific field not only allows the actors to liberate themselves from what prevents them from being free subjects. According to Bourdieu, the way in which the scientific field itself works can be proposed as a social model of the realization of the scholastic values. The scientific field shows a model of what a democratic society could be, since it is the realization of the liberal myth, such as Habermas develops it, where actors are all treated as equals and only compared to each other by the truth validity of their arguments (Bourdieu 1997a: 150).

The analysis of the talk of rules in social sciences by Bourdieu considers this talk as a social practice among others. Yet, it shows that this practice is linked to upholding universalistic values and modes of social organization, through a merciless struggle for power in a field, and through the particular dispositions of the actors. According to Bourdieu, Wittgenstein's analysis of language is a good basis to reach this conclusion, as the author avoids both relativism and dogmatism (Bourdieu 2002: 353). While Wittgenstein also avoided spelling out any ethical position, Bourdieu considers that sociological reflexivity warrants an ethical reflexivity that allows the social scientist to still uphold her own values, but in a sociologically critical fashion (1997a: 143).

Yet, by doing so, Bourdieu attempts to ground the social possibility and the moral superiority of his normative project on what he deems a really true representation of social reality, and thereby steps out of the limits of representation that he had accepted in his critique of positivism. Indeed, he insisted for much of his career that it was illegitimate for social scientists or other intellectuals to mobilize their authority in one field onto other questions where they had no expertise. This was due to the fact that the truth that they could produce was limited to the field of scientific production in which they acted. It did not allow for universal truth, and even less for normative statements. Yet, Bourdieu's moral project must assume at some point the possibility that all humanity uphold the values that he purports. This kind of assumption is not warranted by his sociological descriptions. He is trapped in exactly the dialectics between dogmatism and relativism that he praised Wittgenstein for avoiding. Michel de Certeau's use of Wittgenstein opens a different door to the possibility of proposing new forms of life, which is consistently not warranted by the representational power of the scientific description of the regularities of human action.

De Certeau and the Creative Overcoming of Regularity through the Play with the Language of Representation

In *L'Invention du Quotidien* (1990), Michel de Certeau explicitly bases his analysis on Wittgenstein's linguistic turn. De Certeau considers that all practices can be analyzed as Wittgenstein analyzes language games (1990: 30), and that doing so implies considering the analysis itself as one of its own objects (1990: xxxiii, 19). This leads de Certeau to a critique of the positivist assumptions of bureaucratic and scientific discourse, showing the impossibility of the attempts to represent reality as a single coherent whole. The turn to the multiplicity of everyday life, on the contrary, shows that the latter approach misses a lot of what happens in empirical social reality. But contrary to Wittgenstein, de Certeau's reflexivity is also explicitly ethical. He insists on the effects of all analysis on the reality it pretends to represent. This entails a reflection on the practice of writing social science and on the relation between the authoritative bureaucratic and scientific discourses and the multiplicity of everyday life. Ethical reflexivity entails looking for a way of writing about the regularity of human action in terms that do not enclose it in one single discourse but that, like Wittgenstein's signposts, indicates possibilities of other lives.

The Inner Limitation of Scientific Discourse as the Effect of the Multiplicity of Life

Following explicitly Wittgenstein's analysis of language, de Certeau insists that language is not simply reproductive. The language of coherence and regularity, which pretends to reproduce empirical reality, is not a "picture" of reality, but a performative act that creates an order in that which it names (1990: 227). The use of reproductive language is therefore not a simple reproduction, but a particular use of language in a relation of forces. This is what social sciences do when they categorize classes of people and types of action according to their particular points of view. They pretend to be representing the empirical social reality, while they actually work for the reproduction of the situation of their action, in which they enjoy a particular position in the relation of forces (1990: 66). The use of language as simply "reproducing" reality is therefore the production of an illusion that has as a consequence that the multiplicity of life is erased from the bureaucratic horizon, and therefore from the political agenda (1990: 270–75).

The critique of reproductive language in science, therefore, has a first obvious methodological aspect: it calls for more attention to differences in the details, to the importance of change and of multiplicity. This means, on the one hand, looking for actions that do not correspond to the simplistic logic of a coherent presentation of the whole of social reality (1990: xxxix–xl). But more crucially, it means developing concepts and research tools that allow for observing and thinking a multiplicity that cannot be subsumed in one single view. In particular, de Certeau will insist on showing how everyday life is full of regularities, which he calls "logics of action," which escape a unique and systemic logic and are stable by themselves (1990: 40). The critical approaches that attempt to save the legitimacy of scientific representation by placing it morally above other modes of action actually do not change the reproduction of their own position in the distribution of power (1990: 66). They only create the appearance of a distance from a position that still belongs to the organization of power, which stands on the reproductive use of language backed by a legitimating position. According to de Certeau, while Foucault and Bourdieu do develop a fundamental critique of scientific and bureaucratic action, they do not step out of it, and therefore do not see all that does not correspond to it in empirical reality (1990: 75–96).

Like Bourdieu, de Certeau uses the language of representation as a way to put all human action, including that of anthropologists, on the same level. Wittgenstein's critique of the positivist pretense to represent the world in a unique, faithful manner is then mobilized to show the limits of scientific discourse. But contrary to Bourdieu, de Certeau considers that the inner limits of scientific discourse are linked to the endless multiplicity of everyday life, which constantly goes beyond what this discourse could encompass. Since this multiplicity marks the limit of the ambitions of scientific discourse, all that the latter can do is explore its own limits in order to show the way to what lies beyond its reach, in a similar fashion to what Wittgenstein did in his critique of positivist philosophers who thought they could ground ethics on scientific description and demonstration. This is the thrust where de Certeau develops an ethical reflexivity of anthropological discourse.

Scientific Representation as a Signpost for Its Own Overcoming in Everyday Creative Action

De Certeau's reflection on the relations of power and the use of representative language in them by science and bureaucracy is explicitly a reflection on the way to act against them from the position of the social sciences, that is, using the description of the regularity of human action. This reflection is twofold: it concerns the constitution of the concept of everyday action as a political tool, and a reflection about a way of writing that would not simply replicate that of science and its representativist illusion.

De Certeau considers that the use of the language of regularity in order to talk about everyday practice is a way to legitimize practices that do not fit the systematizing and unifying discourses of science and bureaucracy, and that these discourses tend to present as incomprehensible and irrational, that is, not as valuable as what would be considered legitimate human action. By showing that everyday practice is regular, de Certeau aims to show that it stands on the same ontological and ethical footing as systematic scientific and bureaucratic action (1990: xlii). This allows him, then, to show how the different types of action are engaged in a struggle for power, where the particular bureaucratic and scientific logics are winning, in a way that renders liberal economy and totalitarianism quite similar (1990: 217). To use the language of regularity for everyday practice, for the multiplicity of the ever changing, is then a way to give it a mental space in which it can be legitimately opposed to other practices. It is a way to repoliticize everyday practice, that is, to remind readers that they are engaged in these everyday power struggles and that their difference in relation to bureaucratic and scientific practices is legitimate and worth fighting for (1990: xliv, 250).

At the same time, de Certeau looks for a way to avoid an internal critique to scientific practice that would create only the illusion of a distance to it. In a move that is quite different from Bourdieu's, he does not look in science for a countermodel to that of the relations of power he observes. On the contrary, he looks for a way of writing that would allow the reader to create models other than those of bureaucracy and science. Just like Wittgenstein's signposts were meant to show the possibility of other lives without restructuring them under a new model, be it critical or not, de Certeau attempts to keep openness in his own discourse. He does this by multiplying the differences in his description, and always pointing to the fact that there are infinitely more differences than what he can describe. More crucially, he does this by going back and forth from a representative discourse to a personalist one, thereby avoiding establishing his talk in the authoritative realm of representative science. The reader is constantly reminded that de Certeau's attempt to describe multiplicity is an attempt to open a space for the multiple possibilities within his own writing, a desire to go toward the multiple that is in the author himself, whom he can only find by reaching toward a reader (1990: 281–83). De Certeau considers this back and forth a way to make sense, that is, to inspire in the reader a movement toward life, toward the plural and different, instead of locking him or her in the death of a unified and systematic discourse (1990: 286–87, 1987: 146, 167). The reflexive ethics of the language of rules concerning human action, then, leads to a poetics, that is, the consideration that in all action there can be creation (1990: xxxvii, 48–49) and that the talk of regularity can participate in this creation, either by showing how much is created in the everyday, by showing how the talk of regularity itself is a creative act, or by devising a way of writing that always remains open to and calls for creation by the reader.

Some Methodological Implications of Ethical Reflexivity

These three authors show us at least three possible uses of the representative discourse about human action in terms of rules such as we find it in anthropology: it can bring the reader closer to what is described, this in turn can help to create a critical distance, and finally, it can show the reader the openness in his or her own action as well as in that of which he or she reads a description. These possibilities relate the ethical potential of anthropological discourse to the way in which it describes human action, that is, to the way in which it establishes agency in it. Yet, since the ethical content of anthropology lies not in the self-standing status of its discourse, but in the way in which it relates the author and the readers, the effect of the method of imputation also depends on who reads it. I will briefly explore some of the possible choices one faces when, like myself, one tries to give a description of the professional activities of people working in the financial system. This will allow me to describe how, in my view, we are left with an unwarranted openness in the description that is also an opportunity left for social change.

Imputation and Ethical Content of Anthropological Descriptions

As the example of de Certeau shows, the three ways in which reflexivity about anthropological discourse reveals an ethical content can be at work at the same time. Anthropology has probably always been, even in its infamous colonialist beginnings, an attempt to translate strangeness into familiarity. This has certainly not always been with the idea in mind that all human action would stand in the same ontological plane. But I would contend that it does remain necessary for anthropological discourse to assume the possibility of a certain social reality that could be represented by a discourse in terms of regularity. A certain moment of positivism is necessary in order to establish the first link between the experience of the anthropologist and the reader, a contract of reading in which the latter accepts to consider that the anthropologist indeed saw, heard, tasted what he or she is describing. But this positivism is only a moment if the anthropologist wants to give the possibility to the reader to engage critically not only with what is being described, but also with the description itself. This, in turn, could be an invitation for the reader to experience what is described as something possible and, as such, also as something that could be otherwise. By rendering other people's practices contemporaneous to his or her own (Descombes 2000), anthropological discourse can situate the reader in the realm of action in relation to what she or he reads, but of an action whose possibilities are multiple, open to the reader's own creativity.

Bourdieu and de Certeau, to engage only with the authors explored here, develop very different methods of imputation. While Bourdieu considers himself, his readers, and the people he observed as existentialist subjects striving to liberate their conscience from the conditions of social life, de Certeau considers that action itself defines the actor, in a pragmatist conception of agency where the "subject" is only one of the possible results of interaction. Other authors would imply different agencies and describe their object of study accordingly.

The fact is that different readers will find these methods of imputation more or less appealing, understandable, and stimulating. Bourdieu may seem more poetic to some than de Certeau, and vice versa. What I hope that this excursion that started with Wittgenstein has shown is that it is extremely rich for anthropologists to clarify the ethical possibilities offered by the methods of imputation that they develop in their descriptions. This will not only give those methods an increased conceptual stability. It will also allow the reader to be able to take a stronger position toward them. This is closer to what Weber asked for, with his neo-Kantian method of imputation, when he demanded that scientists render their own values explicit (Weber 1949). I will explore some implications in the case of the description of the everyday practice of financial professionals.

The Case of Financial Practice: What Agency Do We Impute Action To?

The case of the practices of financial professionals, which I have taken up as my object of study (Ortiz 2013, 2014), is interesting because they apply, in their everyday procedures, techniques that are defined by concepts that imply particular financial agencies. Financial analysts, traders, fund managers, and other "front office" employees generally make calculations and deals by applying procedures in which they act as "investors" whose main aim is to maximize return for their clients, their employer, and themselves (usually via the bonus system). In the calculation formulae, as well as in the organization of everyday activities, with the set of contradictions, controversies, strategies, and justifications that they allow for, they also often mobilize concepts such as "market efficiency," or the idea that financial assets have "fundamental," "intrinsic" values. All these concepts are imaginaries that not only organize everyday procedures, but also link them to broader political imaginaries according to which "financial markets" are "efficient" because "investors" gather "information" in them in a way that they would allow for an optimal distribution of resources.

The action of these professionals can be imputed in different, conflicting ways. Financial theory and investment management manuals generally assume that they indeed embody the figure of the "investor" and that the labor contexts and the institutions in which they are employed are close to "efficient markets." I would tend to think of them as participants in institutions with specific financial and political imaginaries, which legitimize with more or less success a quite unequal global distribution of resources. A Marxian approach might tend to link these imaginaries as ideologies to a particular mode of production. An approach from the perspective of the social studies of science might understand them as modes of knowledge that create their own objects, while other approaches might consider that risk is part of human nature. All these descriptions might lead readers to different places, from wanting to change the financial system altogether to considering that the system has only minor problems that need fixing (which seems to be the current approach by regulators around the world, who insist on the issue of "transparency," itself strongly linked to the "efficient market hypothesis") to wanting to help "investors" to "maximize" more.

I follow an approach closer to de Certeau, trying to give the reader the possibility of engaging with the practices of financial professionals in a way that makes them seem not only understandable and familiar, but also changeable, because they are multiple and flowing. But the point drawn from the previous pages is that although I personally communicate better with such a description, that is, it allows me to start doing something with it, to use Wittgenstein's words, some readers might disagree. Clarifying my stance may be the best way for me to effect what I intended, that is, giving readers more tools to be critical and creative with what I describe and with the way in which I describe it. This effect is not warranted, contrary to what Bourdieu expected for his own descriptions. But if it is not grounded on the logical necessity of scientific discourse, it carries with it the strength of all that it leaves open as possibility. Not because it would show the otherness in a totality, according to Foucault's conception of anthropology (1966: 385–98), but, to speak with Deleuze and Guattari (1980), because it would show that there is not just totality, but open multiplicity.

Notes

1. Following the standard, I quote paragraphs and not pages.
2. This point is often missed by many authors who want to find in Wittgenstein an adequate mode of description of practice, close to pragmatism, such as Kripke (1982), Das (1998), and Chauviré (2004). As should become clear below, by doing so they miss the ethical reflexivity of Wittgenstein's approach, and with it its methodological fruitfulness.
3. Bourdieu speaks of his own professional activity sometimes as "sociology" and sometimes as "anthropology." I will use these terms without distinguishing them here, since their possible differentiations are not crucial for my argument.

References

Bazin, Jean. 1996. "Interpréter ou décrire: Notes critiques sur la connaissance anthropologique." In *Une école pour les sciences sociales: De la VIe section à l'Ecole des Hautes Etudes en Sciences Sociales*, ed. Jacques Revel and Nathan Wachtel. Paris: Editions du Cerf-Editions de l'EHESS, 331–47.

Bourdieu, Pierre. 1994. *Raisons Pratiques*. Paris: Editions du Seuil.

———. 1996. *Sur la Télévision*. Paris: Raisons d'Agir Editions.

———. 1997a. *Méditations Pascaliennes*. Paris: Editions du Seuil.

———. 1997b. *Les usages sociaux de la science: Pour une sociologie clinique du champ scientifique*. Paris: INRA Editions.

———. 1998. *Contre-Feux*. Paris: Liber-Raisons d'Agir.

———. 2000. *Propos sur le champ politique*. Lyon: Presses Universitaires de Lyon.

———. 2001. *Science de la science et réflexivité*. Paris: Editions Raisons d'Agir.

———. 2002. "Wittgenstein, le sociologisme et la science sociale." In *Wittgenstein, dernières pensées*, by Pierre Bourdieu et al. Marseille: Agone, 345–53.

Chauviré, Christiane. 2004. *Le Moment Anthropologique de Wittgenstein*. Paris: Editions Kimé.

Das, Veena. 1998. "Wittgenstein and Anthropology." *Annual Review of Anthropology* 27: 171–95.

de Certeau, Michel. 1987. *Histoire et Psychanalyse entre Science et Fiction*. Paris: Gallimard.

———. 1990. *L'Invention du Quotidien*, vol. 1, *Arts de faire*. Paris: Gallimard.

Deleuze, Gilles, and Felix Guattari. 1980. *Capitalisme ou Schizophrénie*, vol. 2, *Mille Plateaux*. Paris: Les Editions de Minuit.

Descombes, Vincent. 2000. "Qu'est-ce qu'être contemporain?," *Le genre humain* 35: *Actualités du contemporain*, February, 21–32.

Foucault, Michel. 1966. *Les mots et les choses*. Paris: Editions Gallimard.

James, William. 1977a. "Pragmatism and Common Sense." In *The Writings of William James*, ed. John J. McDermott. Chicago and London: University of Chicago Press, 418–28.

———. 1977b. "Pragmatism's Conception of Truth." In *The Writings of William James*, ed. John J. McDermott. Chicago and London: University of Chicago Press, 429–43.

Kant, Immanuel. 1998. *Critique of Pure Reason*. Trans. Paul Guye and Allen W. Wood. Cambridge: Cambridge University Press.

———. 2002. *Anthropologie du point de vue pragmatique*. Trans. Michel Foucault. Paris: Librairie Philosophique J. Vrin.

Kripke, Saul A. 1982. *Wittgenstein, On Rules and Private Language*. Cambridge, MA: Harvard University Press.

Lock, Grahame. 1992. *Wittgenstein, Philosophie, logique, thérapeutique*. Trans. Jeanne Balibar, Philippe Mangeot, and Grahame Lock. Paris: Presses Universitaires de France.

Ortiz, Horacio. 2013. "Financial Value: Economic, Moral, Political, Global." *HAU Journal of Ethnographic Theory* 3, no. 1: 64–79.

———. 2014. "The Limits of Financial Imagination: Free Investors, Efficient Markets and Crisis." *American Anthropologist* 116, no. 1: 38–50.

Weber, Max. 1949. "'Objectivity' in Social Science and Social Policy." In *The Methodology of the Social Sciences*, trans. and ed. Edward A. Shils and Henry A. Finch. New York: Free Press.

Wittgenstein, Ludwig. 1965. *Philosophische Untersuchungen—Philosophical Investigations*. Trans. Gertrude Elizabeth Margareth Anscombe. Bilingual ed. New York: Macmillan.

———. 1976. *De la Certitude (Über Gewissheit)*. Trans. Jacques Fauve. Paris: Gallimard.

———. 1984. *Vermischte Bemerkungen—Culture and Value*. Ed. Georg Henrik Von Wright. Trans. Peter Winch. Bilingual ed. Chicago: University of Chicago Press.

———. 1987. *Bemerkungen über Frazers* Golden Bough—*Remarks on Frazer's* Golden Bough. Ed. Rush Rhees. Trans. A. C. Miles. Bilingual ed. Atlantic Highlands, NJ: Brynmill Press.

———. 1993. "A Lecture on Ethics." In *Philosophical Occasions*, ed. James C. Klagge and Alfred Nordmann. Indianapolis: Hackett, 37–45.

———. 2000. *Tractatus Logico-Philosophicus*. Trans. Charles Kay Ogden. Bilingual ed. London and New York: Routledge.

Horacio Ortiz is an associate professor at the Research Institute of Anthropology, East China Normal University, Shanghai and a researcher at the Centre National de la Recherche Scientifique, CNRS, IRISSO (UMR 7170), Institut de recherche interdisciplinaire en sciences sociales, Université Paris Dauphine. Email: horacio.ortiz@free.fr

❦ 6 ❦

HUMAN COCKFIGHTING IN THE SQUARED CIRCLE
Thai Boxing as a Matter of Reflexivity

Paul Schissel

This research was carried out as I apprenticed in Thai boxing (*muay Thai*) alongside a boxing and cockfighting family in northeast Thailand. Rather than developing my own attempts to embody the technical and social aspects of Thai boxing practice, this context—where similar paces were involved in training both birds and boxers—demanded a closer examination of the reflexive relations between the world of Thai men and that of Thai animals like fighting cocks. The locally popular activities of Thai boxing and cockfighting coax participants, including gambling men around the ring, toward a refinement of sidelong movement appropriate to Theravada Buddhist expectations for stillness, making a reflexivity between the world of men and that of animals, and between the Thai realms of life and death. From out of the balanced series of religious materials and learned steps that re-present elders and ancestors in the ring, Thai boxers' animal movements provide bridges to the possibility of personal innovation and new history. In training and competition, by repeating motions that throw their bodies—motions that commit their corporeality to an extensible, unknown, other trajectory—beyond a threshold of the sensible that would preserve perceptible difference, Thai boxers cultivate the ability to enjoin forceful movements of the dead and the other. These carefully timed repetitions, reenacted in the space of the ring, make a space of historical continuity while simultaneously generating new, meaningful events. Thai boxers' use of gendered materials and taboo postures collapse distinctions cultivated in the singular, homosocial realm of boxing and redistribute, for the community gathered at ringside, access to an immensely fertile, nourishing rural Thai world. Describing Thai cockfighting and Thai boxing below, the expectation that these bloody fighting performances are primarily productive of visible physical destruction and domination—an expectation framed briefly herein through Hegelian dialectical programs for conflict and time—is dispelled through accounts of both local Theravada Buddhist cosmology and the durations Thai men become attuned to in animal actions.

Thai boxers, through the motions of animals and the use of foreign and ancestral markers, grant what is other to them a generative position from which the possibility of historical continuity unfolds. This runs counterintuitive to a common conception of otherness or the unknown as that which misleads ethnographers and informants alike, alienating them from authentic, identity-affirming experience. Recalling his gradual indoctrination into a boxing club in inner-city Chicago, Loïc Wacquant notes that he operated with "a *carnal sociology* which fully recounts the fact that the social agent is a suffering animal, a being of flesh and blood, nerves and viscera, inhabited by passions and endowed with embodied knowledges and skills—by opposition to the *animal symbolicum* of the neo-Kantian tradition, refurbished by Clifford Geertz (1973) and the followers of interpretive anthropology" (2009: 146; cf. Wacquant 2005: 467). Along with this commitment to bodily experience—including forewarnings against a neo-Kantian approach that takes epistemological connections as self-evident—the situation of Thai boxing and cockfighting suggests an alternate arrangement for the animal in relation to historicized beings. Rather than positioning man as a type of animal—be that linguistic, symbolic, or suffering—the anthropological approach here is an ontological pursuit that accords animality a position generative of, and intrinsic to, distances from both world and unknown, immanent other—the distances that historicize lifetimes. The Thai cockfighting and boxing examined herein do include practices of making and concealing meaning, practices critical to the parsing of historical conditions at play in carnality. In these contexts, a carnal anthropology finds man's sense of timing closely guided by relations to the animal world: ways of knowing and being that the animal's presence conceals. Embodied experience herein thus includes man's animal aspect, an aspect that extends unto and overlaps the inherently ambiguous and thus generative time of the other. In this time of reaching toward, or preparing for what is other—made prominent in ethnography as in Thai fighting—man's distance from his world may be reconsidered, not as equivalent to a type of animal, be this rational, symbolic, or suffering, but rather, in a time that is given its duration by particular, local forms of the animal. As animals maintain a position of immediacy with the world that reaches both within and outside of human lives—and whereas withdrawing this notion of animality from practical life, the possibility of historical time becomes a universal, rationalized, and ultimately collapsed one—keeping open a notion of animality in practice allows for the continued possibility of grounded, historicized action. At stake in prioritizing the other's reflexivity in this way are the critical grounds in which ethnographers have to locate change or historical movement among groups of others they encounter.

Inside the household compound I stayed at in a rural village in the northeast Thai region of Isan during the rainy season of 2007 (2550 by the Buddhist calendar), preparations for competitions in both the circular cockfighting pit and the square boxing ring were superimposed in a space of daily practice.[1] I slept in a thatched-roof boarding house adjacent my Thai boxing trainers' family home, five steps behind the boxing ring constructed there. While that side of the property held equipment to train young, aspiring boxers from the village, the other side of the family home was reserved for straw-strewn, open-air coops housing well over a hundred chickens in various stages of growth. At mealtimes inside the family home, midsized birds would scamper across the concrete floor of the house, largely unnoticed until they came too close to the pots of sticky rice we shared. Other chickens would dart away from their coops, around the far side of the house and over a layer of bricks, up onto the boxing ring, where they would peck through its makeshift canvas of burlap-stitched bags at the bed of rice husks meant to soften boxers' falls. Shooing them, and the sweeping of their feces, feathers, and dust, was a constant task.

This daily activity with the animal world had a different tenor than the public aspect of cockfighting competitions catalogued in Clifford Geertz's now canonical ethnographic notes on the Balinese cockfight (1973: 412–53). The interpretive position assumed for appraising cultures as texts, where "the anthropologist strains to read over the shoulders of those to whom they properly belong" (Geertz 1973: 452), strains similarly when attempting to understand the distance informants keep between selves and others in their own lives. The validity, or "appraisal" (1973: 16), of any particular interpretation is measured to the extent that it is woven and verified in webs of signification.[2] Where the representational cue of this interpretive paradigm excused anthropologists from efforts to understand the other's ontology (1973: 10) or native point of view, in line with Geertz's critique of Lévi-Strauss's structuralism, attempts to understand the intrinsic—historical-material and political[3]—properties of things were often shelved as well. An interpretive ethnographer's ability to engage critically with any milieu was perennially at risk of being compromised. Among Thai men training fighting cocks or boxers in Isan, on the other hand, interaction did not unfold in self-evident, representational fashion. During the rainy season there, growing forms of life—animals, plants, water—were constantly moving, concealed and then disconcealed, across the horizon of human interaction. Each morning in northeast Thailand, the household woke within the sound of the roosters' crowing, and the near darkness of the day gave movements: geckos, lizards, and wall spiders; the field rat scurrying in the rafters beneath the thatch, back toward the neighbor's rice paddies.

These rice paddy fields right next to the family home had not always belonged to neighbors, but had been sold by the family patriarch, my boxing trainer's father, to pay debts accrued betting on cockfighting and boxing. During planting season, his elder sons now took construction jobs in Bangkok or hired themselves out to plant neighbors' fields.[4] Despite the loss of their arable land, food was still plentiful, with foliage on common grounds throughout the village spilling leafy greens and, when in season, juice-dripping mangos. In front of the family home, a concrete irrigation ditch sluicing water from a hydroelectric dam several miles up the highway had been redirected into a slower-moving pond about ten feet across at its widest point. Fish in the netting submerged there were added to those caught on afternoon excursions to the artificial lake, providing protein to supplement our meals of sticky rice, vegetables, and relishes. My boxing trainer's mother, the household matriarch, kept a close watch on the family purse, selling or exchanging many fish at market to bring home a variety of foods. Memorably, one evening after a boxing tournament she brought home part of a nest of hornet larvae, a rare, sweet side dish for guests gathered to drink beneath the lone fluorescent bulb hung above the ring, men who flicked aside stunned, just-formed wasps as they ate. In the mobility of life and death found sorting honey from hive, the spoils from a day taken up with boxing and gambling renewed communal ties then, and in doing so, reintroduced the men into the community's female spaces.

From a Buddhist perspective, death is not an end, but the beginnings of rebirth. For those gathered around Thai boxing, renewal is constantly cultivated across a space of death. The relation to death made in Thai fighting matches is not based upon pronouncements of the threat of violent, corporeal destruction in the ring. Rather, it is a relation made as Thai boxers take up the matched steps of ancestors and corporeal rhythms making up the time of the dead. The repetitive actions of training everyday produce a flattening of time, a plane through which past times usher forth. In discussing the ritual practices of Thai fighting below, then, "death" is a space wholly other, a grounded place of nonrecognition where the similitude between binary pairings—boxers, bettors, animals—are equalized and extended such that exchanges made across this realm—of death—must necessarily be thrown, sacrificed irretrievably, to give out asymmetrical difference. Each party in *muay Thai* competition prepares for an investiture of equal proportions—contingency is maximized with an equally sized, matched opponent. In these circumstances, making a difference requires action thrown beyond a finitely measurable self-repertoire and a constant sensitivity toward the possible position of one's opponent. Grounded with an attention to what is other from one's self, death therein is also thus a generative space from which the possibility for newness issues. For Thai men who pursue familiarity with these balanced fighting practices, the sting of death—the still moment determining one another—is a wellspring from which the unknowable, outside world may be admitted.

Within the village, the household was a fulcrum upon which the greater community sped by. As a boxing trainee, each morning at dawn I ran up the red gravel road and out of the village, passing monks taking alms along the way, continuing along the shoulder of the highway where trucks, their beds full of huddled migrant workers, would zip past me. When I returned home, most members of the household would already be outside. Though portions of the family home's exterior walls were built of aerated bricks or wooden slats, the air between the corrugated tin roof and concrete floor turned heavy quickly in daytime. My boxing trainer, Chula, was a middle son in a large family. His ostentatious demeanor among villagers gave way to a gentle personality among friends and family. In his midthirties now, with the days and hours of his youth having gone to *muay Thai* training, he slept outside the family home, on the other side of the thatched-roof boarding house. Our beds—his an aged mattress under plastic and mine its warping box spring—were separated by an inner wall of dried leaves woven and tacked between bamboo slats.[5] With thickly cartilaginous, cauliflower ears and numerous scars cutting through his eyebrows, Chula was a self-professed elbow-striking specialist. As complement to the shins, knees, and gloved fists that European or Japanese kickboxers hit with, Thai boxers have the additional option of this elbow strike. Their exchanges may therefore happen in much closer proximity, particularly during the exhaustive fourth or fifth (final) three-minute round, when referees often leave boxers uninterrupted, tangled in a standing clinch, arms clasped loosely enough around each other's shoulders so as to be able to swing askance knee strikes into each other's ribs, but tightly enough to slip closed the space an opponent requires to throw an elbow. The margin for error is slim and blood is frequently spilled.[6] All *muay Thai* takes place standing, above the ground. If a boxer is tripped, points are docked against him and action is temporarily suspended. In the ring, the local posture of resistance to gravity[7] is mediated by rules for engagement between selves and others. In my attempts to become familiar with these bodily techniques, the extent of Chula's mastery involved interrupting me in front of a punching bag hanging from the tree out front of the family home, reminding me to tuck my ankle and pronounce the sharp point of my knee when swinging it, or, another time—*tad mala*—making as though to pull a flower from behind his ear, automatically turning his wrist so as to bring up the sharp edge of the elbow. In the ring, an opponent's presence might be withheld until they were so close as to require force like this, delegated from outside the meeting's immanent frame. Likewise, Chula's direct show of instruction and expertise was of superfluous concern next to the parsing of time and repetition honed in exhaustive everyday training. He rarely instructed the young fighters, most of whom trained almost two hours each morning, and then for three or four more hours every night. Unlike East Asian–inspired martial arts such as karate, aikido, or kung fu, in which the imparting of skill hinges on a master-pupil relationship, younger Thai boxers that came to the yard were left indifferently to shadow the movements of their elders ad nauseam. Technique would only be incorporated into their fighting repertoire to the extent that it was repeated unto physical exhaustion. While Chula's presence as an instructor—as a requisite master requiring subservience or sublation in the Hegelian sense—was never consistent, this time of repetition was prominent. Young boxers continued to fold in their hours, running drills, wrapping hands, pacing, knee-stepping, shadowboxing, and skipping over the compact dirt in front of the smaller bags hung at each edge of the ring.

A whole spectrum of their training exercises focused on the same problem: that of reducing reaction time. Whether working with a hanging punching bag (somewhat effective), with Chula, a parent or elder sibling in the ring holding target pads for them (somewhat more effective), or clinching with a sparring partner (considerably more effective), boxers attempted to reduce the hesitation required to launch an accurate counterstrike, arriving in the place of the other even before their opponent's intention to move was realized. This experience of training—searching, throwing, and transgressing limits at the edges of sensation—extended sense out into the world so that an externalized other could be moved with in an immediate, internalized way. As the boxers made themselves familiar with reflex movement, foregoing any propensity for the inactive paralysis of reflection, the surfaces of their bodies were also made ready for transformation. Each limb invited an aspect of the unseen, invisible, or timeless concealment of action.

Each morning while this training took place, Chula's father would remain at the front of the house, communing with his collection of about half a dozen fully grown, prized fighting cocks stored beneath wicker cages. He rotated the positions of the cages beneath an awning next to the fish farm, conditioning some birds in the heat of sunlight, while refreshing the water and feed pellets held in sliced-open plastic bottles clipped to the inside of their cages. While his toddler-aged grandsons teetered out of the house to chase toads, chickens, or each other, he went about washing the roosters' wings with damp water warmed over a canister of coals, cleaning their gizzards with long tail feathers, and rubbing eucalyptus ointment into the orange-red flesh of their necks. When early in the season I cut my shin during a *muay Thai* match, Chula told me to take this same eucalyptus ointment from the tackle box of cockfighting supplies and apply it to my open wound twice a day, conditioning the skin and keeping bad blood there flowing out. There were injectable steroids, other veterinary salves, and pills I could not identify inside the tackle box. Some days, an old acquaintance of Chula's father or younger men from the neighboring township would come by to inspect or purchase a fully grown fighting cock. The biggest birds could be sold across the Laotian border for even greater profit. When other men brought their own roosters by, a roll of blue foam about three feet high kept at the front of the house was unfurled to make a circular ring with a diameter of about fifteen feet. These afternoon cock-sparring sessions attracted men of all ages, including the toddlers, one of whom would stand on his tiptoes, peering silently over the edge of the blue foam barrier at the fighting birds within. When not faced with each other, the fighting cocks would be resolutely still beneath the hands or haunches of their owners, given to inspection. A detailed taxonomy of anatomical traits and performative tendencies, as well as the reputations of former breeders, would follow each rooster onto market. A fighting cock with two parents from a distant province, or a bird bred outside Thai borders, was especially desirable. I often heard Malaysian or southern birds spoken of favorably among northeastern Thai men.

Similarly, traits that identify a Thai boxer as a distant, foreign other are especially pertinent for *muay Thai* enthusiasts, many of whom are former fighters and all of whom are avid gamblers. The records of each boxer, as well as the reputations of the managers, camps, and villages they graduate from, are relevant for bettors. Where most champion Thai boxers hail from relatively impoverished rural provinces,[8] each peripheral region is said to favor a particular style, southern being more acrobatic, northern using precisely pressured strikes, and northeastern a narrow, rigid stance. For Thai men gambling on boxing matches, Thai boxers bring a type of relentlessly worlding corporeality to bear on established categories of difference. The prowess of these boxers in facing the unknowable result of their match serves to show places and postures from which Thai men may gather forces for meeting the unknowable in their world.

For young Thai boxers, participation also meant opportunities to expand a sense of worldly space. Approximately every second week, I would join Chula, his young, fighting nephews, friends, and gambling men from the village, usually piling into the back of a truck, to travel to a *muay Thai* tournament. Though the route was familiar to their fathers, on trips into tournaments in the regional capital, Chula's eleven-year-old nephew Suthep and his friends would initially stand up in the back of the flatbed on the highway, faces peering into the wind, taking in the surrounding countryside. After fighting early on the card in a tournament that stretched on into the middle of the night, they would sleep up front in the cab the whole way home, even as our driver pulled over to splash his face with ice-cold water. While crowds in the regional, urban stadiums were almost exclusively male, tournaments closer to the village would attract a more eclectic crowd, including mothers, sisters, and younger siblings of the forty to fifty young fighters scheduled to compete over the course of a long afternoon. The first time I saw Suthep fight was at such a tournament, begun at midday on an expansive grassy field in front of the artificial lake, with the rented ring assembled beneath a lone wide tree with roots that had held despite the flooded causeway.[9] This was near enough to the village that Suthep's father, his aunts and uncles (including Chula), grandfather and grandmother, friends, cousins, half brother, and mother were all in attendance. Around the tree and boxing ring, blue polypropylene tarps had been stitched together and tied to posts stretching upward fifteen feet and back to the ground, effectively obstructing any view of the ring from the outside. Their enclosure left only a small open seam through which admission could be charged. The color reminded me of the roll of blue foam that designated the horizon of the cockfighting pit—of having had the sky pulled down to the ground.

Inside this sky-blue scaffolding, the kernels of compossible action were already underway. Suthep was lying on a bamboo mat spread beneath the shade of a snack vending truck parked away from the ring. Already wearing a groin protector and a pair of his uncle's oversized red boxing shorts cinched tight, he sat patiently while Chula wrapped his hands, adding an extra layer of thin cotton wrap not used during training, and then a final layer of white athletic tape over the knuckles and wrist. This same thin white athletic tape is used before a Thai cockfight to cover the sharp heel spurs of each fighting cock. Unlike cockfights in Bali (cf. Geertz 1973: 421–22) or the Philippines, where long razors are affixed to cocks' talons and death comes relatively quickly, a proper Thai cockfight can extend for hours, with up to a dozen twenty-minute rounds and ten-minute breaks during which time handlers wash cocks held still between their haunches, administering food, smoke-heating them over coals, stitching open their eyelids, making incisions with razors in the tops of their skulls and sucking out excess blood there to prevent heavy-headedness.

Though the physiological death of a rooster during a Thai cockfight is a possibility, it is not a prerequisite for determining the match's victor. The Thai cockfight instead ends when one rooster shows itself to be relegated to irrelevance, either by leaping from the ring, collapsing alongside its adversary, or tucking upon the ground instead of fighting standing up. In these cases, the fallen cock's owner will hop into the cockfighting pit and scoop his animal up, conceding the match. In the lead-up to this moment, however, it is difficult to discern a climactic turning point in the bout. Even when a fighting cock has been pecked and scratched to the brink of collapse, it may still stand within neck's reach of its other, completely erect, eyes fidgeting at distance, and then in a blink its whole body will fly forward completely, without reserve, its movement fully invested in attack. In the yard, when two young chickens meet, they may similarly jab and duck beneath each other's wings, clinched together this way for a moment before separating. When these same roosters arrange themselves with an insect upon the ground, they launch forth abruptly, shedding feathers in a flurry, becoming all neck and beak. The commitment with which the chicken carries out its attack is impressive. In Martin Heidegger's appraisal of such behavior, the animal is, exemplarily, captivated by and impoverished within the world. Heidegger's animal *"both has and does not have world"* (1995: 199, emphasis in original). That is, it is capable of action absorbed in its surroundings, yet it is simultaneously "poor in the world," lacking referential meaning, and does not have a world *as such*. Heidegger's bee, dismembered of its stomach, is taken indefinitely, sucking honey (1995: 242), or his moth flies into the light of a flame, burned (1995: 251). Like the chicken moving on continuous, uninterrupted terms with its grounds, Heidegger's animal has no experience of the disconcealment of things that sets man in a time apart from the world. Heidegger's animal does not have the time of its *own* death, and does not die into the world, as it is already there, captive unto its grounds (cf. Derrida 1993: 35, 36, 2008: 144; Elden 2006: 280). For Thai men gathered around the cockfight, the distraction and darting motions fighting cocks make obviate a separate plane of action in the world. As Agamben's reading of Heidegger underscores, the clearing of being from which man experiences things referentially is, at its center, held open by an experience of boredom that suspends and includes an animal's closure with the world (2004: esp. 57–80, 89–92). Animal actions—postures such as clinching or snapping that Thai boxers also take up in time with the animal—offer Thai men moorings to bridge across their finite limits of cause and effect. Where both Thai men and roosters perform alterity in combat, only Thai men have the choice of marking historical duration between each other by pacing off of the animals in their midst. The fighting cocks that move, closed within man's social circle—within their literal circle gathered around the cockfighting pit—are also outside of the open disjuncture men experience in finding life finite in an immanent world. Balanced cockfights, fish fights, beetle fights, and *muay Thai* matches, all popular among men in Thailand, organize potential worldly closure across an otherwise boundlessly open, runaway relation to death. When animal forces are pitted in combat, this potential avenue of control over death in Thailand is withheld, explored, and put under duress, opening spaces for historical repetition.

Midway through the second match of the *muay Thai* tournament, well before Suthep's fight, several police in gray uniforms and white motorbike helmets arrived suddenly upon the scene to extract a licensing fee for the "illegal" gambling. Where moments before the whole crowd had been vociferously engaged in this betting, men now unanimously disavowed the ring, turning to speak affably with each other or unabashedly offer drinks to the police. For several minutes while two policemen talked to the tournament's organizers, the two interrupted boxers sat, ignored on stools in their respective corners of the ring. When an agreement was finally reached, the police rode off and action resumed. After a 1943 wartime fieldwork survey of Thailand, Ruth Benedict wrote that "[p]rivate disputes also characteristically pass off without violence. In the midst of an altercation, one party will suddenly leave off and turn his back on the whole thing" (1952: 37). Time and time again, Thai people have a knack for suspending the moment of direct confrontation. Rosalind Morris similarly describes a northern Thai spirit medium's performance this way:

In the violently climactic last moments of his revelation, when Chuchad [the spirit medium] threaded his cheek with the same rapier that had cut off his pig's tongue, and which he could explain (away) only as a result of bodily training, the audience was unable to summon itself to the task of observation. As though such observation had indeed become a labor, a form of attention no longer propelled by desire. Chuchad had exhausted his audience, and they glanced only distractedly toward the stage. (2000: 343–44)

This distracted distance in moments of contact, "no longer propelled by desire," sets an interpersonal, spatial measure for Thai temporality, and is discernable in both boxing and cockfighting, where danger, risk, and causality are approached with a reserve verging on detachment: a sideways glance, a flick of the wrist, knee, or elbow toward what is other.[10] In the minutes leading up to Suthep's fight, members of his family inhabited a similar distance from the impending conflict. His grandfather set up on a bamboo mat several paces adjacent Suthep in the shade, perched slightly forward on a vinyl and steel-framed foldout stool. His father wandered over to the far side of the ring to speak with friends. After he finished wrapping Suthep's hands, Chula disappeared to join a musician friend on plastic seats behind another vending truck, where they continued to drink beer and reminisce. Two of Suthep's young friends from the village were left to administer his prebout massage, covering his arms, legs, shoulders, and torso in citrus-smelling massage liniment.

When the match drew nearer, Chula found Suthep again to apply a coat of petroleum jelly to the ridges around his eye sockets. Chula also tied a thin red rag, wound into a decorative rope, around Suthep's right bicep. This armlet was made of fabric taken from his grandmother's skirt. Matrilocal kinship ties are considered powerful political forces in Thai villages (Bowie 2008), and careful prohibitions are observed with items that have had contact with sources of matriarchal fertility. In Isan,

[n]ature is personified as both male and female in the form of nature spirits, and both men and women can represent "culture" in different ritual circumstances. Male nature spirits embody the activating powers which fertilize Mother Earth, considered passive and female by villagers. Yet these same male spirits are invited into the village (standing for culture and female) under strictly controlled ritual circumstances. Menstrual blood is perceived as active and threatening the male-dominated ideology of Buddhism. (Sparkes 1995: 65)

An uncontrollable flow of blood (such as during menstruation, or from a boxers' open wound) is evidence of the immense powers of fertility and is antithetical to chaste, ascetic monastic control of this force. Thai men, because they do not menstruate, claim a higher religious authority and sole access to canonical Pali texts (Sparkes 1995: 76). When Suthep wears a strand of the matriarchy's skirt on his upper arm into the ring, it is in keeping with his ritual role, bringing a strand of the immensity of the natural world's power into the midst of the assembled community. Rituals for natural forest spirits are not like the Thai royal ceremonies, which feature Brahmanical symbolism, performing altern power on behalf of a state-sanctioned Buddhist hierarchy. They are instead associated with a third, local religious practice of ancestral spirit cults (cf. Tambiah 1970[11]) and work more readily to address the material needs of villagers. The armlet's position high upon Suthep's arm transgresses norms for Buddhist and gendered hierarchical space, while bringing into relief the lowest, grounded forces of a fertile, forested, unknown, material world. Addressing the aporia of living amid death, boxers from different villages each bring to competitions items carrying local natural and religious force. Not only did this include amulets and, for some, protective tattoos (cf. Tannenbaum 1987), but each time Suthep fought, for example, his father or Chula brought along a large green plastic thermos full of water from their village.[12] This water would be used to cool and wash him between rounds, and again at the conclusion of the match, when a winning boxer would receive a drink from his opponent's village water source, ladled over the ropes by his defeated opponents' trainer. This drink welcomes the winning boxer back into the community while at the same time showing the source of this sustenance to be more broadly available to his supporters.

Male Thai boxers also observe prohibitions on sexual contact with women prior to fighting.[13] When entering and leaving the ring, the comparatively small contingent of female boxers, *muay-ying*, must pass beneath the bottom rope. Their male counterparts climb over the top rope unless otherwise incapacitated. While these rules again minimize the boxer's socially productive role and comply with patriarchal Buddhist norms, they also show the boxing ring to be a space where the immense, generative powers that give life are not acquiesced to, but are ideally kept at arm's length and harnessed as a source of power. By the juxtaposition of female, gendered paraphernalia and masculine bodily space, and as with the control of his sexuality, the boxer makes of himself a generative unit and a means of standing self against the self; a being open to what is other. The Thai boxer thus makes of himself a grounds: a more perfect, balanced position from which, in winning or losing, his actions will stand, or take account of the Thai condition of being caught up in the world.

In the minutes before his match was scheduled to begin, Suthep cut through the crowd and stopped to kneel on the bamboo mat in front of his grandfather, bowing with a *wai*, the Thai greeting, hands held especially high against his forehead when greeting an esteemed elder. Grandfather said a quick prayer and placed the family *mongkon* on Suthep's head. This was one of the rare occasions, outside of the ring, when a Thai man would touch another's head. The *mongkon* is a ceremonial headband approximately a finger's width thick with a rigid tail worn hanging over the back of a fighter's neck. The *mongkon* Suthep wore was made of dark blue, well-worn fabric and had simple gold trim on its tail end—not quite as colorful as some, but not quite as frayed as others I have seen worn by older fighters. When not in use, both the family *mongkon* and armlet were stored in a dark blue briefcase kept hanging high up against the support beam of the family home, away from the ground and all that crawled on it. It is not unusual for *mongkon* to have fabrics tucked inside them upon which local monks have written protective Pali scriptures, or for the entire *mongkon* to be a rolled manuscript written on cloth. After the *mongkon* had been set, Suthep remained kneeling in front of his grandfather. Since the ring had been set beneath the lone arboreal presence that had managed to maintain roots on the flooded plain, fishermen who had favored the spot for cooking had left pits of ash, scattered now beneath the audience's feet. Grandfather dug his fingers into this ash next to the bamboo mat, whispered an additional prayer for the family's dead and ancestors,[14] and sprinkled a thumbful of dust into Suthep's well-oiled, sparse brush cut.[15] After transgressing Thai norms for headspace in this way, when Suthep fought, his sweat, and potentially his blood, would now intermingle with the grounded source of his ancestors' remains.

When Suthep finally approached the ring, his uncles, trainers, and grown men from the village pressed in behind him at the red corner. Opposing bettors did likewise behind the blue corner. Once inside the ropes, Suthep bowed again to each side of the ring, three sides of which were occupied by judges behind tables dressed in the dark, formal shirts reminiscent of off-duty police and municipal officials. These elder men now looked up to Suthep. At that point, the three-piece ringside band composed of a Javanese pipe, drums, and chimes began to sound. The band's notes, and particularly the wail of the Javanese pipe, were amplified through six-foot-tall speakers mounted in the back of a pickup truck parked a dozen steps behind the ring, coloring all activity. The musicians' pace was slow at first in comparison to the insistent rhythm they would take up during each of the five three-minute-long rounds. Inside the first deafening notes of the band, Suthep and his equally sized opponent wearing blue trunks both began their *ram-muay*. Like other teacher-honoring ceremonies (*wai-kru*) throughout Thailand, this dance acknowledges the contributions of predecessors and elders. Suthep and his opponent both first circumnavigated the ring, sliding their right glove along the top rope, pausing in each corner to bow and tap the turnbuckle covers with their gloves. Regardless of what type of *ram-muay* is done, at minimum this sealing of the ring takes place, establishing a space for physical transgressions subverting Thai and Buddhist norms. Suthep had practiced his *ram-muay* in the final half hour of training each evening in the preceding week, overseen by both his father and Chula. The steps he followed in the ring were the same that Chula claimed to have learned from Suthep's grandfather and under trainers and managers at the camps he graduated from during his former career as a boxer. Moving lockstep in the paces of his elders, eliminating his prefight tremors, Suthep repeated each movement of the dance three times—honoring ancestors, honoring the king, and honoring Brahmanical deities. The beginning of each *ram-muay* follows a predictable script, so much so that there was little variation between Suthep's actions and those of his opponent, who all but mirrored his steps while facing the opposite side of the ring. Midway through their routines, both fighters were at mere arm's length, kneeling in the center of the ring, rocking and continuing a series of prostrating bows in opposite directions. The monetary investments around the ring, religious symbolism and gestures, as well as the protracted close proximity of competitors performing their *ram-muay* all heightened tension from a system of equivalence bordering on worldly inanity… and yet, action continued. During the *ram-muay*, Suthep had to stay peripherally aware of his opponent so as not to occupy the same territory, yet at the same time, he had to affect no acknowledgment of the other's presence. Following steps in the *ram-muay* allowed him to remain centered—a focused, coiled, object thing. If their paths or lines of sight did cross, Suthep and his opponent gave no indication of having seen the selfsame boxer opposite them. Hypothetically, in moments of nonrecognition during the *ram-muay*, each "self-consciousness," following Hegel, would be

> self-equal through the exclusion from itself of everything else…. They are, *for each other*, shapes of consciousness which have not yet accomplished the movement of absolute abstraction, of rooting-out all immediate being, and of being merely the purely negative being of self-identical consciousness; in other words, they have not as yet exposed themselves to each other in the form of pure being-for-self, or as self-consciousnesses. Each is indeed certain of its own self, but not of the other, and therefore its own self-certainty still has no truth. (Hegel [1807] 1977: 113)

If the visible physical damage—bloody cuts and bruises—inflicted by and upon Thai boxers was to adhere to Hegel's logic, for the fighters meeting in the ring, to be *for each other* would be to be anchored to the world, and to not have accomplished any overcoming, any assertion of independent consciousness and nondependence upon the other. If the *muay Thai* match was to be understood as centered on the physical annihilation of one's opponent in a Hegelian, dualist sense, being for oneself—independence—would be achieved through a facing of the immediate equivalence and immanence of the other, the realization that one may be *the same* as an other, an element of homogonous, nonsensible world matter. For Thai men, though, before any party in conflict can subsequently find itself enslaved, held down among object things and capable of operationalizing a spirited, dialectical historical process, any such determination is preempted, as the initial moment of immediate confrontation with the other endures. Whereas, as Alexandre Kojève explains, for the Hegelian dialectic, "what is to be 'overcome' is precisely the Immediate" ([1947] 1980: 208), that moment of immediacy has a very different nature in *muay Thai*. Knee- and elbow-deep in the kinesthesia of the Thai boxing ring, immediacy with the other is constantly pursued in movements inside of an opponents' reach, at the very limits of a boxers' sensory horizon, on the articulate edges of fighters' anatomies: in the flick of an elbow, the whip of a shin, or the askance angle of a knee joint held pressed against an opponents' midsection.

Even before this contact transpires, however, the object "thingness" of each boxer and the set of mastered controls and identifications imparted by elders over the match begins to unravel during the *ram-muay*. Though each *ram-muay* varies according to the regions, camps, trainers, and families that teach it, for most of each dance fighters perdure as laboring, warring ancestors and animals. Some fighters rock on their knees, casting nets for fish in the ring, and then bring these fish to their trainers at ringside. Others move as water buffaloes or as hunters scanning the horizon. The main steps in Suthep's *ram-muay* were not uncommon. He walked in rigid time with the wailing orchestra, raising his knees and rotating his hips gently. Reaching the edge of the ring, his arms extended outward, parallel with the ropes: the unfolding of birds' wings. While Suthep's *ram-muay* ended perfunctorily, with bows to all sides of the ring, his opponent's continued to feature a personal addendum to the routine: pointing and firing one of Hanuman's arrows at Suthep across the ring. This first personal derivation from his elders' script happened at the very moment he first acknowledged Suthep's position. The animal motions of the *ram-muay* make a passage between the predetermined steps of elders and this individuation,[16] as well as a passage between strict adherence to religious posture and the transgressions of interpersonal space made when fighting. Inside the orchestra's deafening sound, this animality marks a territory overlapping the self-identical other, displacing any ultimatum for annihilation or fixed identification. To illustrate: a show of direct, vehement aggression in *muay Thai* is never cheered. Judges at ringside award more points to competitors who appear centrally unperturbed by their opponents. In a case where neither boxer stays knocked down, and it becomes necessary to determine the result of a bout that goes all five rounds, a well-executed *ram-muay* may alert judges at ringside that a fighter is familiar with natural, animal forces. Subsequently, during combat, judges will score highly for striking or defensive procedures such as "crocodile sweeps its tail" (for an avoided punch that becomes an opportunity to deliver a kick), "breaking the elephants' tusks" (for an elbowing technique that involves first grabbing your opponents' knees), and even "bird somersaults" (for quick, lower kicks which pre-empt an opponents' attempt at a higher kick) (see Kraitus 1988: 101–2). As command ultimatums during training, these animal descriptors induce the imperative for imperceptibly fast, transformative action on the part of the boxer. By Deleuze and Guattari's estimation, the Thai boxer induces a becoming-animal, not by imitation, but by entering a relation of movement and rest in the proximal territory of the animal (1987: 272–86). His transformative strength comes from eluding or slipping physical form. The speed of each limb the boxer throws harnesses an aspect of the collectivity composing the elephant, the crocodile, or the bird. In contrast to the spirited "Kiai" shout Eastern martial artists focus strikes with, Thai boxers in practice and competition exhale something closer to a growl, snarl, or bark, particularly when throwing *muay Thai*'s whiplashing shin kick, which requires a maximum expenditure of force without reserve. Each boxer makes an unmistakably unique, individual snarl, though this sound is neither kept nor owned as his per se, but pulled from out of a collective, timeless drone of animal sounds. Repeating these becoming-animals unto exhaustion of the physical during training, parts of the boxers' body give out, reject functionality, and become nonsensible, uncooperative matter. The momentum of any thrown punch or kick thus leaves the boxer's core and carries forth through animality to connect in the mattered world of the dead, making historical continuity for Thai men.

The crucial difference between Hegelian and Thai approaches to conflict is most apparent in their respective relation to alterity. In a Hegelian dialectical synthesis, an opposition involves overcoming and a masterful demonstration of individual autonomy, one over the unknown other. In the case of Thai boxing, a balanced conflict with the unknown other is a situation not necessarily to be overcome, but is rather a situation to be extended, expanding new territories of connection, meaning, and receptivity among the manifold, immense thresholds of life and death. In the Thai case, otherness calls not for an opportunity to annihilate, but instead for the possibility of mutual connection. Where boxers' performances also make possible discursive associations between ethnic alterity and animality—one popular metaphor, for example, describes them as having the "lives of hunting dogs" (Kitiarsa 2005)—the specific animals that boxers become also transform social distances on an intimate, corporeal scale. Boxers do not become dogs or cats during competition, but they do become animals such as chickens, tigers, elephants, or crocodiles. Stanley Tambiah notes that in northeast Thailand, dogs and cats both have a significant role to play in systems of classification that designate spaces for life throughout the household—dogs because their behavior is indicative of incestuous relations, and cats because they are cooling and often used in rain-making rituals, connoting fertility (1969: 435–36). Upholding a system of classification relevant to social reproduction, "the dog and cat are not sacrificial animals," whereas chickens, among ducks, pigs, and buffaloes, are readily made victims of sacrifice (Tambiah 1969: 439). The chicken is already outside a mundane, reactive space of social reproduction. In Hindu and Buddhist mythology, it is Garuda, a half-man, half-bird figure, who carries gods and humans between worldly and otherworldly realms (see Wessing 2006; Gray 1991: 61). In Thailand, Garuda is connected with masculine power, included in insignia on the king's royal flags and emblazoned on banks and governmental buildings. As birdmen make these mythic journeys between man's grounds and otherworldly power, Thai chickens are similarly appropriate animals for the test of fighting. Their darting, pecking, and shuffling movements startle, overcoming the static, composed equivalence between sensible and nonsensible matter to give out new turnings toward the world.

The Thai boxer embodies this otherworldly relation to matter by allocating the greatest amount of force at the furthest extension of his limbs, with the least disturbance to his own body's center.[17] It was this way when, with his *ram-muay* completed and *mongkon* removed, the bell rang to signal the beginning of Suthep's fight. As a visible foreigner, I had been ushered close to the ring and was standing next to Suthep's father, shifting my vantage point behind the red turnbuckle cover to see where Suthep had driven the action on the far side of the ring. His strikes landed off-kilter, with sidelong, distal, snapping hesitation. Between Suthep and his opponent there was stillness when I least expected it: a holding of place in favor of direct, crushing force. At times, Suthep and his evenly matched, equally weighted, nearly self-reflecting opponent protracted feints and hesitations approaching one another, becoming tangled, clinched so closely together that there was space only for strikes—sidelong knees, elbows, punches—with momentum gathered from outside of the directly tangible, forward-facing boundaries of the engagement. The *muay Thai* ring became a space for force moving only over a surface of nonrecognition. This surface, where the force that successfully differentiated opponents—the flick of an elbow, perhaps—could only be trained and marked through repetition exhausting the boundaries of a knowable, physically measurable self, mustering its new movement from a fallen, abdicated space of immense possibilities. These forces in the Thai boxing ring kept open a space consistent with that found throughout Thai intercorporeality, where the dead may be prevalent,[18] allowing young men's movements in the ring to revisit, in repetition, those times of elder, ex-fighters in the crowd.

The rest and movement in Suthep's boxing match was parsed out between the temporal churning ascribed by the Theravada Buddhist doctrine of impermanence.[19] Therein, any potentially skin-bound body is known to be transient, already harboring forces able to carry it away, into the world. One Theravada monastic meditation technique

> is to see the three characteristics of impermanence, suffering, and not-self as applying to the body, first over a period of a hundred years… and then in gradually decreasing lengths of time: in three periods of thirty-three years, in each of ten decades, and so on, until he reaches the seasons of the year, the waxing and waning of the moon…. Finally, in each physical movement, such as lifting the feet in the process of walking, the monk is to see the body as changing constantly…. Turning from the facts of bodily change to those of the mind, the monk is to see the very consciousness which perceived bodily change as itself impermanent, unsatisfactory and not-self. (Collins 1982: 236)

This nonself, shot through with the momentary, is comfortable not only in proximity to death, but with a volatile otherness in its midst. Joining Thai monks in their meditations on the corpse, Alan Klima describes a similarly fostered closeness to death unseating his own corporeality. He writes that "[t]o know the body not as an object linked in a string of thoughts to a hypothetical 'me,' but as, say, a heap of bones, an intricate jalopy of a skeleton clunking along, is to glimpse a very powerful form for contemplating death and impermanence" (2002: 208). Once Thai men are introduced to this temporality as monastic apprentices early in life, the actions with which they make meaning and temporal continuity in the world must adjust accordingly.

Though corporeal destruction is a visible output of each cockfight or boxing match, as might be expected from the vantage point of a modernist or Hegelian paradigm for action, Thai men's maintenance of impermanence surrounding the match unsettles the position Hegel would accord others in encounters, leaving blood spilled with the potential to generate new life time. Whereas Kojève explains, for Hegel, "[d]esire, being the revelation of an emptiness, the presence of an absence of a reality, is something essentially different from the desired thing, something other than a thing, than a static and given being that stays eternally identical to itself" ([1947] 1980: 5; cf. Roth 1985: 286), for Theravada Buddhists, abstracted desire as such is a source of ultimate suffering and a means of being kept from worldly being. Desire, as craving for attachment, is seen as exacerbating dissatisfaction, grief, and distress in life (see Payutto 1995: 53–56, 105, 123–25). In Kojève's Hegelian reading, on the other hand, it is by the abstracting of desire pointed toward an other desire that mankind achieves consciousness and superiority over animals and—sparing mutual annihilation—in every meeting, over others ([1947] 1980: 4–6, 40, 191–94). For Hegel, if man were to be wholly given to the world without the absent presence of an unattainable realization of his death, he would be satiated, as an animal, absorbed within the relation of his initial desire, always assimilating what is other to him.

Thus, Hegel designates man as the sick animal,[20] ill suited and held from the processes that give him to the world. This displacement of satisfaction—of desire—gives man to change and history. Whereby in a Kojèvian interpretation, "human history is the history of desired Desires" (Kojève [1947] 1980: 6), ceaselessly pointing desire toward desire would find man at an ends, nameless and speechless, in his species-being. His communication would resonate task as the drone of bees, his buildings would take on the tectonics of massive birds' nests, and his existent love the control of a reproductive, "anthropogenetic" life-form (cf. Agamben 2004: 5–8; Nichols 2007: 81–96). In such a world-historical timelessness, Thai boxing would preoccupy a baseless class with the task of bludgeoning or knocking senseless the cells of meaningful change before they had a chance to affect. Among Thai men, however, desire pointed toward desire—the chasing of an absence in presence, or the negating negativity of self-consciousness by its Hegelian definition—is discouraged in interactions. For Thai men, belligerent acts of direct aggression are often deemed unworthy of interaction—these literally go as *unrecognized*. Given the inadequacy of dualist notions of human, desirous conflict for impacting historicity, event, and temporal continuity in the Thai context, Thai animals may be considered anew as all the more valuable. With attachment to this world called to repose beneath impermanence, animals (fighting cocks), or men thrown, reaching toward generative grounds through animal motions (Thai boxers), make movement that is wholly taken up with the world. For Thai men, the animal holds place both at the center of their being and quite literally, within the centers of their squared social circles during fighting competitions: a center from which, beginning in Thai men's consideration of the category of the animal they share, a temporal, critically meaningful bridge extends over the delimiting of human finitude ascetic monasticism demands closure of, and outward upon the world made thus historically possible. Pitting two balanced animal desires in the test of immanent contact thus gives out active difference and referential historicity—narratives of winners and losers, falling and fallen—over what is otherwise the ever changing, selfless time of impermanence. In choosing animal forces to fix a point outside of homogeneous, impermanent temporality, Thai men thereby answer the imperative to make some historical continuity.

About a minute into the first round of Suthep's fight, I remembered to unpocket my digital camera to try to capture a photo of the action. Instead of the picture I hoped to take of Suthep's snapping punches, though, I have a close-up shot of his father's face turned from ringside, eyes searching earnestly for additional bettors in the back of the crowd rather than watching his son's efforts on the far side of the ring. For weeks in advance of this bout, Suthep had run drills in the yard next to me as I practiced kicks on the large, sedimented black punching bag hung from a tree at the front of the property, gradually conditioning— killing—the nerves in my shins. Watching Suthep in the ring then, I wondered if he might be hurt and not continue there next to me the following day, but I was also caught, quietly in awe of his flexibility, his speed, and his potential strength: his youth. Alphonso Lingis writes of the summons of death that "[l]ong before we feel what physical contact with the dead body of another feels like, we have felt this surge of revulsion on contact with one of our limbs become alien and dead to us" (1998: 152), and that where "[p]ain mires us in ourselves, in the thing, the corpse that will leave us definitively in the midst of the world" (1998: 154), in the final moment, "[w]hen the inconceivable has happened, when the terrifying image of terminal disease is replaced by the disease itself, we find the depths of animal courage we had no idea we had" (1998: 156). This terminal disease—a condition of living—in rural Thailand collects between generations: fathers and sons who go on and give out through motions offering the possibility of moving outside of animal determinacy and into an immensely fertile world. There, this animal courage is hardly the courage of facing nothingness or assuming ownership over the powers of a singular death. Movements with animals maintain salience among Thai men, as these are movements outside the reactive confines of a nihilist or stoic ascetic historic program;[21] motion with the potential for overflowing meaningfulness.

This is not to say that the salience of Thai fighting performances hinge upon a dualistic tension between an animalistic, othered fighter's body and an ascetic, monastic spirit. What is honed within the Thai boxing ring or cockfighting pit is not one side of man, but an animal relation to the world that is both within and without man's conception of his lifetime, thus allowing for the extension of continuity and meaning in the midst of impermanence; in the moment holding just before death's immensity. Even though the perfect masculine monastic Thai type may not occur—particularly in Thailand, where most men step in and out of orange robes throughout their lives—the role of an ascetic monk may be considered as being determined in his renunciation and resignation, through the course of his lifework, to the enjoining of the immense, silent space of otherworldliness and death. While the monk gives himself over to the steady reduction of life force and a reduction of his this-worldly presence, the Thai boxer's pastime involves a relation to grounded force and death that is not necessarily irrevocably determined, resolved, and world-renouncing, but snaps, as with his sidelong strikes, in and back out of the place of death or otherness from which he—like gamblers or cockfighters—musters sensitivity to difference in situations of mirrored equivalence during the competition. Where both Thai boxer and Buddhist monk live a minimalist, temporally repetitive practice consistent with religious austerities,[22] for the Thai boxer, the stasis of equivalent force encountered during fighting competitions fosters a corporeal rhythm familiar with the transference of force—in competitively timely fashion—between measurable, visible stimuli and the unknown, concealed, nonsensing of death; between this- and otherworldliness. Moments marked by this transference of force constitute a sort of temporal, nonlinear abacus, accounting for life's history among Thai men that is full of active potential, and in this way, practically positioned differently from the singular, resolved, temporally homogenous minimalism of monasticism.

Fighting competitions that permit the desire of the animal, and allow for an enjoining of its motion in the world, continue to be vital for Thai men. There is no Thai equivalent to the rodeo or bullfight. For Thai men, the point of the cockfight or boxing match is not to demonstrate mastery over nature or the other, but to show minimal conscription of their corporeal capital—raised fingers in betting or flicked elbows in the ring—to be forceful on a tier of reality traversed by animals, experiencing mobility over the barriers that hide nirvana in their immediate surroundings. Thai "Buddhism and Folk Brahmanism share the assumptions that there is a determinate and knowable level of reality beneath the flux of the phenomenal world, and that their rituals are automatically effective" (Kirsch 1977: 258). The suddenness of a minimized, hidden motion implying great force that skips onto a tier of life-forms beneath the realm of human conscious engagement (or disillusion, as the monks would have it) also makes for a temporal jagging. The chance to connect and be thrown with this transformative ability draws Thai men to reside in the otherworldly space of animals. Northeast Thai forest-dwelling monks, for example, "savored encounters with wild animals" (Tambiah 1984: 283) during hermitages in the forest. Tales of not killing but accepting close proximity to ferocious tigers (1984: 86–91), snake infestations (1984: 286), and even demonic monkeys (1984: 269–70) allowed these monks to accrue prestige on journeys throughout the country. Meditative stillness and minimal disturbance to the body's center while in reach of these unknown ogres was most becoming.

Vital to the authority of the paternalistic Thai religious-political hierarchy is this way of bringing close and extending duration with the foreign other. This reflexivity is visible in the Siamese monarchy's appropriation of European royal iconography presenting political mastery over distant otherness (see Peleggi 2002), or the central upholding of a Thai king "born on a frigid December 5, 1927, in Brookline, a prosperous suburb of Boston, Massachusetts, as far as one could get from the thick tropical air and gilded throne halls in Siam's capital, Bangkok" (Handley 2006: 12). This type of reflexivity is also arguably at the crux of Thailand's hospitable tourist industry, the consumption-friendly production of multilayered—nationally and internationally identifiable—ethnic alterity among northern hill tribes, the political fastidiousness of the Thai monarchy, the pivotal role of the floated baht portending Asia's 1997 economic crisis, and the periodicity of political violence in Bangkok, where death flares suddenly for peripheral protesting generations, only to be subsumed quietly again beneath the despotic interests of an urban, central elite (see Bowie 1997: 18–52; Klima 2002; McCargo 2010; Musikawong 2010; Winichakul 2002). Charles Keyes, reviewing Stanley Tambiah's (1976) study of the relations between religious and state institutions in Thailand, notes that "dialectic tensions do not lead to any fundamental changes; rather, they lead to 'pulsation between modalities' and to temporary 'crystallization' of patterns which 'constitute a limited set of possibilities'" (1978: 158). Where possibility for meaningful historical change beneath patriarchal Buddhist law appears consigned to a limited set of possibilities, the transformative bodies of denigrated, animalian, ethnic others such as those held by young Thai boxers make other narratives and historical times possible—those of matriarchies, families, and communities. Animal fighting actions move outside established patterns of engagement, and the ubiquitous attention accorded them by Thai men refle(ct/xe)s their importance as a source of well-being and material power outside political-religious subjugation. In this respect, activities such as cockfighting and *muay Thai* are not formal reproductions of status quotient wherein man may be posited as an ends via his social utility, as Bentham's co-option in the Geertzian notion of deep play suggests (1973: 432–33). The rest and repetition Suthep and his grandfather enact show that in the time of everyday practice, fighting activities give man a means toward greater meaning, historical continuity, and change. Insofar as fighting entrusts Thai men this historically generative position, I suspect an interpretive turn in anthropology might find this approach to the cockfight an agreeably productive avenue as well. For anthropologists of ritual more generally, the forcibly asymmetrical exchanges in boxing rings and cockfighting pits, as well as the relation made between human and animal worlds, provide a case in which to note how closely the spaces of life, death, and the other can be distanced together through ritual attentions directed to animal forces, thereby opening man up to historical possibility. The notion of time in training and fighting described here alongside a Theravada Buddhist conception of corporeal impermanence expands a moment in which people may avoid a depletion of meaning through practice—practice that, if not relatively recognizable as conflict, opens time through immanent contact with the other.

When the bell sounded to signal the end of the first three-minute round between Suthep and his opponent, Suthep raised his arms above his head, demonstrating a lack of exhaustion to the judges. His chest was heaving. Chula jumped into the ring and lifted Suthep from beneath his arms. Seated in the red corner, Suthep leaned back against the turnbuckle cover and let his arms and legs go slack. Chula set about massaging his limbs while imparting instructions, pouring cupfuls, and then spraying mouthfuls of ice-cold water over Suthep's thighs and chest, kneading his loose arms and legs insistently, whip-snapping them at their extensible limits. When Suthep returned to the center of the ring, both he and his opponent were so drenched that the referee, as is common, first used a towel to wipe their gloves dry before allowing action to resume.

At that point, I felt a finger tap against the inside of my elbow in the crowd. Turning into the suddenly droning amplification of the Javanese war pipe, the words Suthep's mother mouthed to me were obliterated. I stooped down to catch her voice again. "Suthep—*knock-lao*," she repeated. A knockout was coming. I nodded appreciatively and looked back to the ring, but had my doubts. Midway through the third round, on the far side of the ring, Suthep's opponent fell, stunned upon the canvas. His trainers were in the ring even before the ten count expired, shaking his skull and shoulders to reanimate him. To be knocked out while Thai boxing is to lose consciousness, fall to the ground, and return to the world of matter, or of not mattering and not making sense. Suthep began a victory lap inside the ring, kissing his right glove and raising it briefly above his head. Before this circumnavigation could be completed, however, he pulled up, returning to his opponent's corner for the proffered cup of water and then continuing a set of formal bows to the judges. On the canvas in front of the last judge's table, he collected the central bet—a stack of colorful Thai bills—and brought it back to where his family would redistribute the winnings.

Notes

1. In Husserl's investigation of formal grammar, "[t]he combination 'a round square'" ([1901] 2001: 67) exemplifies contradictory absurdity yet still retains the possibility of meaningful relation, as opposed to "[a] heap of words like 'King but or like and'" ([1901] 2001: 71, 67–76), which gather only nonsense. By the same token, oppositional contrasts and imperiled actions in the proverbial, pugilistic squared circle may make for an abundance of meaning. A circle, though never completely rounded, requires a finite measure of linear diameter to begin making its arc.

2. In his essay "'The Native's Point of View,'" Geertz reprises the interpretive anthropologist's role, "searching out and analyzing the symbolic forms—words, images, institutions, behaviors—in terms of which, in each place, people actually represent themselves to themselves and to one another" (1983: 58). Working from this representational framework, the socially validated sphere of public, state theater offered a preferable location in which Southeast Asianist anthropologists looked for cultural change (following Geertz 1980). Concluding a state-of-the-field essay on the anthropology of Southeast Asia, John Bowen writes, "[r]ather than analyzing culture into intrinsically meaningful symbols and meanings, Southeast Asianists have come to see culture as a history of people interpreting public forms"

(1995: 1068; cf. Steedly 1999: 431–34). In this article, by operating inside arm's reach of the other and foregrounding their own engagements with alterity, I am open to finding historical change and meaningful interaction grounded in intimate, day-to-day activities, close to home.

3. For some critiques of gendered, political, and historical context lacking in Geertz's Balinese cockfight, see Levi (2008: 218), Roseberry (1982), and Sewell (1999: 36–37).

4. This substantial loss of land and opportunity between generations was at odds with the representation of social drama and status Geertz notes in Balinese cockfighting, where ultimately, in gambling, *"no one's status really changes"* (1973: 443, emphasis in original).

5. Thai boxers share with monks the auspicious distinction of sleeping on hard surfaces, or literally sleeping closer to the ground and all that might crawl on it. Neither do they participate in gambling, whether on boxing matches, cockfights, or the rocket-firing contests that usher in the rainy season. Both masculine archetypes direct attention away from tasks of social reproduction and toward immanent contact. For monks, though, their brush with immanence is redistributed through esoteric, exclusive channels of authority, while an experience of boxing gives profligate access to worldly powers.

6. The display of blood is so frequent that in casual conversation with Western acquaintances, I have often heard *muay Thai* referred to as "human cockfighting." This writing is in some part an attempt to embrace the ontological implications of such a suggestion.

7. Of upright posture, Erwin Straus writes, "[h]uman gait is, in fact, a continuously arrested falling.… [It] is an expansive motion, performed in the expectation that the leg brought forward will ultimately find solid ground. It is motion on credit" (1980: 148). Thai boxers fixing their gait to animal movements attempt to bring this credit to account.

8. Many of the ex-fighters turned trainers I spoke with at tourist-friendly camps in central Bangkok eventually told me that they had come from villages in Surat, Loei, or Ubon Ratchathani—all provinces in the northeast, closer to Cambodia and Laos.

9. Families from these villages, like others residing along the Mekong River and its subsidiaries since the late 1950s until the present, had been displaced by transnational damming projects financed by the World Bank and privatized/administered by the Electricity Generating Authority of Thailand (see Molle, Foran, and Käkönen 2009; Virtanen 2005). At the peak of the rainy season, a section of the highway, rice fields, and a local elementary school in a neighboring village were flooded for the better part of a week.

10. What Deleuze and Guattari found in the ethnographic record of Southeast Asia as complementary to a notion of becoming was this suspension of direct conflict, or the "substitution of a plateau for a climax" (Bateson 1972: 113; Deleuze and Guattari 1987: 21–22). This plateau is similarly described as a lack of climax in the Freudian readings of Balinese character Gregory Bateson and Margaret Mead carried out (1942). Geertz also noted of person, time, and conduct in Bali, "Balinese social life lacks climax because

it takes place in a motionless present, a vectorless now. Or, equally true, Balinese time lacks motion because Balinese social life lacks climax" (1973: 404). In the Thai case, this suspension of climax is a folding of historically differentiated motion incipiently toward an other who describes a closeness for falling into the world and holding out against permanent selfhood.

11. Cohen, Wijeyewardene, and Hinton (1984), as well as Tanabe (1991), have also described matrilocal spirit cults in northern Thailand.

12. Most of the water towers I saw in rural Thailand were inside the grounds of monasteries.

13. A similar distance between genders is kept by American boxers prior to competition (see Wacquant 1998: 345). The self-denial allied with a competitive Western work ethic, though, does not necessarily feature in the deference accorded matrilocal powers by Thai boxers.

14. Suthep's uncle, Chula's younger brother, drafted into the Thai army, had died approximately a year and a half earlier, hit by a truck along the edge of a highway. Chula told me that once when they were younger and training exhaustively, he had thrown a kick in his sleep, knocking this brother out of the bed they had shared while continuing to sleep himself. In unconscious repetition, time permitting, he would make contact with the dead.

15. Before the square ring was adopted from Western boxing during the 1920s, *muay Thai* competitions were held on open ground, especially at festivals marking the funerals of dignitaries and royalty (see Monthienvichienchai 2004: 24). Currently, "King's Cup" tournaments are held in a public square in front of the royal palace on the king's birthday. In times when sovereignty appears threatened, a balanced *muay Thai* match featuring prayers, libations, and the spilling of blood gives out new life time and amends powers over life and death for the assembled community.

16. Derrida might emphasize here that the animal makes possible the very conception of self-historicizing, autobiographical man (2008: esp. 17).

17. In Thai statues and paintings of a centrally serene, unperturbed Buddha, minute, differential articulations of the hand and fingertips are the means by which great forces are unleashed and blessings cast upon animals, earth, and gods (see Matics 1998: esp. 17–23); Tambiah (1984: 229) also describes the same aesthetic in Thai murals depicting centrally unperturbed dignitaries and kinetically excessive lower classes. I have seen the same revelatory turn of the wrist and flared fingertips characterized in the movements of Thai dancers at parades during Isan's rain-making rocket festivals. Movements co-opting these few joints to reveal great force are not exclusive to Thailand either. Notice Margaret Mead's description of Balinese bodily techniques: "Where an American or a New Guineau native will involve almost every muscle in his body to pick up a pin, the Balinese merely uses the muscles immediately relevant to the act, leaving the rest of the body undisturbed.... The involved muscle does not draw all the others into a unified act, but smoothly and simply, a few small units are moved— the fingers alone, the hand and forearm alone, or the eyes alone, as in the characteristic Balinese habit of slewing the eyes to one side without turning the head" (Bateson and Mead 1942: 17).

18. For some examples of ancestral ghosts prevalent in Isan, see Mills (1995), Sarakan, Phothisare, and Pantachai (2009), and Tambiah (1970: 312–36).
19. In the words of Bhikkhu Bhuddadasa, a prominent Therevada Buddhist forest monk in the latter half of twentieth-century Thailand (the twenty-fifth century by the Buddhist calendar), "[t]he nature of things is described by three characteristics, namely impermanence (anicca), unsatisfactoriness or suffering (dukkha), and nonselfhood (anatta). Not to know this teaching is not to know Buddhism.... By all things being impermanent we mean that all things change perpetually, there being no entity or self that remains unchanged for even an instant" (Buddhadhasa 1989: 23).
20. In a treatise on Hegel's existentialism, Merleau-Ponty explains man's position in a spirited dialectical engagement with his animal side succinctly: "Man cannot be made unaware of death except by being reduced to the state of an animal, and then he would be a poor animal if he retained any part of his consciousness, since consciousness implies the ability to step back from any given thing and to deny it. An animal can quietly find contentment in life and can seek salvation in reproduction; man's only access to the universal is the fact that he exists instead of merely living.... 'Man is the sick animal,' said Hegel" (Merleau-Ponty 1964: 67).
21. Following a footnote Lingis makes immediately prior to his words on animal courage (1998: 156) brings readers to Nietzsche's fourth book in the *Gay Science*, aphorism 326: a counsel warning how stoic priests, "*[t] he physicians of the soul and pain*" (Nietzsche [1887] 1974: 256, emphasis in orginal), forgo the possibility of beauty and change in the world, opting for a petrified endurance of existence. Nietzsche translator Walter Kaufmann here draws attention to Nietzsche's departure from Schopenhauer, whose "Buddhistic negation of the will" (Kaufmann in Nietzsche [1887] 1974: 257) portrayed the world as unavoidably full of suffering.
22. In northern India, Joseph Alter notes how the world-renouncing ascetic, the *sannyasi*, provides a model that local wrestlers identify with in making a disciplined definition of self (1992). In Thai boxing camps, discourse at times similarly associate monks and boxers, particularly in reference to the constraining and conservation of sexual vitality. A practical difference occurs, though, wherein the Thai religious milieu promulgates a doctrine of nonself, making the cultivation of identity assertions and explicitly intellectual platforms of less than vital concern to the boxers' performance in his community—much in the same way that an esteemed Thai monk may never verbalize his own access to a higher state of nirvana before being recognized by his peers as having attained such a state. This does not mean that Thai boxing is a base, unintelligent practice divorced from learned pursuits. Rather, its terms of refinement are approached adeptly within a time often preferably kept concealed.

References

Agamben, Giorgio. 2004. *The Open: Man and Animal.* Trans. Kevin Atell. Stanford, CA: Stanford University Press.

Alter, Joseph S. 1992. "The '*sannyasi*' and the Indian Wrestler: The Anatomy of a Relationship." *American Ethnologist* 19, no. 2: 317–36.

Bateson, Gregory. 1972. *Steps to an Ecology of Mind.* New York: Ballantine Books.

Bateson, Gregory, and Margaret Mead. 1942. *Balinese Character: A Photographic Analysis.* New York: New York Academy of Sciences.

Benedict, Ruth. 1952. *Thai Culture and Behavior: An Unpublished War-time Study Dated September, 1943.* Cornell University Department of Far Eastern Studies: Southeast Asian Program.

Bowen, John R. 1995. "The Forms Culture Takes: A State-of-the-Field Essay on the Anthropology of Southeast Asia." *The Journal of Asian Studies* 54, no. 4: 1047–78.

Bowie, Katherine A. 1997. *Rituals of National Loyalty: An Anthropology of the State and the Village Scout Movement in Thailand.* New York: Columbia University Press.

———. 2008. "Standing in the Shadows: Of Matrilocality and the Role of Women in a Village Election in Northern Thailand." *American Ethnologist* 35, no. 1: 136–53.

Buddhadasa, Bhikkhu. 1989. *Me and Mine: Selected Essays of Bhikkhu Buddhadasa.* Ed. Donald Swearer. Albany: SUNY Press.

Cohen, Paul, Gehan Wijeyewardene, and Peter Hinton. 1984. "Spirit Cults and the Position of Women in Northern Thailand." *Mankind* 14, no. 4: 245–360.

Collins, Steven. 1982. *Selfless Persons: Imagery and Thought in Theravada Buddhism.* Cambridge: Cambridge University Press.

Deleuze, Gilles, and Felix Guattari. 1987. *A Thousand Plateaus: Capitalism and Schizophrenia.* Minneapolis: University of Minnesota Press.

Derrida, Jacques. 1993. *Aporias.* Trans. Thomas Dutoit. Stanford, CA: Stanford University Press.

———. 2008. *The Animal That Therefore I Am.* Trans. David Wills. New York: Fordham University Press.

Elden, Stuart. 2006. "Heidegger's Animals." *Continental Philosophy Review* 39: 273–91.

Geertz, Clifford. 1973. *The Interpretation of Cultures.* New York: Basic Books.

———. 1980. *Negara: The Theatre State in Nineteenth-Century Bali.* Princeton, NJ: Princeton University Press.

———. 1983. "'From the Native's Point of View': On the Anthropological Understanding." In *Local Knowledge: Further Essays in Interpretive Anthropology.* New York: Basic Books, 55–70.

Gray, Christine E. 1991. "Hegemonic Images: Language and Silence in the Royal Thai Polity." *Man* 26, no. 1: 43–65.

Handley, Paul M. 2006. *The King Never Smiles: A Biography of Thailand's Bhumibol Adulyadej.* London: Yale University Press.

Hegel, Georg Wilhelm Friedrich. (1807) 1977. *Phenomenology of Spirit.* Trans. Arnold V. Miller. Oxford: Oxford University Press.

Heidegger, Martin. 1995. *The Fundamental Concepts of Metaphysics: World, Finitude, Solitude.* Trans. William McNeill and Nicholas Walker. Bloomington: Indiana University Press.

Husserl, Edmund. (1901) 2001. *Logical Investigations.* Trans. John N. Findlay. London: Routledge.

Keyes, Charles. 1978. "Structure and History in the Study of the Relationship between Theravada Buddhism and Political Order." *Numen* 25, no. 2: 156–70.

Kirsch, Anthony T. 1977. "Complexity in the Thai Religious System: An Interpretation." *The Journal of Asian Studies* 36, no. 2: 241–66.

Kitiarsa, Pattana. 2005. "'Lives of hunting dogs': Muai Thai and the Politics of Thai Masculinities." *South East Asian Research* 13, no. 1: 57–90.

Klima, Alan. 2002. *The Funeral Casino: Meditation, Massacre, and Exchange with the Dead in Thailand.* Princeton, NJ: Princeton University Press.

Kojève, Alexandre. (1947) 1980. *Introduction to the Reading of Hegel.* Trans. James H. Nichols. Ithaca, NY: Cornell University Press.

Kraitus, Pitisuk. 1988. *Muay Thai: The Most Distinguished Art of Fighting.* Bangkok: Asia Books.

Levi, Heather. 2008. *The World of Lucha Libre: Secrets, Revelations, and Mexican National Identity.* Durham, NC: Duke University Press.

Lingis, Alphonso. 1998. "The Summons of Death." In *The Imperative.* Bloomington: Indiana University Press, 150–56.

Matics, Kathleen I. 1998. *Gestures of the Buddha.* Bangkok: Chulalongkorn University Press.

McCargo, Duncan. 2010. "Thailand's Twin Fires." *Survival* 52, no. 4: 5–12.

Merleau-Ponty, Maurice. 1964. "Hegel's Existentialism." In *Sense and Non-Sense,* ed. Hubert Dreyfus and Patricia Dreyfus. Evanston, IL: Northwestern University Studies in Phenomenological and Existential Philosophy, 63–70.

Mills, Mary B. 1995. "Attack of the Widow Ghosts: Gender, Death and Modernity in Northeast Thailand." In *Bewitching Women, Pious Men: Gender and Body Politics in Southeast Asia,* ed. Aihwa Ong and Michael G. Peletz. Berkeley: University of California Press, 244–73.

Molle, Francois, Tira Foran, and Mira Käkönen, eds. 2009. *Contested Waterscapes in the Mekong Region: Hydropower, Livelihoods and Governance.* London: Earthscan.

Monthienvichienchai, Apisake. 2004. "The Changes in the Role and Significance of Muay-Thai, 1920–2003." MA thesis, Chulalongkorn University.

Morris, Rosalind. 2000. *In The Place of Origins: Modernity and Its Mediums in Northern Thailand.* Durham, NC: Duke University Press.

Musikawong, Sudarat. 2010. "Art for October: Thai Cold War State Violence in Trauma Art." *Positions: East Asia Cultural Critique* 18, no. 1: 19–50.

Nichols, James H. 2007. *Alexandre Kojeve: Wisdom at the End of History.* New York: Rowman and Littlefield.

Nietzsche, Friedrich. (1887) 1974. *The Gay Science.* Trans. Walter Kaufmann. New York: Vintage.

Payutto, Phra Prayudh. 1995. *Buddhadhamma: Natural Laws and Values for Life.* Trans. Grant A. Olson. Albany: State University of New York Press.

Peleggi, Maurizio. 2002. *Lords of Things: The Fashioning of the Siamese Monarchy's Modern Image*. Honolulu: University of Hawai'i Press.

Roseberry, William. 1982. "Balinese Cockfights and the Seduction of Anthropology." *Social Research* 49, no. 4: 1013–28.

Roth, Michael S. 1985. "Alexandre Kojeve and the End of History." *History and Theory* 24, no. 3: 293–306.

Sarakan, Pariyat, Souneth Phothisare and Terdchai Pantachai. 2009. "Cultural Combination of Basic Beliefs of Buddhism, Brahman and Spirit Worship towards the Stability of the Isan Community." *European Journal of Social Sciences* 10, no. 3: 462–67.

Sewell, William H. 1999. "Geertz, Cultural Systems, and History: From Synchrony to Transformation." In *The Fate of "Culture": Geertz and Beyond*, ed. Sherry Ortner. Berkeley: University of California Press, 35–55.

Sparkes, Stephen. 1995. "Taming Nature—Controlling Fertility: Concepts of Nature and Gender Among the Isan of Northeast Thailand." In *Asian Perceptions of Nature: A Critical Approach*, ed. Ole Bruun and Arne Kalland. Nordic Institute of Asian Studies 18. London: RoutledgeCurzon, 63–87.

Steedly, Mary M. 1999. "The State of Culture Theory in the Anthropology of Southeast Asia." *Annual Review of Anthropology* 28: 431–54.

Straus, Erwin W. 1980. *Phenomenological Psychology*. New York: Garland.

Tambiah, Stanley J. 1969. "Animals Are Good to Think and Good to Prohibit." *Ethnology* 8, no. 4: 423–59.

———. 1970. *Buddhism and the Spirit Cults in Northeast Thailand*. New York: Cambridge University Press.

———. 1976. *World Conqueror and World Renouncer: A Study of Buddhism and Polity in Thailand against a Historical Background*. New York: Cambridge University Press.

———. 1984. *The Buddhist Saints of the Forest and the Cult of Amulets: A Study in Charisma, Hagiography, Sectarianism and Millennial Buddhism*. New York: Cambridge University Press.

Tanabe, Shigeharu. 1991. "Spirits, Power and the Discourse of Female Gender: The *Phi* Meng Cult in Northern Thailand." In *Thai Constructions of Knowledge*, ed. Manas Chitrakasem and Andrew Turton. London: School of Oriental and African Studies, 183–212.

Tannenbaum, Nicola. 1987. "Tattoos: Invulnerability and Power in Shan Cosmology." *American Ethnologist* 14, no. 4: 693–711.

Virtanen, Maarit. 2005. "Hydropower Development of the Lower Mekong River Basin: Pak Mun Dam, Northeast Thailand." In *Commonplaces and Comparisons: Remaking Eco-political Spaces in Southeast Asia*, ed. P. Cuasay and C. Vaddhanaphuti. Chiang Mai: Regional Center for Social Science and Sustainable Development (RCSD), Faculty of Social Sciences, Chiang Mai University. Chiang Mai: Within Design Co., Ltd., 199–218.

Wacquant, Loïc J. D. 1998. "The Prizefighter's Three Bodies." *Ethnos* 63, no. 3: 325–52.

———. 2005. "Carnal Connections: On Embodiment, Apprenticeship, and Membership." *Qualitative Sociology* 28, no. 4: 445–74.

———. 2009. "Habitus as Topic and Tool: Reflections on Becoming a Prize-fighter." In *Ethnographies Revisited: Constructing Theory in the Field,* ed. Antony Puddephatt, Steven Kleinknecht, and William Shaffir. New York: Routledge, p. 137-151.

Wessing, Robert. 2006. "Symbolic Animals in the Land between the Waters: Markers of Place and Transition." *Asian Folklore Studies* 65, no. 2: 205–39.

Winichakul, Thongchai. 2002. "Remembering/Silencing the Traumatic Past: The Ambivalent Memories of the October 1976 Massacre in Bangkok." In *Cultural Crisis and Social Memory,* ed. Shigeharu Tanabe and Charles Keyes. Honolulu: University of Hawai'i Press, 248–83.

Paul Schissel is currently a PhD candidate in the Department of Anthropology at the University of North Carolina, Chapel Hill.
Email: paulsch@email.unc.edu

7

PERFECT PRAXIS IN AIKIDO
A Reflexive Body-Self

Einat Bar-On Cohen

Bill, do you know of any sections in this four dimensional space-time continuum which represents "now" objectively?
No… at least not at the present time.

—David Lynch, *The Angriest Dog in the World*

To become animal is to participate in movement, to stake out the path of escape in all its positivity, to cross a threshold, to reach a continuum of intensities that are valuable only in themselves, to find a world of pure intensities where all forms come undone, as do all the significations, signifiers, to benefit of an informed matter of deterritorialized flux, of nonsignifying signs.

—Gilles Deleuze and Felix Guattari, *Kafka: Towards a Minor Literature*

Aikido—the Japanese pacific martial art—is comprised of body movement, which quickly turns into a stance concerning violence, and into a way of life. The relations between *aikidoka* (aikido student or students) begin with an attack, yet aikido practice invariably transforms this aggression into a smooth circular movement, annihilating the effects of violence. While the designated attacker approaches at full speed, the defender firmly leads the attacker, rolls her out of the space of belligerence, and no one gets hurt. The synchronized body movement of the two *aikidoka* engaged in the exercise *is* the world of aikido, and comprises its pacific content in and of itself. Thus, the message of aikido, its ethics—banishing violence—is also made of practice with little recourse to representations.

What is more, by engaging the participants in pure somaticity, aikido performs greater transformation than merely shifting the nature of the relations between the opponents from violent to peaceful; it also alters the mundane relations between parts of the *entire* (nondual) body. While replacing violence with nonviolence, this world also drifts away from unequivocal duality into a world of multiplicity (Deleuze and Guattari [1987] 2005). Aikido engages with the potentialities of the *entire* body to direct the flow between the parts of this body-world through meticulous practice, and bring about a change for the better. The attacking hand is turned into an axis around which an upright stance is continuously replaced by the upside-down position incurred by rolling. Aikido practice perpetually undermines the separateness of each fighter: as the participants revolve, they fuse into one inseparable kinesthetic unit in perpetual, imperturbable movement that transforms the world into a harmonized whole, and a site of peace. The interface between the physical and the mental becomes permeable and dissipates. Unbounded, it comes to include both physical and nonphysical aspects of the *entire* body: muscles, senses, cognition, emotion, and also parts of the surrounding world, the training partner, the hall, and possibly the entire world.

Anthropologists are often concerned with interpreting what the people they study are saying, and so they move quickly into considerations of discourse. They introduce the semiotic gap between a thing and its representation, restating—even if implicitly—the superiority of the cognitive over the somatic and over the *entire* (nondual) body-self, meanwhile reiterating the truth and authenticity of dualism and the consequent falseness and ethereal mysticism permeating the nondual. Anthropology often automatically searches for symbolic, discursive, and representational facets of cultural constructs, and awards them prime importance, while neglecting the role of the actual body and of the social deed. In contrast, an anthropological observation that concentrates on body and practice and then theorizes "practice as it is practiced" (Evens and Handelman 2006: 5) can reinvest them with the primacy they, in fact, hold in social life. In order to reduce the overwhelming presence of discursive disembodied thought pervading our cultural outlook, adopting a somatic point of departure is necessary.

Small-scale social practices—like aikido training settings—operate through the interactions themselves and follow their own pragmatic dynamics. Such face-to-face sociality is the basis of social ordering. Certain situations and interactions allow the anthropologist to enter and participate fully through the somatic, rather than solely through the consciously cognitive. The study of martial arts is such a site; in it the somatic stands out unmasked and prevails over other aspects of social construction, where worlds of signification emerge from sheer somatic social practice. Thus, the study of martial arts contributes test cases of how anthropological reflexivity is related to the embodiment of knowledge experienced during fieldwork. The study of martial arts also reveals how, through this engagement, the anthropologist can discern, in the flesh, the process through which the cultural is formed. Due to the relative visibility of the process of enhancing multiplicity and nonduality in aikido (and other martial arts), the study of these practices leads to a singular take on reflexivity and its ethics. Reflexivity in this case is not the emplotment and employment of abstract notions that approximate reality, but instead unravels sociality in its own right.

All martial arts—and especially aikido—are sites of experimentation and reflection concerning one of the main protagonists of the ethical, namely, violence. Violence is omnivorous; it has a tendency to quickly become a total act, "an act that can have immanent within its process the entire potential and process of human being" (Kapferer 1997: 189). It leaves no space for anything else, as it devours all of sociality and takes worlds apart. Understandably, violence is difficult to observe because of its haphazard, unpredictable, and eruptive nature, as well as its emotional and ethical impact on the participant-observer, taking a heavy toll on all, anthropologist included, rendering her either victim or aggressor. Therefore, in anthropology—despite its tendency to be embedded in the flesh, and despite its centrality to the ethics of sociality—violence is more likely doomed to be talked about rather than experienced as embodied knowledge. In contrast, aikido training lends itself to an embodied study of violence, albeit under controlled circumstances. Aikido endeavors to follow a certain option within the potential social outcomes of violence, while discarding other potential routes. It is concerned with the emergence of violence and its eradication, which are performed through the potentiality of the *entire* body and of violence itself to *do,* to create a reality, and so to synthesize all semiotic levels, including words and signs, into one somatic multiplicity.

Aikido harnesses the potentiality embedded in violence to its pacific ends, to transform this energy into a regenerative force. Consequently, reflexivity also follows the social dynamic as it emerges without ceding precedence to the consciously cognitive; reflexivity, then, depends on the somatic engagement of the anthropologist, within her *entire* body, her effort and the surprise that become manifest while being an apprentice of aikido. Reflexivity is, then, the skill of paying heed to and interpreting a difficulty encountered by the anthropologist training in aikido, somatic as well as cognitive. Questions and issues of somatic knowing that are more easily disguised when the anthropologist engages in semiotic interpretation can then be confronted. These issues include the ethical dimensions, which become the affect and the dynamic directionality emanating from becoming engaged in a certain sociality.

Hence, the question of reflexivity confronts the anthropologist studying Japanese martial arts in three interconnected ways: First, since aikido is utterly embodied, what does it mean to be reflexive with one's *entire* (nondual) body? Second, reflexivity is often understood in relation to cognitive discourse, but forming the sociality of aikido and its pacific project, on the other hand, does not depend on delineated discursive categories; what, then, does nondiscursive, nondual reflexivity amount to? And finally, given that aikido has an ethical pacific project embedded in body movement alone, what does nondiscursive ethical reflexivity mean?

Aikido

As a young man, aikido's founder, Morihei Ueshiba (1883–1969), trained in several martial arts. Out of the arsenal of the older martial arts he selected only those movements that suited his worldview, adding new exercises that he invented (Yoshimitsu 1994). Aikido is thus a renewed tradition, invented in the early twentieth century. Ueshiba was a follower of one of Japan's syncretic new religions, Omote-kyo. While this religion embraced universal, pacific values of harmony between nations and between believers of different religions (Ueshiba 2002: 9), state-sanctioned Shinto, renewed during the same period, placed the emperor at the center of its cosmology, and by its ethnocentricity, played a major role in the patriotic and militaristic period in Japanese history leading to World War II. Ueshiba maintained his beliefs even during World War II, when it was unpopular and dangerous to do so, and it was then, he claims, that he decided to call his new martial art "the art of peace" (Ueshiba 2002: 18). Even today every aikido training area (*dojo*) has a *shomen*—a small Shinto shrine—set on one of the training hall's walls, including a photo of Ueshiba, a copy of Ueshiba's hand calligraphy of the word "aikido," weapons such as training swords, and flowers. All over the world, *aikidoka* respectfully bow to the *shomen* at the beginning and end of each training session.[1]

After World War II, Japan sought to replace its wartime image with a more amicable one. One way was by presenting Japanese cultural treasures to the world, and in particular by emphasizing these assets' universal worth (Befu and Guichard-Anguis 2001). Aikido was a natural candidate for the globalization of Japanese culture; its history as well as its values of peace, harmony, and fraternity facilitated its spread around the globe, and today aikido is one of the most popular Japanese martial arts throughout the world.[2]

Like many other Japanese cultural traditions and neotraditions, aikido is a syncretic assemblage purposefully selected from various origins. From its very conception, thus, aikido is reflexive. It has generated a large volume of literature concerning its worldview, demonstrating the importance and universality of values of harmony and peace by comparing those values in various societies (e.g., Stevens 2001). Yet, like other Japanese martial arts, aikido has no exegesis in the usual sense of the word; rather, its integrity emanates from practice as it is practiced, from solving with one's body the problems that ensue from face-to-face combat. And as in other martial arts, so too in aikido winning is important, but annihilating violence is just as important, and ultimately, according to aikido, it is the pacific end inherent in its exercises that ensures the superiority of this art over other techniques and renders its warriors "invincible" (Stevens 1997).

Thus, aikido exercises vary in detail, but they all have the same teleological design. Aikido exercises are performed in pairs, with each of the two *aikidoka* taking a designated role: defender—*nage*—or attacker—*uke*. Aikido exercises start with the *uke* attacking the *nage*. While moving to *hamni*—the basic aikido stance that resembles opening a door—the *nage* grabs the *uke*'s attacking hand by the wrist, slightly changing the line of the attacker's movement. Employing her body weight and momentum while shifting the angle of her adversary's hand, the defender swerves the attack from its original course of movement, using the captured wrist as an axis. To alleviate the pressure on her wrist and prevent her arm from breaking, the *uke* must roll her entire body around the captured hand, and thus the attacker is rolled out of the zone of belligerence, landing back on her feet unharmed and smiling. The two *aikidoka* then change roles; the new attacker attacks and is thrust and rolled out with even greater momentum and determination, and once again no one is hurt. The initiator of violence always loses, the defender always wins, and no one is ever hurt by the attack. With each attack the movement becomes quicker and more determined, and the smiles on the partners' faces grow wider.

Perfect Praxis

To perform the task of annihilating violence, the body needs to practice the details, to study, learn, and embody movement; it needs "to reflect" until it becomes proficient in praxis. Like any sort of reflection, body reflection means paying attention, putting a certain aspect of the body-in-movement at the center and concentrating on it, exiting the ordinary habitudes of the body and trying to alter the way this or that is done, making an effort to resolve the difference between how a certain movement is performed and how it is supposed to be executed according to a plan, following a teacher's instruction, and imitating her demonstration. Body reflection entails performing a particular aspect of training ever more proficiently than previously. To engender the constantly revolving circle of movement, the *aikidoka* must discover within their bodies how to perform both roles, *uke* and *nage*; they must learn to attack, to react immediately to the opponent's movement, to grab hold of the opponent's hand, to twist it and with it the opponent's entire body, roll, and so forth. Even though what the body learns emanates from the social surrounding and is saturated with culture, body reflection emerges from within. What stems from the intricate Japanese cultural sources is performed each time anew by whoever is practicing aikido. What is learned from the outside—from the teacher's instructions, and through reaction to the opponent's moving body—is revealed as a potentiality of one's own body. The *entire* body reflects and acts on its own.

However, in order to become effective in countering an attack, to perform aikido flawlessly, the body needs to stop reflecting. After endlessly practicing each detailed movement and correcting it, the *aikidoka* can achieve the flow of perfect praxis in which the *entire* body becomes a whole tool, meaning and finality all at once, as the gap between plan and execution is erased. While the participants are rolling in perfect praxis it becomes impossible to tell them apart; moreover, it is impossible to distinguish between the affects of intention, emotion, movement, and cognition. The physical body, thought, emotion, and deed all become part of the moving. Exerting effort and concentration coexist, in perfect praxis, with the effortlessness of floating on the waves of movement, and the active *aikidoka* is also a passive voyager on the undulations of the circular movement. The gap between the formal outline of the exercise—the plan—and the way it actually is done—its execution—is annihilated; as *doing* takes over and fills the social world, the semiotic gap between a thing and its representation is also erased. All semiotic levels then collapse into the perfect doing and done. They come to be kinesthetic, and the movement swallows differences and contraries, idea and deed become indistinguishable, violence and its annihilation inseparable, as are the *nage* and the *uke*.

A revolving cycle of constant movement is formed in which standing upright on one's feet is followed by an upside-down position, the *uke* changes places with the *nage*, and violence is replaced by its annihilation. The *aikidoka* all wear the white karate double-breasted jacket and pants; on top of the white pants, the senior *aikidoka* wear a traditional Japanese *hakama*—a dark, pleated pants-skirt neatly tied at the waist. While rolling, the white top and black skirt of the *nage* mingles with the upside-down *uke*, who is now black above and white below, and the flow of the moving *hakama* brings the ends of the circle to a close. The circular movement seems to be endless, and the constant rolling and exchange of roles between *uke* and *nage* echoes the changing roles between black and white in the yin and yang sign. There is no unequivocal opposition between *uke* and *nage*, between standing upright and rolling, between violence and its annihilation, because these oppositions are temporary and in a perpetual process of interaction, creation, and destruction.

Nondual Cultural Logics and Perfect Praxis

Perfect praxis in aikido espouses Sino-Japanese cultural logics that inform different practices leading to nonduality. Looking briefly at the way these logics propel relations into action reveals the working of perfect praxis, as well as the profound cultural substrata on which aikido is founded. By tilting the relations between parts of a whole, according to these logics, the whole itself is changed. The central common trait between these cultural logics—the principle of actionless action called in Chinese *Wu Wei* and the relations between yin and yang—is that like the aikido revolving unit of two, they both depend on movement. When brought to a standstill they disintegrate.

Aikido follows the lines of the Chinese Taoist practical principle of *Wu Wei* ("effortless action" or "the action of nonaction" [Loy 1985; Duyvenak 1947]) as adapted in Japan. *Wu Wei* is a state of "harmony in which action flow freely and instantly from one's spontaneous inclinations—without the need for extended deliberation or inner struggle—and yet nonetheless accords perfectly with the dictates of the situation at hand" (Slingerland 2003: 7). In *Wu Wei* a system—be it the human body, a family, or the entire state—is set into motion so perfectly that it demands no further effort because it flows in the "right" way. Loy calls the ambiguity of *Wu Wei* "paradoxical" (1985: 73), but paradox assumes the coexistence of two incompatible truths, such as action and nonaction, or effort and effortlessness. The logics of *Wu Wei* and of perfect praxis, however, do not concern static truths but rather two different dynamics of practice that are simultaneously and ambiguously present within perfect praxis: the dynamic of meticulous planning and endless, tedious training polished to perfection, and the dynamic of letting go, of forgoing will and of trusting the body, effortlessly.

The rolling *aikidoka* also follow the logic of the relations between yin and yang. This logic, that of the relations between male and female, is described by Deleuze and Guattari as "the formation of a circuit of intensities between female and male energy, with the woman playing the role of the innate or instinctive force (Yin) stolen by or transmitted to the man in such way that the transmitted force of man (Yang) in turn becomes innate, all the more innate: an augmentation of powers" ([1987] 2005: 157). The same logic of movement emerges between the *uke,* playing the role of attacker, and the *nage,* playing that of defender, the *nage* trapping or transmitting energy emanating from the *uke*'s violence and transforming it into nonviolence, into cosmic energy of peace. The quicker the movement of the two *aikidoka* rolling, attacking, defending, and changing roles, the more intense the exchange of energy (*ki*) between them, and the more undifferentiated they become, resulting in an augmented capacity of the unit of two, and in more energy emitted from it to the world.[3] Thus, instead of sowing destruction, violence becomes a source of vitality, while both *uke* and *nage* perform the universalistic, pacific goals of aikido.

A nondual dynamic is achieved, since the ever turning circle of violence and its annihilation never comes to a rest. Violence is never separated from nonviolence, nor the *nage* from the *uke,* and so they are always in the dynamic process of becoming their contrasts. In aikido the contrasts, like yin and yang, never become dual because they are forever in the making, one constantly becoming the other, dependent on each other to exist; never coming into being as separate entities, they cannot divide into objects—they are never objectified to the full. Perfect praxis ensures that none of the contrasting poles escapes from this dynamic equilibrium; neither gets the upper hand or has a chance for independent objectified life, because if perfect praxis fails, violence may return.

As the *aikidoka* move, the relations between the contrasts become fluid, increasing in proficiency and speed, approaching perfect praxis, blurring the distinction between controlled and uncontrolled movement, so that the energy employed by the *uke* while attacking is harnessed and results in her own downfall. This energy nourishes the defender, the *nage,* and enables her to divert the attack. The result is a synergy in which each kindles the other's energy and also their common cycle of movement. The synergy can then overflow the two opponents and nourish the surroundings, and ultimately even the entire cosmos. The *nage* and the *uke* form a single kinesthetic unit with one center of gravity, which is set between them at the axis of their joint hands—a revolving sphere. They become a vortical microcosmos of inseparable two.

And each time the attacker is vanquished, the ridiculousness of violence is revealed. Violence holds the potentiality to curtail plans and intentionality, to separate people, to engender arrogance, fear, aggression. In aikido all these are replaced by the ever revolving cycle—which is why a smile emerges from within onto the opponents' faces. They are tipsy from turning upside down, and their smiles grow wider as the praxis approaches perfection, as the possibility of separating attacker from defender is obliterated, as they become one kinesthetic unit, dependent on each other to stay afloat. The idea of annihilating violence mingles with the sense of speed and vertigo, and the cheerfulness is a consequence of both, the sheer toppling of thought and emotion into the falling and rising body in its movement. The cycle of movement restores to the fullest the potency of the mind-body, against which the energies of human destructiveness are rendered futile.

The aikido smile is, as Hyers puts it, "the signature of the sudden realization of the 'point' and the joyful approval of its significance" (1974: 23). And this "point" is embedded in constant movement, in the potential of the body to draw on the energy of violence and divert it from its devastating course. The aikido smile also emanates from the realization that "black is not so black and white is not so white, yet black is black and white is white" (Blyth 1959: 212). Humor in the world of Zen has a serious, pivotal role, as it destabilizes the unequivocality of the world and thus pulls it toward multiplicity (nonduality). Yet the agreeable smile of the Buddha also threatens to swallow the world, and so in aikido too, humor is not without threat. It is the expression of release, movement, sociality, control, fun, and victory over aggression, but concomitantly it is also a smile of thrill, a game at the frontier of danger and uncertainty, a smile that threatens to restore violence to the world, this time uncontrollably. Aikido is revealed to have the qualities of a "tendentious joke," dealing with the serious, painful matter of violence and stealing its edge, tricking it into becoming vitalizing energy, forever trapping the ominous threat of violence and the potentiality of harnessing and transforming the menace through performing perfect praxis.

This microcosmos will then overflow so that its benevolent movement spills over—turning the serious into the laughable and the laughable into the serious, creating lines of resemblance between the facets of the world and activating the forces of homology (Bar-On Cohen 2012)—to fill the entire macrocosmos with peace.

Reflexivity

As it is usually understood, reflexivity in science was succinctly formulated by Foucault as "self-examination with respect to thoughts in correspondence to reality" (1988: 46). The need for reflexivity, according to this view, results from the epistemological conundrum; it stems from questions such as: What are the tools of our knowledge and how can these tools correspond to "real" reality? In other words, how do we get to know what we know? Which leads us to another question: In what ways is what we know about reality intertwined with the tools of our knowledge, our epistemological tools, and how do those tools skew our view of reality? Understandably, the epistemological tools that the scientist employs to decipher reality are loaded with her own world and therefore obstruct and distort her view of "real" (objective) reality. Thus, reflexivity is the attempt to free the onlooker from the subjective bias caused by tools of perception—semiotic, situational, emotional, ideological, and more—and bring her position closer to where she can have a relatively unbiased take on the world. Anthropology seeks to understand cultures that operate according to alternative epistemologies (Jackson 2011), and hence the question of reflexivity becomes operative, the practical attempt to free anthropology from its prejudices: How should an anthropologist circumvent her blind spots and see what is hidden from her? How should she proceed in order to overcome the gap between herself and the way reality is seen by the other?

At times reflexivity is considered a method to turn the anthropologist's attention toward the particularities of the culture being studied, a sort of haphazard autoethnomethodology. Ethnomethodology proposes to extract the obvious from its comfortable niche in everyday life, to lure the unreflexive into the open, through generating an intentional provocative behavior that breaches propriety (Garfinkel 1986). So, autoethnomethodology occurs when the anthropologist's behavior breaches propriety as it is lived according to the culture under scrutiny. In this case the breach is not intentional, but is nevertheless noticeable, revealing the unreflexive, the hidden cultural suppositions.

The awkwardness of the anthropologist's conduct and the misunderstandings encountered in the field are indicative of the obvious, of the often unformulated and covert cultural assumptions that the anthropologist, coming from another social reality, lacks. The uncomfortable, sometimes bizarre, encounter between the anthropologist and the social reality being studied is therefore understood to indicate the epistemological inconsistencies between the two cosmologies. Reflexivity thus understood becomes the temporary scaffolding for an understanding that may later be discarded. This sort of reflexivity, conceived as a methodological aid to anthropology, has yielded interesting insights (Briggs 1970[4]); since the collision with accepted norms is reflexive, the anthropologist's encounter with discrepancies fleshes out the underlying social premises.

Bourdieu has labeled this attitude "narcissistic" (2004: 89), since it may at other times divert the focus of attention away from the studied culture and turn the anthropologist herself into the center of scrutiny. The question of reflexivity now becomes what happens to the anthropologist on the occasion of this encounter, and how it helps her overcome her resistance and come to grips with the new conditions. Then, reflexivity is a sort of confession parallel to psychoanalysis—an autosocioanalysis (Bourdieu 2004: 95)—namely, something about the anthropologist herself can be gleaned through the profound *experiential* encounter with the other.[5]

The underlying supposition here is that "we cannot know people unless we are like them," that "similar or identical experiences" are conditions for empathy (Salzman 2002: 808). Pushed to the extreme, through his reactions and sentiments the anthropologist's own sensitivity can be distilled, and through this meaning attached to reflexivity, fieldwork joins the long tradition of forging the character and identity of the anthropologist through travel, the tradition of *Bildung*. Anthropological study becomes a meaningful journey for the anthropologist on the way to discovering himself. A personal, conscious introspection occasioned by a bewildering encounter away from home, the subsequent confession of this profound insight and the confession's cleansing effects, are necessary to accomplish such reflexivity. The culture of interest, in this case, is no longer the studied culture, but rather the anthropologist's own culture, which captures center stage, consequently studying the self instead of the other.

Another, perhaps more widespread understanding of reflexivity in anthropology is an *ideological* one, namely, reflexivity aims to put right the heavy colonial past of anthropology, and to deal with other cultural biases embedded in the hegemonic culture represented by discourse. *Ideological* reflexivity is based on ethical claims of revealing the real face of injustice and emancipating anthropology from the burden of colonial and other wrongs inflicted by Western society on the rest of the world. I label myself a woman, white, middle-aged, and in so doing I bring my bias to the surface. Since reflexivity is intended to safeguard anthropology from unwittingly replicating the norms prevalent in its own worlds of meaning, the confession (again the confession!) purges the cultural bias and, consequently, *ideological* reflexivity is understood as keeping the anthropologist from excluding and patronizing the subjects of study. Nevertheless, the significance of categories such as woman, white, and middle-aged is imported from the world of the anthropologist, which is ruled by categorical thought.

Both the narcissistic autoethnomethodology and the ideological attitudes seem contrary to a basic anthropological stance—perhaps a naïve one—that claims that the field, in its internal life and mode of organization, and not external categories imported to the field from elsewhere, determines what an anthropologist should report and interpret. Ideological reflexivity assumes categories and categorical thought that are prior to fieldwork and that transplant the order, logic, and contents of these categories onto the field of study. Nonetheless, naïveté may very well be a precondition for anthropology, because the ideological reflexivity seems to jam anthropology into a narrow passageway where the impact of the immediate (unmediated) encounter with the other—the major specialty of anthropology (Handelman, this volume)—becomes obstructed. The authority of that encounter and its influence on the anthropologist's views and interpretations are blocked, and thus much of the advantage of anthropology is lost, and with it the question of reflexivity itself. Additionally, ideological reflexivity, which often plays the game of the politically correct, already includes an imported moralistic opinion, and for that reason is also prevented from revealing the ethical dynamics of the other. The moralistic paradigm is already encased within the anthropologist's own paradigm and therefore is a reflection about herself rather than about the other (Kapferer 1997; see also Deacon 2002).

A Reflexive Body-Self

The various understandings of reflexivity mentioned above have one trait in common: they all thoroughly depend on consciousness, on hyperconsciousness, on second-degree consciousness, and on confession. These are understood to have the power to liberate the anthropologist from the shackles of her groundedness in her self, which is understood to be imprisoned by her society and culture. This sort of reflexivity leans on a powerful and omnivorous worldview: the dualistic one. Thus, it is also based on the postulate of a stable self that can perform self-liberation through self-reflection, followed by a verbalization of the results of that scrutiny. It is based on the assumptions and outlines of "the Christian morality of self-scrutiny and the Enlightenment programme of critical rationalism and the belief in political progress" (Due 2007: 17).

More particularly, this understanding of reflexivity tends to describe the anthropologist as a bounded self, facing the world from within the bastion of a separate existence, loaded with her life experience, which obstructs the view of others. This point of departure, however, cannot describe reflexivity in settings such as aikido, which promote (nondual) multiplicity, since the unequivocal differentiation between individuals, their very boundedness, is blurred and replaced by the revolving pair of *aikidoka*. Furthermore, perfect praxis renders the body-in-movement an undifferentiated tool-meaning-finality, thus eliminating the neatness of borders; it questions well-defined categories and swallows the bounded self and the other into a single dynamic.

Deleuze proposes a different view, from which may emerge another sort of reflexivity, more suitable for a scrutiny of aikido, and which I will call somatic reflexivity. For Deleuze and Guattari, the potentiality of freedom and reflexivity is the potentiality of leaving the traced way as one seeps out of one's being though a process of becoming totally other, which they call "becoming-animal," through a "'line of flight' that would begin within a well-defined social group and behavior but then take off in an unknown direction, moving towards as yet unmapped territories, outside of conscious planning and previously known values" (Due 2007: 19). We are constantly remade; we potentially embody a multiplicity of different people and can therefore engage in the dynamics of the other. We have the option of connecting to a line of flight, of seeping out of our habitudes to engage in becoming body, becoming woman, becoming native, becoming animal, becoming dead. "The act of becoming is a capturing, a possession, a plus-value, but never a reproduction or an imitation" (Deleuze and Guattari 1986: 13).

Thus, somatic reflexivity, or becoming other through the dynamic of the other, is not an individual matter; rather, it questions the self as bounded unit, its uniqueness and inextricability, stipulating instead hazy, porous borders between persons and things. Reflexivity, then, becomes a process of following a line with one's *entire* body-self, allowing it to pursue the unfolding of the potentiality embedded in this line and process, landing the anthropologist somewhere else. In it, consciousness is just one aspect of a whole, and confession loses its ethical grip.

Somatic reflexivity shares some of the aspects of autoethnomethodological reflexivity. It too points at the important role played by the anthropologist's engagement in the field and the resultant difficulty throughout the process of discovering the significance of the cultural. This somatic path of discovery, however, is not exclusive to the anthropologist, but is shared by all participants in a particular sociality, since it is not a question of understanding, but rather one of apprenticeship, of *doing*: all must discover within themselves how to perform the cultural. Therefore, in salient distinction from autoethnomethodological reflexivity, when it comes to somatic reflexivity this experiential difficulty is no longer a haphazard occurrence or scaffolding to be discarded, but rather the anthropological finding itself.

While practicing and studying aikido, the anthropologist is no longer solely an onlooker and analyst; she is also engaged in trying to overcome the obstacles and resistance in her own body that hinder the dynamics of dismantling violence. Obstacles stemming from her muscles, coordination, balance, perception, and emotional involvement become inseparable from cognitive obstacles, all impeding the attempt to make sense of what the others are doing and saying. The anthropologist is not only trying to understand them, she is also imitating them, engaging in the dynamics of "becoming them" in this setting. What, for instance, does suspension of disbelief mean when the anthropologist is somatically engaged in the aikido circle of movement? When the anthropologist is merely trying to do what the others are doing? And this clumsy attempt definitely makes her adopt the aikido smile. Creating the vertiginous, smile-inducing movement does not depend, for example, on the belief that *ki* energy "really" permeates the universe,[6] and therefore neither does it generate an epistemological gap. The gap between the anthropologist's cultural understandings and the world she studies becomes a technical problem, one of the technique of the self, while the revolving circle-of-two generates the feeling, the mood, the atmosphere, and the mode of emotional involvement and nonviolent consequences in its own right.

This is the reflexive engagement of the anthropologist with her own somatic learning and changing, while the eyes of the other—the opponent, the teacher, the other participants in a training session—are now directly somatic rather than cognitively interpretive. Such somatic experiential engagement of the anthropologist with hitherto unknown cultural options enables the aim of anthropology to be achieved, namely, making sense of the other not by trying to understand him but rather by entering into a dynamic of "becoming" him by engaging somatically, practically, in the other's way of perceiving and of moving. Such an approach also challenges the subjective anthropologist as a separate entity; it renders the distinct objective and subjective points of view difficult to tell apart unambiguously, as both object and subject are replaced by the process of becoming. Engaging in the circle of aikido, achieving perfect praxis, transforms the relations between participants into nonbelligerence in and of itself, with the anthropologist merely riding the wave. Under these conditions both I and the other become an "expression of a possible world" (Rajchman 2000: 158n14), which can come together, drift apart, or clash.

Deleuze and Guattari and Somatic Reflexivity

Both the idiosyncratic ways and flexibility of Deleuzian thought can be understood as a "tendentious joke" (Holland 1999: 24) that engages with a serious, even painful, matter behind the façade of a jest, perhaps even striking a blow under the guise of make-believe. It simultaneously conceals and reveals behind its peculiar masquerade, providing only a chimera of meaning. Yet is this not precisely the purpose of aikido, to capture and transform the face of violence? To take the serious matter of violent sociality and turn it on its head and make fun of it? Is that not the point, the reason to smile? More generally, is not a good part of sociality, any sociality, constructed in this fashion?

Deleuzian thought as a whole is inherently reflexive; it is malleable and ever shifting and therefore eludes tight definitions; it cannot be explicated in a finite way. It is a world of its own, determining the relations between idiosyncratic wordings and particular concepts. For that reason, drawing on Deleuze is like pulling a tangled thread, dragging the user to explicate ever more of its aspects and particular employment of words. Deleuze and Guattari formulated an alternative both to semiotics and to duality, and for that purpose they have coined notions such as "multiplicity" and "becoming-animal." Their specific, idiosyncratic way of using these terms was deliberately intended to "upset our thinking" (Stagoll 2005: 21), to shake it loose of its snuggly, comfortable categories, typologies, and moral judgments, and especially to overcome the heavy heritage of dualism haunting Western philosophy and thus help portray the world and its continuous (nondual) processes.

Multiplicity is basic to this conception of the nondual. Deleuze opposes "the Dyad One/Many, in all of its forms, with multiplicity," which is "a complex structure that does not reference a prior unity. Multiplicities are not parts of a greater whole that have been fragmented, and they cannot be considered manifold expressions of a single concept or transcendent unity" (Roffe 2005: 176). Multiplicity depends on action to survive; thus, it is immediately embodied and *done*: "Le multiple, il faut le faire" (1994: 13)—"the multiple must be made" ([1987] 2005: 6)—declare Deleuze and Guattari at the outset of their *Thousand Plateaus*. Multiplicity challenges duality by offering the conundrum of duality a practical solution, a solution in terms of *doing*. Moreover, the abstract nature of multiplicity—in stark opposition to the habitual ideas of the abstract—is related to *doing* and not to representation, and this trait permits skewing a fixed meaning (Zayani 2000: 97). Multiplicity accentuates process over fixity, dynamic over identity, and so it does not unite into a bounded entity but remains a patchwork: nothing holds it from without, and nothing transcends it; it has no constant identity. It is not defined in advance; it is revealed progressively, in movement (DeLanda 2002: 26). Dynamics are central to multiplicity, since Deleuze and Guattari "propose to go beyond the spurious question of representation and its corollary the signifier/signified dyad"; thus, the "multiple is neither unified nor totalized but simply unleashed" (Zayani 2000: 98).

Multiplicity has no use for unequivocal categories, ideologies, or typologies; it is not a world of probabilities but of chance. Multiplicity goes into the social without reducing its unruly, rhizomic nature, without renouncing details in favor of ordered principles, and for that reason multiplicity permits a social event to emerge in full. And like the revolving sphere of aikido, multiplicity cannot be divided without changing its nature (Roffe 2005: 177)—like the revolving sphere, held by centripetal forces in continuous imbalance, in ephemeral equilibrium. When the sphere comes to a rest and the two *aikidoka* are back on their feet, smiling, it dismantles and changes its nature.

Replacing the term "nonduality" with multiplicity has several advantages. First, nondual implicitly implies dual, whereas multiplicity circumvents that hurdle. But more importantly for anthropological purposes, multiplicity points at the nonstatic as a necessary condition for untying the knot of unity, which inevitably begets duality. Furthermore, since multiplicity is anchored in process—in the potentiality for "change that inheres in every particular situation" (Roffe 2005: 177), in interaction with others and with the environment, in *doing* as it is done—it permits relating to the many variations found in sociality without necessarily ordering them or trapping them in categories.

Through undoing categories multiplicity unveils the relations between contrasts that do not maintain dual relations, such as the contrasts between attacker and defender, between violence and non-violence in aikido, the relations between actionless and action, or between yin and yang. In multiplicity, the contrasting pairs may seem to show themselves at times, but then they disappear into each other and become trapped, entangled in each other, so both their appearance and disappearance seem ephemeral, perhaps even an artifact.

Deleuze and Guattari point to the traditional "Japanese fighter" as a good example for understanding the irrepressible potentiality of multiplicity, because of the uncontainable dynamic that characterizes his movement. The Japanese fighter is "interminably still… [and] then makes a move too quick to see" ([1987] 2005: 356). He becomes continuously reduced to something other than himself—reduced in the sense that he loses his specific characteristics and in so doing becomes a more general version of himself. The passage between stillness and exact and purposeful movement is erased; no introduction or preparation is necessary; stillness and movement contain each other yet remain contrasts. This unfolding opens up options in the body and in sociality that reach beyond the habitual potentialities, such as challenging the directionality of time (Bar-On Cohen 2007: 7–9).

The Ethics of Multiplicity

Both Cartesian dualism and multiplicity are ethical projects. Cartesian dualism delineates clearly and unequivocally between dual pairs and also determines a moral priority concerning those pairs, in which the right order stipulates that the abstract is ethically superior to the concrete. Body is dominated by mind, objects by thought, words, and other representations, men by God, and practice by discourse. Mind, thought, word, representation, God, and discourse have a higher ethical value than their concrete counterparts, which need to be tamed and subdued so that they can serve the higher order. The ethical project of multiplicity, on the other hand, does not determine such power relations between the concrete and the abstract. Furthermore, multiplicity does not set out to save the other; it does not propose confession as a way of self-scrutiny, because there is no higher authority to provide forgiveness. Multiplicity is in no way transcendental: it is immanent, everything happens within it. The ethical project of multiplicity replaces the individual intention with a collective annunciation. Connecting between planes of the world, in the case of aikido, some of the potentialities of the body, the centrifugal forces and so on. In it the individuals' acts and collective knowledge nourish each other, yet they have no separate existence.

Ethics as we usually understand them depend on a plan, an intention, and a choice. The assumption is that an ethical action consists of choosing good rather than bad on a consciously deliberate plane, at times collectively, but mainly as an individual endeavor (Evens 1995), as if the moral dilemma is always straightforward and formulated as a dual option: right versus wrong. However, if we replace mindful deliberation with ways of organizing bodies and things in relation to one another, ways of "becoming other," as does aikido, and if we replace categories of good and bad with dynamics of *doing*, and in particular of stirring things into different dynamic relations with one another, and if we replace the bounded self with the porous body-self—does forgoing unambiguous categories of good and bad (and most other clear-cut social categories) leave us in an a-ethical state? Of course not. Forgoing clear categories and distinctions does not lead to an ethical void; dynamics of doing have an ethical nature in and of themselves. And in the face of social reality we methodologically pretend that mindful, deliberate, planned, and consciously intended decisions pertain exclusively to the domain of morality and have ethical worth and consequence. We proceed as if the social maze of ethics can be reduced to a deliberate and clearly formulated choice; and again this pretense has consequences, because we concurrently adopt the dualistic ethical understanding.[7] Of course, it is not only within the Japanese framework of aikido that *doing* is of ethical concern; doing is always ethically loaded, since it is from sociality and the way it is put together that social ordering, with all its complex ethical consequences, stems.

Aikido as a pacific martial art is concerned with the ethics of nonviolence. It does not involve disembodied ideas or ideologies, but is rather practically performed through exercises. Inasmuch as all aikido exercises result in the attacker rolling away from the zone of belligerence, in these exercises violence is curtailed time and again and its energy captured, harnessed, and transformed into the energy of vitalization. And this tip of the balance—which permits to annihilate some of the destructive forces of violence and erosion—is dispersed throughout this cosmos. The ethical plan, therefore, demands perpetual effort and effortlessness. The ethical project is to set the world into constant motion and connect it further as it follows its tendency to fall apart and destruct. Obviously, violence and its destructive potential are deemed malicious and vitalization benevolent, but these two contrasts are contrasts of yin and yang: they depend on each other to exist, since out of destruction grows vitality, and vitality inevitably results in entropy and destruction, and for that reason vitality needs to trap violence in order to grow. People enact that revitalization collectively, and in so doing, they perform the ethical.

Eisenstadt claims that it is such a fluid type of moral dynamics that is at the basis of Japanese culture, a culture that puts "an emphasis on reality as structured in terms of shifting contexts rather than discrete, enclosed ontological entities or absolutist, dichotomous categories. Reality, in this view, is conceived of, not in terms of relations involving 'things' on an objective horizon, but rather as something that is constructed or defined by these very relations" (1996: 319). That is to say, a culturally informed ethic of this kind consists of putting parts of the social and physical environment in particular relationships with one another, thus initiating a certain dynamic ensuing from their interaction, and consequently also preventing other potential relations and dynamics from unfolding.

To follow Deleuze and Guattari further still, out of the smooth, undivided, nondual reality of multiplicity springs forth the potentiality of "becoming other" ("becoming-animal"), a potentiality we can all tap into in our bodies-selves (see also Stagoll 2005). That is why the dynamic of the other is always saturated with the social and culturally informed. And so too becoming other by entering the dynamics of the other's world is an ethical matter: it concerns modes of infringement on the other's life space in an active-passive way, which is central to the ethics of multiplicity. While the active *aikidoka* is also a passive voyager on the undulations of the circular movement, the active intentionality is replaced by simple directionality; the active capturing of energy becomes indistinguishable from the passive transmitting of the energy of violence emanating from the attack, and the active self-defense results in the transformation of violence into nonviolence.

Perfect praxis enlists the potentiality embedded within a certain culturally known way of doing to channel the participants into a course of action that is somatically reflexive.[8] Perfect praxis and its reflexive dimension are formed through the feeling of rightness stemming from tacit sensuous knowledge, which is the aesthetic of practice, and not from the consciously conscious alone. Or in Handelman's words, "Unself-consciously, one monitors effectively" (2004: 102, 101–3).

As Japanese philosopher Yuasa puts it (citing Nishida Kitarō), the action of the "self without being a self" is an "animate state with maximum freedom in which there is the least gap between the will's demand and its fulfillment" (Yuasa 1987: 69). The perfect ethical praxis, then, consists of the erasure of the gap between "the will's demand and its fulfillment," or in other words, funneling action in such a way that the conditions to approach erasure of that gap are activated as in

Wu Wei. Monitoring the kinesthetic body-in-movement, the relations between the *uke* and the *naga,* their positioning in space in relation to the other couples practicing around them in a way that is saturated with Ueshiba's call for peace—this monitoring is the passive-active role of the *aikidoka* whirling in the circle of two. And through this culturally transmitted monitoring, the entire scene reflects on violence, on relationships, and on the world while striving to improve it.

Perfect praxis allows the bounded body-self to be overstepped by adopting a passive-active mode of becoming—as the active *aikidoka* also becomes a passive voyager in the ever spinning sphere of two—and augmenting its capacities as it overspills the boundaries of the separated one. Perfect praxis can provoke change within the *entire* body and break the unequivocal boundaries between the participants, opening the *entire* body to potentialities from within, which can only be reached through social practice.[9] It also overflows the microcosm of the spinning two to include more, while engaging the dynamics of entropy and destruction, understood to be at work in the perpetual exchange between the principles of yin and yang, to harness them to the culturally recognized potentiality of energizing and improving the world.

Because the ever spinning sphere taps into the potentiality embedded in violent sociality and simply unleashes it (Zayani 2000: 98), it carries the environment with it. The passive-active, object-subject state can no longer be clearly perceived, because multiplicity shapes the transformation of "becoming" through being captured into the other by chance, by the potentiality to transform that does not permit the contrasts to settle down in a finite way, while also steering intentionally, through the mere engagement with this process, into the other's dynamics.

By polishing these potentialities to a shine, perfect praxis takes on an additional ethical project, which combines the ethical and the somatic aspects of reflexivity, namely, that of coaxing the *entire* (nondual) body into becoming: a body that topples object and subject into one whole that is neither object nor subject, rubbing out the clear distinction between me and other, between inside and outside body-self. The ethical added value of multiplicity stems from its being closer to social life as it is "really" lived. Somatic knowing, integral to living, is made stark and unavoidable. Through such reflexivity, anthropology becomes directly engaged in the politics of somatic living in its manifold forms. Body-in-relation-with-others cannot be reduced to any other significant rendition of existence. Somatic reflexivity is situated in the relations in and of itself. It invites anthropology to look for the more circuitous, rhizomic ways in which sociality and ethics perform their affect.

Somatic Reflexivity

Perfect praxis—erasing the distinction between plan and execution, between me and the other, through practice alone—brackets together the consciously conscious and volition. That is how the tight coupling of people and actions foregrounds an additional facet of reflexivity, one that does not depend on the deliberate intellectual effort of sorting an epistemological conundrum in an active and intentional way. In order to overcome the epistemological gap and to expose the seams of social construction, *doing* must be engaged in an active mode. The body-self must be employed in a specific way to engender a certain dynamic by social actors, one of whom is the anthropologist.

The inseparable personal and common effort that enables this sociality to come into being is reflexive in its resistance both to the participant's disinclination to relinquish her will, and to the natural tendency of the world, embedded in the yin and yang cosmology, to engender violence and to collapse. These forces of resistance are enlisted by cultural wisdom and acumen, and funneled into rejuvenation and the annihilation of violence, engaging the cosmological forces of destruction and turning them on their head. That is why perfect praxis is reflexive in and of itself, and although this reflexivity is not bounded to the individual, it nonetheless engenders an ethical dynamic of reflection on reflection.

Of the many spiritual Japanese practices, Zen is in both aim and procedure somatically reflexive. As part of the Japanese Zen tradition, Japanese martial arts implicitly posit the potentiality of embodied practice culminating in a changed perspective, because relentless practice is the way to enlightenment and such achievements can be attained and comprehended exclusively through experimenting with somatic motion and motionlessness (Hurst 1998; Yuasa 1987, 1993). Enlightenment is a different take on reality, liberated from the many mundane details that clutter life, a reduced point of view and therefore also a more generalized one. The Zen awakening is arrived at unreflectively; moreover, cognitive reflection can only obstruct it, and perfect praxis in aikido, as a variant of the Zen "way" (*do*), also enables an understanding that excludes conscious reflection.

So, to return to our starting point, since the significance of Japanese martial arts stems nearly exclusively from body movement, the anthropological study of this field perforce engages the anthropologist somatically as well. Thus, the questions that somatic reflexivity attempts to answer are: How can one reflect with one's body? And can this reflection be reflexive, that is, can it comment on reflection? How can an anthropologist, engaged in teasing sense and significance out of his, and others' embodied experience in an attempt to describe the world, be reflective in relation to his own, and others' body-in-movement within the revolving sphere of aikido? How can "reflection" be done when it is inextricable from inhaling the world through the senses and exhaling it into movement?[10] A condition for attempting to formulate such reflexivity—and for doing multiplicity in general, which stems from taking the route of apprenticeship instead of limiting one's tools to the consciously cognitive—depends on replacing "what" questions with "how" ones, turning the issue of reflexivity into a practical rather than an exclusively mindful one. Ask how you make yourself a reflexive body-self instead of what it means to be a reflexive body-self (to paraphrase Deleuze and Guattari [1987] 2005: chap. 6). How can we be *directly* reflexive through the lived body and its potentialities to become other?

The issue of becoming reflexive with the *entire* body, in turn, encases a more general question regarding the attitude of the anthropologist to the world: Is there really a difference of nature between reflecting with one's mind and reflecting with one's body? In other words, do we in fact carry out our lives, or at least our intellectual lives, within a mindful self? Or perhaps are we just methodologically pretending and are in practice always also somatically engaged in our anthropological queries? This is already a reflexive question: of course we are always also somatically engaged in whatever we are doing, and doing anthropology is no exception. So what is the price of methodologically pretending to be using our heads exclusively? How does the *entire* (nondual) body, the body of multiplicity—with its physical, emotional, sensuous, cognitive aspects—form and reflectively inform the understanding of the social world?

It engages the anthropologist entirely, her undivided body-self, into *doing*. Her anthropological discovery is abductive; she is startled and surprised by the mere engagement in sociality, and "the scent of truth" (Houser 2005: 455) carries her elsewhere.[11] The directionality of the potentiality embedded in the social process changes her in a way that makes the order of that social dynamics and their ethical consequences apparent. Somatic reflexivity is the process of becoming-animal, which implies to participate in movement, to stake out the path of escape, to cross a threshold, to reach a continuum of intensities, and to find a world of pure intensities (Deleuze and Guattari 1986: 12). Following the movement of sociality wherever it goes is the intensity, the undivided trait of this sociality, its multiplicity. This social dynamic is also the anthropological finding.

Acknowledgments

My reflections in this article are also the result of many conversations with Don Handelman. They are entirely mine, but in a way also entirely his.

Notes

1. Even at temporary locales, such as workshops, a makeshift *shomen* is placed for the duration of the training sessions. The *shomen* is not a representation and does not act as a symbol for the participants of the training session; rather, it is integral to the creation of the world of aikido. It acts to transform and organize the relations between the *aikidoka* and sets the practice into motion (see Bar-On Cohen 2009a).

2. The website of the main school of Aikiki aikido in Tokyo (Honbu Dojo) states that there are 1.2 million people training in aikido in fifty-one different counties (see www.aikikai.or.jp/eng/index.htm). There is no other source of information for assessing the number of *aikidoka* in the world, but aikido is clearly widespread. Moreover, there are other, smaller schools of aikido around the world that are not affiliated with the Aikiki center.

3. This again refers to the Shinto origins of aikido, because many Shinto rituals are made to renew and rejuvenate world energy (see, e.g., Averbuch 1996; Bar-On Cohen 2012).

4. For example, only when Jean Briggs (1970) looked at the pictures she took while her Inuit family was traveling did she notice that the sleigh carrying her gear was much taller than the one carrying the rest of the family's belongings, and only then did she realize the profoundly different attitude to property between her culture and that of her hosts.

5. Alternately, if human consciousness is indeed relatively universal (see Stroeken, this volume), the anthropologist can come to share experience and empathize with her informants with no need to overcome her own psychological or cultural load.

6. The name "aikido" can be translated roughly as "the way of merging the *ki* energy." "Aikido" is composed of three ideograms (*kanji*). The first, *ai*, meaning merging, is sometimes translated as harmony. The second, *ki*, is the somatic and cosmological energy that permeates the universe and enables power and health in the Sino-Japanese tradition. In Stevens's introduction to Ueshiba's book, *ki* is described as "the subtle energy that propels the universe, the vitality that pervades creation, and the unifying force that holds things together" (Ueshiba 2002: x; see also Stevens 1997, 2001). The last ideogram, *dō*, means "the way," implying the way to Zen Buddhist enlightenment (*satori*), and the way of the gods, as the word "Shinto" denotes.

7. Some social settings do operate according to such a morality—for example, the kibbutz in Evens's (1995) analysis—and their anthropological study

naturally follows dualistic tracks, but my claim here is that this is a specific case and not a general universal rule.

8. I thank Terry Evens for urging me to formulate this remark and Don Handelman for helping me formulate it.

9. Perfect praxis enables nondual potentialities—such as the fighting energy of *kime* (Bar-On Cohen 2006), perfect timing (Bar-On Cohen 2007), and the breaking of boundaries in *kibadachi* (Bar-On Cohen 2009a)—to be reached.

10. For some examples of somatic reflexivity, see Tamisari (2000), Ingold (2004), Persson (2006), Smith (2007), and Stephens and Delamont (2006).

11. Despite the centrality of the abductive as a mode of inference for somatic reflexivity, and despite the abundance of literature concerning Peircian "logic of abduction," I will not go into this notion here (see, e.g., Houser 2005; Tiercelin 2005). My understanding of abduction follows Susanne Langer (1979), who insists that in order to perceive at all, in order to make sense of the profusion of information rushing into us from our senses, a logic is employed (not "logical" logic, but rather a holistic one); our mere perception is therefore drenched in interpretation, and in that sense reflexive. It follows that our surprise or awe when faced with the aesthetic holds the potential to make this holistic logic of perception (and of movement) apparent.

References

Averbuch, Irit. 1996. "Performing Power: On the Nature of the Japanese Ritual Dance Performance of Yamabushi Kagura." *Journal of Ritual Studies* 10, no. 2: 1–40.

Bar-On Cohen, Einat. 2006. "*Kime* in Japanese Martial Arts and the Moving Body." *Body & Society* 12, no. 4: 73–93.

———. 2007. "Timing in *Karate* and the Body in Its Own Right in Anthropology." *Social Analysis* 51, no. 3: 1–22.

———. 2009a. "*Kibadachi* in *Karate*: Pain and Crossing Boundaries within the Lived Body and within Sociality." *The Journal of the Royal Anthropological Institute* 15: 610–29.

———. 2009b. "Opening and Closing Ritual in Japanese Martial Arts and the Dismantling of Violence." *The Journal of Ritual Studies* 23, no. 1: 27–42.

———. 2012. *The Forces of Homology: The 1928 Rites of Succession to the Throne of Hirohito, Emperor of Japan* 23, no. 4: 425–43.

Befu, Harumi, and Sylvie Guichard-Anguis, eds. 2001. *Globalizing Japan: Ethnography of the Japanese Presence in Asia, Europe and America*. New York: Routledge Curzon.

Blyth, Reginald Horace. 1959. *Oriental Humor*. Tokyo: The Hokusiedo Press.

Bourdieu, Pierre. 2004. *Science of Science and Reflexivity*. Chicago: University of Chicago Press.

Briggs, Jean. 1970. *Never in Anger: A Portrait of an Eskimo Family*. Cambridge, MA: Harvard University Press.

Deacon, Roger. 2002. "An Analytics of Power Relations: Foucault on the History of Discipline." *History of the Human Sciences* 15, no. 1: 89–117.

DeLanda, Manuel. 2002. *Intensive Science and Virtual Philosophy*. London: Continuum.

Deleuze, Gilles, and Felix Guattari. 1986. *Kafka: Towards a Minor Literature*. Minneapolis: Minnesota University Press.

———. (1987) 2005. *A Thousand Plateaus: Capitalism and Schizophrenia*. Minneapolis: University of Minneapolis Press.

———. 1994. *Mille Plateaux*. Paris: Edition de Minuit.

Due, Reidar. 2007. *Deleuze*. Cambridge: Polity.

Duyvenak, J. J. L. 1947. "The Philosophy of Wu Wei." *Asiatische Studien* 1: 81–102.

Eisenstadt, Shmuel N. 1996. *Japanese Civilization: A Comparative View*. Chicago: University of Chicago Press.

Evens, Terence M. S. 1995. *Two Kinds of Rationality: Kibbutz Democracy and Generational Conflict*. Minneapolis: University of Minnesota Press.

Evens, Terence, and Don Handelman. 2006. "Introduction: The Ethnographic Praxis of the Theory of Practice." In *The Manchester School: Practice and Ethnography Praxis in Anthropology*, ed. Terence Evens and Don Handelman. New York: Berghahn Books, 1–12.

Foucault, Michel. 1988. "Technologies of the Self." In *Technologies of the Self: A Seminar with Michel Foucault*, ed. Martin Luther H., Huck Gutman, and Patrick H. Hutton. Amherst: University of Massachusetts Press, 16–49.

Garfinkel, Harold, ed. 1986. *Ethnomethodological Studies of Work*. London: Routledge & K. Paul.

Handelman, Don. 2004. *Nationalism and the Israeli State: Bureaucratic Logic in Public Event*. Oxford: Berg.

Holland, Eugene W. 1999. *Deleuze and Guattari's Anti-Oedipus*. New York: Routledge.

Houser, Nathan. 2005. "The Scent of Truth." *Semiotica* 153, nos. 1–4: 455–66.

Hurst, G. C. 1998. *Armed Martial Arts, Swordsmanship and Archery*. New Haven, CT: Yale University Press.

Hyers, Conrad M. 1974. *Zen and the Comic Spirit*. London: Rider.

Ingold, Tim. 2004. "Culture on the Ground: The World Perceived Through the Feet." *Journal of Material Culture* 9, no. 3: 315–40.

Jackson, Michael. 2011. "After Understanding: A Memoir of Galina Lindquist." In *Religion, Politics, and Globalization: Anthropological Approaches*, ed. Don Handelman and Galina Lindquist. New York: Berghahn Books, xv–xxvi.

Kapferer, Bruce. 1988. "The Anthropologist as Hero: Three Exponents of Post-Modernist Anthropology." *Critique of Anthropology* 8, no. 2: 77–104.

———. 1997. *The Feast of the Sorcerer: Practices of Consciousness and Power*. Chicago: Chicago University Press.

Langer, Susanne. 1979. *Philosophy in a New Key: A Study in the Symbolism of Reason, Rite and Art*. Cambridge, MA: Harvard University Press.

Loy, David. 1985. "Wei-wu-wei: Nondual Action." *Philosophy East and West* 35, no. 1: 73–86.

Lynch, David. 1991. *The Angriest Dog in the World*. <http://www.davidlynch.de/angry.html>

Persson, Asha. 2006. "Intimate Immensity: Phenomenology of Place and Space in an Australian Yoga Community." *American Ethnologist* 34, no. 1: 44–56.

Rajchman, John. 2000. *The Deleuze Connections*. Cambridge, MA: MIT Press.

Roffe, Jonathan. 2005. "Multiplicity." In *The Deleuze Dictionary*, ed. A. Parr. Edinburgh: Edinburgh University Press, 176–77.

Salzman, Philip Carl. 2002. "On Reflexivity." *American Anthropologist* 104, no. 3: 805–13.

Slingerland, Edward. 2003. *Effortless Action: Wu-Wie as Conceptual Metaphor and the Spiritual Ideal in Early China*. New York: Oxford University Press.

Smith, Benjamin Richard. 2007. "Body, Mind and Spirit? Towards an Analysis of the Practice of Yoga." *Body & Society* 13, no. 2: 25–46.

Stagoll, Cliff. 2005. "Becoming." In *The Deleuze Dictionary*, ed. A. Parr. Edinburgh: Edinburgh University Press, 21–22.

Stephens, Neil, and Sara Delamont. 2006. "Samba no Mar: Bodies, Movement and Idiom in Capoeira." In *Body/Embodiment: Symbolic Interaction and the Sociology of the Body*, ed. Waskul Dennis and Phillip Vannin. Chippenham, UK: Ashgate, 109–22.

Stevens, John. 1997. *Invincible Warrior: An Illustrated Biography of Morihei Ueshiba Founder of Aikido*. Boston: Shambhala.

———. 2001. *The Philosophy of Aikido*. Tokyo: Kodansha International.

Tamisari, Franca. 2000. "The Meaning of the Steps Is In Between, Dancing and the Curse of Compliments." "The Politics of Dance," ed. Rosita Henry, Fiona Magowan, and David Murray, special issue, *The Australian Journal of Anthropology* 11, no. 2: 274–286.

Tiercelin, Claudine. 2005. "Abduction and the Semiotics of Perception." *Semiotica* 153, nos. 1–4: 389–412.

Ueshiba, Morihei. 2002. *The Art of Peace*. Trans. and ed. John Stevens. Boston, MA: Shambhala Classics.

Yoshimitsu, Yamada. 1994. *Ultimate Aikido: Secrets of Self Defense and Inner Power*. New York: Citadel Press Books.

Yuasa, Yasuo. 1987. *The Body: Towards a Mind-Body Theory*. Albany: State University of New York Press.

———. 1993. *The Body, Self-Cultivation and Ki-Energy*. Albany: State University of New York Press.

Zayani, Mohamed. 2000. "Gilles Deleuze, Félix Guttari and the Total System." *Philosophy & Social Criticism* 26, no. 1: 93–114.

Einat Bar-On Cohen is an anthropologist and independent scholar.
Email: einat.cb@mail.hujiac.il

ᘉ SECTION III ᘉ

Reflexivity, Self, and Other

Editors' Preface

Setting it off against Bourdieu's reflexive sociology and materialistic grasp of practice, Paul Clough brings his own argument about reflexivity into sharp relief. Over the course of a year, Clough observed the economic practices of one Fulani farmer cum trader who lived among the Hausa. Like Evens and Handelman, Clough poses a question about the efficacy of ethics. He argues that, while the farmer's behavior is consistent with material self-interest, at bottom it presupposes self-reflection that transcends material concerns. He agrees that the farmer's behavior is open to explanation by reference to Bourdieu's objectivist concepts of habitus and social status, a mode of explanation that tends to see moral beliefs as, at heart, cover for self-interest. But on the basis of inferences drawn from the farmer's everyday discursive interactions, and of direct observation of the farmer's behavior, Clough finds that moral claims in the sense of other-regard effectively mediated material self-interest, and that in fact the operation of the entire economy in which the farmer participated reflected such moral mediation. In effect, he argues that in addition to the materialistic determinism of Bourdieu's "dispositions," the farmer displayed a critical inward or moral agency. In coping with his personal hopes and dreams for the long term as well as with the existential uncertainties of life, the farmer was forced to make autonomous choices, and while these choices were thus self-determined, they were not necessarily self-interested. Keyed, rather, to values such as character, beauty, and responsibility to others, they transcended and could even run contrary to economism. In arriving at this description of the farmer's self-reflection, Clough suggests that his own experience of self-awareness is—in addition to the objective evidence of the farmer's discourse and behavior—what allowed him to recognize the man's inner, agential sense of self. This sort of reflexivity, which features our unique capacity of responsibility, a capacity that grants us the ability to recognize our common humanity (as well as our own otherness), appears to resonate in a general way with Stroeken's notion of cosmopolitan reflexivity, Handelman's appeal to Levinas's ethics, and Evens's emphasis on responsibility.

In his contribution, René Devisch undertakes an expansive retrospective project of vocational reflexivity, one that traverses many decades and nations. Reflexivity serves as the red thread connecting Devisch's ruminations on his family's therapeutic embrace of hedonic conviviality as an ironic hedge against bourgeois values to his fieldwork among the Yaka. But Flemish domestic pleasure functions here as more than a nostalgic sense of hearth and home, for from it Devisch turns to the field by means of a contrast between familial intimacy and the Lacanian notion of extimacy (the latter term referring—as against the received notion, in psychological science, of sheer self-containment—to the diffusion of interiority with exteriority). Looking with Yaka eyes on Flanders and the history of Belgian conquest, Devisch reflexively encounters in extimacy the otherness of intimacy, the cognitively obscure and the affectively traumatic. Interwoven with themes of colonial guilt and historical trauma, the Flemish peasant imperative to enjoy recurs just as irrepressibly as the unspeakable and the uncanny, the vast untold that persists through the generations in Flanders and Yaka. As a narrative, Devisch's focus on pleasure taking in common conjures the hedonic suggestion that humans might be reflexively intersensory even more fundamentally or "primordially" than we are intersubjective.

8

TENSION, REFLECTION, AND AGENCY IN THE LIFE OF A HAUSA GRAIN TRADER

Paul Clough

The Emperor's New Clothes: Agency in the Habitus of Pierre Bourdieu

The apparent power of Bourdieu's theory of habitus lies in its seeming capacity to explain all of the interactions of social life. However, when closely inspected, both his theory and his practice show their weakness: the characters he presents in his analyses have no agency. He therefore cannot explain all that is significant in social life. I will begin this chapter by briefly highlighting the absence of agency, first in his theory, and then in his ethnography.

Throughout the first, theoretical part of *The Logic of Practice*, Bourdieu built up the claim that he had "transcended" the opposition in social theory between objectification (or structural determinism) and subjectivism (or voluntarism) through a theory of habitus—"the systems of durable... dispositions, structured structures predisposed to act as structuring structures,... as principles which generate... practices and representations that can be objectively adapted to their outcomes *without presupposing a conscious aiming at ends*" (Bourdieu [1980] 1990: 53, emphasis added). Essential to his explanation of practice was his recognition of the observable difference between society in past time and society in present time. The whole "accumulation" of past practices generates the *changed* external conditions faced by any individual in the present. Equally, the human "system of dispositions" literally embodies past practices as an internalized "second nature," so that performative skill develops in every socioeconomic niche (Bourdieu [1980] 1990: 56–57). The use of performative skill that is intimately adapted to the niche in which it flourishes makes possible continuous small adjustments to the changed external conditions resulting from past practices: this he calls the "durably installed generative principle of regulated improvisations" (Bourdieu [1980] 1990: 57).

In other words, humans in present time adjust to the changed conditions produced by practices in past time, through performative skill developed in past time. In Bourdieu's theory, "spontaneity *without consciousness or will*" ([1980] 1990: 56, emphasis added) characterizes performative skill. Inherently obscure in the text is *how* past practices generate changed external conditions in the present. The habitus is "practical sense" (Bourdieu [1980] 1990: 57), unconscious performative skill (Bourdieu [1980] 1990: 57), and a "system of dispositions" (Bourdieu [1980] 1990: 53). But how this sense, skill, and "disposition" in past time generate changes *from* the past that are obvious in present time, Bourdieu left obscure. All that he could state with clarity was that performative skill adapts to the social change produced by performative skill. Or practice adapts to the social change produced by practice. Social change itself is unexplained. Readers are left with a statement that is true, but trivially so: practice changes, skill changes.

Bourdieu's prose could be extraordinarily convoluted. He was proud of this: "At the risk of seeming arrogant... what is complex can only be said in a complex way... if you want to hold the world in all its complexity and at the same time order and articulate it... you have to use heavily articulated sentences" (Bourdieu [1982] 1990: 51). And he viewed with disdain the writing of short sentences in the common tongue: "When dealing with the social world, the ordinary use of ordinary language makes metaphysicians of us" (Bourdieu [1982] 1990: 54). In later work, he sought to clarify the meaning of his habitus by reveling in the paradoxical—"cognition without consciousness, intentionality without intention, and a practical mastery... which allows one to anticipate the future without even positing it as such" (Bourdieu [1982] 1990: 12). He attempted to explain habitus through the notion of "strategy," and counterposed the "more or less 'automatic' strategies of the practical sense" with the "projects or calculations of any conscious mind" (Bourdieu [1982] 1990: 62). The principle behind strategies is "the feel for the game... a mastery acquired by experience... which works outside conscious control and discourse" (Bourdieu [1982] 1990: 62). Bourdieu illustrated the unconscious performative skills required to engage in social practices by reference to the game of tennis and the "good" player, who "quite naturally materializes at just the place the ball is about to fall, as if the ball were in command of him—but by that very fact, he is in command of the ball" (Bourdieu [1982] 1990: 60).

Bourdieu's analogy between social practices and sporting games is weak, because physical games, compared with social practices, involve a heavily restricted inventiveness and a speed of action that leaves little room for reflection. Moreover, sporting games require a physical training wherein the role of conscious thought is limited to ensuring speed and accuracy in the achievement of artificially simple goals: these are singularly narrow in comparison with the multiple goals implicit in many social practices. Importantly, the goals in any sporting game are unquestioned by definition. (We all delight in one game or another precisely because games both simplify in a symbolic manner and allow us to escape from the complexity of our social lives.)

Clearly, the thrust of Bourdieu's theory was to criticize analytical approaches that explain social life by conscious adherence to overt rules—or by the freedom of agents to decide for themselves. In the service of these critiques, he developed an emphasis on the wide variety of social practices that emerge through unconscious performances bodily absorbed from childhood. These allow for the human faculty of improvisation. That faculty generates, without any intention intervening, a change in social practices over time, because of differences in individuals' performative skill. The overall effect of Bourdieu's theoretical writing is curiously deterministic.

If we move from the circularity and analogical weaknesses embedded in Bourdieu's theoretical prose to the clarity of his ethnographic analyses, this effect is heightened. Consider his essay on matrimonial practices among the Kabyle in the second part of *The Logic of Practice* (Bourdieu [1980] 1990: 162–99). At the start he outlines a major analytical distinction, grounded in the statistics that he collected in order to go beyond the case-based method of fieldwork, between the small minority of extraordinary and the large majority of ordinary marriages. The former are either patrilateral parallel cousin marriages or marriages of political alliance with distant houses, and they are contracted by the men of the two houses concerned. The latter are negotiated by the women, and include many patrilateral or matrilateral cross-cousin marriages. Thus, from the beginning of the chapter he develops his opposition to the significance of overt social rules (which legitimate Kabyle male control of women) in favor of the well-worn but uncelebrated practices negotiated by women. What is at stake in the matrimonial planning hatched by men and women is their relative social capital (networks), symbolic capital (reputation in terms of the public code of honor), and economic or other pragmatic interests.

Bourdieu develops with great precision the wide variety of possible matrimonial outcomes. These depend on the performative skill with which men and women play the hand dealt to them by history (particularly their relative positions inside any family and patrilineage) rather than on their conscious reflections about the matrimonial system. The political and economic interests of husbands are paramount, because the relationship between brothers is the "keystone and the weakest link" in a patrilineal family structure (Bourdieu [1980] 1990: 192–93). The rule of patrilateral parallel cousin marriage may disguise more pragmatic explanations. For example, an older brother may arrange the marriage of his son to the daughter of his youngest brother because the latter is rich in land but has no sons. And a man without sons may give his daughter to a patrilineal "heir" who comes to live and work for him (Bourdieu [1980] 1990: 178–79). But at the same time, a husband may well be interested in supporting his wife's efforts to negotiate a cross-cousin marriage for their son in order to avoid the dominance of his older brothers. Amid the great variety of possibilities outlined by Bourdieu, he sees each marital undertaking as being the direct result of social vectors.

The final sentence of the chapter is revealing: as soon as the analyst is able to construct the principles that "agents put into practice" when they "immediately identify" the "socio-logically matchable" individuals in a "given state of the matrimonial market," practice becomes intelligible (Bourdieu [1980] 1990: 199). Ultimately, Bourdieu understands agency to mean "variation" within any social system rather than openness of choice. Despite his claim to have produced a unique synthesis from the analytical opposites of structure and agency, none is detectable. His ethnographic analysis of practices is shot through with structural determination. The emperor is not wearing any clothes.

I would suggest that Bourdieu's determinist orientation helps explain the great complexity and length of sentences in his theoretical writing. He was attempting therein to hold for verbal inspection all crucial dimensions in a social situation precisely because he believed that human action could be causally explained by an array of factors that left no room for indeterminacy.

Terry Evens's critique of Bourdieu focuses on the lack of agency in his work, in a manner that links agency to intention and to moral responsibility. Bourdieu not only disavows the significance of intention, he also allows no room for the unprecedented, for the act of creative imagination (Evens 2008: 116). For Evens, the description of human agency entails self-conduction, or genuine choice. Thereby, it implies the attribution of moral responsibility. Bourdieu's practice conceals the "meaningful or moral side of social life and human practice, reducing it to a question of material survival" (Evens 2008: 114–21). Evens contrasts "invention as intention" with Bourdieu's "conductorless, 'practical' ingenuity" of social agents (Evens 2008: 130). Self-reflection by human agents intrinsically involves an awareness that human action is radically open to the future. But self-reflection also contains the awareness of a tension between the self and its surroundings, and more deeply, between self-interest and the demands of others. Awareness of tension between the self and others includes belief in personal responsibility for the resolution of that tension. Thus, the awareness of responsibility—ethics—generates awareness of the reality of self-change (Evens 2008: 128–30).

This chapter examines my field research into the system of rural grain trading in one part of Hausaland, northern Nigeria, in order to explore the kind of understanding that emerges when the researcher reflects on the social interactions of the traders he studied, and on their own self-reflections concerning those relations. Is a structural analysis of "practices"—skilled performances based on indigenous practical knowledge in particular socioeconomic niches—sufficient to explain those practices? Or is the exploration of their self-consciousness also necessary in order to make sense of their actions? What, if any, additional understanding of their actions is provided by a reflection on their own self-reflection? This chapter focuses on the matrix of socioeconomic relations in which was embedded one trader who was at the center of my research into rural Hausa grain marketing.

A Descriptive Analysis of One Year in the Life of a Rural Grain Trader

Background

Abdulkadiri was a Fulani immigrant in the Hausa village of Marmara, in the southern part of Katsina emirate, Nigeria. He still made visits to his home village in the closely settled zone surrounding Kano city. While visiting, he also kept in touch with Fulani kinsmen having herds of cattle. He was very conscious that his paternal lineage had connections with the Fulani ruling class of Hausaland: his father's sister was the mother of the chief (*dagaci*) of his home village. He and the *dagaci* were "joking relatives" (*abokin wasa*), a close relationship between cross cousins among the Hausa and Fulani.

Around 1959, Kadiri had emigrated from his home village to Marmara. For a number of years he pursued grain and livestock trading, but did not farm. Ruefully reflecting on his career, he told me that he did not buy farms when he was still young in Marmara because he was planning to finally return to his home village:

> I have been eighteen years in Marmara—always at my present house. At first, I only followed my occupation [*sana'a*] of trader. Every two or three months I would return to Badumi to greet my mother and father. I did not buy farms here in Marmara because I was always thinking of returning to embrace [*rungume*] my parents. If I had bought farms *then* [in Marmara], while they were cheap, I would now have big farms! Then my parents died, one at harvest, the other in the dry season, within four months of each other. So there was nothing to carry me back home. Only then did I begin to buy farms—but belatedly [*daga baya*], the price had already risen.

The scale of Kadiri's trading and, hence, of his farming expanded slowly between 1959 and 1977. He had limited funds to set aside for the purchase of harvest grain for storage against a price rise, which might have led to more rapid growth. Moreover, a large part of his trade earnings and farm output was reserved for the expansion of his household. By the time that I arrived in Marmara in 1977, he headed a five-man family farming unit (*gandu*)—one of the largest in Marmara. It consisted of himself, his slightly younger married brother, his unmarried young brother, his oldest son, and a more distantly related married kinsman. He maintained a household of fourteen dependents—twice the average size in Marmara.

We can view the results of Kadiri's eighteen years in Marmara by summing up his economic position in December 1977, soon after I arrived in the village. He owned just 6.2 acres of farmland—less than the mean (7.0) but more than the median (4.3) holding. Second, he had a few head of cattle which he reserved as a long-term investment with his Fulani pastoral kinsmen. Third, he had a large household and a big family labor force.

Finally, he had amassed investment funds of around N2,000—a not insubstantial sum in northern Nigeria at that time, before the currency was devalued. Part he kept as cash and part as grain stocks in trade. Kadiri referred to this sum as his *jali*. He used the term to denote the liquid assets available for investment in all economic or social spheres that contributed to the growth of his economic and social position. For Kadiri, marriage payments and expenditures on house building—that is, expenditures which enabled his household to grow—were as appropriate uses of *jali* as were his expenditures on trading and farming.

Toward the end of 1977, Kadiri was poised to set in motion big changes in his life. His oldest son needed to be married. Kadiri himself had been unsuccessful in keeping a second wife, and was intent on having one. And he planned a dramatic expansion of his landholding, to be farmed by both family and hired labor. So he abandoned livestock trading and focused his energies on produce trading and farming. This chapter seeks to elicit how he went about reaching his objectives through the year 1978. Let us begin by exploring his most important social relationships.

Patronage

Kadiri was a client ("boy" or *yaro*) of Alhaji (El Haj) Zubeiru. He referred to Alhaji Zubeiru as his *uban gida* (literally, "father of the house"). *Uban gida* was used by rural Hausa in southern Katsina to denote the person upon whom a man could rely for loan money in trade or other money-creating enterprises. In return, the borrower regularly provided his *uban gida* with services in trade or agriculture.

Although Alhaji Zubeiru's village was some distance from Marmara, Zubeiru and Kadiri met each other frequently in local marketplaces. Kadiri would keep Zubeiru informed of grain supplies and prices around Marmara. From time to time, Zubeiru would give Kadiri money to effect a large purchase from a local farmer, which Kadiri would sell in the distant marketplace of Danbatta, giving Zubeiru the earnings. Kadiri also acted as Zubeiru's local intermediary. For example, in 1976 Zubeiru gave Kadiri money to purchase a grain mill in Marmara, which Zubeiru later collected. In January 1977, Zubeiru gave Kadiri the money to buy ten tons of guinea corn, which he collected in July and sold for twice as much, when prices were much higher.

In return for his services, Zubeiru gave Kadiri a trading loan of N400 at the December guinea corn harvest of 1977. According to Kadiri, this money was to be returned before April 1978, the start of the farming season. He called it *jali,* as he did his own investment funds. In fact, after trading with the N400, Kadiri sank it into farming rather than repaying it, and did not repay it until the harvest of November 1978. Every few months in 1978, Zubeiru would inquire after the money. In the middle of the farming season, he called Kadiri and asked for the money. Kadiri later gave me this wry account of their conversation:

Z: I gave you money so that you would turn it over (*juya shi*). What have you done with it?

K: Farming has eaten it all.

Z: It is not **thus** that we arranged with you (*ba **haka** muka yi da kai ba*). Why did you not tell me this?

K: Why should I tell you what you already know?

This maneuvering between patron and client was based on a mutual assessment of the other's dependability. Aware—and relieved—that he had survived a crucial encounter, Kadiri expanded further on the latitude allowed him: "If Alhaji hears that I have spent his money on buying farms, he is happy. Or if he hears that I am on my farm, he will bring out more money and give it to me. But if he hears that I am in my house, he will send his younger brother to get the *jali* from me."

Nevertheless, Kadiri suffered anxiety before his 1978 maize harvest enabled him to repay the N400 loan. One of Zubeiru's wealthy brothers had had a client-trader arrested and then forced him to sell his house in order to recover a loan. Furthermore, the situation of clientage leads to conflicting perceptions and feelings in the client. On the one hand, Kadiri was grateful to Zubeiru for allowing him to convert a trading loan into a farming loan. On the other, Kadiri was aware that his labor time in buying, storing, and selling grain enabled the patron to make large profits.

Trading Friendship

In order to increase his funds for investment in trade, Kadiri cultivated "trading friends" (*abokanan ciniki,* sing. *abokin ciniki*). These were traders in his own or other lines, and farmers, from whom he borrowed short-term loans without interest (*rance*). "Trading" friendships were understood to be commercial. Sometimes, close personal friendships developed out of trading friendships. In a society centered on the rites of marriage and childbirth, a prospective borrower would often try to initiate a trading friendship by making a donation at the potential lender's household ceremonies. This inaugurated a cycle of gift and countergift at their respective family ceremonies (*bukukuwa,* sing. *biki*).

In developing his trading friendships, a trader was endeavoring to increase not just the total credit available but also the period over which he could use it. Since traders operated mainly in weekly marketplaces, the first step was to increase the period of the loan from one to two weeks. The next step was to borrow the same sum for several, then many, weeks running. If a trading friendship became a bond marked by sympathy, the borrower might obtain a large sum which would be "on call" but not actually demanded for several months. Flexibility, based on trust, was the central feature of *rance* in a society marked by the personal, face-to-face nature of most economic transactions.

As a trader sought to obtain *rance*, he found himself under pressure to give it. And as he was seeking to lengthen repayment periods with his creditors, so too were his borrowers with him. He knew, in borrowing, that part of this credit would be loaned out again. During 1978, Kadiri had a core group of trading friends from whom he could borrow over N1,000 in most weeks of the year. At the same time, he was the trading friend of several core borrowers, to whom he loaned over N200 in most weeks. Kadiri was also continually borrowing from and loaning to a shifting group of other trading friends. His *net* weekly credit fluctuated with the amounts he borrowed in and the amounts he lent out. It actually reached the impressive total of N1,200 in early July 1978.

Of Kadiri's core creditors, four were richer than himself, two of similar income; of his core debtors, one had an income similar to Kadiri, but three were much poorer than he. Thus, many such loans were given *without hope of financial gain*. There was an ethic of mutual help among traders. Although Kadiri's *individual* loans involved dyadic relationships, the direction of this credit flow was from richer persons through the intermediate borrower to poorer ones.

A person's success in accumulating investment funds depended on his character (*hali*). A person with *hali* had many men (*mutane*) from whom he attracted loan money. *Hali* implied truthfulness and trustworthiness (*gaskiya*). But, I would argue, *hali* also incorporated the ideas of redistribution and reciprocal justice. Since the success of most traders depended on the willingness of others to loan *them* money, reciprocal justice required that they lend to those who were still struggling to succeed.

Grain Sellers

Kadiri obtained small amounts of grain by lending money during the preharvest "hungry month" of August, for repayment with grain at the main guinea corn harvest of December, worth at least twice as much as the original loan. It is interesting, but beyond the scope of this chapter, that Kadiri found it very hard to obtain repayment of much more than the money sums originally loaned. Instead, he bought most of his produce at the prevailing market price in Marmara.

Pastoral Kinsmen

Kadiri kept in touch with pastoral Fulani with whom he shared agnatic or affinal bonds and a common area of origin in Kano emirate. At least once a year, he would journey from Marmara to the base camp of the younger brother of his mother. One of this uncle's brothers was a Qur'anic *malam*, who spent Ramadan at his base camp and the rest of the year with Kadiri (a *malam* is an Islamic teacher, across a wide spectrum of learning and ritual practice). Similarly, Kadiri journeyed to greet Alhaji Habu, whose base camp was in western Kano near the border with southern Katsina. They were patrilateral cross cousins: Alhaji Habu's mother and Kadiri's father were senior and junior siblings.

The cattle which Kadiri reserved as long-term savings he kept with Alhaji Audu, whose base camp was not far from Marmara. Kadiri had given him in marriage the daughter of Kadiri's late senior sister. Alhaji Audu honored Kadiri as his father-in-law (*suruki*).

Household

In 1978, Kadiri headed one of the largest family farming units (*gandaye*, sing. *gandu*) in Marmara. The large number of his *gandu* workers enabled Kadiri to concentrate on trade during the farming season—one of the busiest periods of the produce trading year. In return, he provided them, their wives, and their children with two meals a day throughout the year. He paid their annual head tax (*haraji*), their marriage expenses, and made a large contribution at the naming ceremonies of their children.

Kadiri's senior wife (*uwar gida*) had been with him all his married life. She had given birth to his two surviving offspring. Apart from their son in *gandu*, they had a younger son whom Kadiri had sent to the far northeast of Nigeria to study the Qur'an. He returned in 1979 to join the *gandu*. Kadiri's senior wife also kept as her child the unmarried daughter of Kadiri's younger sister. For most of the year, his household also included a Qur'anic *malam*, his maternal kinsman, mentioned above. Kadiri's two junior wives (*amare*, sing. *amarya*) had left him in 1976.

At the 1977 harvest, Kadiri stored most of his output for sale after a price rise, and through 1978, he relied on current earnings in weekly trade to buy weekly food for his household. In this way, he hoped to postpone the sale of his stored output until much later, in the hungry month of August, when grain prices were around their peak.

The 1978 Trading Year

In 1978, Kadiri pursued two strategies in produce trading. He bought and sold produce in the weekly long-distance trade to Danbatta marketplace—"turnover trading," or trading across space. Second, he built up his stock of stored grain for sale after the interseasonal price rise—trading across time.

In the turnover trade to Danbatta, weekly expenditures tended to rise from postharvest into the farming season, and fall sharply thereafter.

Nevertheless, there was great fluctuation in trade expenditures from week to week. In fact, there was only a limited tendency for the trade revenue of one week to be invested in the trade expenditure of the subsequent week. Rather, the money available to Kadiri for weekly trade fluctuated with the amounts he borrowed from, and loaned out to, trading friends. The claims on Kadiri's trade revenue arising out of his various social relationships made it difficult for him to simply reinvest weekly revenue in the expansion of trade expenditure.

Another important reason for the lack of congruence between weekly trading revenue and subsequent weekly trade expenditure was that Kadiri was investing part of his weekly trade revenue in other spheres. To these I now turn.

Agricultural Investments in 1978

In the postharvest dry season of 1978, from January through April, Kadiri embarked on a dramatic expansion of his farmed land. He acquired some by purchase but most by pledge (*jingina*). At the subsequent harvest of 1978, Kadiri more than quadrupled his output over the preceding harvest of 1977.

His greatest single farming expense was the payment of part-time hired laborers. The total cost of this hired labor would have more than doubled if his family workforce had not been available. The money profit from guinea corn, his major crop, would have been eliminated. Thus, the profitability of his farming depended on the deployment of a large family workforce.

In working out Kadiri's profit margin from agriculture, I did not include the social costs of maintaining a *gandu*. (In fact, Kadiri met these costs from his trading.) Since *gandu* services were mainly confined to farm work, these costs ought theoretically to be included in farm expenditure before deriving the profit margin. The expense in 1978 of their food and tax alone would have been sufficient to eliminate the money profits from farming.

But Kadiri did not look at it that way. For the alternative—hired labor—was expensive and its supply uncertain. More deeply, Kadiri *assumed* the situation of a large household. It was the *basis from which* he reflected on the comparative returns of different endeavors.

Social Investments and Expenditures

We turn finally to Kadiri's social investments. In 1978, Kadiri undertook a major expansion of his household. In the postharvest dry season,

Kadiri's oldest son, Haruna, married the only daughter of a rich grain trader near Marmara. Tanko had long been Kadiri's trading friend. Having no male child, Tanko treated Haruna like a son. He gave him farmland. Later, at the guinea corn harvest, he began sending Haruna on trading expeditions to the distant marketplace of Sokoto. After several weeks of trading, he even gave Haruna *jali,* which Haruna returned before the farming season of 1979, when he stopped trading and farmed for Kadiri. Haruna's marriage catapulted him among the most fortunate young men of the hamlet, with more farmland than many household heads, trading capital, and a large trade turnover. Kadiri also benefited. Through his son, he made use of Tanko's produce brokers and wholesale buyers at the distant marketplace of Sokoto.

In August, Kadiri's young unmarried brother in *gandu,* Gambo, began courting a daughter of Audu, the tenth-largest land user in the hamlet. Kadiri fully supported the courtship. Audu had the biggest shop in Marmara. Besides opening opportunities for Gambo, the marriage would strengthen Kadiri's tie to Audu as a trading friend. It would also deepen Kadiri's relationship with Audu's kinship group, the oldest and richest in Marmara.

By the time of the marriage in early 1979, Kadiri had spent N600 on Gambo's marriage (as much as he had spent on the marriage of his son) and over N300 on a room for the couple. In hamlet terms, these were expensive marriages. But if Kadiri had failed in this regard, the young men would soon have left him. Equally, Kadiri saw these marriages as strategic alliances with successful families. His spending was social investment necessary for his farming and helpful to his trading.

In the midst of investments on trading, farming, and household, Kadiri was steadily pursuing a second wife for himself. On his weekly journeys to Danbatta, he courted a young divorcée (*bazawara*). After several months, he married her. But six weeks later, she fled in the night, taking all her goods, he said, "except the bed." When touring his fields, he complained to an old farming woman: "My only fault [*laifi*] is that she was to pound one *tiya* of corn a day. She didn't like this. But did I do wrong, since I gave her no other work? She has disappeared. Perhaps she is still in Marmara, but I do not know." Soon after the flight of his second wife, he began courting another young divorcée on his trading trips to Danbatta. Kadiri's desire for another wife filled his conversation. To one friend he said: "Isa, there are beautiful women in Danbatta, as many as you could possibly want to see."

The wedding to the second divorcée took place in September. Kadiri made arrangements for her to be joined by her daughter from a previous marriage and by her younger brother. The new wife was soon threatening to leave if he did not mend a leaking roof. Household repairs focused Kadiri's mind on a lavish scheme. He planned a large room for his younger brother and a set of rooms, one for his senior and one for his junior wife. The rooms were spacious, with high ceilings and cemented floors, the roofs finished and decorated with white chalk. Kadiri's own marriages and the rebuilding of his compound revealed a willingness to spend on beauty and a capacity for extravagance that I had not earlier suspected.

In 1978, Kadiri's total spending on marriages and house building was N1,732. This was considerably more than his total farming expenditures (around N1,170). It was also greater than the value of his average weekly turnover trade (some N500) and his grain stored for a price rise (N460). Household expansion remained at the center of his thinking about wealth (*dukiya*). By 1979, when he finished house building, it had absorbed some N800—equivalent to the commercial loan from his largest trading friend. Essentially, he had transferred a medium-term loan from his trading account to his house building "account"!

Economic Analysis

We have seen how Kadiri pursued a wide range of purposes. They were guided by a desire for multifaceted expansion. This required heavy borrowing as well as the use of savings. It also required careful calculation, a sense of timing, and the ability to manage a variety of human relationships. Reviewing 1978, Kadiri followed a particular strategy of borrowing, lending, and investment. It can only be understood in terms of the bonds of obligation, and the opportunities arising, between himself and his household, his patron, and his trading friends. Apart from the first three months of that year, when he still had sufficient savings to use as working capital, Kadiri's turnover trading was completely or largely reliant on borrowed funds. Since he bought family food from his balance in turnover trading, household provisions were also, ultimately, dependent on credit. Credit was also essential to his farming. During 1978, credit made it possible for him to:

- Divert his own investment funds from trade to farmland and to household marriages.
- Expand the scale of his turnover trade and, thus, the weekly profit margins available for farming.
- Postpone the sale of his own harvest output until grain prices had reached their peak in the postharvest period, thus maximizing its contribution to his working capital.
- Finance family food purchases.

Patronage and trading friendships enabled Kadiri to shift his own working capital into agriculture, marriages, and house building while maintaining the scale of his trading.

In light of the transformation that Kadiri had accomplished, how are we to assess his working capital at the end of 1978—the commercial value of his liquid assets? As December ended, his liquid assets consisted almost entirely of his own much-enlarged output of guinea corn. Kadiri treated his working capital, or *jali*, as investible in a range of social relations. As a result, he saw his brother's marriage payments, his house building, and the requests for loans from trading friends as charges on his *jali*. At the same time, he was able to make claims on the *jali* of others. Quite separately, Kadiri's intention as 1979 began was to reserve his harvest output as much as possible until the next farming season, when he would sell it to meet farming expenses.

These facets of his thinking were intimately connected. Because he was giving short-term credit to some, he was more likely to attract it from others. And though harvest grain was convertible into money, at least partly they were classified as belonging to separate spheres that were subject to different claims. Money was more liable to diffuse social claims than was harvest grain. It made sense to reserve harvest grain and generate funds for trading through the web of credit relationships.

The value of Kadiri's liquid assets, or working capital, at harvest provides only a suggestive guide to his trading and farming capacity: its real measure was his ability to borrow. The readiness of others to lend him money stemmed from their complex assessment of his trustworthiness, trading skill, and willingness to take on responsibilities for others—in a word, his *hali* (character). If anything, spending on marriages and house building increased his moral stature as a man "of responsibilities" (*mai hidima*)—and therefore, the sympathetic attraction of potential creditors. The complex of personal relationships through which he worked enabled him to break through the limits of economic scale set by his own investment funds and by the human resources of his immediate household.

His Own Voice

My descriptive analysis of a year in Kadiri's life has combined my observations of Kadiri's actions, his own statements, and the observations of others. In its construction, I originally paid particular attention to his actions, and to my own very careful calculation of the money flows between different spheres of his activity. Yet the reader will have seen that in pushing forward the main character of my story, I have found it necessary to invoke his speech. It furnished me with clues, though it was hardly at the center of my analytical attention. But now, I briefly take the reader through my memories of that year so as to foreground the character's voice.

I do not assume that what I will call Kadiri's "thinking"—what he said to himself, and what he said to others—determined his actions. But what is palpable below is that Kadiri was keenly aware of two realities—that he was constantly making plans (from short term to long term), and that there was a discrepancy between his current planning and future reality (or the extent to which his plans were realized). Seen thus, the retrospective seamlessness and coherence of the analytical account disappear. We are left, rather, with a sense of the precariousness of fulfillment, and even of life itself. For continuity among the rural Hausa is itself more uncertain than among those of us who live inside a Western society: even strong men like Kadiri could be felled at any time by disease, as could his household workers or his main creditors. This leaves me with the sense that Kadiri had pulled off a very individual achievement. It involved hard work and, through paying off one loan by contracting another, a kind of sleight of hand. It enacted generosity to others both inside and outside his kin group *and* an effort to appropriate part of the surplus of others (by moneylending to farmers in the preharvest "hungry" period). His achievement was complex.

When he was talking with men whom he respected, in the entrance room to his warehouse or on our tours of his farmland, Kadiri's thoughts were seldom directly addressed to a specific interlocutor; rather, a querulousness barely below the surface of his sentences revealed a kind of shared public meditation on how life was passing by. That curious sense of the need to hurry, and the risk of stumbling, while barely having the time to greet the ships that pass in the night.

In February 1978, at the largest weekly marketplace in the vicinity of Marmara, Kadiri was reviewing with his patron, Alhaji Zubeiru, the relative prices of guinea corn in different marketplaces over a wide area. At one stage he turned aside to me and began talking about something very different. At the time, he was thinking of taking a divorcée in Marmara for his second wife. She was keen on him, but he "had not touched her because [he was] interested in marrying her." To my surprise, he was anxious for my opinion of her. I mumbled lamely that I thought she was "good." This drew the terse reply: "There are many kinds of 'good.'"

In early March, after listing the farms that he had recently acquired, Kadiri told me that he had the intention (*aniya,* with the connotation of "determination" [Abraham 1962]) to farm on a large scale once the rains set in during May. His costs of farming, he said, would be very high because of the need for hired labor in weeding—and without sight of any gain until the harvest in December.

In April, between two weekly trips to his distant outlet market, Kadiri was in trouble (*wahala*) because all of his trade revenue from the preceding trip was loaned out to men as diverse as a poor butcher and a rich farmer. One of them was a small retailer to whom he would lend money regularly on Monday so that this retailer could buy kola nuts, for repayment on Friday after he had sold them. Because of his lending, Kadiri only found money to buy grain by borrowing from others. A week later, he had again loaned out all his weekly trade revenue to an almost entirely different set of men. He even had to borrow from me to buy food grain for his family, until the loans were repaid on Friday.

Kadiri could be honest about times of cash abundance as well as times of shortage. In May, he exclaimed that he had lots of money but few suppliers. He explained how farmers were "hiding" their remaining grain from the previous year's harvest, until such time as they could assess the likely size of the forthcoming harvest. In June, having planted and weeded the seventh-largest acreage in Marmara, he said with satisfaction: "He who has money will add to it. For example, to farm it is necessary to spend. If I did not trade in guinea corn at N800 a week, I could not obtain the money I need to farm." By August, however, Kadiri was angered at the failure of most of the farmer-debtors in his preharvest moneylending of the year before to repay him with either grain or money interest, and worried about the future. Having cultivated a large amount of farmland, his investment funds were finished, and he was deeply dependent on borrowed funds.

Around this time, Kadiri offered a sharp review of his recent life: "Two years ago, I had *jali* of N2,000. I spent N400 on the first marriage of my son, which failed. This year I spent N600 on his second marriage. I spent N200 marrying a woman in the dry season, who left me. I spent N400 on a plot in Malumfashi town, and N400 obtaining farms by purchase and by pledge. By the second month of this rainy season, the N2,000 was finished." Note that in saying this, he accepted the overall priority given to marriages in the use of his investment funds.

We know now that he found the money for continued trading, and paid back the loan of his patron, Alhaji Zubeiru. This left him with sufficient funds for trade. But by the end of the guinea corn harvest in December, Kadiri again faced a cash shortage: "No money! I have given my *jali* to other traders. House building and the marriage of my younger brother—these have taken my money." Notice again the prior claim of family responsibilities and trading friendships on his investible cash reserves.

In early 1979, Kadiri expanded on his recent loans to smaller traders in the hinterland, and said that in return, they stored produce for him. Then he laughed and added: "Just as I give them *rance*, so they give *rance* to others." He offered a revealing summary of his recent past: "For four years, I have not postponed a marriage in my house—for myself, for my son, and for my brother Gambo. If not for this, I would have gone east [to Mecca, on the pilgrimage]." Note that he did not say, "I would have had more money to buy farms or hire laborers." In this case study, we have seen how expenditure on farmland and hired labor was embedded in the consolidation and expansion of his household and the obligations of patronage and trading friendship, within a framework of Muslim belief.[1]

Reflecting on the Self-Reflections of a Hausa Grain Trader

A Structural Analysis?

On the surface, Bourdieu's logic of practice might seem to provide a complete understanding of Abdulkadiri's actions, so let me begin by exploring a structural analysis in Bourdieu's footsteps. The objective of grain trading was the acquisition of wealth in two interconnected senses—the specific accumulation of farmland and the labor power to work it; and the broad-based acquisition of "wealth" (*dukiya*). This latter included material assets of varying degrees of liquidity (from money to productive equipment); and human assets incorporated in social relationships of varying degrees of density (from household kinsmen to trading friends). Borrowing and lending were essential to the process of wealth acquisition.

The most interesting fact about commercial credit is that enormous sums were circulating in the rural areas without interest being charged. Whenever I questioned traders, lenders, or borrowers about "interest" or "profit" (both are *riba* in Hausa), the injunctions of Islam were never mentioned. The basic reason for the absence of a rate of interest is that farmer-traders were subject to such fluctuating claims on their own resources that they could not guarantee the continuous reinvestment of borrowed funds over a specific period. Since borrowers and lenders were subject to the same set of social pressures, it made no sense to charge interest on loans. Their attention was rather focused on a concept of *mutuality*. Through patronage or trading friendship, they aimed by lending to generate a return flow of services or money credit in the longer term. Also, they were aware that commercial borrowing helped them to surmount the fluctuating pressure of social claims. This realization supported a sense of obligation to redistribute resources: borrowers lent money to persons poorer than themselves.

The case study of Kadiri reveals the existence of a flourishing "capital" market in rural southern Katsina—"capital" in the restricted sense of funds for investment in activity that generates income. This market was guided by two principles. First, borrowing proceeds through personal relationships governed by an ethic of reciprocal obligation. Second, these obligations make possible long-term wealth acquisition, but limit the rate at which investment funds can be continuously reinvested.

The case study suggests that the global amount circulating in rural trade as short-term and medium-term credit was much greater than the amount of long-term credit. Thus, trading friendship was more important than patronage in financing the rural grain marketing system, and more generally, the reproduction of social relations.

This conclusion by itself upsets previous analyses that emphasize patron-client relations. It displaces hierarchy—with the concomitant necessity of obedience—with mutuality—and the consequent negotiation of agreements between men of at least similar social and economic standing in such a way as to implant trust. Without trust, money would be neither loaned nor repaid. Focusing on the horizontal lines of negotiation, we can analyze the ways in which the activities of farmer-traders are constructed: they act within a matrix of pressures emerging from Hausa history, ecology, and economy. First, it is imperative for any farmer-trader to finance the marriages of his subordinate kin in order to maintain the family workforce. Second, the imperative to loan out money to other farmer-traders at the same or at a lower socioeconomic level is necessitated by a "disposition" toward diffuse generosity, without which the circulation of investment funds might decline or dry up.

Seen thus, we might follow Bourdieu in recognizing that a local belief in the "moral imperative" to give to one's household or one's trading friends is a misrecognition of what is actually a structural necessity. When Kadiri invoked the "ethic" of reciprocal obligations, he was doing no more than deploying or increasing his symbolic capital, in order to expand his usable networks or social capital (as in Bourdieu [1980] 1990: 112–21). Hence, a full descriptive analysis conveys his habitus—the system of durable dispositions that generate and organize practices and their representations, without any presupposition of a conscious aiming at ends by the actors involved (Bourdieu [1980] 1990: 53).

In these terms, it would seem unscientific to endow a character like Abdulkadiri with "choice" or "decision making." Even what might appear to be his crucial initial decision—to join the circle of farmer-traders in the first place—could be more clearly construed as *a change in social identity*. Kadiri was "undergoing" a change in identity. From being a trader still rooted in the niche of a sedentary Fulani without cattle but with many pastoral kinsmen, he was shifting to the niche of a Hausa farmer-trader. In the terms of Bourdieu's habitus, Kadiri, rather than "deciding," was "responding to" a distinctive set of pressures. Not having the livestock of his pastoral kinsmen, he first emigrated from the Kano closely settled zone to the (then) more land-abundant and fertile region of southern Katsina; and over the subsequent eighteen years came to the belated realization that neither the emotional attachments of home nor the possibility of large-scale cattle trading were open to him. Rather than a process of "free" choices, his deepening involvement in Hausa farmer-trading was predictably inevitable. It was followed, after a time lag, by a change in his self-consciousness.

This kind of structural analysis—in terms of material necessity and the concomitant change in identity—could be rendered even more sophisticated, along the lines of Bourdieu's precision in comparing different marriage strategies with individuals' precise locations inside the same lineage (Bourdieu [1980] 1990: 162–99). Thus, we could explore the ways in which Kadiri drew upon his different identities as upon a repertoire of available practices, tapping sometimes his pastoral affiliations and sometimes his trading networks in order to augment his working capital. Any description of Kadiri's "moral" attitudes becomes thereby a gloss on the behavior needed to advance his socioeconomic position. The explanatory advantage of an analysis invoking the logic of practice is that it shows how, once Kadiri had accomplished a certain oblique movement from cattle trading to produce trading, his own lack of capital committed him to further actions. In these terms, our focus of attention with regard to his self-reflection becomes singularly pointed. For we can see his self-recognition of the ambition to farm on a large scale as an articulation of aims that are perfectly consistent with the most likely path to "wealth" (*dukiya*) or "fortune" (*arziki*) by a man in his *specific* niche of a broader local system of dispositions. In peering upward and outward from Abdulkadiri at the whole social apparatus whirring above and about him, we seem to see that it contains and explains him.

Problems with the Logic of Practice

And yet, a structural analysis based in the logic of practice fails to capture three dimensions of Abdulkadiri's activity. *First, the unpredictability of his search for beauty.* The pursuit of a second wife absorbed time and money. Given his age and that of the women whom he sought as a second wife, this cannot be understood as the desire to acquire a fertile woman who would bear him sons to be contingents in his workforce, or daughters to be pawns in strategic games of alliance building. More deeply, it expressed the desire for a woman, attractive to him, for company and pleasure. Even more economically extravagant, and wholly unexpected, was his rebuilding and expansion of his household compound. *Second, a capacity to dream of a future different from his present—that is, an imagination at work.* Of course, the ability to transform dreams into reality involved the planning of his resources to achieve particular goals. And yet, although "planning" is a kind of instrumental rationality (arguably subsumable under the logic of practice), it cannot analytically disguise the more general endeavor to make concrete a visioning of the future. *Third, his sense of the disjunction, or discrepancy, between dream and reality, between present planning and its future realization, between a relatively certain today and a merely possible tomorrow.* Put differently, he understood the precariousness of human dreams.

Some of this uncertainty is captured by the popular Hausa term for a wealthy man—a man "of fortune" or "of luck" (*mai arziki*). Polly Hill drew on the economic ethnographies of rural Hausaland by M.G. Smith (1955) and Guy Nicolas (1964) to stress that *arziki* incorporates the idea of life as a game of chance that some win and others lose (Hill 1972: 185–86). It denotes the highly individual quality of good fortune, which is here today and gone tomorrow. It cannot be transmitted from its holder to his children. It conveys the sense that men are subject in uncontrollable ways to natural and market forces. This term condenses the multiple meanings conveyed in the Hausa experience of a competitive, capricious rural economy and the unfathomable quality of the power of God (*ikwan Alla*).

If we dwell on these three dimensions of Kadiri's activity as a farmer-trader and head of household, we begin to realize that Bourdieu's structuralism can show how, once the dreaming, imaginative being begins to thread his way through the prickly forest of social relations, he advances step by uncertain step. What structural analysis cannot account for is the existence of a dreaming being *in the first place*. Furthermore, there is nothing in Bourdieu's account of practice that constructs a satisfying mental picture of that contrary urge to extravagance or excess, as when Kadiri blew the loan of his major trading friend on the beauty of a new house rather than on farming or trading. That leap whereby the main character in my story reached out for something not yet real, which he intended with determination (Hausa: *aniya*) to conjure into existence. That picturing of a different and more beautiful future fueled by complex emotions—physical desires for sexual and aesthetic satisfaction, the wish for the security of household laughter, the nostalgic memory of the wives who had left him and the parents who had died back home, before he had time to return and embrace (*rungume*) them. The sad, crazy magnificence of a character who cannot even follow methodically the role in a script of his own devising because, full of longing for a future and nostalgia for a past, he breaks out of it to dance on his own.

So I am brought to reconsider Kadiri's self-reflection. I would suppose that Kadiri, not unlike myself, could at certain times, despite reasons for bitterness at plans blocked or destroyed, be buoyed up by what I will call "humor and delight"—a pleasure unsolicited that opens its mouth in surprise, and then begins to laugh. There was a strange moment, one morning after his return from Danbatta marketplace the previous night, when I found Kadiri laughing out loud in the entrance room (*zaure*) of his warehouse. He recalled his memory of the day before when, killing free moments in that distant marketplace, he stopped to watch *yan daudu*, the transvestite bisexual men of Hausaland, as they were dancing. He went on and on about the grace and humor of their movements. His intonation seemed to suggest that—though sinful in the scriptures—they were beautiful. It was laughter of perplexity—even of thanks.

As I have said, so often Kadiri's speech was not really directed at some other person but seemed more like a public mulling. It was more like talking to himself in the presence of others. Such moments in fieldwork caught me by surprise, because in them, Kadiri seemed to be like me. There was the sense of cultural distance collapsing:

> If we should weep when clowns put on their show,
> If we should stumble when musicians play,
> . . . Will Time say nothing but I told you so?
> If I could tell you, I would let you know. (Auden 1979: 110–11)

Kadiri's self-reflection was more than the expression of habitus, an ideological emanation of material desires reflecting psychobiology, on the one hand, and a specifiable location in the complex of social relations, on the other. Abdulkadiri was also a being caught *between and among*:

- Claims from his wives, brothers, children, and other close kin.
- Claims from the Muslim trading community to which he belonged.
- The pressures of personal desire in a polygynous context.
- The contrary pulls of Fulani and Hausa, old Kano and new southern Katsina, identities.
- His conflicting senses of an aristocratic pedigree and the knowledge that, here and now, he was economically insecure and struggling.

Hence the querulousness I claim to have detected in his tone of voice. Such a being, being between, is somehow aware that he is distinct from the present spheres he seeks to manage, is disjunct from the future that he tries to conjure into reality.

Seen thus, it is difficult to separate "acting" from "thinking," which I earlier defined as the talking that one does to oneself or to others. Human action is the putting into bodily movement of wishes and dreams dogged by worry. Human, that is, mindful, action is a process of self-change that sometimes involves self-expansion.

Here, there is little space to offer a comparison of Kadiri's actions with those of others in Marmara. I will simply say that the majority of villagers enacted their self-change by combining farming with a comparatively risk-free off-farm occupation, in order to expand the number of their domestic and extradomestic bonds; in contrast, farmer-traders took more risks in more milieus. This broad comparison seeks to impart one respect in which villagers differed—in the riskiness of their self-expansion. Among the Hausa, to expand oneself was to make greater demands on others for mutually reinforcing assistance; it was also to expose oneself more to the demands of others.

In a sense, Kadiri was turning himself into a cause that initiates effects. Thus, he became by his actions a part of the "structure" that constrains, or puts pressure on, people, and which people take into account when they initiate actions. In other words, the structure is mobile. It is continuously changing because it is full of initiatory individual actions. In contrast to Bourdieu, who claimed to have transcended the analytical opposition between structure and agency, my reflections on this one farmer-trader suggest, not some synthesis, but rather a reworded solution in favor of agency. This is not weak agency in Bourdieu's sense of "social change," whereby in any society one action induces an array of consequent actions that can be specified predictively given adequate knowledge. Rather, it is strong agency, what Terry Evens calls "self-conduction" (Evens 2008: 114). Self-conduction by numerous inter-actors generates a continuously changing structure—either slowly or rapidly. "Structure" is the assemblage of interacting actions, where by "action" is meant the human translation of dreams and wishes into bodily movement, or some other kind of previously nonexistent reality, while being dogged by anxiety and failure.

Since structural fixity is a chimera, it makes no sense to analytically counterpose structure and agency in the first place. "Structure" as the assemblage of inter-acting actions is shot through with agency and hence mobile. The main limits on the speed of change are: first, that the actions which people author vary in the extent to which and the ways in which they take into account the total assemblage of previous actions; second, the relative sanctional power of the different interacting individuals, groups, or classes gives individuals, groups, and classes highly differential scope for maneuver; and last, people tend to classify the assemblage of previous actions in terms of "what ought to be done" and "what ought to be avoided," and this classification affects the degree to which they follow or depart from previous actions.

The Hausa Notions of "Value" and Agency

I have argued for a strong construction of "agency" in my reflections on the self-reflection of one trader. This still leaves open a rather different question: can a *Hausa* sense of agency be connected to local notions of "value"? The rural Hausa among whom I lived attributed good character (*kyan hali*) or bad character (*mugun hali*) to individuals largely on the basis of their willingness or unwillingness to help those who asked for help. There was also a tendency to ascribe socioeconomic misfortune to the consequences of bad character. Now, this would appear to create a paradox in their thinking. For they often said to me that the will or power of God (*ikwan Alla*) decreed the success or failure, life and death, of every person. For example, while they valued hard work, the outcome of effort was in the hands of God—consistent with their idea of "fortune" or "luck" (*arziki*).

They not only said this, they felt it. I once returned to the village just after a much-liked man had been killed by a bullock that had kicked him down a well while he was watering the beast. As I arrived, I saw men sitting in silence, sadness streaming from their eyes. On hearing the news, I started exclaiming: "How awful!" Immediately everyone vociferously, almost angrily, shouted me down: "It's the will of God!" Surely, however, there is a contradiction between their belief in divine determination and their attribution of responsibility to individuals for their goodness or badness. There is no doubt about the *blame* that they assigned to a person for his bad character. This logically implies a belief in self-conduction: the person could have done otherwise than he did. How can this be made consistent with their belief in the pervasive will of God?

I would argue that there are two ways out of this paradox. The first concerns the Hausa sense of personal culpability. It focused on a person's attitude to others. While goodness or badness was indeed ascribed to actions, moral description concentrated at least as much on the overall character, temperament, or disposition (*hali*) of a person. In consequence, the Hausa were interested in a person's motivations in committing an act. This implies a very introspective concern with intention. It allows for the possibility that intention constitutes the domain of "choice," even if the effects of choice in the world are determined by God. Thus, it was possible for them to *both* believe in the divine determination of effects, and approve or disapprove of the character (*hali*) of others. This is a very interior sense of agency.

A second consideration can be connected to this argument. In conversation, when people attributed good or bad character to a person, they were viewing the person's actions over time—one could say that they were judging a lifetime. This suggests that "choice" is not necessarily apparent in any one action, but is more obviously manifested in the person's striving over time. Striving over time implies that a person is making an effort to align their actions in a certain direction. At the same time, it allows that often, short-term action goes against long-term intention. This is the notion of a *trajectory* of life. A trajectory is viewed by persons other than the actor as a sequence of actions, but at its heart lies the intention (Hausa: *aniya*) of the actor over a stretch of time to translate wishes into bodily movement, with consequence for others.

In conclusion, my discussion implies that what was given value (Hausa: *daraja*) among the rural Hausa with whom I lived was, more than things (such as money, cattle, or a large house) or sorts of social relation (like a pleasurable and fertile marriage or benevolent patronage), *a kind of action and comportment directed toward meeting the needs of others.* There was a Hausa term that, when applied to a person in local speech, singled out his/her value—*hidima*: responsibility shouldered. Dictionaries actually translate *hidima* simply as "serving a person" (Abraham 1962) or "service, administration" (Robinson 1925). But in southern Katsina, it seemed to have the added connotation of "responsibility" and was used especially in reference to a range of family responsibilities—particularly the responsibility to provide oneself and one's children with marriage partners, and to provide for their other needs.

To stress, as Bourdieu has done, the material referents enclosed in local statements of "value" risks losing the sense of tension and dilemma that can invade a person when he compares the various possible actions that he might undertake. Much has been written about giving. We also need to remember that individuals often *give up*—things or opportunities (even with a resentment that must remain hidden)—for the sake of another. Thus, pinning "value" entirely on observable objects or relations risks losing that sense of silent forgoing.

Returning finally to the activity of farmer-traders in Hausaland, Bourdieu argued that local moral rules are the misrecognition of material self-interest, so that "honor," for example, (or *hidima* among the Hausa, I would suppose) is a self-deceiving representation. Thus, the cultivation of personal ties is a technique for overcoming labor scarcity, or capital shortage, in the interest of material accumulation (Bourdieu [1980] 1990: 111). This would imply that "social values"—collectively held principles—exist mainly as verbal generalizations concerning strategic interest incorporated in observable behavior. In contrast, I have argued that the Hausa social value which gives priority to personal relationships is a moral belief. It is an inner mental state. Farmer-traders reflect on their moral beliefs, although I can only infer to their inner states from verbal discourse and observable action. This social value has causal efficacy, for it channels the actions of individuals insofar as they work through their inner tensions in such a way as to implement the value. To that extent, moral beliefs constrain and even deflect the achievement of purely material self-interests. Farmer-traders like Kadiri were very conscious of this. Thus, it is neither obscure nor tautological to say that farmer-traders accumulate personal relationships because that is what they value.

Final Thoughts

Throughout this chapter, I have sought to avoid chasing after an "experience" of choice, or an "ethnographic moment" of decision. On the contrary, I hold that it is logically impossible for the ethnographer to substantiate the insubstantial (Clough 2006: 278–81). I argue for an immaterial—and in this specific respect, a spiritual—dimension to self-conduction and moral reality. Yet in doing so, I seek to persuade the reader by the same rule of method with which we puzzle over tangible experience. Thus, my words and sentences have to be consistent with more of the evidence than alternative explanations.

In reflecting upon time, we become aware of moments in our lives that we remember afterward as a parting of the ways, when we took one path with huge consequences. We are also aware of long periods when we pursue one path doggedly, even resentfully, and stumblingly, so that, with increasing confusion, we despair of our having any agency at all—like a fish on a spear, thrashing from the pain but unable to find its origin. I do not wish to downplay the difference between these experiences of time, the one classically momentary (and remembered as momentous), the other more like a *striving over time*. In both, however, it is difficult to specify mental mechanisms of decision making. Perhaps, then, what the language of choosing or deciding does is gloss an awareness of self-conduction, but in such a way as to render time into a sequence of discrete, momentary points. We should also consider the possibility that when intention is persistent, consistency of purpose leads to gradual self-change over a long period of time. The trajectory of a person's life cannot be described without reference to his or her intentions.

Although the temporal dimension of choice is difficult to specify, the sense of self-conduction is ineluctable. Because I am aware of being a being suspended among present pressures and future possibilities, I am conscious that the self translates possible futures into an embodied present. Pervasive in this sense of self-suspension is the tension between self-desire and other-regard (Evens 2008: 128, 296–97). In a sentence: it is partly through my consciousness of responsibility to the other that I become aware of self-conduction. By my reflections on the self-reflection of one Hausa trader, Abdulkadiri, I have tried to persuade the reader that in what I call "action"—the translation of wishes or dreams into bodily movement or some other kind of previously nonexistent reality—the self becomes most tensely conscious of its difference with its body, of the demands upon it by other selves in like condition, and of the need to decide—what to do, and how to do it.

Notes

1. For further exploration of the connections between Islamic values and the moral nature of the economy, see Clough (2003: 15–16, 2009: 598–607, 2014: 54–58, 334–40).

References

Abraham, Roy Clive. 1962. *Dictionary of the Hausa Language.* London: University of London Press.

Auden, Wystan. 1979. *Selected Poems.* Boston and London: Faber and Faber.

Bourdieu, Pierre. (1980) 1990. *The Logic of Practice*. Trans. Richard Nice. Cambridge: Polity Press.

———. (1982) 1990. *In Other Words: Essays Toward a Reflexive Sociology*. Trans. Matthew Adamson. Cambridge: Polity Press.

Clough, Paul. 2003. "Polygyny and the Rural Accumulation of Capital: Testing a Model Based on Continuing Research in Northern Nigeria." *Etnofoor* 16, no. 1: 5–29.

———. 2006. "'Knowledge in Passing': Reflexive Anthropology and Religious Awareness." *Anthropological Quarterly* 79, no. 2: 261–84.

———. 2009. "The Impact of Rural Political Economy on Gender Relations in Islamizing Hausaland, Nigeria." *Africa* 79, no. 4: 595–613.

———. 2014. *Morality and Economic Growth in Rural West Africa: Indigenous Accumulation in Hausaland*. New York and Oxford: Berghahn Books.

Evens, T. M. S. 2008. *Anthropology as Ethics: Nondualism and the Conduct of Sacrifice*. New York and Oxford: Berghahn Books.

Hill, Polly. 1972. *Rural Hausa: A Village and a Setting*. Cambridge: Cambridge University Press.

Nicolas, Guy. 1964. "Etude de marches en pays Hausa (Republique du Niger): Documents Ethnographiques." University of Bordeaux (cyclostyled).

Robinson, Charles Henry. 1925. *Dictionary of the Hausa Language*. Cambridge: Cambridge University Press.

Smith, Michael Garfield. 1955. *The Economy of Hausa Communities of Zaria*. Colonial Research Studies 16. London: HMSO.

Paul Clough is professor of anthropology in the Department of Anthropological Sciences, Faculty of Arts, University of Malta.
Email: paul.clough@um.edu.mt

$\sim\!$ **9** $\sim\!\!\!\!\!\!\!\!\!\!\!\!$

Reflexivity in Intersubjective and Intercultural Borderlinking

René Devisch

Reflexivity, extimacy, and the borderlinking that this enables are the key concepts of this chapter. The numerous shuttles undertaken for four decades between the Democratic Republic of Congo, other African countries, and my native country of Belgium have triggered a form of autoethnographical reflexivity. Reflexivity enables me, in this chapter, to revisit the development of my anthropological research focus and theoretical interests. In this study, I have come to favor the experiential and intersubjective phenomenology of Merleau-Ponty (1964) coupled with some psychoanalytic insights from Jacques Lacan and Bracha Ettinger (2006) to trace the mutual affect between the anthropologist and the host group. Starting in the first section, the reflexivity revives some memories of my childhood and youth—I was born in early 1944—and echoes my rural Catholic society's positioning in the Belgian landscape of sociocultural othering. I particularly refer to an alienating dynamics at play in the barely conscious transferential exposure of my Flemish-speaking rural society that was blatantly subordinated and otherized by the local French-speaking bourgeois class. The revisit bears in mind my people's way of being and adjusting to adverse otherness, strongly marked by affects beyond wording and unnarratable family histories, and riveted on the propensity of things, the in-between and not-yet-there, as well as life's shadow sides. At play is an intersubjective and intercorporeal mindfulness particularly alert to affliction and trauma. This attentiveness resonates with my ascendant family's durable inscription in the traumatic experience that their generation had, first, during World War I (1914–18) in their home region adjacent to the battle zone and, later, during the German occupation in World War II (1940–44). Moreover, in my memory, the largely unspoken but all the more insistent and passionate family devotion toward life in "doing one's utmost best as a family member" was routinely revived at the family shrine, namely, the marble chimney in the common room.

The second section looks at how the family habitus informed my co-resonance as university student—successively in philosophy and anthropology—in Kinshasa, 1965–71, with the colonial trauma of the Congolese, who were colonized until 1960 by my Belgian nation of origin. As anthropologist from 1971 to 1974, I was welcomed as empathetic and coimplicating participant in the lives of my yiYaka-speaking hosts in southwestern Congo and for annual research stays of some three weeks from 1986 to 2003 in Kinshasa's shantytowns. I was seeking to provide a "com-passionate" and truthful rendition of their worldview and cults of affliction in line with the perspective of their culture and the cultural genius of the subjects. I remained particularly sensitive to the intergenerational memory traces of family or colonial trauma. These were lurking behind the unspeakable and unmentionable, or at the border of words. My peculiar attention was also drawn to the ritual devices seeking to disclose the indefinable or unthought-in-thought.

The concluding section argues how in my eager attention to afflicted people and to the etiology of affliction as well as to healing and appeasement, both the yiYaka-speaking and Flemish-speaking people strongly resonate through me. My "com-passionate" disposition, inspired by my family habitus, toward co-resonating with yiYaka-speaking people's sensitivity thus echoes and indirectly underscores, in a manner surprisingly similar to a looping movement, the look I have been casting back for a few years on my parental Flemish culture while adopting a quintessentially Yaka perspective. Such bifocal attentiveness designates yet again my sense of wonderment at the unthought-in-thought and the holes in the memory of a family or a group that is intercorporeally and intersubjectively shared "here" and "over there." I argue that extimacy is at the core of the intercultural anthropological encounter.

Subjectivity and Family Trauma of War

The main thrust of this first part of the chapter is to revive and echo my feelings and modes of intercorporeality and intersubjectivity in the days of my youth as well as my relation to the topic of affliction. It is paired with a scrutiny of a lingering but barely voiced family and collective history of war and language traumas that, in a first step, I would frame as follows: what does speech expressed in either one's mother tongue or in the adopted language of the colonizing other really mean for and among Flemish-speaking people in Belgium? Approaching such a question hinges on complex issues of both my root identity and the alienating subjectification of the Flemish-speaking people of my breed in the mirror of the Francophone bourgeois other, moreover reawakened by the burden of war. I venture to depict this othering or alienation as effecting some extimacy—a notion coined by Lacan—or alienating shadowy side and unconscious otherness at the very core or intimacy of self. The extimate thus acts as some alien and largely unconscious identity element nestling in and somehow unseating one's innermost self.

Extimacy Grounded in the Sociocultural Field of My Youth in the 1950s and Early 1960s

The uprooting and subjection of Flemish-speaking society was as unsettling for my people as the traumatic experience of the two world wars. On the one hand, it was not until the age of around twelve, through stories of the family and in particular regarding the class divides among Flemish people, that I became aware of what was extimate to my identity as a Flemish speaker. I then started to sense out what was both intimately exceeding and retroactively threatening the core of my identity while provoking uncertainty. I would coin the extimate in my youth as revolving around the following very powerful incentive, short-falling by definition, from within the family group. The family interpellation for "doing one's utmost best as family member, hence as Flemish collective" was abiding in the name of the family's most intimate interiority. I refer here to its ethic of desire, clinging to bare life's survival (see below) above and against the semblance and pretension associated with the Francophone or Francophile bourgeois class in the local society. In my Flemish-speaking milieu, the bourgeois were perceived as eroding bare life by subduing it to a display of privileges and the mimicry of distinction (in the sense of Pierre Bourdieu). But, from the bourgeois perspective, the subjection of Flemish language and its speakers was in the modernist civilizational endeavor part of a remoralization of and by the Belgian nation-state. This arrogation was granting the Francophone a superior state in cultural evolution—because bearing the language premised on Enlightenment rationalism, along the lines of Napoleon's instigation when he created the French Republic (de Certeau, Dominique, and Revel 2004; Von Busekit 1998).

On the other hand, the memory of the war was also very much constitutive of the moral landscape at play in my family and my people when in 1956–57 I began my secondary boarding school at the lyceum in the small town of Veurne. This town was situated close to the North Sea and the French border, in a region of a homogenous indigenous Flemish-speaking population of West Flanders, at that time devoid of industrial development. During this time I joined the KSA Youth Movement consisting mainly of youngsters from Catholic school background. This movement was founded and sponsored by the Catholic Church in an attempt to counter nationalist Flemish leanings in the young generation. I hail from peasant origins and was brought up on a farm. I stood as a postwar witness to the passage my parents initiated from halfway through the 1950s toward a truly modern agricultural enterprise. The farm was situated on the border with France, just a dozen kilometers away from the North Sea. During the night we could see the lighthouse in the port of Dunkirk. The farm stood on a piece of land in Flanders bordering the county of Artois in France. Up to the seventeenth century, this county was joined to Flanders by the old chivalrous nobility, the Catholic Church, and Flemish language and culture. In that border region of Artois in northern France, numerous persons of my parents' generation spoke Flemish, whereas my cousins and nieces over there indulged in the French language adopted by the French state and thus spoken in schools.

The national frontier or border zone was an enigmatic value-laden horizon in my imaginary as a child. During my childhood, on-foot smuggling of farm produce and technology, tobacco, and strong alcohol was rampant. In my imaginary, it turned that frontier into a hunting ground and courageous survival struggle: residents such as my father would help small smugglers who walked by to avoid getting detected by the somewhat rapacious surveillance of the Belgian or French customs officers. In my childhood fantasies and memories, the national border zone thus constituted a driving force of my "family novel" and people's ingenuity and boldness. In the family novel, the border space with France also featured the tension my parents experienced in their own childhood between the Flemish language spoken at home and the colonizing French language then spoken at the secondary school, in well-off bourgeois circles in Flanders, and in the higher ranks of state, church, judiciary, and army. It was this colonial apprehension that they passed onto us, their children. In addition, the national border zone did cast my mind back to family traumas caused by the two world wars that tragically ruined my paternal and maternal family, killing several members, and whose postwar popular vendettas left many moral wounds. Many of my great-uncles and/or uncles were on the battle-field in their native areas either in World War I or World War II: several found death there, or were left incapacitated when the Germans blew over the notorious mustard gas.

The impact of the wars has not stopped living through the generations in my native Flemish society. In the 1950s and 1960s, as young people it was hard for us to remain indifferent to the profession of faith launched by the Frontline Movement, which, reacting to the horrors of World War I, has sought for decades to mobilize Flemish people's consciousness. From 1916 on, in the trenches, it sought to reconnect the Flemish soldiers with their "people's forces" and moral "pride of heart" and to remobilize in them ennobled manners "because women and girls do expect you to safeguard a pure and Christian Flanders." Thus, it was at the front that the dream for the "new order" for Flanders was born. It was a dream marked by "romantic idealism devoid of calculation, hypocrisy or compromise and free from selfishness, and drawing from vital forces, the community spirit and the idea of revival."

In the family, war memory sought to restore some human face to the soldiers the war horror had reduced to complete exhaustion, dehumanization, or annihilation. It was through photographs of family members in military uniforms or bombed farm buildings, now rebuilt, and, more enigmatically, through scraps of conversation with peers that my father transmitted indirectly to us this memory of faith in the inner forces of persons passionately committed to their family and homeland. In this way, my father was actually recounting the mourning process in which his generation was forced to surreptitiously engage. He thereby voiced a collective search to metabolize the baffling humiliation the soldiers had undergone at the hands of the officers, all commanding in French—the language of distinction. On their side, people's loyalty to Flemish language was their affectionate way to honor the blood of so many Flemish soldiers—at the least some 15 percent more than Francophone soldiers—in the 1914–18 trench warfare. My father made us sentient to this effort of conscience and the inevitable attacks of melancholy resulting from the phantoms of the missing persons—and all the monstrous, unthinkable, and undisclosable of the inundated and blood-stained war front. All this fed the dream for revival in the interwar period. Let us recall here the very diverse forms of idealism and social and political activisms that crystallized in memory of the many who lost their lives for their people and their soil. In Flanders starting in the 1920s, the important linguistic reforms in the schools and gradually in the civil service gave force and flesh to this woeful collective memory and mourning of the Flemish-speaking people.

Memories, images, and dreams, crystallized around collective trau-matic events, became surreptitiously associated with ethnocultural and class- and language-bound discrimination. And we may venture to say that the more collective traumas are repressed from public speech, the more likely they are to stage a form of intergenerational comeback (Davoine and Gaudillière 2004). During my younger years—especially between 1950 and 1962 at the secondary school and with the KSA Youth Movement—some of the books and contacts I accessed introduced me to the powerful Flemish spiritual revival and militant political activism of the interwar era. Both the war trauma and reference to Flanders's rich cultural heritage were forcefully nourishing the desire for the Flem-ish-speaking people's emancipation and self-determination, along with some still hesitant community-based idealism. Indeed, just after World War II, the established Francophone or Francophile upper middle class, for example, viewed with suspicion participation in any social or cul-tural movement as evocative of the "Flamingant" militants. Indeed, militants of whatever leaning and in particular communal church-led zeal in the secular public domain were still being associated by many of our generation with a breed of Flamingant idealists—surnamed as the "blacks"—who had collaborated with the Nazi occupation; the mem-ory of their black Nazi-style uniform haunted the popular imagination. Indeed, in the interwar period and during the 1940–44 occupation, these militants had mobilized themselves to obtain from the "German brothers" what the then Belgian national government, predominantly Francophone, proved reluctant to offer them.

As noted above, my native area was both rural and on the border with France. And the fact that this merely agricultural and village-bounded area did not have people from Jewish provenance, yet very conserva-tive and Francophile clerical authorities, undoubtedly explains why the question of deportation and extermination of—to us unacquainted— Jewish communities hardly formed part of the trauma of war there.

The more the war memories remained unspeakable in the genera-tions of witnesses, the heavier their weight on the younger generations. Looking back, it appears depressing to us that the half-spoken allusions in the family to the war, albeit quickly drowned in a heavy and uneasy silence, suggested to us how the end of World War II and its aftermath had stymied the erroneous pro-German community idealism and left the Flemish people deeply wounded, divided, and disillusioned. As far as we were concerned, such accounts brought out a collective form of sa-distic culpability at the core of the Flemish people's genuine aspiration for rehabilitation. My generation was thus not allowed to sympathize with idealistic emancipators of the Flemish people, let alone with the glorification of any Germanic roots and aspirations. The Flamingants were thus jettisoned as having betrayed their people. My generation of those born toward the end or shortly after World War II was summoned to condemn them as nostalgic idealists who lived among us—but who, from now on, were covered with shameful blame. The reason for such a request was rooted in the fear that support for these idealists would significantly undermine and betray our otherwise highly prized sense of loyalty toward the people of lesser means—namely, the majority of true victims of World War II. How often have I heard the following question/affirmation: "Even if they did not go so far as to betray us to the occupying forces, can you tell me how these 'blacks' and their illusions have contributed to the betterment of our living condition or the cause of our country?" The then establishment called upon us to sever our close ties with a glorified Flemish culture. It invited us to rather open ourselves up to new pluralist, future-oriented, and economically realistic horizons, including the Common Market project and the action for the overall development of the newly independent Africa. The memory of World War I entertained a self-image creating the people's community flesh and intersubjectivity for dignity and revival. Contrastingly, until the 1960s any communitarian contact with the somewhat "obscene"—that is, off-scene or repressed—memory of World War II still lingered, causing huge divides and shame or anger.

It was only with the coming of age of our own generation, born around World War II, that the Flemish cause found a novel pluralist and cosmopolitan breath. Let us mention, for instance, the split of the Catholic University of Leuven-Louvain in 1968 and the divestment of national, now called federal, civil service institutions in favor of regional ones for Flanders, Wallonia, and Brussels. In the period between 1960 and 1970, we had witnessed the petrochemical industry initiated in Flanders thanks to investments by US trusts. Here, we also experienced the expansion of port activities in Antwerpen and Zeebrugge—as much as we witnessed Europe's incremental unification and secularization. Thus, on the level of national institutions, our generation revived the Flemish cause, giving increasing attention to lucid self-criticism and transnational openness. Moreover, incited by the successful anti–Vietnam War manifestations at US university campuses, our generation also shared the enthusiasm for two self-emancipating continents—namely, Asia and Africa—to free themselves from the yoke of the colonizing West. In this way, our generation took part in the double openness and hope of that time. The first was a beginning of mimetic respect for the US liberal capitalist model. The second entailed the cosmocratic socialist model and its first leaders, such as Lenin, Trotsky, and Gandhi, using ideas by way of action, namely, Ho Chi Minh, Mao, Cabral, Che Guevara, Castro, Freire, Salvador Allende, Nkrumah, Lumumba, Steve Biko, Nyerere. It was that yearning for emancipation that inspired part of our generation in the 1960s.

This brings me, then, to an awkward but inescapable question: René or Renaat? Does the undisclosed thickness of one's name steer the identity? My Christian name is René, which I inherited from my maternal uncle René who died in Normandy, France, in 1937. In 1914, at the onset of World War I, my mother's family was exiled from its native soil in the battle zone of Yser—in the northeast of West Flanders—where the family farm was located. As this zone had been flooded to stop the advancing German troops, my mother's family was forced to leave a hugely sustainable farm in order to settle elsewhere. In the meantime, from the age of six to fourteen, and accompanied by four brothers and sisters—and many other Flemish refugee children—my mother was settled in a boarding school in Saint-Germain-en-Laye, near Versailles outside Paris; seven other siblings stayed home, two of them mobilized as soldiers in the Yser war trenches.

After the war, as the question of survival was most pressing, many war-stricken Flemish farmers were called upon by their notary or parish priest to find some good farming lands in Normandy, France, for the sake of their entrepreneurial children. In March 1925, my mother, together with three sisters and four brothers, left for Normandy. It is there that her three years' senior brother, René, whom she cared for, died aged thirty-two following a brain tumor. Upon the death of her brother, my mother returned to Flanders and married my father. As adumbrated, she named me after her deceased brother. I remember that as soon as I reached the age of nine or ten, she took special care of me, more than she ever did with my brother and sister. For instance, on Sunday dinner meals she would give me roast beef juice. I soon learned that she had fed her dying brother in the same way. She kept that juice for me "because your uncle René did like it." I felt that, somehow, I was born a replacement for her dead brother, buried near Caen. Did such a name make me and my children heirs to some affinity with death and with a community of unspeakable destiny? (Yet in 1979 I innocently devoted my first book to the theme of "Death, Mourning and Compensations for the Deceased among the Yaka.")

Upon realization of how much my name, René, was French and in the family memory associated with regret for my mother's brother's untimely and disastrous death, adolescent I thought to myself: "I'll have to change René to Renaat" (the Flemish form, also meaning "born again"). But, at the same time, I meant to carry out such a name change to rebel against a form of frustration spawned by Belgicist and antinomic discourses directed to the Flemish identity in my community. Such discourses proved humiliating and spiteful to me, considering the grotesque injustice they inflicted upon our people and culture. For me, taking part from the age of fifteen in the Yser pilgrimage that was held each summer in Diksmuide, at the center of the Yser trenches, to honor our war victims of both 1914–18 and 1940–44, and deftly applying myself to the mastery of the standardized Dutch language, proved to be a genuine way of setting myself against a Francophone bourgeoisie that was appallingly detached from the common people.

I had an uncle who was a butcher and married to one of my mother's older sisters. That uncle would annoyingly make me feel guilty for wanting to inscribe myself within my paternal autochthonous space. He would dangle the prospect of a space of welcoming the Belgicist otherness as though it was a much more liberated good. As he lived not far from our village primary school, I was welcomed at his home for the daily midday lunch. On those occasions he would often refer to his favorite, very Francophone, liberal, and royalist, newspaper, *La Libre Belgique.* He incidentally alluded to his long-standing sympathy for the pro-German Rexist partisans of the mainly Francophone bourgeoisie who projected their political aspirations and social frustrations into the antidemocratic Nazi model of order and authority. In this way, my uncle came each time to poke fun at the narrow horizons of Catholic parish priests, peasants, nostalgic Flamingants, and people of "lesser means" (according to the expression coined by Pierre Sansot) or "people from below" (as Jean-Marc Ela would put it).

In contrast, my father taught me a sense of love for commoners and community life. He owned a large farm and was, during World War II, one of those farmers who wholeheartedly provided assistance to less privileged people from the vicinity in search of survival. These people would come to the farm to ask for the bare necessities, including corn, milk, butter, and potatoes. When he died thirty-five years after the war ended, among the hundreds of people who attended his burial, dozens came to explicitly convey to us their gratitude and regard for having met a truly remarkable man who was motivated by nothing but his spirit of helpfulness and equity. In fact, it transpired only then to me that my father had given or sold them farm produce without making any profit in return—and that he had managed to do this while eluding the requisitioning look of the German occupants.

Because of my mother, I saw French as marked by an imaginary of bivalence. On the one hand, my mother experienced the French language as an opening to fascinating worlds, both urban and rural, namely, the Paris of her childhood and the very "fertile plains" around the industrial city of Caen in Normandy, where she lived until her thirties. To many of her acquaintances, she was known as "the young lady Bertha." Twenty years later, my mother would ask me to go and spend portions of holidays with some of her sisters' family living in large farms near Caen. Whenever I returned to Flanders, I could feel some unwieldiness and closure hardened by authoritarian and moralizing clericalism, and by the unspoken that concealed losses due to wars. This kept some inkling of involvement under the seal of secrecy—an involvement deemed fatal, regardless of whether one supported the so-called Francophile resistance or found oneself offering cooperation to the Germans.

By and large, the language change of my first name from René to Renaat also constituted what for me was my response to those from the rather affluent middle-class universe of entrepreneurs, some of whom were reputed for having made profit out of the war. I learned how some of them had opted for Francophile Belgicist principled ideas. Such a class bragged about their entrepreneurial liberal spirit, while claiming—quite rightly, I presumed—to be more favorable to the country's modern future than the clericalist peasant communities. But, I like to think that, in this ancient Flemish-speaking Flanders haunted by the memories of war tragedies, the French language adopted in bourgeois circles seemed like the idiom of an undue "claim." One can see how, in its appearance, the French-speaking bourgeois positioned themselves with some sort of indecent superiority toward us Flemish speakers of lesser means.

Let me bring yet another tale here of language subordination. The majority of our parental farm was the property of a noble from Brugge (Bruges), who was a Catholic priest and canon. My father was to serve him. During World War II, he traveled some 110 kilometers by bicycle every three months in order to bring butter and ham to the canon. The latter spoke Flemish with his housekeeper. However, when dealing with his family members—some of whom were senior civil servants with the Union Minière du Haut Katanga—or speaking to my father, he would switch to French, thereby positioning himself as both canon and landowner. As a child I took reports on this behavior to indicate that French appeared to be the language of the usurers' class or the privileged few, whereas Flemish conveyed the memory of wars as well as the emotions and aspirations of ravaged people in search of plural emancipation.

Flemish Culture of Bodiliness, the Unfathomable, and the Family Shrine

Many Flemish people of my and adjacent generations identify themselves with a mold of witty disposition in life, corporeal sensitiveness, and intersubjective qualities such as the ones celebrated by Willem Vermandere, an artist-troubadour who was born in West Flanders in 1940. As a singer and poet, he unconceals a forceful, sparkling, and sensual relationship to the body, speech, relevant others, their lifeworld, and former generations that is so peculiar to an autochthonous blend of Flemish-speaking people. He dedicates his artistic work to the memory of his father, a carpenter who fabricated horse-drawn carts. But his songs also reminisce about his mother, whom he portrays as the inexhaustible source of resonance between living and deceased family members, and anything that conjures up life at home, in the vegetable garden, and throughout the neighborhood. Out of doors and on evenings, following a day of musicality and poetry, Vermandere makes rough sculpture out of huge blue-stoned blocks. His poetic songs are expressed in his local dialect and incisively convey the popular vision his generation entertains. It is a nostalgic vision overflowed with verve and energy regarding social and existential issues. Vermandere convenes his public to take sides in important controversies regarding intergenerational and intercultural relations as well as regarding his recollection of World War II and village life in Flanders at the onset of widespread industrialization. Vermandere raises questions about something inherent in the Flemish soul that is frightened of freedom and cannot be spoken about. Whether in playing his flute or clarinet and especially in his subtle and energy-laden choreography, he relentlessly seeks to outreach the limits of the speakable and the showable. Aided by his body talk and musicality, he seeks to tame the undisclosable in the very surprising ambiguity and beauty of transgressive words and voluptuous gestures, joyfully displayed under the imaginary benevolent eye of some invisible matrixial fullness and augury. At play is a domestic culture where commensality, body care, mother, and the homely prevail alongside family values united around the sharing of desire, the zest for life, and the passion "to do your utmost best within the family and with your peers to succeed well in life."

The tangible cradle and focus of my native habitus regarding the unspeakable shaping a complicity and communitarian fellow feeling as family members in the intercorporeal nearness of both ardor and an acute sense of vulnerability is located in what I would define as the true "family shrine." It was the marble chimney surrounding the stove or the hearth in the combined dining and sitting room. In the parental home rebuilt in 1948, that marble chimney was derived from the house of the owner of the farm's core part: we were told that it had been taken out of his bombed and devastated house in the city of Brugge at the end of World War II. On eye level, the chimney was decorated by the main family emblems or photographs and Christian symbols such as the crucifix, Mother Mary's statuette or picture, and/or a particular saint to which the household or the family enterprise devoted itself. It was there where the family met in dialogue, crucial decision making with the aim of "modern development," half-spoken remembrance of—traumatic rather than nostalgic—family traces or thoughts of the past. More importantly, it acted as the only quasi-sacred or "soul-centric" locus in the home: it stood as the place for communal prayer just before bedtime, in particular the enchantingly repetitive rosary. This was followed by the Litany of the Saints, with half-spoken intentions voiced in religious supplications. The prayer developed in a sphere of candlelight and the heat of the stove.

The marble chimney crowned the installation of the house's infrastructure. Alongside daily cooking and common meals, it transformed a house into "our home," namely, a space for communal devotion and looking ahead with hope and determination. Recalling my childhood memories, I wonder whether the abstract and chaotic but sumptuous marble figures oscillating both around and from within empty spaces and holes (Vandenbroeck 2009) was not for the family members setting a scene for the unspeakable or unthought-in-thought, namely, a projective space for the lacunae or empty spaces in the speech and meaning being shared. We may also wonder whether such flux of quaint figures in the marble—of neither light nor darkness, beside any given order or resolution—actually mirrored and molded the subjects' imaginary being torn between, on the one hand, the unspeakable or nonrepresentable shadow side or even holes in their own lives and, on the other hand, the family zest and delight in life. This blend of shadow and vigorousness in life stirred the family passion toward interweaving the allusively transmitted histories of losses, enigmas, and uncanniness in the family novel and the local lifeworlds. These histories were allusively rehearsed at family celebrations of united fervor and entrepreneurial enthusiasm. And these family narratives were moreover interwoven with memory traces of war trauma and social injustice in the local society. My parents, uncles, aunts, nephews, and nieces cherished the sensual corporeal cocelebrating in large family meetings of their "mutual zest, desire, and delight to live life to the brim" (*met levenslust en volle goesting* in Flemish or Dutch). These concepts—almost untranslatable into English—delicately and genuinely conveyed the basic incentive and mood in the family and conjugal intimacy.

To my reflective remembrance, the prayers and intimate conversations at the family shrine did not subordinate the family members to an autonomous ethical order of law—of a patriarchal, Christian, or bourgeois liberal blend. The latter is one that would be centered—in line with some prevalent bourgeois ideals of that time—on assuring some higher comfort, self-realization, and well-being. In my memory, the family shrine figured very much as an imaginary incentive, beyond much wording, to join hands in the—seasonal, existential, and communitarian—regenerative cycle of death and rebirth, loss and redress, the war's wounds and renewed trust. Very much in the manner enacted and poetically voiced by artist-troubadour Willem Vermandere, the family ethic of desire in the native milieu of my breed tacitly but all the more incisively awakened in us a sustained hope for a better future and the audacity to go on opening ourselves to new developments and promising investments in higher education and modern technology. And most ardently, our parents—like also our uncles and aunts—invested in us, the upcoming generation, their principled and passionate search for equity and intersubjective recovery of dignity—as much as they were desperate to expurgate any wickedness and impurity from their own lifeworld and society as a whole. The drama of life and its present sequels were given an encompassing cosmological dimension of fate "lain in God's hands," in the humble awareness of "that's how things are."

The family ethic of desire departed from the much too self-assured and salvific, clerical, and bourgeois programs toward human flourishing and its rational steering. Our families' confrontation with bare life, namely, the wars, human envy, misery, and degradation, and in particular their peasant familiarity with ecology's largely unforeseeable but ceaseless reemerging reproductive energies and reformative potential, had led them to counter their adversities and depressiveness by their sense of dignity and hope, cleanliness and recovery. This sense was very much displayed in their witty and desirous intercorporeality and in the farm's core part, where the newest technology contrasted with the old buildings. All this granted them a marked sensibility for life's regenerative capacities, but also for the suffering, foolishness, and shadow sides in life sucked in—what I label along the lines of Lacan as the undisclosable "real." The crucifix and other devotional figures on top of the marble chimney, like also the communal prayers at this place, expressed the family's eager longing to remain protected from being bogged down into needfulness or adversity, poverty or hardship, namely, what Christian belief calls "the fate of human sinfulness." The holes and empty spaces on the marble may have evoked the doom in life of the uncertainties and chaotic emptied out by evil and the demonic treacherousness of darkness and desire in ourselves, as hinted at in the Christian moral discourse and liturgical celebrations or at Carnival.

Anthropological Co-implication

Late 1960s and 1970s: The Dawn of Post-Christianity, Postmodernity, and Postcolonialism

By the late 1960s, in major cities in the West and Japan, the youth—particularly the student body—and mass culture made their entry on the political scene. Surprising and powerful social and cultural contestation of the established order and truth was being ignited through music and film, Marxism, and surrealism. And it was in particular yielded by the cultural revolutionary right of each to imagination, utopia, liberation, a right that soon would enter onto the political agenda. From that period onward, a number of liberation movements developed in line with the philosophers and/or feminists Nietzsche, Sartre, Simone de Beauvoir, Althusser, Deleuze, Foucault, Hélène Cixous, and Luce Irigaray. Let me mention the movements of social and feminist activism, or for social justice, gender equality, bodily expression, sexual liberation, minority emancipation, counterculture, alternative lifestyles, and ecology. They considered it fitting to question all plain monotheistic intellectual domination, clerical discourses and parochial presumptions of normality, Cartesian disembodied thinking, nonlocalized truth, and (class, male, white) privilege. More importantly, our notions of rational self-control, paternal or patriarchal authority, and moralized normality came under intense scrutiny.

The late 1960s marked also in Flanders the dawn of post-Christianity and postmodernity. In that period, in particular higher-educated categories—some drawing on the aggiornamento in the Catholic Church incited by the Second Vatican Council (1962–65)—started to openly ask questions about a certain Flanders hardened by Catholic and conservative provincialism. They started to distance themselves from those sitting in that ivory tower and to define themselves through the local school, elite (family doctor, notary, parish priest, teacher) or pub, the family patriarch, or the local civil authority. Hence, they engaged in the pursuit of new explorations, wider horizons, and development potentialities. Next to the reign of modernist consciousness and the bourgeois sense of virtue, such quests also involved embracing in new ways the

localized, intercorporeal, and intersubjective flows of desire and the imaginary. Intellectuals were sharing a mood for exploring or supporting
the secularizing, pluralizing, and more gender-sensitive lifeworlds in
the making. They were all the while openly exploring shared expressions of cultural and personal fantasy, ambivalence, in-betweenness,
openly expressed frailty, discordance, divergence, independent-mind-
edness, and polyvalent agency.

Upon arriving in September 1965 as a young man in the Congo
shortly after that country's independence from its colonial master, Belgium, I found myself playing host to those who were not long ago colonized by my fellow Belgians. My immediate feeling was one of genuine
"com-passion" for the trauma Congolese had to endure as a result of
colonial intrusion into their lives; and I sympathized with their response to their grotesque treatment. At that stage, I came to understand
the dawn of the African continent in terms of a solid bond of mutual
trust in social and cultural creativity, based entirely on the shoulders of
each individual. I have relentlessly felt the appeal to such a destiny as
well as to the burdening moral debt that the heirs of the colonial enterprise have to pay.

The fate of colonial and postcolonial Africa, as well as its culpability
effect, which gnawed some of my generation in the 1960s, came into
resonance with the expectations and regrets emerging from movements
of protest, emancipation, and cultural revolution in the West in the
same period. Indeed, the crisis of representation and consciousness in
the late 1960s provided my generation with a powerful incentive for reflexivity and an ability to question ourselves as well as open ourselves
to the "other" face of the world and the human subject. This reflexivity
challenged the alienation of the subject and the unthought in the clash
of civilizations. It also brought under scrutiny the ways of human development and creativity of different cultures. And the traumatic world
wars swelled the sort of humiliation I suffered following denigration
of my mother tongue and peasantry origin at the hands of the Francophone bourgeois. The appeal launched by a militant negritude for
a radical mental decolonization overcame my mind as I was progress-
ing through graduate studies in philosophy at Kimwenza-Kinshasa
(1965–68). The call for decolonization largely influenced my choice to
subsequently study sociology and anthropology at the University of
Kinshasa (1969–71), then called Lovanium.

The break articulated by the young Congolese intellectuals in respect
to the colonial master—as well as the powerful appeal to "recourse to
authenticity" launched by President Mobutu in 1970 for the nation-state
of Congo, known as Zaire between 1971 and 1997, plunged me initially

into disarray. I was not sure what attitude to adopt in the face of such discourses. To which head of a two-faced Janus was I subjected? Given my Belgian origin and unlike my Congolese friends, I faced a real dilemma as to whether to identify myself with those singled out by the Congolese people as enemies, exploiters, and alienating heirs to the colonizer. After all, had I not overtly distanced myself from the colonizing discourses so much imbued with negative othering as they passed off unwittingly and unacknowledged among many Westerners living in the Congo at the time, which no doubt repelled me? Did my compassion for the emancipation struggle in the face of the intruding West not seek to contribute indirectly (at least as far as my fellow students were concerned) to unlock their colonial trauma? Was I, in the aftermath of this traumatic experience, right and able to undertake a repair work as anthropologist by gradually promoting before an international scholarly audience the true aspirations and genius of the Congolese, and more specifically the aspirations of the yiYaka-speaking people? It must be pointed out that these people had fallen victim to prejudicial stereotypes within the Congolese framework because of their initial fierce resistance to colonists and missionaries, and because their soil and subsoil were deemed too poor to contain any meaningful natural resources. For that matter, their Kwaango region experienced no plantations or mining extractions in the hands of colonists-settlers. Neither did it benefit from investments in infrastructure, sustained and widespread public health programs, or the missionary-based education in secondary schools to train administrative, agronomic, veterinary, and paramedical auxiliaries.

What remains certain, however, is that many Congolese and European friends in Kinshasa helped me beyond any measure to keep Janus unveiled, while paying a heavy toll in relation to the cause of decolonization. I can still hear some of my Congolese friends telling me: "Go ahead, give yourself over passionately to the school of our people living in the village or in Kinshasa's shantytowns; make a forceful contribution to the recovery of the yiYaka speakers' national and international dignity." For this reason and in the aftermath of my studies in philosophy and anthropology, I embarked upon an exploratory and adaptive investigation into the local realities of yiYaka speakers, in keeping with basic notions of respect for culture and starting from the experience of spatiality—a dimension that I considered an unprejudiced entryway. However, for me, all these perspectives and intentions were to take a new twist in my participatory research in Kwaango and Kinshasa.

In Kwaangoland, 1971–74: Mutual Adoption by Virtue of Co-affecting Co-implication

From December 1971 until October 1974, I lived as an anthropologist in the yiYaka-speaking society of northern Kwaango along the Angolan border, in the Taanda settlement of thirteen villages—some 120 inhabitants on average, or six persons per square kilometer—450 kilometers to the south of Kinshasa (Devisch 1993; Devisch and Brodeur 1999). From 1985 to 2003, annual visits of some three weeks placed me in direct contact with the emigrants from Kwaangoland living concentrated in some of Kinshasa's shantytowns. In the savannah region of Kwaango, the domestic and public day-to-day life of great—and in the last decades increasing—scarcity is undoubtedly marked by people's modes of production as hunter-gatherers and small-scale subsistence farmers. The patterns of time and space have virtually been unaffected by the small incursions of a cash economy. It is a society devoid of a statist edifice, autochthonous monotheist religion, or any overall master discourse by a centralizing political power. While half of the population in Kwaango—some 350,000 people—have taken advantage of primary or elementary school education over the last decades, it is fair to say that literacy has not been a mutational force and has hardly shaken this society to its foundations and beliefs. Even though we do not have recent statistical data regarding religious affiliations in Kwaangoland, it is reasonably likely that today half of the people have been baptized at the school-going age or have at a later age joined a neo-Pentecostal church.

I enjoyed hospitality in the chiefdom of Taanda—bordering the Waamba River, on the one side, and standing within one-day walking distance from the Angolan frontier, on the other side. It is a grouping of some thirteen villages where daily life seemed well anchored in the local lifeworld. The area had been described in these terms by Léon de Beir, a Jesuit missionary who, in 1938–39, had recorded there in great detail the religious life and ritual practices—and I had brought with me to the field a photocopy of De Beir's book manuscript (1975).[1] I lived in the same village, Yitaanda, throughout the period of my field research, leaving it only for brief stays in surrounding villages. The Catholic parish of Imbela, at some sixty kilometers from Yitaanda, welcomed me several times, as did the University of Kinshasa, for brief stays of concentrated work on my research notes. My wife, Maria, interrupted her teaching of physics and mathematics at the secondary school level in Flanders to join me for the last four months of research in the Taanda chiefdom.

Co-involvement through Transfusion of Phantasms and Receptivity to Feel-thinking

The host community was always welcoming and gave me a helping hand in my endeavors. An attitude of helpfulness and good nature helped me to stand out as a "floating signifier"—as a subject in both excess and default as far as my anticipated identity as a white person was concerned. I intended to mobilize a transferential field where my interlocutors eventually would revise their preconception and feel more than confident to start sharing with me both their erudition and their much cherished cultural practices and institutions. Within family circles and in particular at funerals, I could sometimes experience wise men or notables parodying Western individualistic and probing models—as they went about poking fun of their relationship with the oppressive colonial civil service. I hoped they would as time went by also disclose their traumatic phantasms regarding their experience of "colonized." Furthermore, I expected that I would come to reach their dealing with anxiety in the fields of sorcery, especially when misfortune strikes within the family or community.

A retrospective analysis of my integration into the host group (Devisch and Brodeur 1999: 3–19) shows how the two partners operated what I could only describe as a "transfusion" on both sides of snatches of phantasms and barely articulated memory traces. In January 1972, upon arriving in Yitaanda—where I requested the hospitality of the host group for the duration of my participatory research—I found Chief Taanda Kapata, an octogenarian, on the verge of death. I was quickly invited to administer some "powerful drug" to ease his labored breathing, fever, and acute pain in the chest he was suffering, which led me to suspect that the old man had a bout of pneumonia. He died three weeks later. A delegate of the regional Luunda chief N-saka—standing as a vassal to the suzerain Kyaambvu—showed up at Yitaanda after one month of mourning. His mission was to inaugurate palaver proceedings about the crucial matter of succession (Devisch and Brodeur 1999: 167–77). He publicly addressed me as Taanda N-leengi, a name that connected me to the appearance and disappearance of Taanda Kapata. In fact, this name gave me the power to undo or cast out the bad spell of Chief Taanda N-leengi. The latter chief was predecessor in title to Kapata and was arrested in 1938 by the colonial power. He was eventually exiled to Oschwe in the Lake District in the northeast of Bandundu province. The criminal charges he was facing were that in 1937 he was a member of an anticolonial prophetic movement named Mvungi. Within this historical construct, theorized by the envoy of the Luunda vassal N-saka, and in people's eyes, I came across as somehow linked to a rebirth of Taanda N-leengi, who now reappeared—at the end of the rule of Kapata, which began in 1939—with the white color attributed to the deceased.

As adumbrated earlier, and it bears repetition here, my uncle René, whose name I inherited, died prematurely in 1937. This common fate conveyed through the name of René—which I inherited after my maternal uncle's untimely death—now coupled with the name N-leengi I was given after Chief Kapata's death, awakened in me the enigma of some transfusion of unconscious memory traces in my family—which I would begin to voice only fifteen years later along with my didactic psychoanalysis. Needless to say, my hosts were completely oblivious to the fact that my name, René, literally means "the reborn," a name I inherited from my maternal uncle—for whom my mother had cared until his early death. My uncle René was born in October 1905 soon after his sister Bertha died, aged only one year, thereby preceding my mother, born January 1908, and to whom the name of Bertha was restored.

My integration into the Taanda group has over the years continued to stimulate a reflexivity as well as to trigger some psychoanalytic sensitivity, with the aim of clarifying the transference effects of the anthropological encounter. The overall ambition has been to explain the unconscious memory traces that lie as an enigma or shadow behind the historical and mythopoietic narratives of the chiefdom Taanda as well as behind my "family novel"—which was largely and unknowingly calibrating my life. For an ethnographer, the ideal is to be able to mobilize a transaction between prominent subjects who in their specialist practices or arts "embody" barely voiced memories, unknowingly said knowledge, the usually unmentionable. The more such a transaction between "speaking bodies" deepens, the more likely mutual exchanges acquire the ability to reveal the thought inadequacy between the known and the shadow of the unknown or faint knowledge, such as of social and institutional breakdown or trauma.

Let us now briefly scrutinize the reflexivity learned within such a context and that casts light on the unspeakable and the intercivilizational violence. In terms of the culture, reflexivity would be coined as -yiindulula, which literally means swinging back and forth the ideas I ruminate. The concept is related to toyiniinga, shadow or double; it literally means "something that continues to swing" (-niinga) at the borders of my body and between me and the other—whether person, being, event, or thing—while unsettling such borderspace. My shadow thus propels me beyond my physical limits very much by way of a multisensorial carrying away my imaginary beneath what I can see, feel, or touch.

The Yaka understanding of dreams allows me to elaborate on their concept of shadow, in full knowledge that reflexivity, *-yiindula,* is compared to daydreaming and thus understood as a dreamlike insight. In dreams, my shadow in some way duplicates my body by making me other. My shadow gives me the opportunity to stretch out, beyond my sensory habitus and usual categories of thought and discourse, into an extimate mode of contact between the visible and invisible in some interworld continuity. Indeed, in my nocturnal and daytime dreams, this shadow seems to me to be something extimate, namely, an otherness—or intimate exteriority (Corin 2007)—temporarily suspending my reasoning as long as it makes me follow the impulses of my desire, through anxiety or passion, disgust or attraction. This extimacy connects me to the realm of the unrepresentable and unspeakable of things and to visible as well as invisible or uncharacterizable beings inhabiting this world and the world of the spirits. This extimacy places me in line with what is inexpressible in the trauma, or lurking behind personal and family history, namely, with what is resisting uncovering itself or coming to its true light (*aletheia,* in ancient Greek). Reflexivity, according to the Yaka, is a form of awareness of a perceptual jittering within the borderspace where human subjects intersect alongside forms of animal lives, things, traces of memories, and what punches a hole in such memories—all of which form part of a co-resonant and interdependent universe, either vitalizing or disconcerting.

This reflexivity understood as a form of oneiric insight underlies an ontology of life universes in which the human being participates at the level of borderspaces formed by intercorporeality, intersubjectivity, and interworld co-resonance. Such life universes communicate with each other both through their visible and tangible aspects as well as through their functions and nonrepresentable enigma. They include "the primordial uterine and chthonic source of all life and ceaseless reorigination and reproduction" (*ngoongu*), tirelessly drilled in the here and now as a basal rhythmicity of the (erectile) "life force" (*ngolu ye khoondzu*). It is vividly expressed in the intercorporeal flows of the "uterine life-regenerative vitality" (*mooyi*) that emerge in the pulsative-energetic and affective body, in the sensorium. The life source is also shared in "the innate nature" befalling the individual, and more particularly expressed in the balancing of the upright and mobile body, as well as in the heartbeat and sensorium, physical heat and erectile drive.

Connivance of Being and Shadow of Being

My at times deeply destabilizing interaction in town with school-ed-ucated or so-called "whitened" yiYaka speakers made me gauge the violence underlying intercivilizational encounters in a North-South re-lation of extreme technoeconomic disparity. On 23 and 24 September 1991—at the time I was on a research visit in Kinshasa—a kind of mili-tary mutiny "launched and manipulated behind the scenes" (Yoka Lye Mudaba 1994: 83) broke out and was followed by uprisings and looting that swept through the residential, commercial, and industrial areas of Kinshasa and other cities (Devisch 1995). Hundreds of thousands of men and women of all ages came from slums, including from those predominantly inhabited by yiYaka speakers, and rushed to factories, businesses, warehouses, stores, shops, and homes of entrepreneurs and diamond traders, Western expatriates, and Zaire's "dinosaurs and bar-ons." These Luddites, like a vast collective frenzy, were reminiscent of the Carnival brawls witnessed in rural areas: such incidents of a night of blatant deviance and inversion seek to dispel the specter of a freshly buried but ill-natured person of notable repute and all the ills haunting the community. This night of simulated misrule and extreme license strives to revive and legitimize again the diurnal public order and the conditions of self-determination by self-destructively exorcising their nocturnal opposite (Devisch 1993: 93). Since this looting occurred, yi-Yaka-speaking people in Kinshasa have sought to reappraise through funeral songs their native village environment, the lineage mode of production, and family solidarity patterns in search of a so-called villagization.

In the shantytowns, the survival of many young homeless adults and of those without any genealogical inscription was then defined more than ever by the law of derision of the poor and those devoid of any sustained identity reference. There, survival also implied some occasional predatory economy and resourcefulness in the street at the expense of the better-off and the state. In addition, small predators ap-peared to be an urban reenactment of some imaginary figure in the ru-ral milieu such as a sorcerer or a hunter venturing into untamed areas of deep forests, in the imaginary space-time of the nonsedentary and unsettling zones of uncertainty, ambiguity, and mixture, relating to sor-cery and its so-called night markets (Devisch 1993: 86–93; Devisch and Brodeur 1999: 57ff.).

Notwithstanding a favorable a priori ascribed to individuals and groups who welcomed me in Kinshasa and Kwaango, I found myself increasingly concerned about the paradoxes of modernization initiated according to the canons of my country of origin. I was shocked to discover how much inhuman misery the yiYaka-speaking inhabitants experienced in the slums of Kinshasa, next to the hardships in the Kwaango resulting from malaria, dysentery, kwashiorkor, and varicella epidemics. I was also genuinely shocked by the hard work many women endured in order to secure the survival of their families, particularly by their horticultural work and running some petty trade to pay for their children's education. I would repress my dismay at the local patriarchal gerontocracy that was apparently insensitive to new aspirations of young people, graduates, and many women, as well as to the "politics of the belly" shamelessly pursued by the party-state's civil service (Devisch 1995).

What is more, while in the Kwaango, I felt deeply offended by the self-alienatingly dismissive attitudes of Christian converts—living together in small islands called parishes—toward ancestral religion, divination, healing cults, and the conforming function of sorcery for the local society. By and large, these converts jettisoned all that undergirded their rich classical culture, which incidentally also formed the best part of their upbringing and identity. Suffice it to say that the portrayal of villagers as "pagan and primitive people" by the missionary churches was self-defeating, as I felt ashamed of the pathetic-looking essays of technocratic development and the paradoxes of modernization in Kwaangoland and Kinshasa's slums. It was absolutely central to my position that denying such a rich culture is as paralyzing as to obnubilate one's own provenance.

In its own right, this caricature of the modern West that was hitting my mind by way of a Yaka or shantytown version of *Tristes Tropiques* invalidated the innocence or neutrality of my intellectual tools. In fieldwork, the more I recollected my own taste for Lévi-Strauss's structuralist epistemology while at university, the more frustrated I grew. I like to think that such a feeling remained largely unchanged, however remarkable structuralism's antievolutionary perspective and humanist intent. The reason for my frustration is that this epistemology had the potential to reproduce and impose a logical apparatus and a dualistic thematic that had modernist overtones and was wholesomely phallocentric as well as Eurocentric in nature. These tools erased the original lineaments of logical, epistemological, and ontological engineering of Yaka genius by opposing, along a binary mode, living reality and representation, signifier and signified, facts and thoughts, form and matter, the given situation and the propensity of things.

To illustrate the sociocultural genius of the people in Kwaangoland—in contrast to much mimicry in the parishes and Kinshasa—it appeared to me how much their social identity was not structured in accordance with attributes and classifications of Christian education or the (post)colonial civil service. On the contrary, such identity must be viewed in line with the bearing of totemic animals or of organic meta-phors (e.g., the metaphor of the family "tree" or of "seminal flow and branching of offspring" along the imagery of the nearby river's flow). These metaphors transpose their dynamic form onto sociopolitical net-works and strategies that are viewed respectively as an intricate order of forces (shared and borderlinking in the blood, meals, and mutual help), sources (cosmological, purifying, or reinvigorating ones), or relation-ships (of filiation and descent) and events (that punctuate life within the group and the world order). As one resident confided: "Since we moved here, we eat well and we bring up healthy children." Such was to him a key definition of a vital social and political order.

This view on the intricate order moreover aligns with that on the march of the world intertwining the subjects' desire and momentum of their actions with the forces of their life universe. In this respect, I like to think that for yiYaka-speaking people the order of things and events is not seen as originating in human initiative, but in the tendency, affinity, and resonance in and between beings, events, and things. Crucially, I came to see that in people's view such order is a function of the propen-sity (*yikuma*) or energy (*ngolu*) of the situation (*maambu*). A number of core metaphors seek to stir up this tendency, such as the regulation and renewal of vigor in persons and the living environment following the alternation of day and night and the march of seasons, or in line with the course of the nearby river below the slope. The good luck a hunter is hoping for is to the measure of his zeal, much as his hard-hitting gunshot is respondent to the game's greed, like the overflow of sex-ual craving between husband and wife may prelude the enchantment aroused by a good word.

Conclusion: Bifocal Gaze toward Intercultural Borderlinking

This chapter led me to revisit moves and countermoves that have in-cited some mutually inspirational alliances between anthropology "here" and "over there" as well as between anthropology and psycho-analysis. In all this, I am surprised to find how much my peasant Flem-ish socioculture of provenance yielded a genuine sense of, and basic openness to, the matrixial and the unthought-in-thought, like to some unspeakable or latent but undisclosable images and traces of trauma and regret lingering in the family history.

Valentin Mudimbe (2011: 170–89) has suggested that the polar articulation in mutual resonance of my identity as anthropologist operating in both Africa and my home country—that is, my bifocal gaze and comprehending—could be seen as having as its mirror image the borderlinking figure of blind Tiresias in ancient Greek mythology. Tiresias's art of piercing into and unconcealing the unknowingly said, unspeakable, and unthought-in-thought was characterized by Sophocles, Euripides, Apollodorus of Athens, and Ovid. That borderlinking figure could perhaps help me, first, to further forge the way out of my deep-seated suspicion thrown at exoticizing ethnology—originally at much colonial portrayals that were subduing the local culture to the so-called civilizational enterprise in a hierarchical relationship along the lines of colonizer-colonized. Indeed, my dual position continues to exacerbate a tensional relationship between the pretension, as an allochthonous anthropologist, at laying bare the local cultural genius—even in its unsaid or ethnocentrically overlooked layer—and my learned and relatively aestheticizing anthropological discourse in one of the world languages. The question essentially comes down to: who speaks, for whom, and in the name of which authority?

While addressing a learned audience and pretending to do it from within the socioculture of yiYaka speakers and the rationale of people's practices, organizations, and (ritual) institutions, I seem to provoke now and then some suspicion of whether my enterprise is a science or a version of their mythopoetics. Is it not an alienating shadow play or illusion, unable to critically address—in the Western discourse of suspicion—the group's impediments at genuine emancipation on the world scene and lucid meaningfulness in the mirror of scientific rationality? By all means, I have indeed lived my anthropological field experience as a learning from, and in the terms of those who welcomed me. My anthropological enterprise, moreover, has never ceased to entail a lasting inner scrutiny in my attempt to enduringly welcome my hosts in the clearing of the extimate or otherness in myself. Not only did I not stop submitting my anthropological understanding and wording to my hosts' existential concerns and hermeneutics. But in laying bare much of what is unspoken, unknowingly said, or unthought-in-thought in my Flemish culture and in what my African experience mirrors, this echoic rumination soaks in what Wilfred Bion, Donald Winnicott, Didier Anzieu, and Bracha Ettinger describe as an intersubjective intermediary space of transitionality and intercultural borderlinking.

The very distinctive bifocality at the core of the type of anthropological coimplication that I am advocating is yet a paradox. It advocates understanding local realities through dialoguing and seeing these from the perspective of the subjects concerned, all the while self-reflectively if not critically observing the activity of self and other from one another's perspectives. This is to be reached at before subsequently representing that insight as much as possible in ways that fit the local culture's genius, but that unavoidably are also inspired by Western or North Atlantic academic traditions of clarification and persuasion.

How much, then, does the ethnographic report entail a form of bordercrossing, at the risk of exoticizing if not othering, to the extent that it may lead to representing the culturally different other through methods of reading derived from the Western scholarly traditions of the book, from verbal and scopic scrutiny and distancing? And is the anthropologist's initial tendency toward bordercrossing in fact not rather a search concerned with the estranging stranger or shadowy side within herself? More precisely, is the anthropological engagement in a subaltern society thus basically mobilized by a personal—mostly unclarified or undisclosable—self-healing agenda of both bordercrossing and borderlinking attentive to those dimensions in the host group that reverberate in herself—such as, for example, the family trauma of collective (gender, class) subjection and of war?

I chose to safeguard my anthropological and ethical alliance with the host society by giving these "people from below" a well-deserved, affectionate, and thoughtful attention while avoiding depriving them of their own true genius. In this respect, my focus on the effectiveness of transition rituals and healing cults (Devisch 1993: chaps. 6–7; Devisch and Brodeur 1999: chaps. 3–4) led me to subscribe to a perspectival methodology informed by the local perspective. This heuristic adopts a form of epistemology and outlook informing the given society concerned with how to think through its realities and effectively organize its preferred courses of action. This heuristic tries to grapple with the way that the given society perceives the course of things, the functionality and propensity as well as effectuation of things and beings.

Perspectival ontology is, for example, very fundamental in Yaka divinatory or shamanic practices (Devisch 2012). In fact, in order to scrutinize and uncover the unspeakable and the shadowy side of life, such ontology ascribes the mediumistic diviner's keen perspicaciousness to her strong flair or keen intuition and sharp oneiric insight (Devisch and Brodeur 1999: 93–123). In particular, this ability comes to the diviner via hereditary traits (*yibutukulu*), initiatory or oracular incorporation precisely through borderlinking in the body with a transitional state in the animal world, such as, for example, of "a hen laying an egg and then brooding it until it hatches."

One important outcome of the foregoing reflexivity is that our keen perception of the culturally different other grows along with some lucid insight into the unthought extimacy or alienating otherness inside us. That is an exceedingly important point. Acknowledging that yiYaka-speaking and Flemish-speaking people are worlds apart, it appears that I, however, have not stopped acting as a borderlinker who resonates with sensitivity to the matrixial in each through their extimacies and my own.

Acknowledgments

Research in the Democratic Republic of Congo was carried out in collaboration with the Institute for Anthropological Research in Africa at the University of Leuven and CERDAS Research Centre at the University of Kinshasa, directed by Professor Lapika. It was facilitated by the Institute of the National Museums of Congo. Financial support is gratefully acknowledged from the Belgian National Fund for Scientific Research, the Research Fund—Flanders, the European Commission Directorate-General XII, and the Garry-Frank Guggenheim Foundation. I thank Dr. Paul Komba, fellow of Wolfson College Cambridge, for his invaluable editorial assistance.

Notes

1. Older people in Yitaanda remembered Father De Beir, one of the few Europeans who had repeatedly stayed in that part of Yakaland, the Taanda chiefdom, for a few days. But that souvenir has added to my guilt regarding the Flemish missionary intrusion, spurring my restorative stance in the postcolonial anthropological encounter. My informants related De Beir's condemnation of local dignitaries, in particular those reluctant to Christian conversion. In 1938, before the eyes of the mourners, he had publicly beaten the corpse of a diviner, allegedly as the personification of a heathen institution, hence, of Satan. The narrators characterized this act as *mbeembi*, a term for an unwarranted and chaos-causing assault or an unbearable contravention of their domestic intimacy, auguring misfortune to all who witnessed it.

References

Corin, Ellen. 2007. "The 'Other' of Culture in Psychosis: The Ex-centricity of the Subject." In *Subjectivity: Ethnographic Investigations*, ed. João Biehl, Byron Good, and Arthur Kleinman. Berkeley: University of California Press, 273–314.
Davoine, Françoise, and Jean-Max Gaudillière. 2004. *History beyond Trauma*. New York: Other Press.
De Beir, Léon. 1975. *Religion et magie des Bayaka*. St. Augustin-Bonn: Anthropos.
de Certeau, Michel, Julia Dominique, and Jacques Revel. 2004. *Une Politique de la langue*. Paris: Gallimard.
Devisch, René. 1993. *Weaving the Threads of Life*. Chicago: University of Chicago Press.
———. 1995. "Frenzy, Violence, and Ethical Renewal in Kinshasa." *Public Culture* 7: 593–629.
———. 2011. "The Shared Borderspace, A Rejoinder." In *The Postcolonial Turn: Re-imagining Anthropology in Africa*, ed. René Devisch and Francis B. Nyamnjoh. Bamenda: Langaa; Leiden: African Studies Centre, 197–272.
———. 2012. "Of Divinatory Connaissance in South-Saharan Africa." "Medical Anthropology in Europe: Shaping the Field," ed. E. Hsu and C. Potter, special issue, *Anthropology and Medicine* 19: 107–18.
Devisch, René, and Claude Brodeur. 1999. *The Law of the Lifegivers*. Amsterdam: Harwood.
Devisch, René, and Francis B. Nyamnjoh, eds. 2011. *The Postcolonial Turn: Re-imagining Anthropology in Africa*. Bamenda: Langaa; Leiden: African Studies Centre.
Ettinger, Bracha L. 2006. *The Matrixial Borderspace*. Minneapolis: University of Minnesota Press.
Merleau-Ponty, Maurice. 1964. *Le Visible et l'invisible*. Paris: Gallimard.
Mudimbe, Valentin Y. 2011. In *The Postcolonial Turn: Re-imagining Anthropology in Africa*, ed. René Devisch and Francis B. Nyamnjoh. Bamenda: Langaa; Leiden: African Studies Centre, 143–96.
Vandenbroeck, Paul. 2009. "The Energetics of an Unknowable Body." In *Backlit Heaven: Power and Devotion in the Archdiocese Mechelen*, ed. Paul Vandenbroeck and Gerard Rooijakkers. Tielt: Lannoo, 174–204.
Von Busekit, Astrid. 1998. *La Belgique: Politiques des langues et construction de l'Etat—de 1780 à nos jours*. Bruxelles: Duculot.
Yoka Lye Mudaba, André. 1994. "Mythologie de la violence à Kinshasa." *Zaïre-Afrique* 34: 83–88.

René Devisch is Emeritus Professor, Catholic University of Leuven, Institute for Anthropological Research in Africa.
Email: Renaat.Devisch@soc.kuleuven.be

≈ SECTION IV ≈

Reflexivity, Democracy, and Government

Editors' Preface

In his contribution, Yaron Ezrahi, a political theorist, focuses directly on democracy. In doing so he brings to bear a sense of reflexivity quite different from what we have seen so far. In relation to the apparent meltdown of today's democracies, he addresses the question of reflexivity as it bears on the problem of the erosion of the Enlightenment synthesis of politics and rationality. In principle, reflexivity, considered as conscious reflection, functions as both a premise and practice of democratic government, and as a posture that challenges and temporalizes everything eternal in this mode of governance. Ezrahi clarifies this situation by distinguishing species of reflexivity—most particularly, reflexive and "unreflexive" reflexivity—that function variously to support or undermine consensual governance. Entailing awareness of the faults as well as the benefits of any particular democratic regime, reflexive reflexivity can promote change in, as well as distrust of, the regime. By contrast, unreflexive reflexivity, in which the government is simply presumed by the people to conduct itself in their interest, allows for institutional conservation and stability. If because of unbridled reflexive reflexivity "the people" comes to see as mere pretense its own role as the democratic sovereign power, then the legitimacy of the democratic regime is severely undercut. Ezrahi suggests the instrumental solution needed is a balance between reflexivity and unreflexivity, a balance to be engineered and struck by the government. But given the current growing distrust of democratic regimes, distrust fostered by increasing technological access to information suggesting corruption and illegitimate governmental acts, the durability of democracy is thrown into question. Ezrahi is therefore led to wonder if, in the face of the loss of faith in the realness of their principled ontological foundations, democratic governments can be preserved by ethical commitment of the citizenry. In effect, posing a question of the efficacy of ethics, Ezrahi asks if the sheer moral desirability of democracy can move people to keep faith in this form of government even when governmental practice flagrantly belies the democratic ethos. Here reflexivity, being seen largely in terms of reflection or conscious thought, is subject to governmental manipulation. To highlight the significance of this sense of reflexivity, we add, in view of Ezrahi's argument, that how a democratic government informs the people has an immense impact on the ability of the voting public to think critically about choices and therewith the legitimacy of the democracy. Take, for instance, a democratic regime that, for one reason or another, decides to go to war. Declaring war, and therewith implementing an *exceptional state* of national affairs, positions the government to adopt what amount to fascistic powers and persuade its people of the need to do so. In the event, the democratic regime waxes indistinguishable from an authoritarian one.

THE LATENT EFFECTS OF THE DISTRIBUTION OF POLITICAL REFLEXIVITY IN CONTEMPORARY DEMOCRACIES

Yaron Ezrahi

When Narcissus falls in love with his own image reflected in the water, we have an allegory of unreflexive reflectivity. Narcissus is unaware of his prior causal relation to the image that he treats as independent of himself. In the story of Narcissus, such a lack of reflexivity is self-destructive. But in the sociopolitical context, unreflexive reflectivity can be a powerful conserver of social behavior, agencies, and institutions insofar as it encourages individuals and groups to take them for granted. By contrast, reflexive reflectivity, insofar as it generates individual and group awareness that the polity comes into being largely by means of their own performance as agencies, consciously or unconsciously, actually enacts liberal-democratic imaginaries of the political order. Such enactments may trigger reformative or even revolutionary actions. I regard political reflexivity in the democratic context as combining the individual's sense of his or her own political agency, a measure of critical understanding or intuition of the assumptions or fictions on which the hegemonic political order rests, and finally an awareness of the individual's reciprocal relations with the regime, including the individual's own power to participate in bringing about a change in the "system." But the preservation of changes induced by such actions requires a switch from reflexive back to unreflexive reflectivity, at least among a large part of the population, a shift to unreflexivity that restores the capacity to naturalize and constitutionalize at least parts of the induced political changes as stable givens.[1]

Between what can be called radical reflexivity that may be self-paralyzing and radical unreflexivity or literalness that can unleash violence in the name of utopian visions, I would like to suggest a third possibility that I will call deliberate, or reflexive, unreflexivity, meaning a willing and conditional suspension of self-referential knowledge and skepticism. Such an orientation may indicate a considered decision to temporarily treat some aspects of experience, or of the observed world of subjects and objects, as unproblematic pregivens in order to enable the behavior that advances some goals.

Scientists may follow such a course as part of a larger conceptual or theoretical strategy of advancing a certain kind of knowledge by parceling out phenomena. The differentiation of scientific disciplines is usually accompanied by the subdivision or regrouping of research objects. The boundaries of these research objects are usually fixed by strategies of conceptualization that deliberately suspend some questions in order better to focus on others, and use matching research instruments. This is often indicated by a discipline's name, like elementary particles physics as distinct from astrophysics. Also in the context of liberal-democratic politics one can discern a policy, or an intuitive tendency, to suspend distrust in the "objective" reality status of aspects of the social world perceived as external to the human subject as well as in the very pregiven reality of the subject itself. Scientists often produce "objectivity" as a necessary or desirable regulatory norm of their professional discourse (Daston and Galison 2008). Political actors often produce "objectivity" as a necessary or desirable regulatory norm, or a classifying category, of political discourse and action.

Democratic politics heightens the sense that legitimation is created, and can be lost, at any moment. "Presentism" as a part of the logic of democratic politics, as the politics of the living, is in some respects a double embodiment of both constructive and disruptive reflexivity in public affairs. By focusing on the legitimacy of current structures and actions, it tends to erase the past, create the present, and aim at the near future; it often undermines conventional hierarchies and generates new ones. This does not mean, of course, that democratic political leaders do not employ counter- and antireflexive strategies such as naturalization, realism, legalism, and even the authority of tradition in order to stabilize their authority. Also, historiographies can at times serve the attempt to safely fix a deterministic imaginary of the sources of political authority that sets boundaries to the open flow of the reflexive reformative or revolutionary "presentism" of ongoing democratic politics. Only by temporally distancing, constitutionalizing, or mythologizing an earlier revolution can radical revolutionary reflexivity be sufficiently detached and bounded in time to prevent revolutionary orientations from spilling over and disrupting stabilized postrevolutionary democratic politics. Here again we can see the combined role of reflexive and unreflexive orientations in the construction, transformation, and stabilization of political systems.

This, of course, is also why so much energy and cultural resources are invested by hegemonic elites in the means to transform what is made by, and still depends upon, voluntary performance into a given, a reality, that requires automatic or "rational" compliance. As a matter of fact, the very category of reality, beyond any reflexive interrogation, is postulated in diverse forms of behavior that by virtue of adapting to it are often praised as rational, pragmatic, and so forth. Clustering "realism" with "rationality" or "pragmatism" can be seen as a group of strategies deployed to repress the potential effects of destabilizing reflexivity on a particular imaginary of reality. So one can regard shifts between social and political creativity, deconstruction and conservation, as the result of the sequential, and often simultaneous, dialectics of individual or group reflexivity and unreflexivity. A similar concern with the disruptive potential of reflexive orientations can be discerned in the field of law. In discussions of proposals for an Israeli constitution held in Israel's Democracy Institute around 2003, Israel's former chief justice Aaron Barak characteristically warned against too much interrogatory reflexivity on the origins of legal authority.

Reflexivity and Citizenship

Reflecting on the dialectics of reflexivity and unreflexivity is a permanent feature of Western political life due to the growing recognition of the groundlessness of the contemporary political order that lost its earlier presupposed safe, unreflexive anchors in the religious metaphysics of transcendence, nature, tradition, and historical or social laws. What seem to have changed over time are both the degrees of political reflexivity and the ways of inducing unreflexive (literal) orientations as strategies of legitimizing political hierarchies and the political order.

A balance between radical reflexive subjectivity and stable and transparent social "reality" is a necessary requirement of democratic agency. Sometimes the degree of reflexivity and its timing can become contested, reflecting diverse social values and political agendas. Take, for instance, the debate between political theorist Sheila Benhabib and philosopher Judith Butler on the question of whether individual agency should be regarded as pregiven or as formed in the course of social and discursive performance (Stern 2000). The imaginary of a pre-given subject is often politically and legally more potent in encouraging a consciousness or an orientation of resistance to illegitimate authority than the imaginary of a non-pregiven subject, which according to Butler, following Foucault, is continuously formed in the network of power relations. Butler writes that "the subject itself is a site of ambivalence in which the subject emerges both as the effect of a prior power and as the condition of possibility for a radically conditioned form of agency" (Butler 1997: 14–15). While Butler is no less concerned than Benhabib with the possibility of resistance, I think Benhabib reflects in her rejection of thick or deep, and her support for a more moderate and less open-ended individual reflexivity, a more politically "realistic" understanding of democratic individualism and its commitment to strong agency. By proposing a different distribution of reflexivity and unreflexivity within the consciousness of the individual subject, she may be described as trying to balance individual reflexivity with a measure of intuitive or deliberate unreflexivity that is more consistent with emancipatory and effective conceptions of democratic political agency (Benhabib 1992). Butler may, on the other hand, actually provide a more convincing view of what behaviorally and psychologically happens in the relations of power and subject formation. Still, the recent historical record indicates that as legal-political imaginaries, theories of human and citizen's rights that were predicated on a pregiven individual proved both more socially diffusible and politically influential.

Selective Suspensions of Reflexivity in Science and Technology

A most pervasive example of such a strategy that was able to synthesize and augment the powers of nature and rationality to depoliticize power and authority has, of course, been modern science. Science, as suggested above, is in itself an internally most reflexive enterprise. Science, which was characterized by the American sociologist Robert Merton as a social form of "organized skepticism," has been transformed by the modern state into a most potent means of repressing popular reflexivity about "reality" and of "depoliticizing" the actions of state bureaucracy. Many modern social scientists have for a long time crowned physics as a model for "scientific" social science facilitating a deployment of physical-like concepts of social facts. This enabled some French positivistic philosophers already in the eighteenth century to call sociology "social physics," presented as a neutral apolitical basis for state actions. It is as if there was a tacit agreement between the modern state and some social sciences to contain and compartmentalize skepticism and reflexivity in endless discussions of methodology and procedure within relatively secluded professional elites, while promoting faith in unreflexive certainties among laypersons. In some fields, such as education and anthropology, the spread of radical ethical reflexivity often appears in conjunction with reduction in the social authority of scholars as men or women of knowledge and reform, leaving more space to the unknowable subjectivity of his/her subjects (Handelman, this volume). Especially, but not only, in the social sciences, radical ethical or political reflexivity can easily have spillover effects that divide the scientific community and diminish the social authority of the relevant bodies of knowledge in the context of public affairs.

The dialectics of reflexivity and unreflexivity, the selective spreading, for example, of popular political reflexivity and unreflexivity, can, depending upon timing and location, serve both totalitarian and democratic states. In both these forms of governments, physical, military, economic, and social "facts" that are authoritatively certified by experts have been used to present government actions as apolitical and instrumentally rational responses to objective situations. But in democracies there are obviously free forums of criticism that can challenge such certified facts. This is partly why democratic political orientations are more reflexive in the sense that critical attitudes toward official descriptions of factual reality are publicly accessible and are more closely linked with citizens' capacity to politically act. At times, however, political reflexivity has been effectively repressed in democratic states when the coexistence between general trust in science and a free but not sufficiently investigative journalism has enabled one opinion to unreflexively prevail and become dogma. In democracies, publicity, claims of transparency, and an exaggerated sense of individual autonomy have often cultivated a false sense of public knowledge and participation, while actually glossing over arbitrary or uninformed political actions (Jasanoff 2005; Ezrahi 2008).

At least since Marx, the struggle between "naturalizers" and "politicizers" of the market has been continual. During the second half of the twentieth century, economics was elevated to the status of the most scientific of the social sciences, and troops of economists were deployed by democratic governments as guides and advocates of a wide range of "scientifically" warranted public policies. Facilitated by statistics and mathematical arguments that are invisible to the public, economics has become perhaps the most effective governmental tool of depoliticization and of repressing public political reflexivity in many areas of democratic action. Economic knowledge and the liberal-democratic state have combined to form what Foucault called a "regime of knowledge and power" (Foucault 1980: 109–33). Such regimes are the result of what some sociologists of science call the "co-production of knowledge and the social order" (Gibbons et al. 1994). From our perspective here, we can look at the knowledge part or, more accurately, the "social scientism" component of this cluster as combining a solidification of the "reality" bases of the social order at the level of the larger public with partly compartmentalized professional methodological and theoretical reflexivity on parts of elite economists.

It is particularly interesting in this connection that those like the late Israeli sociologist of science Joseph Ben-David, who believed that science, as the core culture of rationality, is the most potent and appropriate constraint on the revival of fascism, had strong objections to the sociology of knowledge (not to the sociology of the scientific community, to which Ben-David made a substantial contribution). He feared its potential to focus reflexivity on the foundations of knowledge, thus weakening the capacity of science to resist ideology and politicization and undermine its reputation as a reliable neutral arbitrator between conflicting political opinions (Ben-David 1981). Again we see in this example the dialectics and the differential distribution of reflexivity and unreflexivity in the construction and deconstruction of political structures.

Repressing Reflexivity by Disciplinary or Organizational Divisions

A measure of control over reflexivity has often been achieved by various forms of departmentalization and division of labor. This is the case in such diverse contexts as the differentiation within science between disciplines to which I alluded before, and within the bureaucracy between departments. In both, specialization reinforces unreflexive reflectivity that enables a local standardized cooperative language-action system to set boundaries for discourse, action, and the imagination. Bureaucratic departmentalization or scientific divisions of labor may constrain radical paradigm shifts or even lesser innovations. The gains of reasoned crossing of such boundaries are amply illustrated by the example of the rise of biochemistry from the "migration" of some chemists into biology. Combining methodologies that grew in different scientific traditions, these scientists triggered reconceptualization of the study of chemical processes in cells.[2] There are, of course, many other such cross-disciplinary innovations associated with the unexpected encounters between distinct systems of disciplinary presuppositions and their attached respective professional communities of specialists. Among the unexpected effects of such encounters or cross-disciplinary migrations one often discerns conceptual innovations triggered by the spread of reflexivity that questions given disciplinary boundaries.

But when bodies of knowledge are appropriated as bases of authoritative scientific definitions of reality or of instrumental technology in order to stabilize political structures, even creative yet destabilizing scientific reflexivity is feared because of its potential political consequences. This is one of the primary sources of tensions between, on the one hand, the stabilizing and regulatory impulse of bureaucracy to protect its institutionalized classificatory system (what Handelman often includes in his concept of "bureaucratic logic") and the revolutionary impulse of science constantly switching theories, instruments, and methodologies in search of better and more potent knowledge (Handelman 2004). These tensions are often manifest also in the relations between university administrators and research faculty and their respective judgments concerning policies and the allocation of resources.

The Reflexivity and Unreflexivity Balance

As I pointed out above, every political regime must rest on a particular balance between reflexive and unreflexive orientations, between the awareness of citizens of their powers as individuals and as members of groups to influence the structure and course of the government (and in the wider sense of the larger political system) and citizen's unreflexive compliance. The ethos and the political ideology of the Enlightenment attempted to achieve a balance by welding political reflexivity in the form of freedom and democratic politics and lay unreflexivity induced by popular versions of the authority of factual, scientifically certified reality. As such, the cultures of science and rationality were expected to set morally neutral and therefore unproblematic limits on political power, freedom, and arbitrariness. The commitments to science and rationality were largely driven by the intuitive fear that a new consciousness of freedom, the spreading of radical political reflexivity of the kind that can erase established modern forms of authority, could lead in some social contexts to revolutionary action or anarchism, while in others to politically deleterious skepticism, declining political participation, and passive compliance. Be it as it may, since the balance between reflexivity and unreflexivity was meant to be implicitly achieved by a balance between political freedom and the constraints of scientifically certified reality (often referred to as nature), any significant rise in reflexivity directed to scientific knowledge could contribute, and indeed have contributed, to the unsettling of earlier democratic balances between reflexivity and unreflexivity or naturalized conceptions of factual reality.[3] Nevertheless, a significant, moderate level of political reflexivity associated with the consciousness of freedom and political efficacy has always been fundamental to democracy. Students of comparative political cultures tend to associate weak democracies with citizens' unreflexive orientations toward their own role in shaping politics, their low sense of political efficacy, and, more generally, with underdeveloped political culture (Almond and Verba 1989). In politics, either empirically warranted or unwarranted citizens' faith in their actual (not only their right to) political freedoms can produce freedom-enhancing actions, whereas disbelief in the existence of such freedoms, whether they exist or not, only facilitates indifferent compliance with established authority.

The liberal democratic political order has been then distinguished, among other things, by moderate but not radical reflexive orientations toward both the rules and contents of politics. Insofar as in such a regime power is legitimized largely by adherence to agreed-upon constitutional rules, it is characteristic of such a regime to focus public political reflexivity on the stability, changes, and applications of the rules of the political game beyond the narrow professional reflexivity of lawyers, legislators, and political leaders. The belief that the "people" is the cause of the government is fundamental, of course, to a measure of constructive political reflexivity that also enables elections as a culminating moment of political participation in political self-governing. When participation fails to produce a new government or support the necessary political fiction of government by the people, there is always the danger that it will lead to a crisis in the regime, to radical destructive awareness of the fragile imaginary basis of the democratic political order, and disrupt the level of popular unreflexive credulity that is necessary for the electoral process to create legitimation. This is what happened to some extent during the 2000 elections in the United States. The Supreme Court, which had to handle the political crisis that developed without encouraging too many doubts about the system, deliberately refused to look too closely at the adequacy of the practice of the election procedures, fearing it might reinforce distrust of the system and encourage an imbalance between the amount of unreflexivity and reflexivity that allows the system to work (Miller 2004).

With respect to the focus of reflexivity on politically relevant contents, insofar as the liberal democratic regime delegitimizes any attempt by the state to unilaterally privilege and fix as hegemonic a particular religion or ideology, such attempts tend to heighten awareness of the illegitimacy of such content protectionism by an incumbent power against competing alternatives. The French political theorist Lefort properly articulates this position. He characterized the core of the democratic state as an empty space that is periodically and sequentially filled up by contents introduced by the parties that temporarily switch their positions between opposition and government (Lefort 1988). Precisely because the liberal democratic polity resists in principle—although much less in practice—any effort to legislate and institutionalize contested coherent and comprehensive systems of beliefs, such an empty space at the core is a necessary condition for the dynamics of political freedom in liberal democracies. Since usually only a part of the spectrum of existing political forces and interests can govern at any period of time, rotation between the political contents and powers that can enter and occupy the empty space that Lefort is talking about secures a wider representation of political viewpoints and powers in the long run.

I would like now to come back to my earlier distinction between politically constructive or creative reflexivity and a politically self-paralyzing or self-destructive one in the context of a brief discussion of the impact of the electronic mass media on the distribution and quality of political reflexivity in the contemporary democratic state. As the main mediator between citizens and their government, the electronic mass media has heightened the awareness of the public of the elusive yet weighty role of the shifting collective political imagination. Periodic changes in hegemonic political imaginaries and even faster transformations of public moods alert the general public of the temporary validity of former concepts of causality and reality and consequently also the anachronism of former policies and expectations. Not surprisingly, as consumers and unconscious producers of political imaginaries, citizens are increasingly reflexive about the limited life expectancy of these imaginaries and their impact on politics. To reiterate, the Enlightenment ethos of a democracy, in which political reflexivity and a self-awareness of the rights and potential of political freedom encouraged public political participation in what was perceived as a stable universe of objective, certain, public facts, a universe in which arbitrary uses of government powers could be checked by the authority of science and certified facts, has been gradually replaced and discredited by distrust in the very existence of any authority to define such "final" facts.[4] Put yet another way, I would claim that without the check of such certified "reality," without even the myth of a given reality, democratic politics usually appears to be gradually reduced to public rituals of legitimation for ambiguously chosen officials who mostly posture rather than govern.

In the past, the trust in the "hard facts" of perceptual realism was supported for a time by illusions about photography. In the 1870s the German scientist Wilhelm His accused his colleague Ernst Haeckel of using handmade drawings to illustrate his scientific objects, which he believed cannot be free from subjective bias, holding that by contrast "the photograph reproduces an object with all of its particulars, including those that are accidental, in a certain sense as raw material, but which guarantees absolute fidelity" (cited in Daston and Galison 2008: 194–95). The idea that photography ensures absolute fidelity to nature is inconceivable today. It is widely understood that photographs only embody points of view. Hence, attempts that were made to transfer the objective desubjectified authority of photographs from objects of nature to objects of politics cannot hold water today. A plea, made in the spirit of Kant's "What Is Enlightenment?" by the well-known British statistician Karl Pearson in 1892, urging citizens to control their emotions and model themselves after dispassionate scientists would sound ridiculous today (Daston and Galison 2008: 196). Whereas photography was accompanied from the beginning by a debate on its place between science and art, public expectations encouraged by the mass media profession, by the reality claims of documentary films, and by spectacular scientific uses of photography, as in ethnographic recording, have sustained in some popular circles a view of the camera as a reliable neutral window into reality. But the cumulative experience of failures to repress subjectivity (and therefore posturing and theatricality in politics), the widespread intuition that almost everything on the small screen as well as on the big one is a staged production mixed with art and/or the economics of profit, have redistributed reflexive reflectivity, as I claimed above, extending it also to what was formerly successfully presented as objective photographic representations of sociopolitical "realities."

The gradual erosion of science and photography as political resources for the authority to define reality and depoliticize the public appearance of power brought about a significant change in the very foundations of contemporary democratic political cultures. A wider recognition of this change is delayed, however, by an anachronistic vocabulary that continues to entertain Enlightenment concepts of deliberative democracy and rationality in public affairs,[5] and by popular commonsense attachment to realism (Rubin 2005). At present, deliberate arguments against beliefs in the givenness of the world as an external object available to us as sentient beings are discernible mostly in the more esoteric forums of the scholarly community. The philosopher John McDowell, for instance, has been developing an influential philosophical perspective that rejects what he and Wilfrid Sellers have been calling "the myth of the given," claiming that our primary sense experience is already mediated by concepts (McDowell 1996). In a different context, David N. Rodowick's study of the shift from film to digital photography as a change from a chemical process of *recording* images of objects to a computational-algorithmic-electronic process of *making or emulating* images of objects describes the ontological decline of the object as a physical referent in the increasingly pervasive environment of digital photography (Rodowick 2007). Referring to digital photography, he says that "computational algorithms may model processes and aspects of the physical world according to the criteria of perceptual realism. However, these models have no causal relations or references to physically existent objects or states of affairs" (Rodowick 2007: 139).

As I have indicated above, such scholarly awareness of the decline of the idea of an external world capturable by untutored perception or mechanical devices like the camera is repressed at the more politically significant level of popular culture. While digitization, much more than chemical film photography, could have induced a deeper awareness of our participation in making up the pictures of our world, the older commonsense perceptual realism, supported by and large by cinematography, still prevails in the environment of digital photography as a genre. It has superior rhetorical powers because it conceals or belittles the active subject's participation in making the visible world. We can redescribe this popular trend as reflecting intuitive popular inclination to limit reflexive critical orientations toward both the reality of the world as a picture and of the individual as its observing subject.

These recent developments raise many questions about the future course of democratic regimes. What kind of a balance between political reflexivity and unreflexivity, and between politically creative and politically corrosive reflexivity, can eventually evolve from the ruins of the declining Enlightenment synthesis of rationality and politics? Can an ethical commitment to factual reality replace its disappearing ontological foundations? How can power that rests on faith in the possibilities of transparency and accountability be protected from deteriorating into arbitrary power without effective guardians of "objective facts"? Was Ben-David right in his fear of the sociology of knowledge, or was he fighting a losing battle against the rise of modern popular political epistemology that denies former safe dichotomies between truths and illusions, facts and fictions? Finally, and more generally, how can the democratic ethos live with the recent spread of radical reflexive reflectivity in both science and politics?

Notes

1. In my book *Imagined Democracies: Necessary Political Fictions* (Ezrahi 2012), I take up the general issue of political reflexivity concerning the nature of political regimes as enacted collective political imaginaries. The denial of this performative aspect of political ontology, the relentless effort to protect the theatrical foundations of the political from public reflexivity, become, therefore, a major preoccupation of politicians, judges, bureaucrats, and intellectual advocates of the regime.
2. On biochemistry as a hybrid discipline and its evolution, see, for instance, Beinert (2002).
3. I see a connection between the declining social authority of science and the rise of its image as a reliable mediator between citizens and political leaders, but I shall not discuss that here.
4. On the role of science in certifying public facts as a basis for the rise of "instrumental politics" in modern democracies, see Ezrahi (1990).
5. On the anachronism of the terms of the current discourse on democracy, see Rubin (2005).

References

Almond, Gabriel A., and Sidney Verba. 1989. *Civic Culture Revisited*. Newbury Park, CA: Sage.

Beinert, Helmut. 2002. "Bioinorganic Chemistry: A New field or Discipline? Words, Meaning and Reality." *The Journal of Biological Chemistry* 277: 37967–72.

Ben-David, Joseph. 1981. "Sociology of Scientific Knowledge." In *The State of Sociology: Problems and Prospects*, ed. J. F. Short. Thousands Oaks, CA: Sage Publications, 40–59.

Benhabib, Seyla. 1992. *Situating the Self: Gender, Community, and Postmodernism in Contemporary Ethics*. New York: Routledge.

Butler, Judith. 1997. *The Psychic Life of Power*. Stanford, CA: Stanford University Press.

Daston, Lorraine, and Peter Galison. 2008. *Objectivity*. New York: Zone Books.

Ezrahi, Yaron. 1990. *The Descent of Icarus, Science and the Transformation of Contemporary Democracy*. Cambridge, MA: Harvard University Press.

———. 2008. "Controlling Biotechnology: Science, Democracy and Civic Epistemology." *Metascience* 17: 177–82.

———. 2012. *Imagined Democracies: Necessary Political Fictions*. New York and Cambridge: Cambridge University Press.

Foucault, Michel. 1980. *Power/Knowledge*. Ed. Colin Gordon. Brighton and Sussex: Harvester Press.

Gibbons, Michael, et al. 1994. *The New Production of Knowledge: The Dynamics of Science and Research in Contemporary Societies*. London: Sage.

Handelman, Don. 2004. *Nationalism and the Israeli State: Bureaucratic Logic in Public Events*. Oxford: Berg.

Jasanoff, Sheila. 2005. *Designs of Nature: Science and Democracy in Europe and the United States*. Princeton, NJ, and Oxford: Princeton University Press.

Lefort, Claude. 1988. *Democracy and Political Theory*. Trans. David Macey. Oxford: Polity Press.

McDowell, John. 1996. *Mind and the World*. Cambridge, MA: Harvard University Press.

Miller, Clark A. 2004. "Interrogating the Civic Epistemology of American Democracy: The Stability and Instability the 2000 US Elections." *Social Studies of Science* 34, no. 4: 501–30.

Rodowick, David N. 2007. *The Virtual Life of Film*. Cambridge, MA: Harvard University Press.

Rubin, Edward. 2005. *Beyond Camelot*. Chicago: Chicago University Press.

Stern, David. 2000. "The Return of the Subject: Power Reflexivity and Agency." *Philosophy and Social Criticism* 26: 109–22.

Yaron Ezrahi is a professor of political science at the Hebrew University of Jerusalem and Senior Fellow Emeritus at the Israel Democracy Institute in Jerusalem, Israel. Email: yaron.ezrahi@huji.ac.il

~~~ Postscript ~~~

REFLEXIVITY AND SOCIAL SCIENCE

Terry Evens

Objectivity and Basic Ambiguity

If one considers the enormous impact of Bourdieu on anthropology and sociology, and of Gödel, Heisenberg, Heidegger, Wittgenstein, Kuhn, and so forth on modern science and the philosophy thereof, the theoretical concern for reflexivity can be in no doubt. It may be true that in the course of everyday life most of us do not sit around contemplating (reflecting on) our reflexive capability (at least not as such). But in view of the consideration that reflexivity does nothing so much as distinguish our very *anthropos,* the fact that people in general tend to take for granted this more or less incomparable faculty makes it anthropologically not merely worthwhile but absolutely requisite to ponder it. As pointed out in the introduction to this volume, anthropology and selfhood are by definition reflexive.

I do not mean to suggest that disciplinary concern with reflexivity is beyond criticism. Hardly. Although bent on showing the anthropologically illuminative value of "reflexivity," most every chapter in this volume is decisively critical of the constricted way in which the concept has so far been understood and treated in the discipline. What is more, the consideration that a number of the contributions here focus on reflexivity as a demonstrable feature of the cultures and societies ordinarily subject to ethnographic study makes plain the critical role of reflexivity in culture and society. In turn, this consideration elucidates that professional anthropology, as a kind of culture and society in its own right, is also inherently reflexive. What kind of culture and society is anthropology? It is, as especially Bourdieu's work in reflexive anthropology and sociology highlights, a social scientific kind.

What appears to bother many critics of the methodological and analytical turn to reflexivity is that it seems to take the life out of science, which is to say, out of objectivism. For this reason, the turn is often associated with postmodernism. This is not unreasonable. Since postmodernism (along with poststructuralism) fundamentally questions scientific positivism, it is easily seen as undermining the very idea of objectivity, seeming to leave nothing but subjectivism as the basis on which research can proceed. Supposing that all reality is mediated at least by language, that is, by a veritable terminological screen, reflexivity too seems to reduce reality to subjective fancy.

The trouble here, however, is the all too easy leap from the critique of objectivism to pure subjectivism—indeed, solipsism—as what alone remains. The literature of postmodernism is hardly uniform in character. In my view, though, the cutting theoretical shift in this movement is most essentially a turn not toward pure subjectivity but away from the immaculate distinction between the objective and the subjective. Instead of self-containment or identity, postmodern thought ascribes ontological primacy to relationism or betweenness or withness, thus defining objective and subjective in basically relative terms. That is, none of us can ever be perfectly objective or subjective, but rather more or less so. We are innately capacitated to detach ourselves by degrees from what interests us, thus assuming what we ordinarily regard as a perspective that is objective to some degree or another and, it follows, subjective in variable measure. But one can no more achieve complete objectivity than one can take up a stance wholly outside the world.

Wittgenstein and Language

Even should we dwell on the common thesis of language (see, e.g., Lawson 1985), an essentially reflexive phenomenon, as that which filters and in this sense shares in the "construction" of reality, we need not conclude that there is nothing but subjectivity. It may be the case, as Wittgenstein held (1961: 115), that "the limits of my language mean the limits of my world," but he later struggled mightily to cut through the attendant implication that there is no connection at all between the reality of the world and the way we speak or write about it. He made clear that he did not mean to suggest that we are in error when we observe, for instance, that while this volume goes to publication (2015) South Sudan remains in the throes of a civil war, the Greek euro crisis may (or may not) be approaching its endgame, and America's Republican and Democratic political parties remain radically opposed to each other for all intents and purposes.

What is in question here is Cartesian dualism, the logic of which makes knowledge of the mechanicophysical world not merely mysterious but virtually impossible. For if the difference between mind and body is total, then the former, whatever the language in use, can know nothing of the latter. In relation to the role of language, Wittgenstein's response to this problem is laboriously self-critical and richly complex. Perhaps most profoundly, his solution appears to come down to the consideration that language is not only mindful but also corporeal, that is, a matter of physics. Words are embodied in mechanical sound waves; when written, they are materially visible; when embossed, they become tactile; and so on. This means that in the *saying* (by which I mean also the writing and the thinking) of them, words partake directly of the stream of life with which their *said* can never truly catch up. How could the words as said, that is, as already fixed in time, draw level with the stream of life without distorting that very stream by bringing to a halt its flow, its very essence? Conversely, being *of* this stream in actually *saying* them, words are always already in contact with it, and thus have access to it. Speaking of the "spatio-temporal nature" of propositions, Wittgenstein made the following critical observation (cited in Stern 1995: 154–55) about the possibility of verifying propositions pertaining to the dynamic of existence: the "spatio-temporal nature [of propositions]… must be related to their commensurability [with the stream of life] as the corporeality of a ruler is to its being extended—which is what enables it to measure." In other words, because the actual *saying* of a proposition participates directly in the stream of life, it may, depending on time and place, constitute a verifiable measure of that stream. We suppose that this observation stands together with Wittgenstein's famous proposition that the most basic meaning of a word is not in the dictionary but in the word's application in practice, that is, in its *immediate* use.[1]

Thus, the prison house of language, for all the great height and thickness of its walls, is not at the end of the day perfectly secure. Like all boundaries, linguistic ones too both separate and connect, as between, in the present relevance, mind and body. In effect, language's contact with the reality of the world is quite natural, even if it can never succeed in capturing the stream of life to the fullest extent and must therefore always miss something in its descriptions.

One can illustrate this relative, though ultimate, incommensurability between language and action by appealing to Thomas Kuhn's notion of paradigm change. Take Kuhn's (1970: 118–19) probing discussion of the difference between the way Aristotle and Galileo saw "a heavy body swinging back and forth on a string or a chain until it finally comes to rest." Whereas Galileo saw it as a perpetual motion machine, and developed a new dynamics on the basis of that perception, for Aristotle it was simply a heavy body falling arduously and ever so slowly to rest. Kuhn surmises that many readers would say both Aristotle and Galileo saw a pendulum, but that each interpreted it differently. However, the point that Kuhn (1970: chap. 10) is keen to make is to the contrary: that in a critical sense, with the shift of paradigms "the world" itself had changed, such that the medieval Italian thinker and the ancient Greek one were not in fact seeing the same thing. To expand Kuhn's point, although the two perceptions, Aristotle's and Galileo's, are opposing, both are, as Kuhn points out, accurate. This must mean that each necessarily overlooks a truth that the other distinguishes. The example from Kuhn, then, might be seen to suggest, in addition to the possibility of different objective perceptions of dynamic movement, Wittgenstein's thesis of an ultimately intractable incommensurability between language and what it refers to: that at the end of the day and for all the force and reality of *saying*, the dynamic reality of the stream of life and the world cannot be perfectly caught by the *said*.[2]

Deleuze and Guattari and Ontological Ambiguity

The upshot of Wittgenstein's (and Kuhn's) position amounts to a picture of fundamental ontological ambiguity. For yet another powerful twentieth-century philosophy dwelling on, in different terms and philosophical character, the essential ontological betweenness of reality, we can look to the work of Deleuze and Guattari. Taking their cue directly from physics rather than language per se, Deleuze and Guattari draw a distinction between molarity and molecularity.[3] Whereas the molecular refers to relations defined by difference and openness, thereby denoting indetermination, movement, and change (as in, say, entropy), the molar, compressing and delimiting the molecular into abstractions (concepts, ideas, representations, things, etc.), takes on the guise of stasis, closure, and settled identity. Put another way, with molarity, difference is eclipsed (but by no means eradicated), producing what amounts to an abstraction from the molecular, namely, sameness owing not to identity per se but to repetition. Nonetheless, because the abstract appears only insofar as it is materially embodied (as in, e.g., voice, word, book, body, brain, etc.), the molar cannot "transcend" the molecular without, paradoxically, registering it. Likewise, as a primarily relational event, the molecular too entails materiality (if only, e.g., atoms and subatomic particles), and therefore necessarily augurs molarity, that is, the "actual" as distinct (but not wholly separate) from the "virtual" (potentiality), or, in Deleuze and Guattari's even more distinctive idiolect, the body *with* rather than *without* organs.

With the terminological dyad of molar and molecular, Deleuze and Guattari aim to bypass the philosophy of consciousness and its defining (Cartesian and Kantian) dualism of mind and body. Far from being immaculate, the distinction is cast in terms of a decidedly nonteleological "dialectic": a dynamics of *fundamental* ambivalence or ambiguity. In other words, although the molar versus molecular distinction constitutes a duality, it not only has nothing in common with dualism—which is to say, with absolute mutual exclusion—but also refutes it as a basically acceptable image of reality (or, if you like, as "stupid," by which Deleuze and Guattari mean senseless, as in "stupor"). For them all dualities are decidedly relative, such that the lines of bifurcation are fundamentally capacitated to both separate and connect all at once—as in, for instance, the fold of a doubled-over sheet of paper (Deleuze 1993).

Seeing molecularity in terms of "logic" of "multiplicity," Deleuze and Guattari might be understood to afford the molecular (as does, to hark back to the introduction, Luria for the Infinite or *Ein-Sof*) a qualified axiological primacy, the primacy of creation or genesis or, indeed, life itself. I say "qualified" because Deleuze and Guattari by no means discount the necessity of the role of the molar. (How could they, since, for all their remarkable efforts to molecularize the telling of their philosophy, they cannot do so save by means of concepts and representations?) What is more, multiplicity also characterizes molarity. Whereas molar multiplicities correspond to spatial divisions, and are therefore numerical, molecular ones, having nothing to do with the common distinction between the one and the many, are a question of qualitative rather than quantitative differences; therefore, they bespeak temporality or duration rather than spatiality. Multiplicity, in Deleuze and Guattari's usage, amounts to the potential for processive "bifurcation," which is to say, creative selection. Such selection comes in two types: on the one side, natural, and, on the other, imaginative or thoughtful. Obviously, the division between these two types parallels that between molecularity and molarity: on the plane of the latter, bifurcation creates space, whereas on that of the former, bifurcation does not mark time so much as make it, thus creating becomings.

Of the multiplicity of paths prompting bifurcation, whichever one is selected, it is selected at the expense of all the others. For this reason, bifurcation (and, therewith, multiplicity) involves duality (yet not dualism proper). What I have called "paths" here, Deleuze and Guattari speak of as "singularities." A singularity, though, according to these two *penseurs,* is not a self-contained and well-defined phenomenon, but a multiplicity in itself. As such, it is an opening, singular only in its being inaccessible to circumscription and classification, and in its offer of radical novelty and shocking difference. Thus, the duality composed by a (naturally or imaginatively) "chosen" singularity and all the singularities that are left unsounded is irreducible to the division between the one and the many, for by definition no singularity can be characterized by oneness as such. Given the principle of crossing or reversibility in Deleuze and Guattari's ontology, concrete oneness is fundamentally precluded. That is, in light of the chiasma between multiplicity and singularity, oneness per se is impossible, since any singularity always exceeds utter oneness to begin with (as is true also of Luria's god figure, the eccentricity of which is defined by the abnegating act—a crossing and inversion—of cosmic contraction and the concomitant becoming of a new, creational world comprised of various beings as becomings). Indeed, perfect ontological resolution (a state of being and absolute identity logically defined by Descartes's dualism and explicit in his *cogito*) would amount to the denial of molecular process. That is, it would convey stop-time (the complete or totalistic "time" of the pre-Lurianic figure of God drawn in the received Genesis of Judeo-Christianity). Of course, numerical oneness does hold on the plane of molarity, but only as an abstraction or approximation—its actual, taken-for-granted forcefulness in our lives notwithstanding.

Thus, in Deleuze and Guattari's philosophy we find posited a wild, incongruent ontology keyed to basic ambiguity: essential vagueness, uncertainty, indistinctness, immeasurableness, whether we have in mind rhizomatic or arborescent models—that is, respectively, multiplicities or root-and-branch dualities. In this critical respect, this ontology brings to mind Luria's cosmological account of genesis. Perhaps "theological" is not an adjective Deleuze and Guattari would want applied to their philosophy, and they would likely reject the kabbalistic idea of an eventual cosmic correction (the *Tikkun*) of the imperfection described by ambiguity. Nevertheless, it is arguable that in a sense their philosophical ontology entertains the mystical, for between mystery and *essential* incomprehensibility there is obvious semantic affinity, if not synonymy. Insofar as the empiricism of these two thinkers rests on ontological ambiguity, seen from a perspective that is predicated on identity proper—which is to say, a rational perspective—the empiricism verges, if not turns, on mystery. In their unreserved efforts to do away with the dualism of immanence and transcendence, Deleuze and Guattari, taking a cue from Spinoza, deployed the word "substance" to describe whatever it is that underlies the crossing relationship or paralogical connection between the molar and molecular. But there seems no denying (as also remains the case for Spinoza's ontological argument) that their use of "substance" does not, for all their talk of immanence, elude the sense of mystery that is intrinsic to fundamental ambiguity.[4] In other words, an ontological foundation of basic ambiguity—in effect, *a foundation that is not a foundation, and an ontology that is not an ontology*—is irreducible to rationality proper or the logic of identity, thus allowing one to see and think the abiding and ultimate indeterminateness or openness of what there is.

Science and Objectivity

The overall point at this juncture is that there is nothing in postmodernism and reflexivity, *at least not in the way that we, in this volume, have used and represented these concepts,* that necessarily denies the possibility of objective, empirical research. To the contrary, if anything, by exposing as a perfectibilist exaggeration the picture, deeply entrenched in Western thought, of objectivity and subjectivity as absolutes, we position ourselves to better grasp who and what we (human beings) are and are becoming. It is hard to deny the effectiveness of Western dualism, the great power of which is only too evident in (among other things) the technological ability to exploit natural resources to the point of their exhaustion. By bringing into relief, though, the "stupid" side of this power, the side that binds thought in thrall of pure identity, totality, and absolute control, the concept of reflexivity puts both subjectivity and objectivity on a more concrete, and in this sense saner, basis. By acknowledging (what should be by now) the empirically obvious, that between these two attitudinal perspectives there is a fundamental zone of indistinction, the idea of reflexivity reveals that each of them is both the same as and different from the other. This relation of basic ambiguity rings at once true and explanatory, so long as the identity of each faculty to the ambiguity, subjectivity and objectivity, is grasped as a matter of degree and in terms of becoming. Given that we are in and of the world, objectivity cannot be perfect. But it remains—what science, soft or hard, never fails to demonstrate—a relative yet evidential matter. For me there is no question but that reflexivity does not deny reality, which is to say, the real world. In which case, the idea of reflexivity must also be capable of addressing real anthropological problems.

To be sure, the language of science presents itself and tends to be received as not just another tongue with its own view of the world, but the tongue whose view *formally* speaks universal truth. This self-presentation depends on the claim to objectivism, which, scientists presume, distinguishes scientific language from all others—even if many of the latter languages also do not doubt, without predicating this as such, the world borne by them. The issue, then, reduces to the principle of objectivity: is it the case that the practice of science reveals the objective world as such, a world that goes unmediated by the language through which it is demarcated?

I think that science's claim to universal truth, although misleading to a consequential extent, must be taken seriously. Who can deny the extraordinary practical efficacy of science? If, for some reason or other, you wish to put a man on the moon, you can do so *virtually* by slipping him a hallucinogenic (as Carlos Castaneda's [fictitious] Don Juan did) or by *actually* putting him there. The difference between these two means of transportation is a difference that makes a difference, one that is indeed substantial.[5] At this point the question becomes that of the relation between objectivism and technological efficacy. Of course, the drug is also a technology, one no doubt having emerged originally, way back when, from an accidental consuming of the wrong mushroom—in effect, an unintended trial. Today, to be sure, this process of discovery is perpetuated in pharmaceutical laboratories around the world, with the difference that it has been formally systematized as trial and error. In other words, despite the difference between the two ways of putting a man on the moon, there is a plain continuity between them. Yet the difference reveals much about the nature of an objective stance.

Objectivity amounts to a sustained effort to detach oneself from one's own feelings and prejudices, in order to better think through the object of one's interests. While understanding can serve as an end in itself, in general it is at least implemented if not always sought in the interest of manipulating to one's own advantage the object in question. In other words, objectivity may be construed as a kind of tool—a sophisticated, attitudinal prosthesis, artificial in the manner in which all second nature is artificial, and given as a potentiality of that nature—to develop further the practical toolkit of human beings. Paradoxically, objectivity issues from a subjective decision to stand back from the world in order to better cope with it. It is subjective because it makes sense only in respect of creatures abundantly endowed with selfhood, creatures that can mindfully (reflectively) decide for themselves to systematically restrict or (as the phenomenologists say) suspend their immediate (subjective) responses, in order to see the world *as if* they stood outside of it, that is, objectively. When executed, this decision results in the endeavor to stop and think (reflect) before committing oneself to action proper. More comprehensively, the decision also occasions the creation of a logic to facilitate the act of thinking (reflecting), a logic that helps to ensure the efficiency and productivity of thought, namely, rationality proper. In its classical form, this logic is based on the canonical principles of identity, noncontradiction, and the excluded middle. As is given in their very names, these principles ensure that the logic cuts with an edge of perfection, such that in practice it can yield only truth or falsity, but nothing in between. Conducted in accordance with this perfectibilistic logic, the experimental procedure of trial and error becomes stunningly efficient at finding what works, that is, at producing practical success. This success gets formalized as scientific theory, a stock of knowledge that serves in turn to guide the procedural deployment of trial and error.

To be sure, such success more than suggests that reality corresponds in imposing degree to the scientific findings. For this reason, Charles Taylor (1985: chap. 5) argued that wherever it is exported, science normally commands respect. Nevertheless, because the success is generated by *logically* precluding a defining aspect of the real, the aspect of the in-between, such success comes not only with significant benefits but also at great costs to us and our world. If it is the case, as a moment's reflection tells us, that everything is the same as and different from everything else, then we are compelled to consider a notion such as Deleuze's "substance" or Merleau-Ponty's "flesh of the world." In other words, what makes the world *both* whole *and* open becomes a critical consideration if we are to come to viable terms with reality. But, as we have just described, by excluding the middle, the success of exact science is achieved precisely by systematically neglecting the openness of the whole, the dynamic in which the whole unfolds in ever untold and untoward ways—Wittgenstein's "stream of life."

Heidegger and the Costs of Scientific Reductionism

To assess the cost of this immensely powerful reductionism, we can look at "the question concerning technology." That question is given profound attention in Heidegger's famous essay (1993) by that name. In encapsulating Heidegger's argument here, it is well to keep in mind his well-known notion (1978: 32) that *Dasein* (English: "being there") "is distinguished by the fact that, in its very Being, that Being is an issue for it." In other words, man is defined by Heidegger in terms of the capacity for reflexivity.[6] Here are the key points, as I understand them, of his influential argument concerning technology.

Seeking the "essence" of technology, Heidegger begins by telling us what we all already "know," that technology is a means to an end, that is, an instrument. This is true, of course, not only of modern technology but also of premodern technology, such as, for example, handicrafts. The difference rests, though, with the degree of mastery, modern technology being bent on *complete* instrumental control. Modern technology, Heidegger suggests, omits to acknowledge the relative "in-itselfness" of what it sees as a mere resource, something to be wholly dominated. This difference insinuates the question of the relation between the grasp of technology as merely a means and the problem of essence, for if technology has not always been motivated by the objective of total control, then there must be more to its essence than instrumentalism per se. To disclose this "more," Heidegger points out that instrumentalism may be understood as a causal phenomenon: the end is the cause, and the effect the means or technology. It follows that where the definition of technology as exclusively instrumental prevails, there man, when taking himself as master of the world, is, ironically, nothing but (as in Hegel's master-slave dialectic) the effect of the end, that is, a kind of instrument or object of technology. Seeing himself in the reflection of godly prodigious technology, man makes of himself a prosthesis to a machine. He becomes something to be ordered and automated, as if he were simply another natural resource—one more "standing-reserve," as Heidegger calls it. This circumstance is, Heidegger holds, perilous.

To be sure, man is innately given to the development of technology—he is, as Karl Marx and the physical anthropologists (e.g., Kenneth Oakley) have called him, man the toolmaker (*Homo faber*). But is he this above all? Still pursuing the question of the essence of technology, Heidegger proceeds to complicate the picture by thinking of causality as, instead of two events, the second of which results from the first, a multifaceted, dynamic whole, in which man's capacity for thought is a crucial component but by no means the only occasioning cause in the production of technology. Rather, speaking ontologically of this dynamic whole, Heidegger reasons that what there is amounts to potential that is hidden but open to being revealed and developed. In this holistic dynamic, man, by virtue of his capacity for reflection, plays the role of midwife, bringing the embryonic reality into the open and subsequently actualizing it. The trouble is, though, that by competing with ("challenging," says Heidegger) instead of nurturing this potential, modern technology poses a grave danger. For in its totalistic designs and correlative failure to respect the potentiality that it helps to open up, modern technology threatens man's "freedom." It does so by erecting an epistemic blind that makes it impossible to see the true essence of technology, which is not instrumentalism but the creative process itself. In effect, Heidegger is arguing that the essence of technology is not the means-ends relationship, but, as he puts it, poetry (*poiesis*), in the sense of creative process. For this reason, the *primary* danger is not technology moving us to physically destroy the environment on which we depend (though surely that too is critical), but rather the reduction of human being to nothing more than means. In other words, we have rendered reflexivity primarily in terms of might and mastery, blocking our ability to see life, including our own, in relation to its capacity to create, and as indebted to and dependent on the continuance of that which we technologize.

Descartes's Dualism

Heidegger's argument about technology, thus, boils down to the predication of a perverse or deleterious reflexivity. Under the sway of this reflexivity, human beings see the difference between themselves and everything else as immaculate, such that everything else is taken in terms of its use value alone. In the interest of mining coal for energy, we are inclined to perceive a mountain not as such or magnificent in its own right, but as "standing-reserve," says Heidegger. In effect, the "truth" (to use Heidegger's word) of life and the creational dynamic is largely eclipsed. This perversion, I suggest, amounts to a play on Cartesian dualism, in which the cogito (the "I am" in Descartes's "I think, therefore I am") presents itself as hermetically sealed, to the point that whatever is not "thinking stuff" (*res cogitans*), including one's own body, is wholly bereft of reason (which is to say, for Descartes, of godliness). Consequently, under this *radically* asymmetrical divide, the material aspect of things (*res extensa*), insofar as it exists at all, does so only to be set upon by the "I" of pure thought, the "I" that cannot recognize corporeality as, even in a relative sense, something characterized by its own creational contribution.

In light of man's capacity for reason, Descartes took an ethereal figure of God as the mirror of himself, leaving only the gravitative fact of his embodiment to explain the transparent imperfection of his self next to so picture-perfect an image of the on-high. Had Descartes allowed his rational faculties to understand himself directly in view of its embodiment, he would have had to conceive of the nature of not only body but also mind as fundamentally compromised, that is, as essentially ambiguous. By contrast, today's scientific view of the mind as reducible to the brain is nothing more than a logical conclusion of Cartesian dualism. Given the absoluteness of the boundary it defines, this dualism can only be resolved by positing a faultless monism: that *in reality* one of the two principles of the dualism must be utterly reducible to the other. Whereas Descartes made reason the master key, in science it is the supremacy of the material principle that is taken for granted. Plainly, Cartesian dualism, with its logical and ontological (but not ontic, as Descartes himself had to admit) separation of mind from body, remains a colossal and immensely consequential projection in the West. St. Augustine ([1942] 2006: book 7, xvii), whose influence on Descartes is transparent, held the body to be "a load upon the soul." I am inclined to think, though, that in today's Western thought there is no greater load upon our thought and reason than that of Descartes's dualism and the unconditional reflexivity it has fostered regarding the difference between mind and body.

By defining man's essential being solely in terms of his mindfulness, Cartesian dualism transforms him into sheer interiority, an illusory, out-of-this-world figure. To Descartes, each man is indeed an island. Momentously, this figure of the individual cuts across all social and cultural differences among men, from class and caste to race and creed. As Kant put it, since each man enjoys the capacity of reason, so each is an end in himself, deserving of the accordant moral respect. We have here the principle of equality on which modern democracy finds, in prominent part, its presumptive basis. Ironically, though, the same figure of *the* individual logically divides one person from another in absolute terms, for if each is wholly self-contained, then, *by definition,* ordinary experience notwithstanding, the other is exactly not-self.[7] In the event, from the standpoint of the self, the other and all otherness appears, on some deep and impelling plane of perception, as grist for the mill of instrumental treatment, a veritable consumer good. This phenomenological circumstance helps, I propose, to understand why it is that in, say, the United States, a country that presents itself as the archetype of modern democracy, there prevails, increasingly, a tendency to practice the reverse of what is preached on the basis of equality: power, greed, and deceit instead of (a mantra that has come truly to live up to its comic-book origins) "truth, justice, and the American way." Today's all too easy presumption that what comes natural to humans is self-interest rather than other-regard finds a basis in this view of the individual as wholly self-contained. The presumption is insidious on two counts:

first, because it tends to justify the conduct it presumes; and second, as both self-interest and other-regard issue from the second nature that essentially defines our humanity, neither can be more or less "natural" than the other.

Marx and Labor Power

The Cartesian form of reflexivity is perverse because, through the stupefying power of his technology, man is goaded to transform himself preeminently into a creature of that very technology. An inspired account of this transformation is found in Marx's concept of labor value, which pictures human beings as just another commodity to be bought, sold, exploited, and dominated.[8] In effect, we are reduced to the very mechanical stuff from which Descartes was at such great pains to detach man. Keyed to the goal of surplus production, capitalism is inclined to commoditize everything (land, water, air, fossil fuels, human beings, other creatures, etc.). In *Key Largo,* John Huston's 1948 classic film, a vicious gangster, having been asked by one of his hostages what it is that he wants, responds with, "More. That's right! I want more!" "More" is another name for the politicoeconomic system called capitalism, and modern technology constitutes a crucial means of producing more and more, lastly in the form of profits. Strikingly, labor power too enters into the capitalist equation by reference to profits, just as if there were no difference between this kind of power and technology. Although the market value of labor power may be determined as a function of the commodities necessary to produce that power, it remains always undervalued relative to its own contribution to production. Were that not so, the resulting productivity could not produce an excess of income over expenditures, that is, profit. Moreover, owing to market competition, a corollary of capitalism, there is constant reinvestment of surplus value in the interest of enhancing the means of production, which results in an ever widening range of commoditization, so extensive as to encompass the globe and everything in it. Inasmuch as capitalism has the effect of eclipsing the essence of life (Heidegger's "truth") and making labor or use value the bottom line of existence, we might wish to speak of this expansionism, and the concomitant pursuit of nothing more than more, as a necrotizing process. For if one of capitalism's products is the primary presentation of ourselves to ourselves as machines, then we will have killed our humanity and that aspect of the world that bespeaks the wonder of life.

Virilio and Technology

The expansionism is, however, not only spatial but also temporal. Here we turn to Paul Virilio's ingenious and provocative work on modern technology and its effect on our humanity. Unlike so many French intellectuals, Virilio diverges from Marx's preoccupation with economy. For Virilio, as for Heidegger, it is the desire for total control that moves humans to technologize themselves, leaving their essential humanity behind. What is representatively at stake, as Virilio sees it (2006), is the state's power to move things, including bodies, with supreme efficiency. The upshot is chronic "military" competition over, not class differences, but "speed," by which Virilio means the most proficient technological means of control. The exemplar of these means has long been, of course, armaments proper. But today it is information and communications technology that, in this regard, begins to reign supreme. In the current state of things, a countless number of humans are being conducted and informed by this technology.[9] But most exemplary in relation to the "prostheticization" of human beings is our mechanismic attachment to the computer itself.

A critical phenomenological result of this technology is the acute contraction of space, whereby we live increasingly in the virtual reality projected on our computer screens. We no longer need to leave our homes in order to shop, play, travel, visit, explore, or make war. With this shrinkage of space, time slouches toward the instantaneous. Our terminological screens are themselves computer mediated by the digital display, the process being programmed by binary numerical operators (1 and 0). Although this technological emphasis on speed and instantaneity may not wholly eradicate past and future as concerns, the critical force of these two temporalities is considerably blunted: living so neatly enclosed in the instant, concerns of past and future become doubly abstract, to the point where their phenomenological bite increasingly fails to break the epistemic skin of the user, therewith scarcely registering an impelling concern. "The whole world suddenly becomes endotic [by contrast to exotic]," writes Virilio (1997: 24–25): "And such an end," he continues, "implies forgetting spatial exteriority as much as temporal exteriority ('no future') and opting exclusively for the 'present' instant, the real instant of instantaneous telecommunications."

Consequently, despite the extraordinary proficiency and power of information technology, the partial but profound eclipse of the real world tends to impede an intelligent and viable approach to the reality found in the flesh rather than on an electronic display. Sitting in a room with remote controls, it becomes all too easy for the controller to "disappear" other humans from afar, as if these latter were mere avatars in a computer game of pilotless aircraft. The death resulting from such action extends, in a different but still substantial way, to the controller, since by operating the remote device, he himself waxes robotic, a creature of a computer game, but with real lethal consequences.[10]

Given that Virilio, dwelling on the grave dangers posed by this extraordinary technology, ignores its "benefits," his critique is transparently hyperbolic. Nonetheless, it plainly forges a warning of consequences so dire that we can disregard it only at our peril. Prodigious technology projects the temptation of titanic power, effectively eroding awareness of our earthly finitude. In the event, we are all too often given to ignore the symbiotic nature of our relation to the resources that sustain us in our humanity (air, land, water, forests, other beings, etc.). In doing so, can we altogether avoid points of no recovery? Virilio is arguing that the power of this technology is also the power that leads us down the road of tragic foolhardiness. By inventing the ocean liner (Virilio's example), we invite the kind of dreadful accident that befell the *Titanic*. This understanding of the causal continuity between formidable technology and fearful accidents alerts us to the fact that we can count on unintended consequences. As was demonstrated in the 2011 earthquake and tsunami that brought down the nuclear power plant in Japan, wreaking terrible destruction, almighty power occasions almighty accidents. We our not in total control and never will be.

In all cases the resources on which we rely are subject to pollution and depletion. In light of the advent of the combustion engine, what is troubling about a crisis of fossil fuels is not that it may be upon us, for it is bound to happen in due course. What is troubling, rather, is that we have arrived at its coming so irresponsibly, with a speed occasioned by anything but care for our humanity and the world in which we live, and without due preparation for the event. Virilio is arguing, as I see it, that with the invention of digital technology, we have also opened ourselves up to the destruction of our humanity, an "accident" to which, given this technology's commanding instrumental "success," we largely remain oblivious. This invention bespeaks, he says, a failure to consider the "path" of our humanness, producing a descent—indeed, a "fall"—into inhumanity. As Virilio puts it (1997: 30, emphasis in original), "The *path's being* defines *the subject's perception* through the object's mass. The falling body suddenly becomes *the body of the fall*." Put otherwise, this time exhibiting a postmodernist rather than biblical sensitivity (Virilio 1997: 24), "Between the subjective and the objective it seems that we have no room for the 'trajective.'"

Humanity may be regarded as a resource in its own right, but one that belies the sheer instrumentalism connoted by the term "resource." If the quality of being human is a matter of self-construction, such that man is greatly capacitated to determine his own ends, then it describes a reflexivity so pronounced as to bring into high relief a "natural" (but not for that reason inexorable) subordination of instrumentality to value qua value. This is because such an ideal manifestation of reflexivity, in which objectivity emerges as a subjective possibility, bespeaks the relative transcendence of value over use, that is, of what is better over what is more powerful. In his moral philosophy, Kant speaks here of an end in itself, by which he means something the value of which is irreducible to use. Virilio's work is suggesting that what is merely a means to an end, high technology, is rapidly becoming its own end, thus redefining in terms of sheer means the notion of "end in itself"—much as, in Marx's critique of capitalism, accumulation of wealth becomes its own end, reducing value to measurable properties. The result is the *devaluing* of everything, including human beings, into means or prostheses to machines. For Virilio, by tempting us to replace bodily perception simply with information, discarding the immediate experiences of the actual world, the experiences from which any information ultimately derives, we risk the depletion of the resource called humanity. Virilio describes this depletion as "the losing of one's soul, *anima*" by virtue of having lost the "being of movement" (1997: 25). In evolutionary terms, our gift for self-construction amounts also to a power of self-destruction through a process of *unnatural* selection, which is to say, through choices that issue from humankind's second nature. Insofar as modern technology manages to hide from us our own finitude, leading us to regard the world as our oyster but not our responsibility and to delegate our ethics to mechanical deliberations, we will have, ironically, denied our humanity, to say nothing of the state of (so-called) civilization and the world.

The Self and Its Ground: Hans Jonas's "Ontological Surprise"

We have seen that Heidegger pictures the human practice of reflexivity in terms of *poeisis* or aestheticism. But as a number of contributions in this volume help us to understand, this practice of creation is also a matter of ethics. In the introduction, the editors contended that reflexivity constitutes a critical descriptor of being human and that it therewith affords a certain advantage to social science among the sciences. At this point we can see that this advantage bears on the question concerning ethics. As the capacity of *self*-determinacy, reflexivity is fundamentally an ethical becoming. So long as "ethics" is defined *primarily*, as it is here, by reference to a process of *choosing* ends rather than to a fixed code of the ends thus chosen, wherever there is self-fashioning, *all* choices, no matter how trifling, routine, quotidian, and less than conscious, become, either explicitly or implicitly, questions concerning ethics.

In the interest of emulating positive science and educing determinacy, social science can work (and has worked) to disregard ethics as a dynamic of self-determining. But, without making nonsense of itself, social science cannot wholly eradicate this dynamic, for the dynamic finds a basis in biology. All living things, plants and animals alike, including human animals, present a metabolic exchange between themselves and their environment. But with humans, this exchange has undergone a qualitative inversion, or as the late philosopher Hans Jonas says ([1966] 1982: 79–80), "an ontological surprise." Whereas the life of other living things is first and foremost mediated by what they consume, humans are, in a dramatically singular way, not primarily what they eat. While on one plane of their being, they depend on the ingesting of plants and animals, their lives, *as lived*, are primarily mediated by their sense of self. Jonas speaks here ([1966] 1982: 80) of the human organism as "its own continuous achievement," describing "the relation of the organism to its material substance" as a "double nature": it is, he says ([1966] 1982: 80, emphasis in original), "a dialectical relation of *needful freedom* to matter." This relation is summed up by him succinctly as follows: "[I]nstead of saying that the living form is a region of transit for matter, it would be truer to say that the material contents in their succession are phases of transit for the self-continuation of the form."

Clearly, as applied to humans, the metabolic exchange readily lends itself to description in terms of a self-other relation. Because we can distinguish between, say, a plant or a nonhuman animal and its environment, we might also apply this nomenclature, of self and other, to the botanical or zoological world. But doing so smacks of anthropomorphism, seeing as selfhood entails well-developed self-consciousness. In the case of the plant or animal and its environment, the form of life is largely reducible to "a region of transit for matter," whereas with human beings life takes on a critical sense of self as (if still only relatively) conspicuously transcendent of matter. Trying to capture the wonder of this ultimately limited but nonetheless consequentially transformative difference, Merleau-Ponty wrote (1962: xiii): "Reflection does not withdraw from the world towards the unity of consciousness as the world's basis; it steps back to watch the forms of transcendence fly up like sparks from a fire; it slackens the intentional threads which attach us to the world and thus brings them to our notice; it alone is consciousness of the world because it reveals that world as strange and paradoxical." In other words, human existence brings into high relief the basic ambiguity of life, the sense in which the material nature of life is an abstraction from a vital dynamic of essential betweenness, an "ontological" dynamic in which materiality is ever cut, intrinsically, to one degree or another, by the immaterial. With the emergence of the human organism, the degree reaches a kind of tipping point, such that the material aspect, although ever present, is *for lived purposes* deprived of its ontological primacy, in favor of the immaterial or what Merleau-Ponty calls "reflection" or "[self-]consciousness" or the "invisible" (1968). These lived purposes are thus so distinguishing that they occasion the appearance of a qualitative leap—a reversal of right of way, so to speak—from matter to form, when form is rendered in the dynamic terms of self-identifying.

Put another way, human being describes an organism in which the reflexive relationship holding between one thing and another is internalized in the thing itself to so arresting a degree as to distinguish the individual as an "individual"—a *person*. That is to say, what we, from our unique (so-called sapiential) vantage point in the animal kingdom, are inclined to perceive as a *predominantly* external relationship between a thing and its surround (Jonas's metabolic exchange relationship) is transformed into an *apparently* interior relationship, in which mindfulness envelops the body for lived purposes, occasioning the manifestation of reflex action as "reflection," that is, thought, and, accordingly, well-developed self-consciousness or selfhood.[11]

Under this condition, the self stands out against its ground, almost as if its connection to the latter were superfluous, as if the ground were alien to the self. It has been argued that this primal alienation, between ourselves and our ground, is registered phenomenologically in upright posture (cf. Straus 1980), inasmuch as this bearing may be seen and felt to constitute a force of opposition to the very ground on which we stand, a dynamic "resistance" to being *earth*bound. Thus, our material nature comes to represent the other in the self-other relationship, a conceptual turn disposing us to see our*selves,* which is to say, our reflexive, conscious being, as our true ground. Given this heightened experience of selfhood in conjunction with awareness of the irremovable backdrop of our mortality or reduction to the ground, the reassignment of this self-begotten ground to yet a higher consciousness, a god figure, seems destined. But even here, as the

Judeo-Christian story of Genesis frankly narrates (and shares with so many other theological and mythological narratives of the origin of humankind), selfhood is pictured as ever conflicted between contestation with and allegiance to any such celestial ground.

The most emphatic point I want to make, though, is not theological but ontological: *insofar* as our sense of self depends on standing against our ground, and our ground has become our*selves*, selfhood amounts to a dialectical dynamic of negation and creation in which the self can make itself *only* by standing (out) against itself. In other words, by continuously negating—and in this sense "sacrificing"—itself, the self creates and re-creates itself, making of selfhood a fundamentally paradoxical phenomenon if ever there was one. In effect, the dynamic describes self as essentially a self-other relation in its own right, an autodynamic of reflexivity. Were the self not at once other to itself, there would and could be no self at all.

In the wake of poststructuralism, it is often maintained that the self is a fiction, meaning that it is nothing but a construct. Yet, this way of looking at it, though fruitfully disconcerting, remains too shallow. For even if we do not possess a self as we do a heart and lungs, selfhood is nonetheless imposed on us—it comes with the human territory of singular mindfulness, and is therefore for all practical purposes real. This reality is indeed that of *self*-constructing, in which case, inasmuch as this kind of construction is also mindful, it becomes a matter of responsibility, such that one cannot but be in good part accountable for one's worldhood, the world one constructs and inhabits. In other words, determining our own ends, if only as an effect of self-consciousness, amounts to deciding, relatively, our good and our bad, our right and our wrong. What we are constructing, then, is ethics, in the broadest sense of this term, the sense in which ethics is not primarily a bounded philosophical or moral discipline but, more fundamentally, the continuing process of deciding, always in the face of others and otherness, our own ends or good. Whether we have in mind society or the individual, the process of deciding is innately social, not only because the very idea of the individual is social, but also because selfhood in itself amounts to a self-other relationship.

Meontology: The Primacy of the Between or the Social

We can return now to the question of the implicit advantage of social science vis-à-vis the positivist sense of science, the sense on the basis of which social science has typically sought to model itself. The advantage, however, is precisely that the subject matter of social science shows, brightly and stubbornly, the limitations of positivism. Indeed, in light of its innate resistance to its own material makeup, humankind, in its very being, exposes a veiled pretense of hard science, namely, the presupposition of sheer objectivity.

Social science points to a different, more encompassing sense of reality, a nonontological ontology in which nothing/no thing is perfectly identical to itself—that is to say, in which identity is ever relative. Such ontology is well conceived of in terms of (the Greek) meontology, that is, the reality of betweenness or basic ambiguity, of what stands between being and nonexistence. Beyond or irreducible to being or nothingness, such reality is never really settled but rather ever on the move, always in-between, and therefore constantly becoming other to itself.

The difference this "ontology" makes is radical, picturing reality in terms of a paralogical holism, in which everything is *both* distinguishable from *and* essentially linked to everything else. Such basic ambiguity describes a tensile relationality—an open totality, so to speak—in which differentiation or creation is ongoing. Take, for example, a sightless person and his walking stick.[12] Because we, in the West, are culturally predisposed to construe the world as made up of discrete entities, that is, things abstracted from their circumstances, we have no difficulty telling the person from his stick. But were we to conceive of the blind man as person-in-action—which is to say, without conceptualizing "him" as set apart from the concrete world—then where does he end? Where his hand touches his cane? Where the cane touches the pavement? Where the pavement meets the street? And so on. Conceived of in this way, in the concrete flow of reality, it is not possible, as Yeats penned, to tell the dancer from the dance—*at least not unambiguously*. That is, telling the one from the other supposes a *circumstantial*—and therewith incomplete—relationship between the seer and the seen, such that the determination of the seen will differ depending on how the seen and the seer are situated; thus, a poetic point of view yields a different phenomenon from that of the positivist. The question here is why we are inclined to regard as real only the product of the latter perspective. Indeed, one might wish to think that, in reality and for all the amazing efficacy of science, it is the poetic perspective that enjoys ontological primacy.

Obviously, circumstantiality implicates temporality. Thus, although it remains possible to demarcate the blind man relative to one's perspective, in the holistic reality at point the blind man is also defined in terms of all of the possibilities mentioned above: as an aspect of the walking stick, the pavement, the street, and beyond. Plainly, in this open and holistic ontology, reality is apprehended not only in terms of entitativity but also potentiality. Borges, in his "The Garden of the Forking Paths," captures just this sense of time and reality (1965: 91): "Differing from Newton and Schopenhauer, your ancestor did not think of time as absolute and uniform. He believed in an infinite series of times, in a dizzily growing, ever spreading network of diverging, converging and parallel times. This web of time—the strands of which approach one another, bifurcate, intersect or ignore each other through the centuries—embraces every possibility. We do not exist in most of them. In some you exist and not I, while in others I do, and you do not, and in yet others both of us exist." In this picture of reality, while "existence," which is to say, actuality or being, enjoys a special relationship to "absolute and uniform" time, more basically the real pertains to a multiplicity of relative times that together hold "every possibility" or becoming. In other words, given the dynamic nature of this polymorphous sense of time, the virtual rather than the actual constitutes the more encompassing reality. Many peoples of this world—our (as Borges put it) "ancestors"—understand this. But because, for reasons of scientism cum rationalism, so much anthropology has been blind to this sense of reality, the discipline itself—for all the light shed by intensive ethnographic research—has largely failed, in at least one particular but very profound way, to understand such peoples. Dismissing as nonsense or symbolism the kind of ontology at issue here, anthropologists have been broadly inclined to fail to perceive the particular ontological truth of the reality projected by the so-called primitive or traditional or atheoretical peoples on whom modern anthropology cut its teeth.

A fair amount of recent anthropology has been influenced by actor-network theory (ANT), in which agency is attributed not only to humans but also to all other things, animate and inanimate. The example of the blind man's stick seems to resonate with this position. But my aim is more ontological than methodological, and it acknowledges that despite the irrefragable relationship of continuity between, on the one hand, humans and, on the other, nonhumans and things, that relationship nonetheless describes a difference that makes a difference, one so crucial that to fail to acknowledge it is to toss the baby out with the bathwater. I too wish to highlight *as ultimate* the meontological notions of the in-between, open holism, and reflexivity, notions that help to account for the universality of "agency." But in this meontological ontology, as Heidegger and Deleuze and Guattari stress, difference remains absolutely critical. While it is just a conceit of humankind to see all but themselves as lacking agency, when it comes to producing effects it would be a mistake to discount, or even make light of, the difference made by developed mindfulness and selfhood. The agential reflexivity between the blind man and his stick is asymmetrical, by which we mean that the stick's agentive role is imaginatively carved out ("unconcealed," says Heidegger) or allowed to manifest itself by the man, in accordance with the stick's potential. To be sure, tools have a way of turning against their maker, even to the point of transforming the latter into the prosthetic pole of the reflexive relationship.[13] But, as so much science fiction features (from the golem stories to Mary Shelly's *Frankenstein* to Stanley Kubrick's *2001* and so on), these reversals of influence and control are driven by the agency with which man endowed the tool. Taken as a cane, the stick is, as with selfhood and language, a product of *Homo faber,* a reflection of an elevated imagination and capacious creativity. The creative plasticity afforded by human consciousness is distinguished by its magnitude. That we can determine our own good, and are irrecusably self-responsible (even should we refuse responsibility), bespeaks, as Hans Jonas submits, the "ontological surprise" of nature transcending itself: a second nature.

Such a nature throws a wrench into the works of science proper. It does so not by denying science's transparent success and powerful grip on reality, but by suggesting that this efficacy is nonetheless gained at the price of a costly—jarringly in respect of humans—impoverishment of reality. At bottom, science proper proceeds on the basis of synchrony and entitativity, therewith thematizing and fixing "things." In this sense, science is constructivist, which does not mean, however, that it is just arbitrary. Insofar as these constructions are instrumentally effective and resist falsification, they do indeed reveal a substantial aspect of reality. But they do so by putting out of play other circumstantial aspects of the real, most conspicuously apparent contingencies and uncertainties. These make plain that science, for all its success, is not simply abstract, but in a fundamental way decidedly so—the success of science depends on the conceptual exclusion of these circumstances as well as other possible perspectives on the object of inquiry.

At this juncture, it suits my purpose—my emphasis on reflexivity—to feature one circumstance in particular. I have in mind the observer's share. The exclusion of this circumstance as a relevant consideration in scientific practice has been principled and routine. Were it not excluded, the absolute claim to objectivism could not stand. If the observer, simply through the act of observing, can inform and affect what is being observed, then science would seem no more scientific and objective than what passed for the pursuit of knowledge at the time when the willful intervention of a god figure into the course of nature was generally taken for granted. As is well-known, quantum mechanics has struggled with an issue of this kind. The vexed but fascinating matter of what has been called, in this revolutionary branch of physics, the "observer effect" has led at least some scientists to conclude that consciousness in itself can cause change in the phenomenon under observation. Whether these physicists are on to something or not, it is plain that in social science the question of the beholder's share, as the editors introduced at the outset of this volume, has always dangled on the horizon and today looms large. In anthropology this question of reflexivity is hard to dispel, because the relationship between a people under study and their ethnographer is precisely a "social" relationship, characteristically a face-to-face one (see Handelman 1973, 1977). Such a relationship is, by definition, mutually affecting and informing.

I have linked reflexivity to open holism and betweenness. In a reality defined in these terms, everything is not only relatively different from but also identical to everything else. This ambiguity, of difference and identity, conceptually subsumes that of self and other. Indeed, speaking with abandon but still deliberatively, everything has a "social" coefficient to it; this is so whether we have in mind a creature and its environment or, for that matter, a rock and its hard place. Therefore, one might want to say that everything manifests a self-other relationship, even (as I showed with the example of the blind man walking) a multiplicity of such relationships. The difference between this all-inclusive sense of sociality and the routine conception of the social is found, most basically, in the fact that among humans the self-other relationship holds not only between one individual and another but also, imposingly, within each individual. While nonhuman creaturely social orders present critically important intermediary cases, they do not rise to the level of the inverse difference—the "ontological surprise"—described by Jonas's thesis about metabolic exchange. It is this difference that in a far-reaching way complicates matters, mitotically but still chiastically, dividing reflexivity into bodily or involuntary reflexiveness on the one hand and cognitive *reflection* on the other.

The major internalization of the self-other relationship is, then, a difference that makes an arresting and consequential difference. But even though it greatly amplifies individuality, this difference must not be taken to entail the ontological primacy of the individual. For sheer individuality remains a chimera. As Durkheim demonstrated long ago, the very idea of the individual is a social phenomenon. Hence, there is no need to explain, pace Hobbes, how individuals manage to overcome their individuality and join together to form a social order—individuals are always already social. The internalization of the self-other relationship into a singular body and being is both continuous with and subsequent to the self-other relationship found at large. It follows that the universality of the latter enjoys the potential to make the former possible. The human individual is nothing but a skin-bound, finite, and writ-small reflection of the internality of the infinite multiverse or open whole. If this rings true, then consciousness, both rudimentary and developed, is inherent in what we moderns are inclined to think of as the "material" cosmos. In other words, the purely material conception of the universe amounts to an abstraction from what lies betwixt and between being and nothingness, the visible and the invisible—in a word, becoming.

A more acute awareness of the beholder's share has helped move many anthropologists and other social scientists to rethink the nature of their disciplines, in the direction of placing a premium on reflexivity. But insofar as that premium is basically methodological, it fails to grasp the full force of reflexivity and its implications for doing social science. This force is ontological, depicting reality in terms of basic ambiguity. For decades the proscription against ethnocentrism fortified anthropologists in the (pretentious) supposition that they could save their research from any and all subjectivist bias, thus allowing for a constituting dedication to scientism. In more recent times, though, the prescriptive elevation of reflexivity has encouraged, as a significant trend, a neglectful inattention to the question of objectivity, in favor of overt social activism on the part of the researcher. But when reflexivity is taken as a sine qua non of humankind rather than a mere method, its disciplinary proscriptive nature is greatly complicated, in a way that reflects the ultimate indeterminacy of nature and the rhizogenic openness of reflexivity.

Describing reality primarily in terms of basic ambiguity, reflexivity manifests itself as a dynamic of becoming. This dynamic takes the general form of self-other relationism. Among human beings, though, this phenomenon is highlighted in terms of a mind-body equivocality in which selfhood and mindfulness enjoy a certain preeminence, turning the tables on, in a limited but nonetheless astonishingly consequential manner, otherness and embodiment. This exceptional state of being, ideologically parsed in terms of "freedom" and "transcendence," presents the openness of nature in an exemplary fashion, making the existential condition of intrinsic indeterminacy terrifically hard to discount by appeal to the causal face of reality. If openness, as critically highlighted in human existence, is innately registered in reflexivity, then the purely instrumental deployment of reflexivity is bound to be self-defeating. For, in studying human beings, the social scientist is by definition studying himself. In which case, he is no more absolutely free of the condition of existential indeterminacy than are those subject to his deliberative inquiry. Insofar as, by reason of the proscription against ethnocentrism, he continues to see the principal goal of his research in terms of absolute, rather than relative, determinacy, he is bound to miss and therewith conceal that which is presupposed by normative order and conduct, namely, man's second nature. That nature amounts to the extraordinary dynamic capacity of man to determine his world in conjunction with his self. And because that capacity is possible only so long as there is ontological openness, that is to say, essential ambiguity, man's strategies to assume, on behalf of objective inquiry, a stance of clean detachment cannot succeed in the final run. Notwithstanding the slackening of his ties to the world, man ever remains caught within it. In other words, no more than his understanding of others can his self-understanding be conclusive—it must always be tentative.

The question arises, if the social scientist can never truly be bias-free, what, if anything, distinguishes his professional reflexivity from that of the people he is studying? I think that the answer continues to rest with the determined efforts to assume an objective perspective, that is, one that is "disinterested." By that I mean the social scientist's professional interest in turning back on himself, in a reflexive effort to suspend his "value judgments." But it is the effort, not objectivity qua objectivity, that basically signifies here. If only because it is subjective, the decision to effect disinterest and indifference can never assure the immaculate detachment entailed by the dualist distinction between subjectivity and objectivity. Indeed, objectivity per se might well be conceived of as an *as if* reality, a kind of illusion supported by logic qua logic, which is to say, an organon that epistemologically equips and constrains one to decide cleanly between truth and falsity. To be sure, objectivity is also supported by empirical results, that is, by what appears to work for the time being. So powerful a logic coupled with such results is undeniably imposing. Nevertheless, when taken as conclusive in the absolute, it is shortsighted, even deceptive. We are not only in the world but also of it, and no matter how hard we try we cannot step out of it to observe it from nowhere. The very possibility of *choosing* a posture of objectivity presupposes a reality of basic ambiguity, of betweenness—the reality expressed in reflexivity. As such that choice necessarily conveys, even in its own case, uncertainty. Regardless of its intention to suspend all value judgments, then, it should not be surprising that there are always such judgments that go undetected—if only the ethnocentric one of *faith* in science. In fact, the choice of objectivity is an ethical decision in which the value of science is given a certain priority. The ethical nature of the choice is made transparent by the strong, current trend in social science to prioritize political commitment on the part of the researcher, a decision that renders objectivity, if not moot, at least a subsidiary choice and value. That reflexivity has been deployed both to enhance objectivity and to pursue, in the face of this absolute standard of scientific rigor, a politicomoral persuasion goes to show the fundamental limits of objectivism.

But we go too far. For on the basis of our ontological understanding of reflexivity, the illusory quality of objectivity must also characterize subjectivity. If reflexivity conveys essential ambiguity, then subjectivism too must be, by dint of objectivity, basically relative. This is the case despite the standard portrayal of reflexivity as wholly subjective, as an airtight loop from which there is no escape whatsoever.

In the philosophy of science, as suggested above, objectivity is typically justified by appeal to logic as such—that is, rationality in the strict sense of the term—and to empirical corroboration. Leaving aside the question of whether or not these two modes of proof can themselves be proven (I am thinking here of Kurt Gödel's famous "Incompleteness Theorem"), I suggest that there is a deeper, more compelling basis of objectivism, namely, ontology. Any formal determination of what there is, that is, any ontology, necessarily already depends on our sensory experience of the sensible universe. That experience—however formal ontologies diverge from one another—records everything as different from and the same as everything else. How could it be otherwise? Entailing congruity as well as incongruity between the beholder and the beheld, human behavior and perceptibility cannot help but project just this paradoxical state of things. Put another way, ontological thinking presupposes meontology, the experiential primacy of betweenness. Merleau-Ponty addressed this condition in terms of the "flesh" of the world. By this he did not intend substance per se, but a fundamental relationality between one thing and another—what I have deemed, paralogically, wholeness that is no less open than closed. Conceived thusly, the whole describes anything and everything as at once what it is and not what it is, which is to say, as always less than identical to, or incommensurable with, itself. Both the *apparently* external relationship between a thing and its environs as well as the *apparently* internal relationship between a thing and itself define wholes in this sense. In other words, this comprehensive, unexpected sense of the whole muddies the distinction between inside and outside, and therefore, focusing now on the self-relationship that identifies personhood, the distinction between subjectivity and objectivity. In which case, since they define and delimit each other, both perspectives are essentially relative matters, subjectivity being no more nor less illusorial than objectivity. The point is that at bottom both are semblances, but not for that reason ineffica- cious. Constructed by humans on the experiential platform of the basic ambiguity of reality, they constitute quasi-actualities.

At this juncture it is easy to see that open holism and reflexivity amount to the same dynamic: fundamental relationality in which iden- tity is unceasingly cut by difference. In other words, it is a crossing dy- namic the crux of which constitutes openness to change. This dynamic displays, to the human eye, a preponderance of "external" relations between one thing and another in the world at large. When, however, the dynamic is internalized roundly within a single, skin-bound being, as is the case with humans, it occasions Jonas's "ontological surprise": self-consciousness. The development of this acute sort of consciousness generates in its host a tantalizing divide between mind and body, the mind definitively given to reflect on it*self*, yielding thus a sense of her- metic unicity that naturally moves the mind toward alienation from its own corporeality or otherness. In Western thought, a conceptual op- timization of this outcome is, as shown earlier, Descartes's cogito, in which the very existence of the body is doubtful, the mind being the sole reality about which, in Descartes's reasoning, we can be certain. Driven by the sheer mindfulness of logic qua logic, however, Descartes got it backward, for the bodily constitution of mindfulness remains a constant. In his cosmological efforts to unravel the genesis of self-con- sciousness, Merleau-Ponty's ambiguous usage, "flesh," intimates pre- cisely the meontological intertwining that is body-mind/mind-body. The restriction of "reflexivity" to reflection is, then, in the end a function of the mind's capacity for self-deception. That is, it is a consequential conceit. While it fosters exceptional creativity on the part of humans, it tends to eclipse the sensible basis of just this possibility. Ultimately, thinking and perceiving begin with our being not only in but also of the world. In other words, the basic relation presented by reflexivity is not that between the mind and itself, but rather that between somatic reflexivity, as in a conditioned reflex, and reflection as deliberation.

In effect, the dynamic of reflexivity opened up a stunning reversal in the flesh of the world, yielding a phenomenon in which matter, for the time of being, is put in the service of form rather than the other way around. The result is humanity, a species that, although indubita- bly continuous with all other creaturely life, is capacitated to resist the world's gravity to an exceptional degree, liberating man to creatively construct himself and his world in a still provisional but uniquely com- manding way. This extraordinary creative capacity is what makes the social and human sciences special in the field of scientific studies. By bringing into high relief this distinctive faculty, these sciences do not lend themselves so readily to the exactitude required by hard science. By the same token, however, precisely because they constitute a glaring exception to the presumption of consistent determinacy, they capture a fundamental aspect of what there is: openness. Here I am not in a position to say how this picture of reflexivity might serve in some (if any) meaningful measure as a corrective to science proper. But it certainly suggests that the embedded effort of social science to emulate the hard sciences in the quest for determinism is bound to make too little of the qualitative difference man represents. For all man's plain continuity with other creatures, his creative capacity distinguishes him, sharply. Although he is no more than mortal, the degree of "freedom" he enjoys, that is, the patent extent to which he can keep his ground at bay, gives him, remarkably, the unique deliberative ability to destroy as well as to nurture the world as he finds it. No other creature possesses this ability, by virtue of which every choice humans make—whether personal, domestic, economic, political, religious, aesthetic, and so forth—constitutes and reflects ethical process, since it is by definition a construction of the "good." Social science is positioned not only to focus on but also to demonstrate the exceptional ontological gravity of this ability. And while this "scientific" position is a metaperspective, it remains an ethical one too, which is to say, a construction of the "good." For it supposes that by striving for objectivity, and in this particular way taking advantage of our creative capacity, the result, instrumental and/or intellectual, is in itself valuable, and therefore a good. Moreover, by exposing the limitations of determinism and, correlatively, of itself, objectivity can serve to disclose the defining role of reflexivity and the creative or ethical process for our peculiar form of life. In doing so, it makes plain not simply the existential ambiguity that describes us but the accompanying responsibility such ambiguity imposes on us.

Notes

1. I should note that Wittgenstein held meaning to be relative in yet another sense, one related to his well-known argument about "private language." Since every language as such is essentially social, different languages ("language games") necessarily yield different meanings according to the socio-cultural context to which they correspond (see Kripke 1982). Nevertheless, there is for Wittgenstein the possibility of bridging even these semantic differences. In his critique of James Frazer (1979: 8E), he tells us, for example, that there "is something in us too that speaks in support of those observances [i.e., magical notions and practices] by the savages." In this essay,

he appears to appeal to human experience (the "spirit" or "inner nature of a practice") (14E) as a basis for cross-cultural understanding, since the "evidence" for reaching such a translation includes "the thought of man and his past, the strangeness in what I see in myself and in others, what I have seen and have heard" (18E). Of course, science presents itself as different from all other languages, on the ground of objectivity. Most ordinary languages take for granted their connection to reality. But, by virtue of logic and rationality, the language of science sees itself as genuinely universal and therefore the only language strictly true to reality. In the last century it has been argued, an argument brought to its head in postmodern and poststructural thought, that at least in good part this presumption is, importantly, not altogether warranted.

2. The terminological distinction between the saying and the said is due to Emmanuel Levinas (e.g., 1991: 170).

3. See Deleuze and Guattari (1987: 272ff.), Brian Massumi (1992: 47ff.), Holland (1999: 93ff., 99ff.), and Rajchman (2000: 80ff.).

4. Cf. Curtis Brown (n.d.) on the *logical* infelicities of Spinoza's argument, and Jonas (1974: chap. 10) on Spinoza and the idea of two different perspectives on the same thing (substance). Descartes too used "substance" (*res*: things, objects, material) to apply to both mind and body. But, needless to say, he saw these two phenomena not as the same thing but as two *totally* different things. Leaving aside the epistemological difference made by modern science, one might wish to see Spinoza's usage of "substance" as anticipating the notion of the Higgs-Boson particle, given the scientific conjecture that this atom is the glue that makes all mass. In this connection, it is also worth citing M. Merleau-Ponty's notion of the "flesh of the world." He coined this usage to propose that we can "know" all the other things of the world because basically they and we are of the same stuff, a proposition that seems to resonate with Wittgenstein's observation about the substantive way in which language participates in the reality to which it refers. Deleuze and Guattari's distinction between the molar and the molecular evokes Wittgenstein's affirmation of the commensurability between language and the flow of life, while their Spinozist spin on "substance" speaks to the way in which the two elements of the distinction are just two perspectives on the same thing. Given that in his usage the word "flesh" is basically ambiguous between immanence and transcendence, Merleau-Ponty may be closer to Wittgenstein's grasp of the matter. But we should not forget that even though Deleuze and Guattari found regrettable Merleau-Ponty's appeal to "flesh" (they regarded it as too close to Christian dogma), Deleuze spoke of his own philosophy as "transcendental empiricism."

5. Even if in certain respects one could argue that there is no difference, as when the (fictitious) Don Juan, replying to Castaneda's question regarding the reality of his drug-induced experience of flying, responded that the question was senseless, given that Castaneda truly experienced himself flying.

6. Instead of "man," Heidegger used the term *Dasein*, or "being-there," in an effort to get away from the ontological baggage carried by the standard usage. For my limited purposes here, I will make do with ordinary language.

7. Hence, the notorious philosophical problem of other minds, which Merleau-Ponty regarded as absurd (1962: 349): "The constitution of the other person does not fully elucidate that of society, which is not an existence involving two or even three people, but co-existence involving an indefinite number of consciousnesses." In a nutshell: "The existence of other people is a difficulty and an outrage for objective thought." (Merleau-Ponty 1962: 349).

8. I have drawn heavily here on Eugene Holland's excellent exposition of this point (1999: 112ff.).

9. For a rather clever example, George Myerson (1997) observes that what is most basically communicated when using a cell phone is "use mobile phones," a commercial dispatch that has instructed a huge portion of humanity.

10. See, e.g., Bumiller (2012).

11. Here Barfield's (doctrinally tendentious) thesis (1977) of the internalization of godliness in the skin-bound individuality of Jesus Christ is provocative. From a non-Western perspective, we might also cite the difference between the figure of the leopard-skin priest and that of the prophet among the Nuer of East Africa (Evens 2012: 39–41).

12. Although I have developed it for my own purposes, the basic example is lifted from Gregory Bateson (2000: 318). It is also worth citing Merleau-Ponty in a strikingly similar vein (1962: 143): "The blind man's stick has ceased to be an object for him, and is no longer perceived for itself.… In the exploration of things, the length of the stick does not enter expressly as a middle term: the blind man is rather aware of it through the position of objects than of the position of objects through it.… There is no question here of any quick estimate or any comparison between the objective length of the stick and the objective distance away of the goal to be reached. The points in space do not stand out as objective positions in relation to the objective position occupied by our body; they mark, in our vicinity, the varying range of our aims and our gestures. To get used to… a stick is to be transplanted into [it], or conversely, to incorporate [it] into the bulk of our own body."

13. In this regard, see Ellen Ullman's (2002) compelling argument bearing on the project of artificial intelligence and the definition of life.

References

Augustine. (1942) 2006. *Confessions*. Trans. F. J. Sheed. 2nd ed. Indianapolis: Hackett.

Barfield, Owen. 1977. "Philology and the Incarnation." In *The Discovery of Meaning and Other Essays*. Middletown, CT: Wesleyan University Press, 228–36.

Bateson, Gregory. 2000. *Steps to an Ecology of Mind*. Chicago: University of Chicago Press.

Borges, Jorge Luis. 1965. "The Garden of the Forking Paths." In *Fictions*. Translated from the Spanish. London: John Calder, 81–93.

Brown, Curtis. n.d. "Spinoza on Why There Can Only Be One Substance." http://www.trinity.edu/cbrown/modern/spinozaPartI.html.

Bumiller, Elizabeth. 2012. "A Day Job Waiting for a Kill Shot a World Away." *New York Times*, 29 July.

Deleuze, Gilles. 1993. *The Fold: Leibniz and the Baroque*. Trans. Tom Conley. Minneapolis: University of Minnesota Press.

Deleuze, Gilles, and Felix Guattari. 1987. *A Thousand Plateaus*. Trans. Brian Massumi. Minneapolis: University of Minnesota Press.

Evens, T. M. S. 2012. "The Phenomenology of a Stateless Society: Non-dualism, Identity and Hierarchical Anarchy among the Nuer." In *Contesting the State: The Dynamics of Resistance and Control*, ed. Angela Hobart and Bruce Kapferer. Wantage, UK: Sean Kingston, 21–54.

Handelman, Don. 1973. "Gossip in Encounters: The Transmission of Information in a Bounded Social Situation." *Man*, n.s., 8: 210–27.

———. 1977. *Work and Play among the Aged: Interaction, Replication and Emergence in a Jerusalem Setting*. Assen: Van Corcum.

Heidegger, Martin. 1978. *Being and Time*. Trans. John Macquarrie and Edward Robinson. Oxford: Basil Blackwell.

———. 1993. *Basic Writings*. Ed. David Farrell Krell. Rev. and exp. ed. San Francisco: Harpers.

Holland, Eugene W. 1999. *Deleuze and Guattari's Anti-Oedipus*. New York: Routledge.

Jonas, Hans. 1974. *Philosophical Essays: From Ancient Creed to Technological Man*. Englewood Cliffs, NJ: Prentice Hall.

———. (1966) 1982. *The Phenomenon of Life: Toward a Philosophical Biology*. Phoenix ed. Chicago: University of Chicago Press.

Kripke, Saul A. 1982. *Wittgenstein: On Rules and Private Language*. Cambridge, MA: Harvard University Press.

Kuhn, Thomas S. 1970. *The Structure of Scientific Revolutions*. Enlarged 2nd ed. Chicago: University of Chicago Press.

Lawson, Hilary. 1985. *Reflexivity: The Post-modern Predicament*. La Salle, IL: Open Court.

Levinas, Emmanuel. 1991. *Otherwise than Being or Beyond Essence*. Trans. Alphonso Lingis. Dordrecht: Kluwer.

Massumi, Brian. 1992. *A User's Guide to Capitalism and Schizophrenia*. Cambridge, MA: MIT Press.

Merleau-Ponty, Maurice. 1962. *Phenomenology of Perception*. Trans. Colin Smith. London: Routledge and Kegan Paul.

———. 1968. *The Visible and the Invisible*. Trans. Alphonso Lingis. Evanston, IL: Northwestern University Press.

Myerson, George. 1997. *Heidegger, Habermas and the Mobile Phone*. London: Totem Books.

Rajchman, John. 2000. *The Deleuze Connections*. Cambridge, MA: MIT Press.

Stern, David G. 1995. *Wittgenstein on Mind and Language*. New York: Oxford University Press.

Straus, Erwin. 1980. "The Upright Posture." In *Phenomenological Psychology*. New York: Garland, 137–65.

Taylor, Charles. 1985. *Human Agency and Language: Philosophical Papers*. Vol. 2. Cambridge: Cambridge University Press.

Ullman, Ellen. 2002. "Programming the Post-human: Computer Science Redefines 'Life.'" *Harper's Magazine*, October.

Virilio, Paul. 1997. *Open Sky*. Trans. Julie Rose. London: Verso.

———. 2006. *Speed and Politics*. Trans. Marc Polizzotti. Los Angeles: Semiotext(e).

Wittgenstein, Ludwig. 1961. *Tractatus Logico-Philosophicus*. Trans. D. F. Pears and B. F. McGuinness. London: Routlege and Kegan Paul.

———. 1979. "Remarks on Frazer's *Golden Bough*." Trans. A. C. Miles and Rush Rhees. *The Human World*, no. 3 (May): 18–41.

Terry Evens is Emeritus Professor of Anthropology at the University of North Carolina, Chapel Hill. Email: tmevens@email.unc.edu

Index